LAND LORDSHIP IN ANGLO-NORMAN ENGLAND

John Hudson

CLARENDON PRESS · OXFORD

OXFORD HISTORICAL MONOGRAPHS

Preface

> In any body of law we are likely to find certain ideas and rules
> that may be described as elementary. Their elementary cha-
> racter consists in this, that we must master them if we are to
> make any further progress in our study; . . . as regards the law of
> the feudal time we can hardly do wrong in turning to the law of
> land tenure as being its most elementary part.
>
> *Pollock and Maitland*, i. 231

With the venerated exception of Maitland, historians of law have too
often seemed to be separated from other historians by their interests,
their approach, and even their language. Their insights, therefore,
have not always been properly appreciated. This book is a study of
Anglo-Norman society, and the working of ideas and power therein,
which seeks to unite such insights with the broader approaches and
interests of other historians.

In legal terms, this work could be seen as an essay on the early
stages of the emergence of Common Law property. Historians of
'property' have generally concentrated on 'real property', in particular
land. I have followed this tradition, whilst recognizing its limits.
Hence I do not, for example, discuss the relevance of possession of
chattels to notions of ownership. Within land law, I concentrate on
three areas again central to previous writings, a position they owe
partly to their importance in modern definitions of ownership, partly
to their historical importance: security of tenure, heritability, and
alienability. In these areas, therefore, my intention has been to bring
different evidence and new interpretation to an area of established
importance.

Certain omissions should be noted. I have concentrated on illuminating seignorial power through land-holding and the working of
law. I have sometimes drawn on other evidence in order to modify
received views of the honour, but have not attempted a complete
political and social reassessment of the history of lordship. For example, I have not made a general analysis of the effect on seignorial
power of 'feudal geography', the distribution of fees within the honour.
Whilst I have examined the possibility of regional and honorial variation

of custom, I have made no special study of the marcher lordships or
of the honours which were to develop into the great palatinates. My
primary interest has been in those areas which were to be directly
subject to Common Law. The problems of evidence have led me to
concentrate on the higher levels of society. Hence I deal primarily
with land held for military service, and do not, for example, consider
the development of socage tenure. Certain other forms of land-
holding have been examined only in passing, or omitted altogether,
for example curtesy.

As always in a first book, thanks are due to many people, only some
of whom can be named here. The writing of the thesis and the book
were supervised at various times by Jim Holt, Paul Hyams, and
Paul Brand, and my debt to them is enormous. David Corner read
an entire draft, and made many trenchant and useful comments.
Professor Milsom examined the thesis in a generously open-minded
way; I have greatly appreciated his comments then and his encoura-
gement thereafter. I hope that the influence of James Campbell,
as undergraduate tutor and since, is at least sometimes apparent.
Peter Cramer, David Crouch, and George Garnett attempted in their
different ways to make sure that I saw both the wood and the trees; I,
like many others, am also indebted to Dr Crouch for access to his
large collection of transcripts of twelfth-century comital charters.
Mark Philpott, Steve White, and Patrick Wormald generously shared
with me their ideas and their unpublished work, and I am also
grateful to Julia Boorman, Paul Dalton, George Garnett, Lorna Walker,
and Graeme White for allowing me access to their unpublished
theses. Errors and eccentric arguments are my own.

   Rather like one who survived ordeal by water according to the
Assize of Northampton only to face the penalty of banishment, Lise
McAslan's fate after surviving ordeal by book completion was the
dubious one of becoming my wife. My parents first aroused and then
sustained my interest in history, and my mother has also read much
of this work at various stages. To them the book is dedicated.

J. H.

St Andrews
February 1993

Contents

Abbreviations

AJLegH	*American Journal of Legal History.*
A-NS	*Anglo-Norman Studies.*
ASC	*Anglo-Saxon Chronicle*, tr. D. Whitelock, with D. C. Douglas and S. I. Tucker (London, 1961).
BIHR	*Bulletin of the Institute of Historical Research.*
BNB	*Bracton's Note Book.*
Bracton, Thorne	'Bracton', *De Legibus et Consuetudinibus Regni Anglie*, ed. and tr. S. E. Thorne.
BSAN	*Bulletin de la Société des Antiquaires de Normandie.*
CChR	*Calendar of Charter Rolls.*
CDF	*Calendar of Documents Preserved in France illustrative of the History of Great Britain and Ireland.*
CHJ	*Cambridge Historical Journal.*
CLJ	*Cambridge Law Journal.*
CMA	*Chronicon Monasterii de Abingdon.*
CP	*Complete Peerage.*
CPR	*Calendar of Patent Rolls.*
CRR	*Curia Regis Rolls.*
Domesday	*Domesday Book*, ed. A. Farley (2 vols.; London, 1783).
EHR	*English Historical Review.*
EYC	*Early Yorkshire Charters.*
Fauroux	*Recueil des Actes des Ducs de Normandie*, ed. M. Fauroux.
Glanvill, Hall	'Glanvill', *Tractatus de Legibus et Consuetudinibus Regni Anglie*, ed. and tr. G. D. G. Hall.
Hinschius	*Decretales Pseudo-Isidorianae*, ed. P. Hinschius.
HKF	W. Farrer, *Honors and Knights Fees.*
HMC	Historical Manuscripts Commission.
JEcclH	*Journal of Ecclesiastical History.*
JMedH	*Journal of Medieval History.*
JSA	*Journal of the Society of Archivists.*

L&HR	*Law and History Review.*
Leges Henrici, Downer	*Leges Henrici Primi*, ed. and tr. L. J. Downer.
Liebermann, *Gesetze*	*Die Gesetze der Angelsachsen*, ed. F. Liebermann.
LQR	*Law Quarterly Review.*
MGH	*Monumenta Germaniae Historica.*
MTB	*Materials for the History of Thomas Becket.*
P&P	*Past and Present.*
Papsturkunden	*Papsturkunden in England.*
PKJ	*Pleas before the King or his Justices, 1198–1202.*
PL	*Patrologia Latina.*
Pollock and Maitland	Sir Frederick Pollock and F. W. Maitland, *The History of English Law.*
PR	*Pipe Roll.*
PRO	Public Record Office.
PRS	Pipe Roll Society.
RCR	*Rotuli Curiae Regis.*
Recueil	*Recueil des Actes de Henri II.*
Red Book	*Liber Rubeus de Scaccario.*
Regesta	*Regesta Regum Anglo-Normannorum, 1066–1154.*
RHDFE	*Revue Historique de Droit Français et Étranger.*
Sawyer	P. H. Sawyer, *Anglo-Saxon Charters: An Annotated List and Bibliography.*
SSC	Stubbs, *Select Charters* (9th edn.).
TAC, Tardif	*Très Ancien Coutumier*, ed. E.-J. Tardif.
TRHS	*Transactions of the Royal Historical Society.*
TVR	*Tijdschrift voor Rechtsgeschiedenis.*
VCH	Victoria County History.

1

Introduction

ONE day soon after his appointment as Abbot of Glastonbury, Henry of Blois was travelling—as any good lord should—through the lands of his lordship, and moved round the boundaries of his manor of Brent Marsh. As he progressed, he hit upon a field which was partially protected by a round bank and by a deep watercourse, and, he tells us in rather Wordsworthian tones,

I saw there a shiny golden harvest, sweetly rustling in a light breeze, presenting a wide and even surface without any excrescence of weeds or anything to separate adversely the stalks that were standing close together, and offering the harvester bundles rather than ears.

Now this cornucopia came to him as something of a surprise, since the land had been obtained by a knight from Henry's predecessor on the grounds that it could never be of any use to the Church.

As I asked what that field was called I heard that the aforesaid knight had given it the name of 'Useless'. So when on the appointed day this great fraud was unveiled to the numerous people who had been convoked, I received back through their judgment the aforesaid land, whose name was suitably changed.[1]

This story, for once from an autobiographical source, introduces many of the key themes of this study. Notably, it illustrates the ways in which legal processes, such as hearings in court, were used by parties to obtain their ends. It reveals how lordship had to be actively exercised, and, unusually, it shows how the economic value of land could determine the amount of effort a lord would expend upon it.

Control of land was a crucial aspect of power in Anglo-Norman England, and land-holding has been central to legal historians' consideration of the same period.[2] Yet despite their vital interrelationship,

---

[1] Adam of Domerham, *Historia de Rebus Gestis Glastoniensibus*, ed. T. Hearne (2 vols.; Oxford, 1727), ii. 307–8.

[2] Note, however, that land-holding was not always central to the relationship of lord and man in this period, and the personal bond could exist without any tenurial link; see

studies of power within the honour and those of land law have
remained largely separate. This book examines seignorial control of
land in order to illuminate both the power of Anglo-Norman lordship
and the functioning and development of law within society. I therefore examine the areas of co-operation or conflict between kings,
lords, and vassals. To what extent was the honour an independent
social and political unit, and how did relationships and land-holding
within honours work? What were the characteristics of a good lord,
what constraints existed upon the exercise of seignorial power and
patronage? What were the aspirations of vassals, especially with regard
to land?

Above all, I ask how the aims and actions of lords and vassals were
facilitated or constrained by power and ideas, and particularly by
what might be referred to as legal norms. The close connection and
indeed the continuity between legal and other activities must be
emphasized, and I am far from suggesting that a completely discrete
category of exclusively legal matters existed. However, I would argue
that some loose description of certain affairs as legal is still valid, both
in terms of analytic utility and of the thought of the time. Certainly
power had an effect on the normal conduct of affairs concerning
land-holding and law, but the use of power to flout the workings of
law and justice was condemned.[3] According to King Arthur, or at
least Geoffrey of Monmouth, 'nothing which is acquired by force and
violence is justly possessed by anyone'.[4] Clearly, also, there were men
such as canonists who were self-consciously concerned with the legal.
Furthermore, men were aware, for example, of customary descent
patterns, and again one can refer to this subject-matter as 'legal'. In
addition, people perceived certain acts as separated from everyday
transactions by their formality, for instance having a Latin charter
drawn up to record a gift or ensuring that a dispute was heard in
what they considered a proper fashion before a properly constituted
court.

To adopt such strategies was one of the various ways in which

below, p. 16. I am thus primarily concerned with one very important aspect of lordship.

   [3] See e.g. *Liber Eliensis*, ed. E. O. Blake (Camden Soc., 3rd Ser. 92; 1962), 226–7
on the Clares.
   [4] *The Historia Regum Britannie of Geoffrey of Monmouth*, i. *Bern, Burgerbibliothek, MS.
568*, ed. N. Wright (Cambridge, 1985), 114. See also Jordan Fantosme, *Chronicle*, ed.
and tr. R. C. Johnston (Oxford, 1981), ll. 217–18, where Henry II states 'E ço quë est
a force u pris e purchaciez, | ço n'est dreit ne raisun; ço est suvent jugiez.'

lords and vassals sought to attain their shared or contrasting ends. Examination both of disputes and of documents seeking to reinforce control of land can reveal much about lordship and land-holding. Consideration of inheritance and of participation in land grants, for example, helps to determine the scope and varying influence of kinship. Analysis of cases illuminates the workings of honorial politics. Problems faced by lords or vassals, for example, may be related to the distribution of social and political power, as may different types of settlement. The paucity of evidence unfortunately makes it impossible to attempt a finely tuned investigation of the relationship of economic and legal change.[5] Even on a much more particular level, it is all too rarely possible to sketch the economic circumstances of a dispute, but some instances do hint that areas of increased value were particularly disputed.[6] The frequent appearance of certain kinds of dispute can reveal points of wider tension, for example between lay and ecclesiastical views. Such a broad approach both ensures the wider relevance of conclusions, and provides the best understanding of legal change.

My concern is with the upper levels of society, primarily with seignorial relationships amongst kings, barons, and their vassals. Only for them do the sources allow the type of analysis undertaken. At these levels in lay society, the Norman Conquest and settlement marked a distinct break. As is well known, Domesday Book recorded only two English lay tenants in chief of any significance. The Norman settlers brought with them their own notions concerning lordship and land-holding.[7] However, there also remained a very important

---

[5] e.g. the possibility that the sale of land was very common in the Anglo-Saxon period renders questionable any firm conclusions on the relationship between the later development of alienability and of the land market; see J. Campbell, 'The Sale of Land and the Economics of Power in Early England: Problems and Possibilities', *Haskins Society Journal*, 1 (1989), 23–37; cf. R. C. Palmer, 'The Economic and Cultural Impact of the Origins of Property: 1180–1220', *L&HR* 3 (1985), 375–96.

[6] See below, p. 99. Key objects of capital investment such as mills were often involved in disputes: e.g. *CMA* ii. 64–5; J. Loengard, 'The Assize of Nuisance: Origins of an Action at Common Law', *CLJ* 37 (1978), 149–51. Stephen White informs me that mills were often the subject of dispute in the west of France in this period.

[7] See esp. E. Z. Tabuteau, *Transfers of Property in Eleventh-Century Norman Law* (Chapel Hill, NC, 1988); J. C. Holt, 'Feudal Society and the Family in Early Medieval England: II. Notions of Patrimony', *TRHS*, 5th Ser. 33 (1983), 193–220. Note the problems which arise in studies such as S. E. Thorne, 'English Feudalism and Estates in Land', *CLJ* (1959), 193–209, from seemingly treating the late 11th cent. as a *tabula rasa*.

inheritance from Anglo-Saxon England, particularly the powerful
administrative inheritance, manifest for example in certain royal rights,
the county court, and the writ.

Ideally arguments concerning the development of land law might
be tested from official normative texts and from a variety of official
and unofficial records of conveyances and disputes. Unfortunately,
our sources do not permit a complete history of this sort. They
are almost all in Latin, whereas gift ceremonies and other court
proceedings would generally have been in French or perhaps sometimes English. Reference to vernacular literature can provide only a
very partial solution to this problem. The increasing amounts of
evidence may lead to the post-dating of developments which are
previously hidden by the lack of sources. Moreover, particularly in
the earlier part of our period, any document recording a transaction
involving laymen may well stem from an abnormal situation, generally
one of conflict. Simpler transactions would be oral. The situation is
made still more difficult by the fact that the written documents often
try to hide the very abnormality of the situation as they aim to restore
workable social relations, and the fact that almost all provide ex-parte
statements.[8] Charters from England can be frustratingly terse compared with those from France. The English draftsmen's prevailing
use of a limited variety of phrases often drives one to place excessive
reliance on illuminating but exceptional documents.

I weave into my analysis four main historiographical strands. First,
there are analyses of the workings of the honour. Since the 1930s,
the classic description has remained Stenton's *First Century of English
Feudalism*. Stenton was intent on restoring a balance within contemporary historiography, 'to leave the standpoint of the king and his
court, and to consider, from within, the community of knights and
barons over which they presided'.[9] Stenton was not primarily interested in law or even land-holding but he did produce important
evidence on, for example, the composition of courts, and also noted
the flexibility of the norms by which the honorial court worked. He

[8] See in particular P. R. Hyams, 'The Charter as a Source for the Early Common
Law', *Journal of Legal History*, 12 (1991), 173–89. See below, pp. 73–4, on disputes
behind charters which seem to record simple regrants. For a fuller discussion of the
sources, see J. G. H. Hudson, 'Legal Aspects of Seignorial Control of Land in the
Century after the Norman Conquest', D.Phil. thesis (Oxford, 1988), 10–17.
[9] F. M. Stenton, *The First Century of English Feudalism, 1066–1166* (2nd edn.,
Oxford, 1961), 6.

connected this with its sovereignty, the fact that the honour was an autonomous 'feudal state in miniature'.[10]

Secondly, there is the history of government and the structure of politics in the period, dealing with such questions as the extent of royal power and the sophistication of administration. I would include within this strand studies of the royal administration of justice, as distinct from studies of the law of the time. Whilst such matters are of concern throughout the book, they only take centre stage in the last chapter.

Obviously these two strands, the honorial and the political and administrative, intertwine.[11] Here it is important to note that historians often write of royal intervention in the affairs of lords and men, but overemphasis on royal control and on enforcement perpetuates too confrontationist a view of Anglo-Norman history: kings and barons, if sometimes in opposition, also had many shared interests. For example, the honour court can be seen not as an essential threat to royal power, but rather one means by which the conquerors ruled their conquered acquisition. Henry I, for example, surely did not see the earl of Leicester's settling potentially violent disputes between his tenants, or even perhaps involving others, as a threat to royal power, but rather as the act of a loyal vassal and companion of the king. Similarly, kings sometimes willingly helped lords to control recalcitrant tenants. Lords on occasion would have seen the presence of royal officials in their courts not as interference but as a welcome benefit. Rejection of the confrontationist view, of the notions simply of royal 'interference' in the honour, allows a more sophisticated view of power and of lordship.[12]

Yet the Anglo-Norman kings, like Henry II, held certain ideas incongruous with a purely passive role. Sometimes they could act aggressively in a way which some regarded as unjust.[13] However, at their coronations they swore to prevent iniquity and to ensure justice. The threat that the king would act was recorded in the clauses of

---

[10] Stenton, *First Century*, chs. 2 and 3, quotation at p. 51.

[11] As Stenton himself was well aware; cf. *First Century*, 51, just cited, with pp. 218–22.

[12] For co-operation by a hierarchy of lords up to the king, see e.g. *Chronicon Abbatiae Rameseiensis*, ed. W. D. Macray (London, 1886), 255; note also *Glanvill*, viii. 11, Hall, 102–3.

[13] Note e.g. *Early Buckinghamshire Charters*, ed. G. H. Fowler and J. G. Jenkins (Records Branch of Bucks. Arch. Soc. 3; 1939), No. 1, a charter of *c*.1160 promising warranty against all men 'besides royal violence'.

writs stating that unless the addressee did justice, a royal official or even the king would do it.[14] The royal concern for peace and the royal right and duty of hearing cases of default of justice led the king to seek to settle land disputes. The increasing amount of evidence makes this clear from Henry I's reign, whilst in addition occasional chronicle references, such as that to Ralph Basset's hanging of thieves at Hundehogge, show concern with crime.[15] The language of crime could occasionally be applied emotively to actions involving land,[16] and distinctions between criminal and land law were surely not foremost in the minds of the king and his advisers. The common factor was the maintenance of peace and justice, and such could lead to assertive royal action.

The third historiographical strand is that of recent studies of the 'social attitudes' to land-holding and transactions involving land, most notably in France, rarely in England. By 'social attitudes' are meant those which are not strictly legal—particularly those in a society where universally applied legal rules do not exist as a discrete group, differentiated from other norms, be they for example social, religious, or moral.[17] Here one immediately feels the pervasive influence of Marcel Mauss. Land grants are presented as total transactions, that is activities which are simultaneously 'religious, legal, moral, and economic'.[18] Within this context, a gift created a lasting social and moral bond, dissimilar to the discrete and complete conveyance of the modern sale of property. Moreover, each transaction was only one of a series, it was part of a total relationship.[19]

---

[14] *Royal Writs in England from the Conquest to Glanvill*, ed. R. C. van Caenegem (Selden Soc. 77; 1958–9), 148, 154–7, 162–3.

[15] *ASC*, 191, s.a. 1124.

[16] e.g. *The Ecclesiastical History of Orderic Vitalis*, ed. and tr. M. Chibnall (6 vols.; Oxford, 1969–80), iv. 106.

[17] For works on France in English, see e.g. S. D. White, *Custom, Kinship, and Gifts to Saints: The* Laudatio Parentum *in Western France, 1050–1150* (Chapel Hill, NC, 1988), B. H. Rosenwein, *To be the Neighbor of Saint Peter: The Social Meaning of Cluny's Property, 909–1049* (Ithaca, NY, 1989). For French studies, see notably the works of Bloch, Duby, and Fossier. For England, see e.g. T. M. Charles-Edwards, 'The Distinction between Land and Moveable Wealth in Anglo-Saxon England', in P. H. Sawyer (ed.), *Medieval Settlement* (London, 1976), 180–7, cf. Campbell, 'Sale of Land'. More generally, see A. Gurevic, 'Représentations et attitudes à l'égard de la propriété pendant le Haut Moyen Âge', *Annales ESC* 27 (1972), 523–47.

[18] M. Mauss, *The Gift*, tr. I. Cunnison (London, 1954), 1.

[19] See e.g. Rosenwein, *Neighbor of Saint Peter*, 132; such transactions need not always have been friendly, and Rosenwein, e.g. p. 135, stresses the part played by claims within such relationships.

Fourthly, and most obviously, there are lawyers and legal historians writing within the English Common Law tradition. They have tended to treat the century before 1166 as, at best, a preface for the 'Angevin Leap Forward', and one of my purposes is to treat Anglo-Norman law for its own sake.[20] Because of the peculiarities and difficulties of their approaches, it is useful here to set out briefly the differing interpretative frameworks of key writers. These involve the relations of lord, vassal, and land, and of land-holding, jurisdiction, and norms, and have generally been presented in terms of rights, interests, and claims in land and on persons.

Basic to Maitland's framework is his belief that, in this period, 'at the same moment several persons might have and be actually enjoying rights of a proprietary kind in the same plot of ground'.[21]

The tenant in demesne, the tenant on the lowest step of the feudal scale, obviously has rights in the land, amounting to a general, indefinite right of using it as he pleases. But his lord also is conceived as having rights in the land. We have not adequately described his position by saying that he has a right to services from his tenant. Of him as well as of his tenant it may be said that he holds the land, not indeed in demesne but in service, that the land is his land and his fee, and even that he is seised, that is, possessed of the land.[22]

The totality of each person's rights of this type, which lawyers call 'real rights', Maitland referred to as their interest in the land.[23] Dependent tenure consisted of such 'real rights' and of 'personal rights', for example the services by the tenant to his lord, and the defence and warranty normally owed by the lord to his tenant.[24]

---

[20] Maitland's main interest was 'the land law of Henry III's day', or, more generally, 'the law of the age that lies between 1154 and 1272', Sir Frederick Pollock and F. W. Maitland, *The History of English Law before the Time of Edward I* (2 vols.; 2nd edn. reissued with a new introduction by S. F. C. Milsom, Cambridge, 1968), ii. 1 and 672 respectively, whilst S. F. C. Milsom, *The Legal Framework of English Feudalism* (Cambridge, 1976), 1, seeks 'to reconstruct what may be called the feudal component in the framework of English society in the years around 1200'. Note also how D. M. Stenton, *English Justice between the Norman Conquest and the Great Charter 1066–1215* (Philadelphia, 1964), divides the Anglo-Norman material between chapters on 'The Anglo-Saxon Inheritance' and 'The Angevin Leap Forward'.

[21] Pollock and Maitland, ii. 35; see also e.g. ii. 82.

[22] Pollock and Maitland, i. 236–7.

[23] e.g. Pollock and Maitland, i. 355.

[24] Pollock and Maitland, i. 236. Maitland sometimes sought to keep separate analysis of personal and of real rights, but elsewhere let the distinction disappear. Thus he noted 'an indeterminate right of the lord to prevent alienations which would

Land-holding was further complicated by the personal bond of homage and fealty, and by rights of property 'shading off' into rights of
sovereignty and jurisdiction.[25] The Angevin legal reforms constituted
a shift in jurisdiction rather than a fundamental change in the nature
of rights in land.[26]

Many subsequent studies, often without any great self-
consciousness, have simply taken over Maitland's framework of a
complex of rights in land and rights in the person. However, Maitland's
framework has been criticized by Thorne and most fully by Milsom.
They lay considerable emphasis upon two key points, one historical,
one legal: first, Stenton's view of the Anglo-Norman world as one
composed of sovereign honours, focused on the seignorial court;
secondly, tight Common Law-based definition of key terms, such as
'rights', 'inheritance', and 'ownership'. Such definition helps them to
make clear what they see as key elements of pre-Common Law
practice. Thorne argued that seignorial control of land was fundamental to land-holding before 1200 in a way for which Maitland had
not allowed. In the early twelfth century, when a tenant died, 'land
which had been the lord's all along, subject to the tenant's interest,
became his free of that interest... his rights in it revived in their
entirety'. The dead tenant's heir 'had no rights in the land but merely
a claim to succeed his ancestor as the lord's feudal man'.[27] The
tenant only became the true owner of the land in *c.*1200, following
Henry II's reforms.

For Milsom, land-holding, jurisdiction, and the nature of norms
are inextricably linked. It was the emergence of royal jurisdiction
which created the substantive rules and framework of rights in land
described by Maitland.[28] He rejects as inappropriate the notion of

seriously impair his interests', Pollock and Maitland, i. 346, but did not define whether
this was a right in relation to his tenant or his tenement.

[25] Pollock and Maitland, i. 68, 296, 585.

[26] However, according to Maitland, the reforms, as well as other causes, could lead
to changes in the balance between the various holders of rights in land; see e.g. Pollock
and Maitland, i. 344 on alienation.

[27] Thorne, 'Estates in Land', 196-7.

[28] A claimant could now force an unwilling lord to accept his claim by resort to
royal authority; this change from claims and obligations to real rights, from personal
to proprietal relationships, constituted 'a transformation of elementary legal ideas';
Milsom, *Legal Framework*, 37-8. The new jury procedures also created a new type of
law: they allowed 'the facts to come out', and 'substantive law is the product of
thinking about facts'; Milsom, *Legal Framework*, 2, Pollock and Maitland, vol. i, p.
lxvii—and note especially Milsom's 'Law and Fact in Legal Development', *University
of Toronto Law Journal*, 17 (1967), 1-19.

ownership for the analysis of land-holding before the late twelfth century: the essential elements were personal, between man and lord, not proprietal, between man and land. In a world of sovereign honours, 'transactions and litigation mainly happened in the vertical dimension', that is between man and lord. Of an essence are reciprocal obligations, not rights good against the world.[29] Men had only claims against the lord, and if, for example, an heir was passed over at the time of succession, 'he cannot by litigation seek the ouster of the one preferred'.[30] 'Seisin itself connotes not just factual possession but that seignorial acceptance which is all the title there can be.'[31]

Thus such writers have often placed considerable reliance on modern legal terms. When employed sensitively, these can certainly be of considerable help in clarifying argument, although they must not lead to neglect of the vocabulary of the time. Thus I shall distinguish between principles, norms, and rules.[32] Principles and norms arguably are better seen as a continuum, with principles as the more general, not being essentially connected with specific contexts such as land-holding.[33] Their nature is best spelt out by an example: thus the principle that a man must act well towards his family produces the norm that a man must not disinherit his heir, but the closeness of the relationship between heir and donor may affect the influence of the norm in a particular case, as might other factors. Hence the weight of principles and norms varies with circumstances.

---

[29] Pollock and Maitland, vol. i, p. xlvii; Milsom, *Legal Framework*, ch. 2, esp. pp. 37–9. For further discussion, see J. G. H. Hudson, 'Milsom's Legal Structure: Interpreting Twelfth-Century Law', *TVR* 59 (1991), 47–66.

[30] Milsom, *Legal Framework*, 181, although note the qualification at p. 41.

[31] Milsom, *Legal Framework*, 40; on such an absolute bind, see also p. 183, and for criticism, see P. R. Hyams, 'Warranty and Good Lordship in Twelfth Century England', *L&HR* 5 (1987), 464, D. W. Sutherland, *The Assize of Novel Disseisin* (Oxford, 1973), 215, and below, pp. 132–3.

[32] Usage is not settled amongst lawyers, and differing definitions have produced disagreements between historians. My thinking here starts from H. L. A. Hart, *The Concept of Law* (Oxford, 1961); J. Raz, *Practical Reason and Norms* (London, 1975); R. M. Dworkin (ed.), *The Philosophy of Law* (Oxford, 1977); P. Bourdieu, *Outline of a Theory of Practice*, tr. R. Nice (Cambridge, 1977); S. Roberts, *Order and Dispute* (Harmondsworth, 1979), ch. 10; R. M. Dworkin, *Law's Empire* (London, 1986).

[33] Norms may be important in obtaining outside help during a case, but the outside authority's decision is also affected by other considerations such as his favour or disfavour to the claimant. One principle or norm may outweigh another in a case. However, because of their nature and because of the absence of a strict notion of precedent during this period, the defeated principle or norm, though possibly weakened, need not be invalidated for another, similar case. On the other hand, repeated successful appeal to a norm could strengthen it for the future.

Rules I take to be certain norms regularly enforced by superior
authority.

I attempt throughout to explain the functioning and development
of law both through underlying structures and through eleventh- and
twelfth-century perceptions of lordship and land-holding. Thus I
seek to analyse the workings of land-holding and law in terms of
parties pursuing their aims in various ways. For example, rather than
laying down at once a court framework which ought to have applied,
one can examine the problems facing parties, to which courts they
took them, and how far such were matters for courts at all. In
particular, I stress two themes which have often been lacking in
previous writings on legal history. First, I emphasize the importance
of power in its effect upon law and lordship. Secondly, I analyse the
importance of changes in thought on reasoning concerning law and
land-holding.[34] For example, the study of the emergence of Common
Law has not really been connected with the various changes known
as the 'Twelfth-Century Renaissance', which have tended to be the
preserve of historians of 'ideas', that is of academic rather than more
mundane thought. Yet changes in the practice of law can be seen
as part of this Renaissance, and law provides an ideal field for
examining 'the application of rational discourse to ordinary life'.[35] I
also emphasize the various points of view upon land-holding, for
example the contrasting attitudes of ecclesiastics and laymen, and
suggest that such differences were of notable influence. Both of these
themes will become apparent in my discussion of cases, and allow a
more nuanced picture of the working of law within society.

I arrange the book in three sections, concerning security of tenure,
heritability, and alienability. These reflect areas of concern for both
lord and tenant. Take the latter's point of view. He will have received
his land, either as a new gift from his lord, or as his ancestor's land

---

[34] For a much broader—and controversial—discussion of the effect of these changes
on Western law and society, see H. J. Berman, *Law and Revolution: The Formation of the
Western Legal Tradition* (Cambridge, Mass., 1983).

[35] The phrase is from R. W. Southern, *Robert Grosseteste* (Oxford, 1986), 50. For
the moment, see e.g. R. C. van Caenegem, *The Birth of the English Common Law* (2nd.
edn., Cambridge, 1988). In a slightly different context, see also P. R. Hyams, 'Trial by
Ordeal: The Key to Proof in the Early Common Law', in M. S. Arnold *et al.* (edd.),
On the Laws and Customs of England: Essays in Honor of Samuel E. Thorne (Chapel Hill,
NC, 1981), 90–126, and R. Bartlett, *Trial by Fire and Water: The Medieval Judicial
Ordeal* (Oxford, 1986). The effect of such practical abstract thought will be most
clearly illustrated in my discussion of life-grants, below, pp. 97–101.

to be held of that lord. The former would be referred to as his acquisition, the latter as his inheritance.[36] During his lifetime, the man would desire that his tenure be secure, but it might be threatened in various ways. For example, he might come into conflict with his lord over services, or his position as the rightful heir might be challenged, be it by the lord or a third party. The tenant would also wish to dispose of his lands as he saw fit. This could involve ensuring that they passed to his heirs after his death, or giving them to others in his lifetime. Such choices would be determined by various considerations and customs. For example, in post-Conquest England, inherited lands generally passed to the eldest son, but acquisitions might be granted more flexibly. Clearly all these concerns are interconnected, and at times they might conflict: thus an heir might not be happy to see his father granting away the family lands. Added complexity is brought by the fact that each individual would simultaneously or consecutively have various roles: lords were also tenants, heirs became fathers. Not just one, but the combination of these roles helped to shape the ideas and practice of land-holding.

[36] See below, pp. 209–10.

PART I

SECURITY OF TENURE

2

Security of Tenure: Homage, Distraint, and Warranty

Those who serve him for the lands which they hold are already rooted and grounded, and have no fear of being torn up so long as they conform themselves to their lord's will.

Eadmer, *Vita Anselmi*[1]

LORDSHIP was a key element in land-holding in the Anglo-Norman period. Tenure—the relationship of lord, tenant, and land—and its security have been areas of considerable interest for historians both of law and of politics. In particular, the termination of such relations has been examined as a key to the relative power of the parties. Amongst legal historians, Maitland wrote that escheat 'forms as it were a basis for all [the lord's] other rights', and Milsom placed his consideration of 'Disciplinary Jurisdiction' prominently at the start of *The Legal Framework of English Feudalism.*[2] Similarly, many historians see the capacity of Henry I and his Angevin successors to disinherit tenants in chief as a key element in their power.[3]

From where, then, did this disciplinary jurisdiction and this claim to escheat stem, and how much more can be discovered about the way in which it was exercised? I first deal briefly with connections between homage and land-holding, for some previous scholars have taken the homage relationship to be central to both the creation and the termination of tenurial bonds. The bulk of the chapter is then

[1] Eadmer, *The Life of St. Anselm, Archbishop of Canterbury*, ed. and tr. R. W. Southern (2nd edn., Oxford, 1972), 94.

[2] Pollock and Maitland, i. 351. See also R. C. Palmer, 'The Origins of Property in England', *L&HR* 3 (1985), 6–7.

[3] The discontinuities in the descent of lands at this level, especially under Henry I, stem from forfeiture not from any weakness of routine succession; see below, chs. 3–4. On Henry II's limited use of forfeiture, see J. E. Lally, 'Secular Patronage at the Court of King Henry II', *BIHR* 49 (1976), 160.

devoted to distraint and the enforcement of services. Distraint, the removal from the vassal of chattels or land, is seen as the main process by which a lord could discipline his tenants, although of course many other informal pressures could be brought to bear. I close with a discussion of good and bad lordship, with particular attention to the warranty of land. Examination of these areas reveals the considerable security of tenure enjoyed by vassals in Anglo-Norman England.

HOMAGE, LAND-HOLDING, AND FORFEITURE

The bond between lord and vassal was most clearly expressed in the homage ceremony. Maitland wrote that 'Glanvill and Bracton seem to lower their voices to a religious whisper when they speak of homage.'[4] According to *Glanvill*, homage, unlike oaths of fealty, necessarily involved land-holding: 'homages are only done about lands and free tenements, services and rents precisely fixed in cash or in other things. Homages are not owed to anyone for mere lordship, except to the king [*excepto principe*].'[5] However, *Glanvill*'s statement must be treated with caution. Naturally there is a danger of projecting his views too far back into the twelfth century. Conceivably he was making an ex-parte statement. Moreover, his emphasis on the close tie between homage and land-holding must stem in part from his purpose; he was not interested in other aspects of homage.[6] Evidence from other sources, notably vernacular literature, emphasizes the continuing possibility of a personal homage involving no tenurial link. These reinforce *Glanvill*'s stress on the mutuality of the bond, and, for example, the man preserving his lord's earthly honour in all things. They recall the ideal that a man should love whom his lord loves, hate whom he hates.[7]

[4] Pollock and Maitland, i. 297. On homage, see also J.-F. Lemarignier, *Recherches sur l'hommage en marche et les frontières féodales* (Lille, 1945), esp. ch. 3; J. Le Goff, 'The Symbolic Ritual of Vassalage', in his *Time, Work and Culture in the Middle Ages*, tr. A. Goldhammer (Chicago, 1980), 237–87, 354–67.

[5] *Glanvill*, ix. 2, Hall, 106.

[6] See similarly S. D. B. Brown, 'Military Service and Monetary Reward in the Eleventh and Twelfth Centuries', *History*, 74 (1989), 25, on *Bracton*.

[7] I learnt much from Stephen Brown's unpublished paper on 'The Significance of Homage in the Creation and Definition of Lord–Vassal Ties'. See also P. R. Hyams, 'Warranty and Good Lordship in Twelfth Century England', *L&HR* 5 (1987), 449; *Glanvill*, ix. 4, ix. 1, Hall, 107, 104. *Glanvill* adds the proviso 'saving the faith owed to the lord king and his heirs' to the obligation of honour.

If the homage bond often but not necessarily involved land-holding, did land-holding generally or necessarily involve homage? In the modern literature, the strongest claim for the connection has been Thorne's:

In feudal theory, a fief was given to a vassal in return for his homage and service. It was to provide his maintenance and give him the means of furnishing his lord with the service due. Thus it was his for no fixed period, but only as long as the personal relationship of vassalage, the tie of homage between lord and man which constituted his title, continued.[8]

Various twelfth-century texts reveal links between homage and the creation of a tenurial relationship. According to *Glanvill*, 'homage should be done in the following form: he who is to do homage shall become the man of his lord, swearing to bear him faith about that tenement for which he does his homage.'[9] As such statements may lead us to expect, many charters refer to grants being made in return for homage. Henry I gave back to Abingdon ten hides in Sparsholt which Hugh fitzTurstan held; Hugh and whoever held after him were 'to do homage therefrom and fealty to the church and abbot'.[10] Other charters state more tersely that the gift was made 'for his homage and service'.[11]

However, such evidence need not mean that land could be granted only in return for homage, even in *Glanvill*'s day. The passage from *Glanvill* just cited continued 'but homage should not always be done about all lands', and the writer mentions that homage is not owed, for instance, for land given in free alms, or for dower, or, until the third heir, for frank-marriage, or for the fee of younger sisters holding of the eldest.[12] In addition, homage would not have been taken for

---

[8] S. E. Thorne, 'English Feudalism and Estates in Land', *CLJ* (1959), 196.
[9] *Glanvill*, ix. 1, Hall, 104.
[10] *Regesta*, ii. No. 683.
[11] Examples from the first half of the 12th cent. include F. M. Stenton, *The First Century of English Feudalism, 1066–1166* (2nd edn., Oxford, 1961), No. 30; *Reading Abbey Cartularies*, ed. B. R. Kemp (2 vols.; Camden Soc., 4th Ser. 31, 33; 1986, 1987), No. 577. S. F. C. Milsom, *The Legal Framework of English Feudalism* (Cambridge, 1976), 85 n. 2, has uncovered early plea roll cases where the tenant successfully claims land from a lord who has taken his homage but not delivered the promised land; all involve claims also relating to charters or to homage before the royal justices.
[12] *Glanvill*, ix. 2, Hall, 106. Some groups of persons were excluded from doing homage; *Glanvill*, ix. 1, Hall, 106, excludes females. See *S. Anselmi Cantuariensis Archiepisc. Opera Omnia*, ed. F. S. Schmitt (6 vols.; Edinburgh, 1938–61), iv, No. 223, for Pope Paschal II laying down that clerics are not to do homage to laymen for lands. The controversy between Anselm and Henry I may well have sharpened thinking

more limited grants, for example for terms of lives.[13] It would seem
therefore that *Glanvill* did not regard homage as necessary to all
complete grants of land; this contrasts to his attitude to livery of
seisin, without which he considered a gift a 'naked promise'.[14]

Furthermore, charters referring briefly to grants 'for his homage
and service' only become particularly common in the second half of
the twelfth century.[15] Usage even then was inconsistent; charters
referring to apparently similar or connected grants sometimes mention homage in one case and not in another.[16] Arguments from
silence are of course extremely dangerous, and the rarity of mentions
of homage in earlier twelfth-century charters might mean that homage was so important as always to be assumed. A Ramsey agreement
from 1114 × 30 recording a gift 'without homage' furthers the
ambiguity; does it prove that homage was normally done, hence
the need for this explicit statement, or that gifts without homage
were perfectly conceivable?[17] Comparison with the regular statements
that grants were made in return for services may well indicate that
homage was not necessarily done for every gift. Occasional charters
link land-holding with fealty rather than homage.[18] Even in the case

---

concerning the relationship between homage and land-holding. The final compromise,
of course, allowed bishops elect to do homage to the king, but, according to *Glanvill*,
ix. 1, Hall, 106, 'consecrated bishops are not accustomed to do homage to the lord
king even for their baronies, but swear fealty accompanied by an oath'.

[13] Pollock and Maitland, ii. 113.

[14] *Glanvill*, vii. i, Hall, 69–70. Milsom, *Legal Framework*, 160 n. 2, cites examples of
'the taking of homage as evidence that a tenant was seised'.

[15] *The Beauchamp Cartulary: Charters 1100–1268*, ed. E. Mason (PRS, NS 43;
1980), provides no examples from before 1170, Nos. 10, 11, 310 could be from the
1170s but may be later, and e.g. Nos. 180–1, 214, 216, 287, 327, 335, 345–6 may be
from the 12th cent. but are certainly after 1180; among the Honour of Richmond
charters in *EYC*, iv and v, note from the 1150s or 1160s Nos. 244–5; later in the
century, e.g. Nos. 143, 309, 322, 395; the *Stoke by Clare Cartulary, BL Cotton Appx. xxi*,
ed. C. Harper-Bill and R. Mortimer (Suffolk Charters 4–6; 1982–4), provides a
similar pattern, No. 30 coming from 1166 × 73, many more from later in the century,
e.g. Nos. 246, 248, 439.

[16] See e.g. *Charters of the Honour of Mowbray, 1107–1191*, ed. D. E. Greenway
(London, 1972), Nos. 366 and 367 (both *c*.1170 × *c*.1181).

[17] *Chronicon Abbatiae Rameseiensis*, ed. W. D. Macray (London, 1886), 263–4.

[18] See e.g. *Ramsey Chronicle*, 245–6. *EYC*, iv, No. 31, for Kirkstead Abbey, specified
that the lands were granted as freely as any alms could be, 'not doing fealty or any
other worldly service'. Note also the unusual arrangements in a Norman cirograph,
*Earldom of Gloucester Charters: The Charters and Scribes of the Earls and Countesses of
Gloucester to A.D. 1217*, ed. R. B. Patterson (Oxford, 1973), No. 70.

of some charters which do refer to homage, it is unclear whether the homage and gift were more than temporally linked.[19]

Was homage particularly linked to one form of land-holding, most probably holding in fee?[20] The *Leges Henrici* draw a distinction between disputes concerning a person and his farmer 'who is not his man' and those between a person and one who holds a farm 'in fee and has done homage for it'.[21] The Assize of Northampton, clause 4, concerns lands of free tenants which it refers to as fees: 'if the heir is under age, the lord of the fee is to accept his homage and hold him in wardship as long as he ought'.[22] On the other hand, concerning the lord of the fee's obligation to take homage from the heir, *Glanvill* states that 'thus I say if those fees owe homage'.[23] Perhaps *Glanvill* was here using fee in the very general sense of 'holding', rather than land specifically held 'in fee'. In the charter evidence, however, one can find instances where grants in fee did not involve immediate homage.[24] More importantly, one may ask whether a further gift in fee by a lord to a man who had already paid him homage, whether every increment given to a vassal, required a fresh homage. Sometimes grants were explicitly made for services and homage already rendered. Especially telling is a Ramsey grant 'in fee and inheritance' to Nicholas 'Mercenarius' made 'since we did not wish to lose his homage and service'.[25] Here it sounds as if a single act of homage had been done some time in the past. Such a grant of land might even sometimes be a reward for faithful service in a homage

---

[19] e.g. *Regesta*, ii. No. 511. The relationship between homage, land, and services in *Feudal Documents from the Abbey of Bury St Edmunds*, ed. D. C. Douglas (London, 1932), No. 168, the Bury charter regarding the Conqueror's knight Peter, is far from clear. Cf. the comment of E. Z. Tabuteau, *Transfers of Property in Eleventh-Century Norman Law* (Chapel Hill, NC, 1988), 122, on the scarcity and brevity of mentions of homage and fealty in 11th cent. Norman charters.

[20] On the meaning of 'holding in fee', stressing its lasting nature, see below, Ch. 3. *Bracton*, fo. 84, Thorne, ii. 244, sees those holding in socage as being bound by fealty rather than homage. Other evidence does refer to some socage tenants doing homage; see Pollock and Maitland, i. 306 and references at n. 3.

[21] *Leges Henrici*, 56 1–2, Downer, 174; note also *Feudal Documents*, No. 127.

[22] *SSC*, 180.

[23] *Glanvill*, ix. 1, Hall, 103.

[24] e.g. *Sir Christopher Hatton's Book of Seals*, ed. L. C. Loyd and D. M. Stenton (Northants Rec. Soc. and Oxford, 1950), No. 429, homage when a gift of twenty librates is complete.

[25] *Ramsey Chronicle*, 309, although the granting verbs may suggest that this was a confirmation rather than a new grant. Note p. 272, where the grantee is referred to as 'our man'.

relationship which had previously had no tenurial element. Thus even the temporal links between gift and homage may be loosened.

Such conclusions distance the connection between homage and land-holding, compared with the close and necessary connection suggested by *Glanvill*, but they do not completely destroy it. That a link did exist is further illustrated by disciplinary escheat. Breaches of homage constituted felonies, and these could bring the homage, and hence the tenurial, relationship to an end.[26] Honorial examples of lands escheating to the lord for disciplinary reasons are hard to find, but some can be uncovered. They arise, for example, from failure to serve or to answer in court.[27] Thus a narrative concerning the foundation of Biddlesden Abbey states that

in the time of King Stephen, when there was a very great war, Robert [of Meppershall] stayed at Meppershall and left Biddlesden, and as neither he nor anyone for him rendered service for it to the earl of Leicester, the land escheated to the earl, who gave it to his steward Ernald de Bosco for his service.[28]

Such specific examples back up the general statements of the *Leges Henrici* and of *Glanvill*. The *Leges* state that 'anyone who commits theft, is a traitor to his lord, flees from him in an encounter with the enemy or on the battlefield, or is convicted of having committed felony, is to forfeit his land', and *Glanvill* records that generally a man

may not, without breach of the faith of homage, do anything which works to the disinheritance or bodily dishonour of his lord. . . . If anyone does anything to the disinheritance of his lord and is convicted of it, he and his heirs shall by law lose the fee which he holds of him.[29]

---

[26] Note, however, the change in the meaning of the word 'felony', away from this specifically feudal context to cover instead serious crimes punishable by death or mutilation; Pollock and Maitland, i. 303–5.

[27] *Regesta*, ii, No. 1314. Often the reason for escheat cannot be discovered, e.g. *HKF*, iii. 323.

[28] *Monasticon Anglicanum*, ed. Sir William Dugdale, rev. J. Caley, H. Ellis, and B. Bandinel (6 vols. in 8, London, 1817–30), v. 367; note the fear of continuing insecurity with regard to this land; for comment, see D. B. Crouch, *The Beaumont Twins* (Cambridge, 1986), 80. See also *CMA*, ii. 140–1, and esp. 'The Charters of the Earldom of Hereford, 1095–1201', ed. D. Walker, in *Camden Miscellany*, xxii (Camden Soc., 4th Ser. 1; 1964), No. 38 which specifies that tenants are to pay their rent 'as they love their holdings'.

[29] *Leges Henrici*, 43 7; note also 43 3–4, and the lesser penalty for leaving the lord

General statements are not confined to law books. The Abingdon chronicler, writing probably in the 1160s but concerning events at the start of Henry I's reign, recorded the case of William the king's chamberlain who refused to do homage to Faritius, the new abbot of Abingdon. His failure to serve against Robert Curthose's invasion was proved by the abbot and, the chronicler wrote, 'in accordance with the law of the country it was decided that he deservedly should be deprived of the land'. Certainly in practice disciplinary escheat was sometimes reversed or tempered by compensation, as in fact occurred in the case of William the king's chamberlain.[30] This might result from a prejudice against the extreme action of severing the lordship bond or from the practical limitations of lordship. Still, the norms to which appeal was made are revealing. Breach of homage could end the relationship of man and lord, and therefore also the land-holding arrangement which was one aspect of that relationship. This mixture of the personal and the tenurial is well illustrated in an order by Bishop Nigel of Ely: the addressees were to obey 'just as you love me and the fee you hold of me'.[31]

Having abandoned *Glanvill*'s apparent certainties, perhaps one can only conclude that homage was generally central to the bond of man and lord, and was therefore closely linked to the land-holding elements of that bond. Homage would precede the initial creation of a holding in fee, but it need not have been specific to that holding. A structure to explain twelfth-century land law cannot, therefore, happily rest upon the act of homage as peculiarly constitutive of the holding of each tenement by the vassal from the lord.

---

without permission mentioned in 43 2: all Downer, 152. J. Biancalana, 'For Want of Justice: Legal Reforms of Henry II', *Columbia Law Review*, 88 (1988), 452, takes *Leges Henrici*, 43 4, Downer, 152 specifically to refer to services; it seems rather to refer to answering in court ('esse ad rectum' = 'to be to justice'). *Glanvill*, ix. 1, Hall, 104; see also vii. 12, p. 85, for forfeiture because of marrying off daughters without the lord's consent, ix. 13, p. 115, for forfeiture because of a tenant making a purpresture against his lord.

[30] *CMA*, ii. 128–9. For another general statement concerning the justice of forfeiture, see *Cartularium Prioratus de Colne*, ed. J. L. Fisher (Essex Arch. Soc. Publications, 1; 1946), No. 39, a case from *c*.1175. For compensation, see also e.g. *CMA*, ii. 104–5. Compromise, as well as the typical problems of investigating the internal affairs of the honour, thus helps to explain the shortage of specific evidence of disciplinary escheat.

[31] *Liber Eliensis* ed. E. O. Blake (Camden Soc., 3rd Ser. 92; 1962), 381.

SERVICES AND DISTRAINT

Even if performance of the classic feudal due of serving as a knight in
the host was rather less common in Anglo-Norman England than
once believed, desire for service was a vital element underlying the
creation of the bond between lord and man, and homage, together
with the oath of fealty, can often be seen as intimately linked to
service. Performance of service was the most obvious recollection of
homage.[32] When a lord gave his vassal a man's homage, the most
obvious lasting effect would be the performance of service to the
donee instead of the donor. As I have already noted, failure to serve
might amount to disloyalty, and hence terminate the bond.

For the vassal, certainty concerning services was a sign of holding
freely.[33] The capacity to exact his dues and the tenant's to resist
unjust demands were therefore essential features of the balance of
power in seignorial relationships. Some, but by no means all, charters
record the amount of knight service owed. Very few give detailed
information on other dues and obligations.[34] Even were such matters
settled orally at the time of the grant, room for dispute was likely to
remain, even if the parties did not deliberately struggle to improve
their relative position. Effective lordship rested on the lord's ability to
display and, if necessary, to use his might in order to enforce his
will. Many different means might be employed, as appropriate to
circumstances, but amongst these distraint was crucial as a method of
exerting pressure to various ends, including service enforcement.[35]
The noun *districcio* itself could mean forceful pressure, and it was
used by victims to suggest that the pressure was unjust.[36] Lords
surely distrained not merely to end a temporary refusal of service,

---

[32] See esp. F. Joüon des Longrais, *La Conception Anglaise de la saisine du xiie au xiv^e
siècle* (Paris, 1925), 262; note also Anselm, *Opera Omnia*, iv, No. 223, *Bracton*, fo. 78b,
Thorne, ii. 228. See below, Ch. 7, for services as a primary consideration in permitting
or forbidding alienation.

[33] See A. W. Douglas, 'Tenure *in elemosina*: Origins and Establishment in Twelfth-
Century England', *AJLegH* 24 (1980), 100–1; also P. R. Hyams, *Kings, Lords, and
Peasants in Medieval England* (Oxford, 1980).

[34] For one unusual example, where a donor sought to impose lay obligations upon
an abbot, see *Ramsey Chronicle*, 274–5.

[35] The one book devoted solely to distraint is F. A. Enever, *History of the Law
of Distress for Rent and Damage Feasant* (London, 1931), but Enever's arguments,
particularly concerning the period before 1200 are not very trustworthy.

[36] e.g. Hugh the Chantor, *The History of the Church of York, 1066–1127*, ed. and tr.
C. Johnson (Edinburgh, 1961), 31.

but to teach the offender a lesson, and to encourage obedience in the other barons of the honour. These considerations suggest that distraint sometimes constituted only semi-tamed force.[37]

Yet historians have generally represented distraint as a closely controlled legal process. In part, they can do so because of the relatively numerous mentions of distraint in twelfth-century law books, and the scarcity of evidence concerning actual practice. Few surviving documents record processes for exacting service, and barely any disputes can be substantially reconstructed. Much outside intervention within the lordship may be hidden because, starting informally or by plaint to the sheriff, it produced no record.[38] When a relevant writ does survive, it is rarely possible to tell from what stage in a dispute it comes. Lack of evidence also helps to explain historians' disagreements over distraint.

Apart from considerations of the administration of justice, legal historians have tended to neglect the practical needs which helped to determine procedures for enforcing services. Distraint could be a strategy adopted at one stage in a continuing dispute. It could provide the lord with a bargaining counter against his recalcitrant vassal. Moreover, even if distraint was sometimes forceful, it might also be regarded as a ritual act, a statement or gesture, to be interpreted by the interested parties.

Depending on particular circumstances, distraint could aim at bringing the distrainee into court, or directly at gaining the services required, or both.[39] Milsom cites an assize of 1204 which refers to the tenant being distrained not to answer in court concerning the services, but to do them there.[40] Lords desired public performance and hence public admission of due service, and the lord's court

---

[37] See below, pp. 42–45; also 42 n. 133 for evidence that the Church in Normandy saw lay attitudes to distraint as needing further taming. Such are of course the attitudes the conquering lords brought to England.

[38] See below, p. 41.

[39] Many historians distinguish distraint to force a tenant to perform services from distraint to compel appearance in court, the latter being part of mesne process; see e.g. Pollock and Maitland, ii. 593 on distraint to force appearance in court in personal actions. Milsom, *Legal Framework*, 8–13 esp. 11 argues that, on the contrary, mesne process and distraint for services were not separate in the 12th cent.: distraint was part of the usual procedure to force a tenant to answer at court, in this case concerning failure to serve.

[40] *CRR*, iii. 133: cited Milsom, *Legal Framework*, 14 nn. 1–3. The plaintiffs lost, partly because they distrained by fee without a previous taking of chattels, thus contravening royal court rules.

was one very suitable forum for such demonstrations of obedience. Furthermore, even if a tenant eventually did service away from court, he might still have to answer for his earlier failure. In this sense distraint was intended both to exact immediate performance of service and to force the tenant to answer in court.

I now deal first with cases where the tenant admitted holding of the lord but withheld service or disputed the amount owed, secondly with instances where the distrainee disclaimed tenure from the lord. I concentrate upon military service and rent. Since my primary interest is lordship, I leave aside, for example, distraint for debts between men with no seignorial link, which might be dealt with in other courts, by other procedures. I argue that in some circumstances distraint had to obtain swift obedience, and that such needs helped to form Norman attitudes to proper distraint. Even then, distraint had to be reasonable, although the criteria of reasonableness might be flexible, and one man's view of reasonableness would of course vary according to circumstances and his perspective as either distrainor or distrainee.

The Norman lords who came to England with William I must have been aware that, in certain circumstances, distraint had to be swift to be effective. Vassals were summoned to bring their knights for an expedition, meeting at a fixed place and time. The recipient may have been unprepared. Unlike rent, military service was not rendered at established dates, after which the lord could proceed against his tenant. The recipient would face his lord's wrath and action if he failed to bring a satisfactory body of knights, and hence had rapidly to exact the service owed to him.[41] Even were the lord summoning the men for his own purposes, swift enforcement might be a matter of victory or defeat, life or death. A lengthy process would be useless. Such pressures must have helped to determine the notions of distraint which the conquering Normans brought to and developed in England.

How far they saw the same process of distraint as appropriate for dues other than military service in person is unclear. Not all disputes

---

[41] J. C. Holt, 'The Introduction of Knight Service in England', *A-NS* 6 (1984), 104, argues that the king demanded a satisfactory turn-out, not exact fulfilment of the quota owed. However, see *CMA*, ii. 128, where the abbot sends a substitute for a knight who failed to answer his summons. This suggests that exact fulfilment may have been required.

were so serious, and non-payment of rent, for example, can hardly have been seen as failing one's lord in his necessity. In such cases the procedure may have been less peremptory. Moreover, summons of the host became rarer in Anglo-Norman England, certainly from Henry I's reign. When military service was demanded, it may often have been as scutage.[42] This possibly made peremptory action less likely. Although lords had sometimes found substitutes for non-attending vassals, it was probably easier to absorb a vassal's recalcitrance with regard to scutage; the shortfall could be met from the lord's other revenues, including the scutage raised from knights enfeoffed in excess of royal requirements. In addition, it is questionable how often lords in England summoned men for their own, rather than royal, military purposes, at least outside the Marches and Stephen's reign.[43] Yet on other, non-military, occasions personal service must still have been urgent. Some peremptory procedure must lie behind the development of distraint in Anglo-Norman England.

If exaction sometimes was peremptory, even so it should, no doubt, have been reasonable. Few lords can have been able regularly to ignore the customs and opinion of their court. The *Leges Willelmi* specified that no one was to take distraint 'rashly [*temere*]'.[44] In *Glanvill* one reads that lords distraining for aids should act 'according to the consideration of their court and reasonable custom'.[45] Obviously the criteria of reasonableness might vary with the position of the parties in the dispute; the same man might apply different standards when distraining or being distrained. The circumstances of what in the lord's eyes constituted his vassal's failure might also have an effect. Conceivably there were variations between the customs of different honours. And the criteria expressed or acted upon might vary with the relative power of the parties involved, taking into account the ability of both to rally support within the honour and to

[42] C. W. Hollister, *The Military Organization of Norman England* (Oxford, 1965), 195–204. However, T. Keefe, *Feudal Assessments and the Political Community under Henry II and his Sons* (Berkeley, Calif., 1983), 87, argues that Henry II was not intent on wholly substituting scutage for knight service. The situation in Stephen's reign is obscure, but wider violence may well have encouraged peremptory action.

[43] For the need to obtain immediate military service in the Marches against one's enemies, see the Magna Carta of Cheshire, c. 10, *The Charters of the Anglo-Norman Earls of Chester, c.1071–1237*, ed. G. Barraclough (Rec. Soc. of Lancs. and Cheshire, 126; 1988), No. 394.

[44] *Leges Willelmi*, 44, Liebermann, *Gesetze*, i. 517: the French version does not include an equivalent of *temere*.

[45] *Glanvill*, ix. 8, Hall, 112.

obtain outside help.[46] On all these questions, evidence is too scarce
for clear conclusions. However, certain key issues do emerge.

First, was a court judgment required?[47] The evidence is ambiguous, and it is perfectly conceivable that on some occasions judgment
did occur, on others it did not—the variations being at least partly
explicable by the kind of considerations just outlined.[48] In addition,
absence or other circumstances might render manifest the failure
to perform properly the required service. In 1088 William Rufus
summoned, amongst others, William bishop of Durham to serve.[49]
The bishop failed to fulfil his obligation, his lands were seized, and
he was brought to trial, where Hugh de Beaumont put the king's
case. In Hugh's hearing, the king had summoned the bishop to ride
with him:

you answered to him that you would willingly go with the seven knights
whom you had there and would with haste send to your castle for more; and
afterwards you fled from his court without his permission, and took with you
certain of his household, and thus failed him in his necessity.

Whilst the plea concerns desertion, not simple failure to respond to
summons, the two were not very different in effect—both might be
regarded as failure to help the lord 'in his necessity', as felonies.[50]
The king's party at the trial seems to justify the earlier seizure of the
bishop's lands by his manifest guilt: Hugh had heard the original
summons, non-performance was obvious.[51] In contrast, a case might

---

[46] See below, pp. 35–40; however, no higher authority was available for lay tenants
in chief, and only the Pope for ecclesiastics.

[47] Most historians hold that a judgment was required: e.g. Pollock and Maitland, i.
353–4, ii. 575. The contrary position is taken by *Select Cases of Procedure without Writ
under Henry III*, ed. H. G. Richardson and G. O. Sayles (Selden Soc. 60; 1941), p.
xciii n. 1.

[48] See also P. A. Brand, 'Lordship and Distraint in Thirteenth Century England',
in P. R. Coss and S. D. Lloyd (edd.), *Thirteenth Century England, III* (Woodbridge,
1991), 6–8.

[49] See Simeon of Durham, *Opera Omnia*, ed. T. Arnold (2 vols.; London, 1882–5),
i. 170–95. I follow Southern, *Saint Anselm and his Biographer* (Cambridge, 1966), 148,
and F. Barlow, *The English Church, 1066–1154* (London, 1979), 281 n. 46, in taking
this text as providing a near contemporary account of the case. For the contrary view,
see H. S. Offler, 'The Tractate *De Iniusta Vexacione Willelmi Episcopi Primi*', *EHR* 66
(1951), 32–41.

[50] Simeon of Durham, i. 181. See also *Glanvill*, ix. 1, Hall, 104–5. Felony and
treachery were often associated, sometimes in a phrase such as 'plus fel que Judas'.

[51] Distraint for damage feasant—damage done by animals encroaching on another's
land—never required a judgment, presumably because the offence was often manifest
and needed to be stopped speedily in order to prevent further damage. A swift process

be unclear, for example concerning the amount of service due,[52] the continuing relevance of an earlier one-off remission,[53] or the date at which rent was owed. Judgment here might be particularly necessary if the decision could affect the lord's other tenants.

Few specific instances of distraint mention judgment.[54] In the early twelfth century there arose a case between Abbot Faritius of Abingdon and Ermenold, a burgess of Oxford, concerning arrears of rent. After Ermenold withheld the rent in one year, the abbot the following year, at harvest-time, ordered that all the chattels which could be found on that land be taken in distraint, and that some sort of action be taken in relation to the land itself—perhaps forbidding the tenant access to it (*terram prohiberi*). The chronicle records no court judgment, and only after the distraint did court procedure begin, with Ermenold finding sureties that he would plead on an appointed day.[55] Nor do the occasional charters providing for future distraint give any hint that judgment should precede distraint.[56]

Possibly, everyone assumed the need for judgment. The *Leges Henrici*'s statement that 'no one may distrain another, without judgment or permission [*licentia*]' may give some indication of seignorial court procedure, but Richardson and Sayles correctly pointed out that it referred specifically to the hundred court, and it derives at least in part from a law of Cnut.[57] One charter of the early 1160s

may also have been permissible when the grant to the tenant made express provision concerning default of service; see examples below, p. 34.

[52] e.g. *CMA*, ii. 129. *Red Book*, i. 204, records a case where the tenant seems to have argued successfully for a lower quota.

[53] Probably the situation envisaged by the *Leges Willelmi*, 32, Liebermann, *Gesetze*, i. 514.

[54] *Regesta*, ii, No. 1865, shows that distraint to attend the abbot of Reading's pleas in his private hundred court required the judgment of the hundred.

[55] *CMA*, ii. 140. The case is also discussed by Brand, 'Lordship and Distraint', 5.

[56] e.g. *Documents Illustrative of the Social and Economic History of the Danelaw*, ed. F. M. Stenton (London, 1920), Nos. 175, 181; *The Registrum Antiquissimum of the Cathedral Church of Lincoln*, ed. C. W. Foster and K. Major (10 vols.; Lincoln Rec. Soc., 1931–73), No. 2124; *Historia et Cartularium Monasterii Sancti Petri Gloucestriae*, ed. W. H. Hart (3 vols.; London, 1863–7), No. CXLVII; see also below, p. 34. The same is true of royal writs referring to distraint; see for example the instances cited by Brand, 'Lordship and Distraint', n. 16. Such documents could of course record exceptional circumstances.

[57] *Leges Henrici*, 51 3, Downer, 166, cf. II *Cn.* 19 2, Liebermann, *Gesetze*, i. 322–3; *Procedure without Writ*, p. xciii n. 1. See also Brand, 'Lordship and Distraint', 5, on this passage. Dr Brand has suggested to me that 'licentia' might mean that lords by their very position were licensed to distrain. I am not convinced that 'licentia' can be so interpreted. However, see also J. Goebel, *Felony and Misdemeanor: A Study in the*

points clearly to judgment before distraint. Robert earl of Leicester notified his men that he held ten librates of land in Knighton hereditarily from the bishop of Lincoln. If he or any of his heirs failed to do or observe their homage, 'the bishop of Lincoln will distrain [*cohercebit*] him by that land according to the judgment of that court, according to the *statutum regni*'. *Statutum regni* may simply mean the custom of the realm, but I think that it probably refers to a royal decree. If so, had Henry instigated a new requirement that distraint be by judgment? A general prohibition of the abuse of distraint is also possible.[58] However, even if this charter points to a general requirement for judgment concerning distraint by land, it need not imply that judgment was needed for distraint by chattels which could have been seen as a less weighty matter.[59]

Glanvill's evidence must be used with caution for the earlier period, since by his time legal change was probably already affecting procedure. Nevertheless his discussion is notable. Writing of a man's disloyalty to his lord, he stated that 'anyone can of right, by judgment of his court, bring his man to trial and distrain him to come to his court', and likewise the lord might distrain for reasonable aids 'by judgment of his court'.[60] Yet, as Brand has pointed out, *Glanvill*'s treatment of distraint for services is different:

although it is said that the distraint is to secure the tenant's appearance in the lord's court to answer for withholding all or part of his service, nothing is said of this distraint being made by the judgment of the court, and responsibility for making the distraint is ascribed solely to the lord.[61]

History of English Legal Procedure (New York, 1937), esp. pp. 211–12, on the relation of the *bannum* and *districtio*; also M. Bloch, *Feudal Society*, tr. L. A. Manyon (2 vols.; London, 1961), ii. 367, on 'low justice' and distraint.

[58] *Registrum Antiquissimum*, No. 313. On the basis of this charter, Stenton, *First Century*, 40 n. 2, argued that 'by itself *statutum* means nothing more than "that which is appointed" . . . No legislation can ever have been put forth on so fundamental a matter of feudal organisation.' He apparently regarded legislation as necessarily involving radical change. Yet coronation charters decreed on matters as 'fundamentally feudal' as relief. If one man was likely to know of such a decree and mention it in a charter, it was the earl of Leicester. That the charter speaks of 'statutum regni', not 'statutum regis' need not rule out legislation. For the tenurial background, see D. B. Crouch, 'The Foundation of Leicester Abbey, and Other Problems', *Midland History*, 12 (1987) 4–6.

[59] On this, see Brand, 'Lordship and Distraint', 6.

[60] *Glanvill*, ix. 1, 8, Hall, 105, 112; see also vi. 10, p. 63.

[61] Brand, 'Lordship and Distraint', 5; *Glanvill*, x. 1, Hall, 105.

Similarly, Brand notes, amongst the early plea roll cases concerning replevin, none of the plaintiffs alleged that distraint was wrong because it occurred without the judgment of the lord's court.[62]

On balance, the evidence does not suggest that there was a general requirement for judgment before distraint. Often a lord may have sought at least the assent of his court. He may have desired this not only to ensure backing from his barons, but also to publicize the action, sometimes to justify to his neighbours the reasons why a body of armed men would soon be riding purposefully across the county. He might need help against a powerful vassal. A single official could take a few of the distrainee's beasts, but sometimes the lord particularly needed the backing of his court since they might be the very men who would have to enforce distraint by fee. On the other hand, a lord with a strong household force relied less on the enfeoffed knights of his court. The relative power of the parties and the scale of the operations could often have a major influence.

A second criterion of reasonableness was regard for peace. Improper seizure of goods could constitute theft or robbery. A miracle story concerning Thomas Becket tells of a certain Ailward who was convicted by ordeal of water for theft, after he had distrained his debtor by breaking into his house.[63] My failure to find similar examples involving seignorial distraint for services may result partly from the paucity of evidence, but also from the social standing of those involved. Lords must have been expected to display their might, and great men taking goods from their tenants would not have been associated with common thieves. The criterion may therefore have been that they act without undue force, particularly force likely to have wider repercussions. No instance of a clear standard for excess force survives, and the limits of legitimate exercise of power must have been unclear. Especially during political disorder, distraint shaded into extortion.[64]

Were there definite provisions for what might be taken and in what order? The set stages which appear in the court rolls, from summons to distraint by chattels and then by fee, could be the product of regular royal control. In addition, distraint as part of mesne process for compelling attendance at court may have required a succession of measures of gradually increasing intensity. But the situation for lords

---

[62] Brand, 'Lordship and Distraint', 6.
[63] *MTB*, i. 155–8; ii. 173–182.
[64] See below, pp. 39, 42.

distraining for service might be different. Here even *Glanvill* seems ambiguous: lords distrain for reasonable aids 'by the chattels they find in their fees or by the fees themselves if necessary'.[65] Was distraint by fee needed because the tenant had not complied after his chattels were taken or because no chattels could be found? Or had the lord and his court from the first judged that only distraint by fee would be effective?[66] There is no hint of successive measures when the Abingdon chronicler, having recounted Ermenold's failure to pay rent, stated that 'in the following year, therefore, the abbot at harvest-time ordered to be taken in distraint all the chattels which could be found on that land, and forbade Ermenold access to it [*terram prohiberi*]'.[67] Many documents in the century after the Conquest specify distraint by land without any suggestion that it should be preceded by the taking of chattels.[68] Even when both lands and chattels are mentioned, there need be no implication of a correct order. In 1155 Henry II ordered all men who ought to hold of the church of Reading to do service to the abbot, as it had been done in Henry I's time. Otherwise, the abbot was to 'justice' them by their lands and chattels.[69]

In practice, chattels may often have been taken as a first step, but not because of any strict legal requirement. The taking of chattels could act as a ritualized threat. The lord was accusing his tenant of having done wrong, and warning of his power to crush him.

---

[65] *Glanvill*, ix. 8, Hall, 112; cf. *Coutumiers de Normandie, ii: La Summa de Legibus Normannie*, ed. E.-J. Tardif (Société de l'Histoire de Normandie, Rouen and Paris, 1896), iii. 2, pp. 7–8.

[66] *Glanvill*, x. 3, Hall, 117, discussing cases concerning debt, states that 'it is not the custom in the court of the lord king to constrain anyone to come to court in any plea by distraining his chattels; therefore in such a plea he may, if the court so decides, be distrained by his fee or by attachment through sureties, as is customary in other pleas'. Perhaps other powerful lords might customarily not distrain by chattels for appearance at court.

[67] *CMA*, ii. 140.

[68] See e.g. *CMA*, ii. 167–8; *Reading*, No. 1076. From after 1166, see e.g. *Beauchamp*, No. 334. Note further a problem with the translation of *pecunia*, which is generally taken to mean chattels, but can occasionally refer to all possessions, movable and immovable.

[69] *Reading*, No. 24. See also E. Miller, *The Abbey and Bishopric of Ely* (Cambridge, 1951), 281, for a later writ of Henry II; *Danelaw Documents*, No. 219. Again it may be helpful to posit some cruder notions of distraint, which influenced thought, but were rarely put into practice in most of England outside Stephen's reign; distraint might approximate to a squeeze, even a harrying, of the vassal's possessions, hence distraint by land and chattels.

However, as a good lord should, he was allowing the tenant the possibility of answering the accusation and of reaching a settlement. At the same time, he ensured that the 'reasonableness' of his distraining was apparent to outsiders. Individual circumstances might also demand distraint by chattels, notably when the man owing service held no land. In addition, removal of some animals, for example, might be simple, and could be performed by one or two of the lord's servants—the typical chattels distrained were not merely movables; with suitable direction, they would move themselves. Seizure of land was likely to meet greater resistance, require greater support.

Did forms of distraint vary according to type of service? Royal writs enforcing suitors' attendance at private hundreds generally specify distraint by chattels, never fee.[70] Otherwise, one finds inconsistency. Sometimes distraint by chattels was specified for non-payment of rent, sometimes distraint by fee.[71] Henry II ordered the knights of the church of Ely to do due ward service on the Isle of Ely, otherwise the bishop was to justice them by their chattels and the fees they held of him, whilst writs of Henry I and II to those owing ward at the castle of Rockingham specified distraint by chattels.[72] Overall, apart from the case of attendance at private hundreds, no rigid association of particular forms of distraint with particular services is apparent.

In order to be reasonable, the distrainor had to treat the distrained goods and lands in a certain way. They had been taken not so much into full possession, but as a bargaining counter whereby the recalcitrant tenant might be pressured. Animals, and perhaps other goods, were to be kept in a pound, whence the distrainee should not seize them back.[73] The *Leges Henrici* mention the offences of *pundbreche* and *excussio*—that is anyone 'taking away and re-appropriating his distrained property'—in a section on the hundred, but its phrasing may suggest wider applicability.[74] Moreover, the

---

[70] *Regesta*, ii, Nos. 1771, 1812, 1865; iii, No. 753, see also No. 490; *Registrum Antiquissimum*, No. 155.

[71] Fee: e.g. *Registrum Antiquissimum*, No. 2124; chattels: e.g. *Regesta*, ii, No. 1387.

[72] Miller, *Ely*, 281; Regesta, ii, No. 563; *Beauchamp*, No. 175. Both of Henry I's writs which definitely concern knight service specify distraint by fee, *Regesta*, ii, Nos. 553, 697; both were to Abingdon, and issued in the first five years of the reign. *Regesta*, ii, No. 1860a, to Ramsey, may be a contrary example; see also *Ramsey Chronicle*, 275, which may concern knight service.

[73] See e.g. *Red Book*, vol. ii, p. cclxix, one of the returns to the Inquest of Sheriffs.

[74] *Leges Henrici*, 40 2, 51 8, Downer, pp. 144, 168. *PR 13 HII*, p. 156: Adam As Gernuns owed 5m. 'pro namis excussis'.

distrainor should not grant away the lands, nor consume or sell the goods. William bishop of Durham complained that the king had swiftly granted his lands to other men.[75] Yet despite such provisions, one still finds lords who did sell distrained goods, and seem to have got away with it.[76]

After the distraint had been made, the distrainee should offer gage and surety as guarantee that he would answer the claim for services, in return for which the distrainor must release the possessions. The burgess Ermenold, having been distrained, sent Walter archdeacon of Oxford and Richard of Standlake to Abbot Faritius and regained his goods on their surety.[77] Although we have no clear evidence from the century 1066–1166, it seems probable that land taken in distraint should similarly have been returned. This requirement could in part derive from or be reinforced by learned ideas, coming from Canon and ultimately Roman Law, and be asserted more strongly under the influence of Gregorian reform. The canonical collections frequently emphasize that bishops should not be judged whilst despoiled of their goods or ejected from their sees.[78] William of St Calais used the idea in his defence against Rufus: to show his good will, he once offered to answer even while disseised, but at another point he refused to answer 'until it is justly adjudged that I ought to plead despoiled'.[79] The *Leges Henrici* extend the idea beyond bishops, repeatedly specifying that no one is to plead disseised:

[75] Simeon of Durham, i. 173; see also e.g. *The Chronicle of Battle Abbey*, ed. and tr. E. Searle (Oxford, 1980), 210–12.

[76] See below, p. 281. See also Richard Fitz Nigel, *Dialogus de Scaccario*, ed. and tr. C. Johnson, rev. F. E. L. Carter and D. E. Greenway (Oxford, 1983), 110–12, describing royal distraint for debt, including arrears of scutage, deals at length with the sale of the distrainee's movables. The evidence does not reveal whether this was a special royal right. Possibly, if a distrained tenant at length admitted that he owed the services, but claimed inability to pay, his goods might be sold.

[77] *CMA*, ii. 140. See also below, p. 40, on replevin. *Red Book*, vol. ii, p. cclxxviii, a return to the Inquest of Sheriffs, records that the earl of Clare's officials had not returned a horse even after the scutage owed had been paid. Similar circumstances were to be a constant source of friction in the 13th cent.

[78] Cambridge, Trinity MS B 16 44, pp. 36, 47, 53, Hinschius, 133, 184, 237; Ivo, *Pannormia*, bk. iv, cc. xlii–lii; Gratian, *Decretum*, C. ii, q. ii. On this, see also D. M. Stenton, *English Justice between the Norman Conquest and the Great Charter 1066–1215* (Philadelphia, 1964), 22–3; Goebel, *Felony and Misdemeanor*, 430 n. 340. The Trinity MS of the *Collectio Lanfranci* was probably produced at Bec in the late 11th cent. Matters concerning the *Collectio Lanfranci* are much clarified by M. Philpott, 'Archbishop Lanfranc and Canon Law', D.Phil thesis (Oxford, 1993).

[79] Simeon of Durham, i. 174, 182 respectively.

no one who has been obliged to provide sureties or has been outlawed or unjustly disseised by his lord is to be impleaded by him before lawful restitution. . . . And no one is to plead disseised except concerning the disseisin itself. And after anyone disseised has pledged his law and justice to his lord, and added sureties if needed, he should be seised.[80]

Disseised could here simply refer to goods,[81] but the ecclesiastical evidence already cited suggests that it would apply both to goods and land. Meanwhile, the parallels to known procedure for replevin of goods are sufficiently close to suggest that the passage is not simply an invention of the writer of the *Leges*, but represents contemporary practice in lords' courts: lands distrained should be given back to those who showed themselves ready to answer concerning their services.

If the initial steps of distraint by chattels or fee proved ineffective, the final result of failure to perform services could be forfeiture of the lands which the tenant held. Late in Henry I's reign, Battle Abbey lost a holding at Barnhorn for alleged failure of service.[82] In 1166 William of Mountfitchet reported that he held in his hand 'two-thirds of a knight' for default of service.[83] Was forfeiture limited to those lands for which the tenant had failed to serve, or did it involve all the lands he held of the lord? *Glanvill* is unequivocal: a man should answer his lord's complaint that he is withholding service, and battle or the grand assize might result; 'if the tenant is convicted of this, he will be disinherited by right of all the fee which he holds of his lord,' and his opinion tallies with that of the *Leges Henrici* on forfeiture.[84] Such is the principle. In practice, partial forfeiture may have been common. In part, this reflects ambiguity as to whether services rested

---

[80] *Leges Henrici*, 53 3 and 5–6, Downer, 170; see also 5 3, 29 2a, 61 21, pp. 84, 132, 200.

[81] F. W. Maitland, 'The Seisin of Chattels', in his *Collected Papers*, ed. H. A. L. Fisher (3 vols.; Cambridge, 1911), i, esp. 332.

[82] *Battle Chronicle*, 118, 210–18; see E. Searle, 'The Abbey of the Conquerors: Defensive Enfeoffment and Economic Development in Anglo-Norman England, *A-NS* 2 (1980), 160–2; J. C. Holt, 'More Battle Forgeries', *Reading Medieval Studies*, 11 (1985), 75–86. Interpretation of the case is not entirely clear. I take 'pro beneficii recompensatione' to mean service rather than a relief-like payment, and the phrase 'abbas manum omnino retraxit' as meaning the abbot refused to give in, rather than, for example, that he gave up the land.

[83] *Red Book*, i. 350. See also the two cases recorded by Henry of Blois concerning the lands of Glastonbury; Adam of Domerham, *Historia de Rebus Gestis Glastoniensibus*, ed. T. Hearne (2 vols.; Oxford, 1727), ii. 313–15.

[84] *Glanvill*, ix. 1, Hall, 105; see above, n. 29 on the *Leges Henrici*.

on land or personally on tenants.[85] When a charter specified that a
man and his heirs were granted a piece of land so long as they held it
lawfully and performed due service for it, failure surely resulted only
in the forfeiture of that land.[86] Secondly, partial forfeiture may have
arisen through compromise. The balance of such settlements would
be determined, for example, by the seriousness of the offence, the
relative power of man and lord, and the lord's desire to retain the
vassal.

A formal hearing would often precede forfeiture.[87] A hearing was
desirable for various reasons. To disinherit a man was a serious
matter; he should be allowed his day in court. The hearing provided
a last chance for an amicable settlement. It would help to convince
the other vassals that they were not seeing, nor were themselves
in future liable to be threatened by, an act based solely on the
lord's will, that rather they had a good lord. Hearings might also
settle difficult cases, for example as to whether the lands were free
maritagium for which no services were owed.[88] Formal judgment
before forfeiture would contrast with any more peremptory judgment
before distraint. This suggests that distraint by disseisin of land differed from forfeiture in more than duration. Contemporaries surely
distinguished between the two in terms of seriousness, dishonour to
the tenant, solemnity of procedure, and permanence.

Not all cases of distraint would pass smoothly, nor would they all
be confined to participants within the honour. The expectation of
trouble may be suggested by the appearance from the 1120s of
written clauses concerning distraint for failure to serve. Vincent,
abbot of Abingdon between 1121 and 1130, made an agreement with
Simon the king's dispenser, that if Simon or his heirs failed in
rendering the farm for the manor of Tadmarton, it was to be reseised
into the church's own demesne.[89] Such written specifications might

---

[85] e.g. *Red Book*, i. 309–10, the 1166 *carta* of the knights of Wallingford: two entries
attribute the duty of knight service to specific lands; see also Pollock and Maitland, i.
236–7. See below, Ch. 7, on the effect that a tenant's grants of land had on his lord's
capacity to distrain that land for service.

[86] e.g. *EYC*, i, Nos. 264, 312, 539, 607, 627; iii, No. 1303.

[87] See e.g. *CMA*, ii. 128–9, *Glanvill*, ix. 1, Hall, 105.

[88] e.g. *Red Book*, i. 217. The dispute over Barnhorn, involving Battle Abbey, may
have turned on genuine doubt as to whether the abbey had been acquitted of the
service owed to the donor's overlord; see above, p. 33.

[89] *CMA*, ii. 167–8. Note also charters of St Mary's, York, cited above, n. 86.

be seen as lords preserving powers of peremptory distraint. They were, at least, attempts by lords to reinforce their position by use of writing.

A lord might be faced by a powerful vassal or a vassal with a powerful protector. The lord's decision to distrain, if necessary to enforce forfeiture, and his success in putting these decisions into effect, would depend amongst other factors on his power relative to his recalcitrant vassal. Even at the highest level, such calculations were not limited to considerations within the honour. For example, the king of England's action could be affected by the vassal's relationship with the king of France. Lower in society, the exercise of distraint and the enforcement of forfeiture might depend equally or even more upon political and power relations both within and without the honour.

Glanvill speaks of 'the lord not capable of justicing his tenant for his services and [*vel*] customs'.[90] Arguments that this refers to courtless lords seem unnecessary; often it must have been simply a matter of power.[91] Sometimes a lord was unable to do anything in this situation. In 1166 the bishop of Salisbury reported rather helplessly that Walter Walerant held the fee of one knight for which he had served the bishop's predecessors. Now he only did the service of half a knight, having deforced the bishop of the service of the other half since the time of war.[92]

A lord might seek outside help. The obvious source was his own lord. Thus Rannulf earl of Chester gave Bisley to Miles of Gloucester, and in 1129 × 41 Rannulf addressed a writ to Richard de 'Veim' and his other vavassours of Bisley, ordering them to do service to Miles 'the constable' as willingly as they ever had.[93] Such writs may refer to specific disputes. Even if, on the other hand, they were only intended to back up a grant by ensuring that tenants would do their new lords service, they could be taken as promises of help in

---

[90] *Glanvill*, ix. 1, 8, Hall, 105, 112. On the powerful protector set up against his own lord, see the passage of the *Leges Henrici*, cited below, p. 46.

[91] Cf. Milsom, *Legal Framework*, 33. The affairs of lords who had no court of their own might often have been dealt with in their overlords' courts.

[92] *Red Book*, i. 237.

[93] *HKF*, ii. 51; Stenton, *First Century*, No. 1, Chester, No. 47 and note; Stenton, p. 21, takes this as evidence that 'vavassour' need not refer to sub-tenants; I would see this as another instance of the use of the word in that very sense. See also e.g. *Earldom of Gloucester*, No. 152.

the case of future dispute. Such support constituted good lordship.[94] Additionally, overlords' own services might be threatened if their sub-tenants disobeyed the mesne lord. In 1166 the abbot of Westminster stated that Walter 'del Meine' owed the service of one knight, 'but William of Staunton, who holds that fee from him, deforces half'.[95]

There are also hints that lords sometimes looked to the great men of the area for help. In their *confederatio amoris*, Robert earl of Gloucester promised Miles earl of Hereford help to guard 'his rights and his inheritances and his tenements and his acquisitions ... and his customs and dues [*rectitudines*] and his liberties'.[96] None of the terms need specifically indicate services from vassals, but the intention seems to be to help in any claim and hence implicitly to include such services. Again it is notable that this example comes from the reign of Stephen, when other channels of aid may have been reduced.

Most evidence of support for lords exacting services concerns royal involvement in ecclesiastical honours, but even so the extent of royal aid is extremely unclear, especially before 1100. Lords may have turned to royal officials for help, but we are unlikely to know of this unless a writ was obtained. Some general orders of William I that churches should have their lands and customs do survive, but nothing more specific.[97] Then Rufus ordered the sheriff and faithful of Suffolk to do full justice to those who detained the dues [*rectitudines ... retinuerit*] of St Edmund.[98] He and subsequent kings also issued general confirmations of customs.[99] Such charters may have swayed later cases, or have helped to obtain more specific royal orders. During Henry I's reign appear precursors of the later writ of 'customs and services'. Thus Henry ordered a certain Ruallon to do the service and aid to the abbot of Ramsey which he justly ought to do from his land; otherwise the abbot was to 'justice' [*justificet*] him by

---

[94] If exercised in favour of the Church, there was the further motive of spiritual benefit; see e.g. *Stoke*, No. 31, where Roger earl of Hereford orders his steward, whilst he himself is away, to act if any of the men of the monks of Stoke by Clare withhold their rents or tithes.

[95] *Red Book*, i. 189. On overlords and services, see below, Ch. 7.

[96] *Earldom of Gloucester*, No. 95.

[97] e.g. *Regesta*, i, Nos. 49, 153.

[98] *Regesta*, i, No. 394; see also No. 420.

[99] e.g. *Regesta*, i, No. 304; ii, Nos. 499, 669, 913; iii, Nos. 128, 187, 215; *Cartae Antiquae, Rolls 1–10*, ed. L. Landor (PRS, NS 17; 1939), No. 141, *Feudal Documents*, No. 79.

his movables until he complied.[100] Evidence for Stephen becoming involved in cases involving services is very scarce, and suggests that the king and his rivals were less involved with enforcing services owed to lords than Henry I had been.[101] In contrast, Henry II rapidly became involved in such affairs. From the first half of the reign come a series of royal charters ordering restorations to Malling Abbey. One, addressed to the tenants, orders that they serve Abbess Emmelina their lady for the lands which they held of the abbey as fully as service had been done in the time of Henry I. Otherwise, she was to justice them by their fees.[102] A few similar writs survive, and by the end of the reign *Glanvill* took as normal that a lord who could not justice his men to serve might have recourse to a royal writ and thence the shire court.[103]

Kings were asked by lords to intervene. Many passages of the *Cartae* of 1166 sound like direct requests for help. Lambert d'Etocquigny complained that Richard 'de Haia' had done no service for Lambert or the king for his knight's fee, except two marks, since Henry's coronation: he asked the king 'that you send me your judgment [*placitum*] about Richard de la Haye, who detains the service of that fee from me, and I cannot have it except by your order'.[104] In such circumstance, lords might have to pay for royal favour. Although the Pipe Rolls of this period include perhaps surprisingly few relevant entries, it is possible that not all payments for such favour were accounted at the exchequer.[105]

Kings were also protecting their own interests.[106] Certainly a lord

---

[100] *Regesta*, ii, No. 1860a; see also e.g. No. 789.

[101] For Stephen's actions, see e.g. *Regesta*, iii, Nos. 264, 265. For writs ordering attendance at private hundreds, see iii, Nos. 668, 753; see also No. 490.

[102] *CChR*, v. 60; note also v. 58 (No. 17).

[103] e.g. *CMA*, ii. 225; see also *Early Charters of the Cathedral Church of St Paul, London*, ed. M. Gibbs (Camden Soc., 3rd Ser. 58; 1939), No. 45; *Glanvill*, ix. 8, Hall, 112–13.

[104] *Red Book*, i. 385–6.

[105] On the financial role of the chamber, see e.g. J. A. Green, *The Government of England under Henry I* (Cambridge, 1986), 31; H. G. Richardson and G. O. Sayles, *The Governance of Mediaeval England from the Conquest to Magna Carta* (Edinburgh, 1963), ch. XII.

[106] Note also the distinction between intrinsec and forinsec services discussed by Pollock and Maitland, i. 237–9. Use of the phrase forinsec service only became quite common in the later 12th cent., see e.g. *Danelaw Documents*, No. 5. I have not been able to establish any clear correlation between the forinsec nature of disputed services and royal intervention. See also *Regesta*, ii, No. 576, which concerns payment of geld. Note that several royal writs survive concerning suitors' attendance at private hundreds, none about attendance at honorial courts.

had to fulfil his obligations to the king even if he could not raise the full service from his vassals. He might find substitutes for defaulting knights, or pay full scutage. Yet in practice the king's own service might be endangered if sub-tenants refused to serve their lords.[107] Guard obligations at royal castles caused particular problems. In 1105 Henry I ordered the barons of the abbey of Abingdon to do castle guard at Windsor as they had previously done and as Abbot Faritius had ordered.[108] Similar writs to other ecclesiastics survive.[109] Quite possibly these lords were facing not individual defaulters, but a wider revolt of their vassals. Because of the outside requirement for these services, the lord could not strike a compromise with his men. On the other hand, the lord's position within the honour was eased by the likelihood of royal support, for the king had an interest in his success.

Outside help might be useful not only to the impotent lord but to one needing a swift result. A royal writ may also have made it difficult for the distrainee to claim that the distrainor had acted wrongly. Henry I ordered Robert Mauduit to do service to Abbot Faritius for the land he held as his ancestors had in Abbot Adelelm's time, 'and unless you do so, I order that the said abbot do his will about his land which you hold'.[110] The last phrase, providing for distraint by fee, is unusual and emphasizes the abbot's power to act freely and swiftly now that he has obtained royal backing.

Those whose services were demanded sought support too. Evidence is scarce for overlords helping their sub-tenants. However, a lord's confirmation of his vassal's gift, stating that the donee should hold freely, might extend to protection from unjust exactions by the donor or his heirs.[111] Unusually, a mid-twelfth-century confirmation

[107] See the earl of Arundel's *Carta*, *Red Book*, i. 200–1, for Henry apparently imposing his own authority within the honour through a recognition, when a disagreement arose amongst the knights of the honour about an expedition to Wales.

[108] *Regesta*, ii, No. 725; see also iii, No. 6.

[109] e.g. *Regesta*, ii, No. 1606; Miller, *Ely*, 281. See also *Regesta*, ii, No. 563. *Feudal Documents*, No. 90; *Beauchamp*, No. 175; *Red Book*, i. 394; *The Chronicle of Jocelin of Brakelond*, ed. and tr. H. E. Butler (London, 1949), 65–7.

[110] *Regesta*, ii, No. 697. The reference to the land as 'the abbot's, which you hold' is noteworthy. Unfortunately, too few similar writs survive to allow satisfactory analysis of usage of possessives in such contexts. See also *Regesta*, ii, No. 651, another writ ordering that the abbot of Abingdon do his will concerning specified lands.

[111] e.g. *EYC*, v, No. 389. See also *Book of Seals*, No. 177. The overlord may in some cases have been seeking the sub-tenant's homage, thus excluding the mesne lord—see also below, p. 44; certainly in some circumstances disputes arose about mesne lords losing their tenants' homage to the overlord.

by Roger de Mowbray to Uctred son of Dolphin ended by ordering that Uctred was to be placed in no plea over the land concerned except in Roger's presence, 'since he is my man for this and I his protector [*presidium*]'.[112] Also, in a world of competition for services, men might often find other powerful helpers who foresaw profit from providing such aid.[113] Aid offered to churches being vexed for services might bring spiritual reward.

Again the chronology of royal involvement is very vague. Even if fairly minor lay tenants did often receive writs protecting them from unjust vexation, the chances of such documents surviving would be small. If help was often obtained by plaint to the sheriff, no record need have been produced. All kings issued confirmations ordering that the beneficiary should hold 'freely and quit'[114] and some, particularly to churches, specified that they were not to be vexed or distrained.[115] However, more specific evidence is scarce even for Henry I's reign. In 1104 Robert Gernon gave Robert fitzHervey and his lands to the queen who in turn gave them to Abingdon.[116] Robert seems to have disturbed the gift for in 1106 Henry ordered him to allow Robert fitzHervey and his land and goods to be in peace, as on the day he had given them to the queen and she had given them to Abingdon. Scanty evidence of Stephen providing protection against unjust exactions does survive,[117] but there is also extensive evidence of lords exacting unjust services against whom Stephen provided no protection. Thus in the late 1140s, William d'Aubigny earl of Chichester admitted that he had been making 'many exactions on the churches and the lands of those in the bishopric of Chichester', which his predecessors had never done.[118]

---

[112] *Mowbray*, No. 392.

[113] On competition for services, see e.g. P. R. Hyams, ' "No Register of Title": The Domesday Inquest and Land Adjudication', *A-NS* 9 (1987), 132 and n. 23; E. King. 'The Anarchy of King Stephen's Reign', *TRHS*, 5th Ser. 34 (1984), 138.

[114] e.g. *Regesta*, i, No. 412a; ii, Nos. 831, 1479, 1494; iii, Nos. 37, 50, 145; Henry II: *Registrum Antiquissimum*, No. 154.

[115] e.g. *Regesta*, ii, Nos. 1312, 1327; Henry II: *Gloucester Cartulary*, No. DCCCXXI. In Henry's reign, an increasing proportion of charters specifies that no one is to harm the beneficiary: e.g. *EYC*, ii, No. 1005, *CPR, 1408–13*, 300, *Gloucester Cartulary*, Nos. CLV, CCLXXXVIII, *Cartae Antiquae, Rolls 11–20*, ed. J. C. Davis (PRS, NS 33; 1960), No. 477.

[116] *Regesta*, ii, Nos. 674, 676, 742; *CMA*, ii. 97–8.

[117] e.g. *Regesta*, iii, Nos. 401, 404, the latter almost certainly issued after the Treaty of Westminster.

[118] King, 'Anarchy' 133, 136; I quote King's translation. William was also called earl of Arundel.

Henry II, the evidence suggests, strove to regulate distraint more tightly than had his predecessors, although specific recorded interventions remain fairly scarce up to 1166.[119] Richard fitzNigel's description of distraint for royal debts suggests a decree on the subject in the first decade or so of Henry's reign.[120] I have already mentioned Robert of Leicester's charter of the early 1160s, allowing that the bishop of Lincoln justice him and his heirs by the judgment of his court, 'according to the *statutum regni*'.[121] The assize of novel disseisin was at least in part aimed at unjust distraint by lords, and Henry also enforced the replevying of goods: thus in the mid-1160s Hugh de Mortimer owed the king £100 since he had not released to his knight his animals for pledge, as the king had ordered by his writ.[122]

By 1189, crucial protection came from the sheriff, by the action of replevin.[123] Thus *Glanvill* includes a writ ordering the sheriff 'that, in return for gage and sureties, you justly and without delay make G. have his cattle, which he complains that R. took and detained unjustly for the customs which he is demanding of G., who does not admit owing them.'[124] A thirteenth-century tradition held that under Henry the plea of replevin was granted to sheriffs, acting as the king's justices.[125] If there was such a transfer of jurisdiction, the Pipe Rolls suggest that it occurred in the last years of the reign, for entries from the 1170s into the early 1180s show eyres dealing with replevying.[126] Who heard such cases before the 1170s? The transfer of jurisdic-

---

[119] In 1154 × 8, Henry ordered Conan earl of Richmond to allow Roald the Constable to hold in peace and justly specified land. No one was to vex Roald or unjustly place him in plea, otherwise the king's justice or the sheriff would take action; *EYC*, v, No. 178. The last phrase may suggest that Roald was being vexed for unjust services, although other explanations are possible, notably the competing claims of the Rollos family.

[120] *Dialogus*, 112.

[121] See above, p. 28.

[122] Milsom, *Legal Framework*, 11–14; cf. D. W. Sutherland, *The Assize of Novel Disseisin* (Oxford, 1973), 30. *PR 12 HII*, 104, *PR 14 HII*, 150.

[123] These matters will be greatly illuminated by Dr Brand's work on replevin, an early draft of which he kindly allowed me to read. The brief discussion of the subject in S. Painter, *Studies in the History of the English Feudal Barony* (Baltimore, 1943), 106–7, is not very satisfactory. Note also that the sheriff was the addressee of the writ of customs and services, and thus might be involved in the enforcement of dues on behalf of the lord; see above, p. 37.

[124] *Glanvill*, xii. 12, Hall, 142.

[125] *CRR*, xv, No. 1968a.

[126] Note esp. *PR 22 HII*, 68, 214; *PR 29 HII*, 5, 116; *PR 31 HII*, 70, 151, 182, 185; *PR 32 HII*, 46.

tion would suggest that in Henry's reign replevin was originally a crown plea. I argue below that it concerned default of justice and possibly breach of the peace, two other particular interests of the king. Hence disputes would be heard by royal justices, be they based in shires, itinerant, or sent out specially, and probably also by sheriffs. The thirteenth-century specification that sheriffs did so only as royal justices was more important after Magna Carta, c. 24, which forbad sheriffs to hear crown pleas, than it would have been in the early twelfth.[127] Then, conceivably, the shire often heard such cases, especially those not involving breach of the peace which might attract special royal concern. The changes under Henry II should, no doubt, be related to wider administrative developments. One possibility is that the disappearance of local justiciars and the greater regularity of eyres produced the shift visible in the Pipe Rolls of the 1170s and early 1180s. The eyres of those years may have been so overburdened that full responsibility for replevin was granted to sheriffs, acting in the place of royal justices.

Why did the king and his officials help those owing service, be it through the enforcement of the release of goods or, for example, by orders that the tenant should not be vexed for unjust services? Richard fitzNigel saw lords as men's 'domestic enemies', and unjust exactions were an obvious sign of tyranny.[128] To protect the weak, the *pauperes*, from this was a major royal duty; thirteenth-century tradition saw the change in the administration of replevin as for the benefit of poor free men, and the resultant hastening of justice as a way of preventing harm to their animals and goods.[129] Similarly, kings had a duty to protect the Church, and churches may often have faced distraint for services claimed from land which they themselves held to be quit of worldly dues.[130]

Furthermore, the king again was responding to men's requests for favour. A tenant could buttress his case in various ways. He might

---

[127] On sheriffs as royal justices, see G. D. G. Hall, review of Van Caenegem, *Writs*, *EHR* 76 (1961), 319. *Leges Henrici*, 10 4, Downer, 108, notes that 'dominica placita regis' do not belong to the sheriff in his farm except if specifically pre-arranged; this may simply mean that the sheriff must render for such pleas separately from his farm. Note also the case recorded in *CRR*, xvi. 27.

[128] *Dialogus*, 101. King, 'Anarchy', 135–9.

[129] See Hyams, *Kings, Lords, and Peasants*, 261–2; *CRR*, xv, No. 1968a; *Bracton*, fo. 155b, Thorne, ii. 439. See also *Dialogus*, 110–11, on goods by which the king's officials should not distrain for debt, lest the distrainee be permanently impoverished.

[130] e.g. *EYC*, v, Nos. 159–60.

claim that his lord had distrained with undue force, had demanded services not due or not in arrears, or had carried out the distraint unreasonably, perhaps refusing to replevy the possessions taken.[131] Those with royal confirmations stating that they were to hold free of service, or for specified services, might first use these to try to check their oppressors, and if this failed, to obtain royal help.

Worry about distraint was closely linked to concern for peace. Some documents associate distraint with violence or at least theft.[132] The influence of the Peace of God movement, which sought to restrict distraint, was felt in Normandy, and the reform movement sought to prevent churches being distrained.[133] Charters to churches associate distraint with harming: thus Henry I confirmed various gifts to St Peter's, York: 'and I forbid that any of my officers make entry into their houses or lands to take distraint and do harm.'[134] Such pressure would have reinforced the king's own desire to keep the peace. Violent distraint may have been common in troubled areas under Stephen. Attempts by lords to squeeze increased services from their men produced disputes in the next reign. Henry II, intent on restoring order, had to end such activities.[135] *Glanvill* in the 1180s associated disseisin and violence: 'the defeated party, whether he be

---

[131] On unjust taking and detention against gage and surety in *Bracton*, see below, n. 139.

[132] See above, p. 22, on the use of *districcio* to mean forceful pressure. In the mid-13th cent., a letter of Simon de Montfort concerning Gascony referred to extra-judicial distraint as 'the beginning of all wars'; C. Bémont, *Simon de Montfort*, tr. E. F. Jacob (Oxford, 1930), 77. It may also be notable that for *Glanvill*, theft, like replevin, was a viscontiel plea; *Glanvill*, i. 2, xii. 12, Hall, 4, 142.

[133] See e.g. Orderic Vitalis, *Ecclesiastical History*, ed. and tr. M. Chibnall (6 vols.; Oxford, 1969–80), iii. 32, the decrees of the Council of Lillebonne, 1080; also P. Chaplais, 'Henry II's Reissue of the Canons of the Council of Lillebonne of Whitsun 1080 (?25 February 1162)', *JSA* 4 (1973), 631. A council at Rouen in 1096 decreed strict observance of the Truce of God, 'so that no man assault or wound or kill another, nor anyone take distraint or plunder'; Orderic, v. 20. On the Peace movement in Normandy, see H. E. J. Cowdrey, 'The Peace and the Truce of God in the Eleventh Century', *P&P* 46 (1970), 59–61; F. M. Powicke, *The Loss of Normandy, 1189–1204* (Manchester, 1913), 93–8; see also *Regesta*, ii, No. 1908. The Legatine Council of Westminster, Dec. 1138, recorded similar concerns in England; *Councils and Synods with other Documents relating to the English Church*, i, ed. D. Whitelock, M. Brett, and C. N. L. Brooke (2 vols.; Oxford, 1981), ii. 774–8. Papal decrees against laymen invading church lands may in part have concerned what the lay 'invaders' would have considered distraint; see e.g. Gregory VII's decree which became Gratian, *Decretum*, C. xii, q. ii, c. iv.

[134] *Regesta*, ii, No. 1327; see also e.g. *EYC*, iv, Nos. 24, 67.

[135] King, 'Anarchy', 135–9; it is noteworthy that the legislation following the civil war of Henry III's reign also dealt with distraint.

the appellor or the appellee is always in the king's mercy on account of violent disseisin.'[136] Here the use of appeal language again could be taken to associate the procedure with that for crime. Bracton too stated that unjust detention of distrained possessions was 'against the king's peace'.[137]

It could well be that royal involvement first became regular in cases involving or threatening disorder. Admittedly, the common penalties for lords' abuse of distraint were far from those specified by *Glanvill* for theft and breach of the king's peace, that is death, loss of limbs, and disinheritance of heirs.[138] Yet *Glanvill* himself might not have felt such penalties proper for all those who could be seen as breaking the king's peace, regardless of their status; a powerful man should be treated differently from an insignificant one. Still, concern for peace does not fully explain royal interest in unjust distraint, certainly not the more complete regulation which developed under Henry II. A second crucial element was the king's claim to hear cases of default of justice. Both wrongful taking of distraint and unjust detention might constitute such an offence.[139]

Violence and default of justice were anyway intimately connected.[140] On the one hand, royal hearing of cases of default of justice need not simply have been a favour granted to the weak; it also offered a peaceful strategy to the aggrieved tenant who might otherwise have resorted to violence against his lord.[141] On the other hand, seignorial

[136] *Glanvill*, xiii. 38, Hall, 170, on which see Sutherland, *Novel Disseisin*, 27–8. For a description of a violent disseisin, see R. C. van Caenegem, *The Birth of the English Common Law* (2nd edn., Cambridge, 1988), 118 n. 20. Note also *The Letters and Charters of Gilbert Foliot*, ed. A. Morey and C. N. L. Brooke (London, 1967), No. 176.

[137] *Bracton*, fo. 158b, Thorne, ii. 446.

[138] *Glanvill*, i. 2, vii. 17, Hall, 3, 91.

[139] If the purpose of distraint was at least in part to ensure appearance at the lord's court, the tenant might argue that the lord's refusal to replevy constituted a refusal to allow the case to proceed in a reasonable fashion, i.e. default of justice. Indeed, the tenant might claim that he was being forced to plead whilst disseised, of lands or goods. For *Bracton* writing of breach of the peace, it was unjust detention against gage and surety which caused replevin to be treated as a plea of the crown, whereas cases of unjust taking could properly be amended simply by neighbours, *Bracton*, fo. 158b, Thorne, ii. 446. Such a nice distinction seems more appropriate to the time of *Bracton* than of, say, Henry I.

[140] It is notable that the ecclesiastical equivalent of 'unjustly and without judgment' was, for example, 'violently and without judicial order [*et absque ordine iudiciario*]': see e.g. Biancalana, 'Legal Reforms of Henry II', 473, van Caenegem, *English Common Law*, 122 n. 58.

[141] See e.g. *Regesta*, ii, Nos. 975, 997, *Facsimiles of Early Charters from Northamptonshire Collections*, ed. F. M. Stenton (Northants Rec. Soc. 4; 1930), 12–15, Stenton,

violence and default of justice need not have been discrete categories, at least in most men's mind during most of the period. The very survival of the list of royal rights in the *Leges Henrici*, which includes breach of the peace and default of justice, has encouraged too simple a view of discrete crown pleas. Somewhat similar actions might again be perceived differently according to the status of the participants. Not unusually forceful but still unjust distraint might be perceived as theft if carried out by a minor man, as default of justice if carried out by a more important lord. Elsewhere, the *Leges Henrici* link 'default of justice' with 'violent denial of right [*uiolenta recti . . . destitutio*]'.[142] In practice, denial of justice may often have involved force or at least its threat, and this is especially true of a procedure such as distraint which rested heavily on the exercise of power.

I now turn more briefly to certain disputes in which a man refused service on the grounds that he did not hold the relevant lands from the lord demanding the service. They could stem from real doubt as to where services lay, previous grants perhaps having led to confusion, or from tenants attempting to exploit seignorial weakness and perhaps aspiring to hold as freely as possible. Pleas of non-tenure might occur with an heir refusing homage to his ancestor's lord, or with a newly succeeding lord demanding homage from his predecessor's tenants. Alternatively, an overlord might be seeking to cut out the mesne lord and establish immediate lordship over the latter's tenant, who might therefore disclaim tenure of the mesne lord. Disclaimers might also be made when men were summoned to serve, or to answer for failing to serve.[143]

A lord could reseise into his own hand land which had been granted in return for service and which the man now denied holding of him. As in cases not involving disclaimer, the lord might have good reason to wish to act swiftly. Moreover, disclaimer, by its very nature,

---

English Justice, 138–9, for a case where a tenant seizes the lord's harvested corn and livestock from a disputed piece of land, about which he believed himself to have been denied justice.

[142] See also above, p. 42. *Leges Henrici*, 33 1a, Downer, 136; see also 59 19, p. 188. *Leges Henrici*, 10 1, Downer, 108, which might seem to provide a list of precise and discrete crown pleas, is the work of a learned man working partly from written sources, rather than a reflection of everyday thought.

[143] Additionally, in a dispute between two lords over a piece of land, a tenant might well disclaim tenure when his service was demanded by the lord whom he was not backing, but I leave aside such cases, as spin-offs from wider disputes.

was likely to be manifest: the man refused homage to the lord. Yet we possess little evidence of lords acting peremptorily. Perhaps this is because most of the recorded disputes come from Church honours, whose lords may have been less able or willing to exert force. Yet the *Cartae baronum* show lay and ecclesiastical lords experiencing similar difficulties. The *Carta* of the honour of Clare states that Stephen de Tours owed one knight from whom the earl had never received homage, relief, or service.[144] There is no sign that Stephen claimed to hold of another lord.

The evidence reveals court hearings rather than swift disseisin. At the beginning of the twelfth century, Nigel d'Oilly was a prominent tenant of Abingdon. He held a meadow at Oxford, a hide at Sandford, and another at Arncott, lands which his predecessor Robert d'Oilly may have obtained improperly. For a long time after Abbot Faritius's succession in 1100, Nigel did neither homage nor service:

therefore the abbot took action in court against him [*contra ipsum diratiocinando egit*], that he do homage to the church and abbot for the things he held, on the condition that he recognize for all time that the church was quit of all royal geld and that he would serve the abbot everywhere as his lord.

The verb *diratiocinare* suggests certainly a formal court hearing, perhaps an offer of battle, although the chronicle does not specify the court: it may well have been the abbot's own.[145]

Peremptory action may have been unusual partly because of the purposes of lord and man. Lords sometimes wished to retain tenants who disclaimed their tenure. Those disclaiming need not always have intended to maintain their cases to the last, but have hoped for favourable settlements, having tested their lord's strength.[146] A gradual process might allow reconciliation. The power of some vassals must also have deterred or prevented peremptory action. A lord wishing to take back the land may have been unable to eject the man in possession. It is notable that some deeds involving particularly strong vassals make careful provision concerning disclaimer by the

---

[144] *Red Book*, i. 405.

[145] *CMA*, ii. 132–3.

[146] See esp. *CMA*, ii. 128–9, 132–4. Here we are seeing disclaimer as a strategy adopted within a relationship, rather than a final action leading to the application of clear rules of tenurial and jurisdictional logic. However, these disputes involving 'strategic' disclaimers might also lead to the man claiming to hold of another lord; below p. 46. Among other possibilities is the situation where one sub-tenant incurred the king's enmity and the king regranted his land to another; e.g. *CMA*, ii. 125–7.

46 *Part One*

vassal.[147] Even if the tenant was not particularly powerful, forcible action might cause him to seek help from another lord. The *Leges Henrici* speak of the man who, through arrogance, created an advocate for himself against his lord, and state that such a man was to lose what he held of that lord.[148] On occasion in practice, however, the distraining lord may have suffered permanent loss to the man's new protector.

Lords faced with sitting tenants disclaiming tenure may often have needed royal help in pressuring the men into doing homage. Occasionally a man might, as a tactical move during a dispute, claim to hold of the king. If so, the lord might well need royal help to regain control of the tenant. In other instances, a lord might seek royal support because of his opponent's power. Walter Giffard the younger held Lyford from the abbey of Abingdon. Before 1066, the sons of Alfyard had held from the abbot but were not to go elsewhere without the abbot's permission. Still, they commended themselves to Walter. When Faritius became abbot, Walter strove to avoid service, and appears not to have done homage. Faritius obtained a royal order which led to a hearing in Oxford at the house of Thomas of St John, where the abbot was currently holding his court. In the presence of Roger of Salisbury, Robert bishop of Lincoln, and many of the king's barons, Walter became the man of the church and abbot, on the condition that he render the service of one knight from that land in the same way as the church's other knights did service. The hearing thus seems to have been before a court which can be considered either that of the abbot, afforced by powerful friends, or one of mixed composition, partly royal, partly honorial.[149]

In addition, there was a jurisdictional logic forcing lords to seek royal help. A man disclaiming tenure was also denying any obligation to answer in the lord's court concerning the relevant lands.[150] The lord might still wish to get the man to answer in his court, preferring to keep a desirable vassal, rather than take the land back in demesne

---

[147] e.g. *Registrum Antiquissimum*, No. 313, on which see above, p. 28.

[148] *Leges Henrici*, 43 3, Downer, 152.

[149] *CMA*, ii. 133–4; *Domesday*, i, fo. 59a. For such courts, see also e.g. *CMA*, ii. 128–30. Cf. *Leges Edwardi*, 9 2, Liebermann, *Gesetze*, i. 633.

[150] See Milsom, *Legal Framework*, 30, 44 n. 1. The situation would be more complicated if the tenant held from the lord other lands, whence the services were not disputed.

or grant it to another. Sheer force was one way to bring such a man into court, but this might not be a viable option because of the balance of power between lord and disclaimant, and might anyway lead the latter to seek outside help. A better solution for the lord could be to obtain a royal writ to force the man into court. The cartulary of St Frideswide's, Oxford, preserves one likely instance, which is probably datable to the later years of Stephen's reign. A knight called Edward held a hide of land from the church,

for which he refused to do homage or any service to Prior Robert and the canons of St Frideswide, wherefore the said prior claimed to hold the said hide in demesne by a writ 'of right' [*breue de recto*] in the court of the earl of Leicester. And the case took its martial course and was decided by judicial combat fought in the court of the said earl ... Finally, after many blows between the champions and although the champion of Edward had lost his sight in the fight ... they both sat down and as neither dared attack the other, peace was established as follows; the said Edward did homage for the hide to the said abbot and should hold it by hereditary right.[151]

Thus the case, like many others involving disclaimer, eventually ended in compromise.[152]

The king would also sometimes have aided those disclaiming. Imposition of seignorial-style exactions on other men's tenants, as we have seen, was a feature of the 'tyranny' which barons exerted under Stephen, and to a lesser degree quite possibly of competitive lordship in other reigns. It could be both the king's duty and in his interests to protect such men. Moreover, even if the man had not at first specifically claimed to hold of the king, the king may have desired the man's homage and therefore aided him.

Parties in cases involving disclaimer probably also looked to other sources of support, be they royal officials, overlords, or local great men. Overall, the surviving evidence does not suggest that people

---

[151] *Cartulary of the Monastery of St Frideswide at Oxford*, ed. S. R. Wigram (2 vols.; Oxford Hist. Soc., 28, 31; 1895–6), ii, No. 1123. The dating comes from a phrase preceding the quotation, referring to this case occurring at the time of the composition made between the monks of Bec and the canons of St Frideswide in the presence of Pope Eugenius III, a composition datable to 1147. Crouch, *Beaumont Twins*, 162 dates the case to *c.*1166 on the basis that it started with a writ of right, but the general phrase *breue de recto* need not point to such a date.

[152] The proportion settled thus is unfortunately very hard to discover. Although some settlements entirely in the lord's favour might produce quitclaims, documents would commonly only be produced to record and regulate the settlement for the future relations of the parties, that is when a compromise had been reached.

acted very differently in these disputes compared with those not
involving disclaimer. The sources may hide many lords reseising
lands which vassals had disclaimed holding of them, or many men
successfully disclaiming the seignorial bond. If not, two main reasons
suggest themselves for the similarity to actions not involving disclaimer. First, considerations of power were likely to produce resort
to outside support, whether or not disclaimer was involved. Secondly,
refusal or disclaimer of homage was sometimes a ploy aimed only at a
favourable settlement with the lord, not at permanent separation from
him.

The above picture is one of flexibility, defined by various criteria
of reasonableness. Custom, the lord's assumptions and interests,
together with the pressure of his court, gave weight to the restrictions. The power of the lord in relation to his vassal would help to
determine his remaining freedom of action. For example, a vassal
holding land far from the centre of the lord's power might be particularly hard to discipline.[153]

Moreover, interpretations of the pre-Common Law period which
emphasize seignorial discretion assume that it was the lord who
throughout the period had control of the most desirable resource,
land. Possible sources of services are taken as plentiful, and if one
failed, it would simply be removed and replaced by another. Implicitly,
the need for a man to obtain a grant of lands is seen as greater than
the need for a lord to find followers. Such a picture is of course too
simple. Connections other than those of land-tenure and services
make such a market based model misleading. Moreover, at some
times and in some places, the need for lords to attract vassals,
particularly men of existing local influence, may have been strong.[154]
Vassals were not always weak, and indeed the balance of power may

---

[153] Note e.g. the case of Henry de Lacy cited below, p. 215. For a study of such
relations for one county, see P. Dalton, 'Feudal Society in Yorkshire', Ph.D. thesis
(Sheffield, 1989), esp. ch. 7. Note also P. A. Brand and P. R. Hyams, 'Seigneurial
Control of Women's Marriage', *P&P* 99 (1983), 125.

[154] As a tenant's hold on his land strengthened, so his bargaining position with his
lord might improve, thereby allowing him to strengthen still further his hold on his
present lands and those he might acquire. The situation suggested in some ways
resembles that presented by historians of lords seeking to expand their affinities in the
later Middle Ages. For such competitive lordship, see also *Monasticon*, i. 596–7, on the
activities of Aethelwig of Evesham; Hyams, *King, Lords, and Peasants*, 225–7, 239, on
the context of early 12th-cent. writs for the retrieval of peasants.

have shifted towards at least some of them during this period.[155] Even at the time of Domesday, lords had some powerful tenants.[156] However, their numbers almost certainly increased and a rank of landed tenants not easily controlled by their lords grew larger.[157] The troubles of Stephen's reign may have accelerated such change. The treaties between the magnates during the last years of the reign had the reassertion of control over lesser men as one of their concerns. Henry II may well have come to the throne at a time when men were particularly unwilling to take the decision of the honour as final. With the reassertion of peace, the disgruntled tenant could no longer fight, but he might turn to the king against his lord. The *Cartae baronum* of 1166 are very revealing of the kind of problems lords faced.[158] Occasionally lords had tenants considerably more powerful than themselves.[159] A few lords had enfeoffed a large proportion of their lands to one vassal.[160] The *Cartae* repeatedly record lords, many ecclesiastical but some lay, who were unable to enforce their will on their tenants.[161] Some returns sound like requests for royal help.[162]

[155] Cf. J. Boussard, *Le Gouvernement d'Henri II Plantagenet* (Paris, 1956), 584, who suggests that the resources of 'les hobereaux angevins et limousins' probably remained static, whereas those of great or even middle-sized lords increased.

[156] See e.g. C. Lewis, 'The Norman Settlement of Herefordshire under William I', *A-NS* 7 (1985), 208; also R. Mortimer, 'The Beginnings of the Honour of Clare', *A-NS* 3 (1981), 137, 'Land and Service: The Tenants of the Honour of Clare', *A-NS* 8 (1986), 195; S. Harvey, 'The Knight and the Knight's Fee in England', *P&P* 49 (1970), 6–7; Dalton, 'Feudal Society in Yorkshire', 226. Painter, *Feudal Barony*, 21–3, comments on subinfeudation by 1086.

[157] See e.g. Stenton, *First Century*, 143 ff.; Dalton, 'Feudal Society in Yorkshire', 246–7, 254–5; Harvey, 'Knight and Knight's Fee'. Harvey is criticized by R. A. Brown, 'The Status of the Anglo-Norman Knight', in J. Gillingham and J. C. Holt (edd.), *War and Government in the Middle Ages* (Cambridge, 1984), 18–32, and D. Fleming, 'Landholding by *milites* in Domesday Book: A Revision', *A-NS* 13 (1991), 83–98. Mortimer, 'Land and Service', 196, found that most families with large holdings in the honour of Clare in 1086 grew more powerful thereafter.

[158] On subinfeudation in the *Cartae*, see Painter, *Feudal Barony*, 23–30; also 178–9 on the honour of Striguil, and 179–80 for the rather different history of the Berkeley estates.

[159] Powerful sub-tenants: e.g. Geoffrey de Ver, i. 217, 226, 298, 352; see 274–5, 355 for his tenancy in chief. Ralph de Chahaines, who owed four knights in all, had Walter Giffard amongst his tenants, i. 218. See also William de Bosco, who was not a tenant in chief, but held of many lords: i. 203, 217, 291, 360, 362, 395, 397; he may well have been more powerful than, for example, Geoffrey de Valognes, from whom he held one knight, i. 349. Also the sub-tenancies held by Philip of Kyme, i. 375, 377, 381–3, 390, 416; *HKF*, ii. 118. See also Boussard, *Gouvernement d'Henri II*, 61–2.

[160] e.g. *Red Book*, i. 219, 229.

[161] See esp. the problems of the earl of Warwick, *Red Book*, i. 326–7; see also e.g. i. 196, 228, 243, 254 for lay lords, 200, 204, 251 for ecclesiastical lords.

[162] e.g. *Red Book*, i. 251, 386, 415.

Moreover, the *Cartae* illuminate only the relations of king, tenant in chief, and vassal. Subinfeudation would have had similar effects lower down the social scale.

Thus social change, by weakening seignorial control, may have increased the demand for involvement from outside the honour in processes of distraint and the enforcement of services. The extent of such involvement is extremely hard to determine. At first, one-off provisions of favour may have predominated. However, even early in the period, superior authorities were probably involved more regularly in disputes potentially affecting their own dues. Churches may have been more regular recipients of help, perhaps particularly from kings. Royal action may also have been likely in cases involving breach of the king's peace. Even this degree of involvement would limit the exercise of the lord's will.

Moreover, royal involvement could be self-perpetuating. If one party had royal support, the other might also have to turn to the king. Lords might be faced by recalcitrant tenants claiming to be protected by royal privileges. The *Leges Edwardi*, dealing with those who possess the king's peace, stated that 'because of this peace they are not to withdraw service of their lord nor dues if they owe these to their neighbours; since he is not worthy to have peace who does not love to observe peace.'[163] Moreover, if the preponderance of royal writs concerning churches is not simply a product of the survival of records, churchmen's actions may have furthered the feeling that such inter-vention was fairly normal, impressing themselves upon other lords, who then followed suit. Royal responses to churchmen might form the basis of remedies later used more generally. In such ways, royal involvement could snowball.

There is at least one more reason for the extension of royal control of distraint. Throughout this section, the *Cartae baronum* have been a major source for lord–tenant relations. Although the king seems to have requested the names of tenants primarily because he was demanding an oath of loyalty [*ligantia*] from them,[164] the *Cartae* provided Henry, his counsellors, and administrators with much ad-ditional information on relations within honours. Might this not have influenced their future approach to disputes over services, not directly by using them as reference sources but by removing residual inhi-

---

[163] *Leges Edwardi*, 26 1, Liebermann, *Gesetze*, i. 650; note also *Regesta*, ii, No. 1812.
[164] *Red Book*, i. 412.

bitions on the propriety of royal interference? And would not other inquiries, such as the Inquest of Sheriffs, have had similar effects? Such information-gathering may have been another force behind the more generalized royal involvement of Henry II's reign and after, which contrasts with the probably extensive and influential but still irregular involvement of Henry I.

Flexibility probably only disappeared with regular royal involvement emerging from the 1160s. By the time of the first court rolls, royal justices gave little consideration to local custom or specific circumstance, but applied generally the rules of distraint appropriate for forcing a defendant to answer in the communal courts, rules which may only have become rigid in the twelfth century.[165] Eventually, royal participation helped to change the nature of distraint so that by the second half of the thirteenth century it had become an extra-judicial process, requiring no court judgment and limited to taking the chattels of the defaulter.[166]

WARRANTY

The performance of service represented the action of a good vassal. The lord had in return to observe his obligations in the relationship, he had to be a good lord. Even if the particular tenant concerned was likely to feel some injury, the reasonable exercise of distraint would help a lord to appear good in the eyes of his other vassals. Services, homage, and good lordship can also be seen coming together in notions of warranty; indeed some warranty clauses specifically make their promise in return for the service for the tenement.[167] Here my

[165] The Anglo-Saxon laws suggest precise, unvarying procedure, but provisions in the 12th-cent. *Leges* seem to contradict one another; cf. *Leges Henrici*, 29 2, 51 3, Downer, 130, 166; *Leges Willelmi*, 44 1, Liebermann, *Gesetze*, i. 517. Enever, *Distress*, 79–80, also draws attention to this contradiction. As always, it is hard to tell, even for the communal courts, how far these sources reflect actual practice, which may have been more flexible.

[166] Pollock and Maitland, i. 353. Note esp. Milsom, *Legal Framework*, 34–5, *Historical Foundations of the Common Law* (2nd edn., London, 1981), 137–43, on the origins of novel disseisin and its unintended effects. Also *Legal Framework*, 29–31, for arguments on the way in which the requirement for a writ in cases concerning a free tenement affected disputes concerning the quantum of service.

[167] *Danelaw Documents*, No. 98, *CChR*, ii. 431, *St Paul's*, No. 175 (which also mentions a countergift made in part for the promise to warrant). All these examples come from after 1150. Cartae Antiquae, Roll 24, m. 2, No. 15, a charter of Henry II, promises warranty in return for past service. (Photograph courtesy of Professor Holt.)

concern is warranty in connection with the security of tenure of any individual tenant, not the heritability of the warranty bond.[168] My survey is brief, since Hyams's fine article on 'Warranty and Good Lordship in Twelfth Century England' has covered the major themes in depth.

Hyams summarizes 'the warranty of early land law' in the following terms:

in his warranty, the grantor made two different commitments. He made a positive promise, that he (and his family) would maintain the grant against outside challenge.... If they were unable to do this, the grantee had to be compensated for his loss, as by an exchange [*escambium*] of an equivalent holding. Developed warranty also had a negative aspect, ... once the grant was complete, neither he (nor his family) were to try to resume any part of the property conveyed.[169]

Hyams argues that warranty may first have applied to chattels, perhaps beginning in livestock markets.[170] It therefore seems right to hold that warranty of chattels stemmed originally not from homage or lordship but from gift, grant, or sale, at least in cases where the two parties maintained a direct relationship.[171] This would help to explain, for example, the warranty of land given in alms, over which—at least in the Church's opinion—the donor ceased to exercise lordship and for which he took no homage.[172] However, in Anglo-Norman and Angevin England, the granting of land was generally very closely connected to lordship. Therefore, with regard to land, warranty was often a manifestation of good lordship: 'a man

---

[168] Hyams, 'Warranty', 459: 'it appears that from well before the advent of the common law warranty was, in principle, a heritable obligation, which normally bound the heirs of both principal parties'; see also 469–73. This fits well with my view of inheritance, below Chs. 3 and 4.

[169] Hyams, 'Warranty', 440. Some charters help to add to Hyams's discussion of the procedure for exchange: some specify that exchange is to take place before disseisin, e.g. *Earldom of Gloucester*, No. 71, *Facsimiles of Early Charters in Oxford Muniment Rooms*, ed. H. E. Salter (Oxford, 1929), No. 42, *Chester*, No. 86; others provide that the exchange is to be from the warrantor's inheritance, e.g. *Chester*, No. 71, *Registrum Antiquissimum*, No. 149, *Danelaw Documents*, No. 60. Note also *Cartae Antiquae, 1–10*, No. 95, a charter of Henry II from 1181 which explains that the equivalence is to be set 'by oath of four lawful men of that area [*prouinicie*]'.

[170] Hyams, 'Warranty', 445. Note also the use of warranty language in Henry I's decree concerning the coinage, issued early in his reign; Liebermann, *Gesetze*, i. 523.

[171] Hyams is not very explicit about this point: my interpretation rests on the passages cited in the next two notes, and his statement at 456 that warranty was 'a general obligation on all grantors'.

[172] See Hyams, 'Warranty', 442.

owes a duty to support and protect in their material honour the vassals on whose support he depends'.[173] Warranty should also be associated with the various forms of protection a man sought from his lord.[174] In particular, it was closely linked to notions of maintenance, a voluntary obligation to support vassals, in some cases if necessary by force.[175] As Maitland wrote,

Happy then was the tenant who could say to any adverse claimant: —'Sue me if you will, but remember that behind me you will find the earl or the abbot.' Such an answer would often be final. . . . he has a lord who may use carnal weapons or let loose the thunders of the church in defence of his tenant.[176]

General warranty obligations had become common in Normandy by *c.*1100, and it seems likely that 'the same kind of customary expectations of good lordship already existed early in the eleventh century'. Early developments in England and Normandy are hard to trace because of the lack of charters, particularly those recording grants from one lay person to another. Warranty obligations pre-dated the rise of charter clauses expressly promising warranty, and 'precocious examples apart, warranty clauses are hardly found before the middle of Henry II's reign and are still not completely normal at the end of the century'.[177] However, Domesday Book reveals warranty-style procedures for the establishment of land claims, and 'even confirms that men were familiar with the warranty terminology itself'.[178] As early as Henry I's reign, charter draftsmen were, for

[173] Hyams, 'Warranty', 439.
[174] For continental parallels, which provide vital background to the English situation, see P. Duparc, 'Le Tensement', *RHDFE* 40 (1962), 43–63.
[175] Hyams, 'Warranty', 449–51; see e.g. Stenton, *First Century*, No. 46—a charter from *c.*1150 which is very concerned with the dangers of war. See also J. C. Holt, 'Feudal Society and the Family in Early Medieval England: III. Patronage and Politics', *TRHS*, 5th Ser. 34 (1984), 24 for a letter from the dying Warin fitzGerold to Henry II asking that the king maintain his gift to Bury. Again, the lordly act need not have been connected to land-holding; a lord might just as easily maintain a non-landed follower in a dispute. In the later Middle Ages, maintenance was considered an abuse, see e.g. J. G. Bellamy, *Bastard Feudalism and the Law* (London, 1989), ch. 4.
[176] Pollock and Maitland, i. 306–7. An indication of warranty becoming in a sense artificial, or at least tied to courts, is provided by e.g. *Beauchamp*, No. 183 (*c.*1182 × 6), where a weak man promises to warrant a strong one.
[177] Hyams, 'Warranty', 456–7, 474, 479, quotations at 457, 474; Tabuteau, *Transfers of Property*, ch. 9. Note the earlier view of Stenton, *First Century*, 161 and n. 3.
[178] Hyams, 'Warranty', 458 and n. 87. Cf. Tabuteau, *Transfers of Property*, 196, who sees charter clauses as involving the concept of warranty even when they do not use the verb 'warrant' or the noun 'warrantor'. She points out that these words only appear in

example, including clauses denying the obligation to provide an exchange, and Hyams concludes that 'when draftsmen take the trouble to exclude expressly a possible corollary, the existence of the primary obligation is so clear as not to require mention'. Thus from the middle of Henry I's reign, 'the good lord was routinely expected to warrant his man's tenure'.[179] Nor was warranty simply a claim resting on the lord's good faith. Others might be called upon to regulate this element of the relationship of vassal and lord; 'men probably thought first of an overlord, then of some other magnate prepared to claim the lordship'.[180] Royal enforcement became gradually, if not steadily, more common. A few Pipe Roll entries and the occasional writ 'encourage one to believe that Henry I could be persuaded for a price to lend his support in a claim for warrant or exchange', and a wider range of writs came to be available under Henry II. Thus it can be argued that gradually the situation was arrived at where 'by Glanvill's time ... warranty approximated tenant-right'.[181]

This overall picture seems highly convincing, and fits well with the development of land law put forward in my later chapters. Vernacular literature emphasizes more strongly the connection between warranty and personal lordship, as well as land-holding. It stresses protection against third parties and is associated with other words of the same general sense. Roland, seeing the many French dead at Roncesvalles, mourned

> Barons franceis, pur mei vos veis murir;
> Jo ne vos pois tenser ne garantir
>
> (French barons, I see you dying for me
> I cannot protect nor warrant you.)[182]

Such lines remind us both of the continental context of notions of warranty and the fact that they were far from confined to courts.

---

four 11th-cent. Norman charters. For early evidence concerning exchange to value in England, see *Regesta*, i, No. 206.

[179] Hyams, 'Warranty', 456, 457.

[180] Hyams, 'Warranty', 466–7, also 442 n. 14. On the possibility of bad faith, see e.g. *Danelaw Documents*, No. 105, a charter of the late 12th cent.

[181] Hyams, 'Warranty', 486, 453. However, on the problematic position of the tenant in chief in relation to the king, see J. C. Holt, *Magna Carta* (2nd edn., Cambridge, 1992), 157–63.

[182] *The Song of Roland: An Analytical Edition*, ed. G. J. Brault (2 vols.; Pennsylvania, 1978), ll. 1863–4; see also l. 1354, and *Raoul de Cambrai*, ed. and tr. S. Kay (Oxford, 1992), ll. 495–6: 'li rois meîsmes ... | dont devons estre tensé et garanti' (The king himself ... who should be protecting and warranting us).

Examination of charters beyond even Hyams's wide range also raises a few points. First, whilst he is right to state that explicit warranty clauses emerge only slowly in the twelfth century, there may have been an initial burst during Stephen's reign, perhaps followed by a temporary decrease. This pattern is found in the charters of the earls of Chester, which include an early group of warranty clauses in the 1140s and early 1150s, whereas such clauses are rare in the later twelfth century.[183] All three clauses for laymen relate to grants which may have been particularly in danger during the troubles of Stephen's reign. From this it may be concluded that such special circumstances led to the writing down of the obligation.[184]

It may also be questioned whether firstly exchange and warranty and secondly the negative and positive aspects of warranty were immediately so closely linked as Hyams argues. An unusual mid-twelfth-century charter recording a grant by Walter of Bolbec to the abbots of Ramsey does not mention warranty or exchange, but specifies that if a challenger were to

> prove his right to that land, then he should hold the same from Abbot Walter and his successors without any exchange of land or repetition of the payment which the lord may give to this abbot or his successors; and the abbot shall hold it from Walter of Bolbec and his heirs.[185]

Such an arrangement suggests a flexibility of solution greater than that allowed by Common Law warranty and exchange.

The early Chester charters to laymen, on the other hand, made explicit the lord's obligation concerning exchange: 'and unless I can warrant to them that tenure of Fifehead, I will give them exchange to

---

[183] See my 'Diplomatic and Legal Aspects of the Charters', in A. T. Thacker (ed.), *The Earldom of Chester and its Charters* (Journal of the Chester Arch. Soc., 71; 1991), 173–4. Amongst the early examples, those to the Church are similar to the later standard formulae, *Chester*, Nos. 20, 76, 107, including the warrantor's heirs and noting the perpetuity of the obligation. Those to laymen are different. They make no mention of perpetuity or of the warrantor's heirs, although one does include the warrantee's heirs; *Chester*, No. 86; the other two relevant grants are Nos. 56, 71; see also No. 66. For another early instance of a warranty clause, see *The Coucher Book of Furness Abbey*, edd. J. C. Atkinson and J. Brownhill (2 vols. in 6 parts; Chetham Soc. NS 9, 11, 14, 74, 76, 78; 1886–1919), ii, pt. ii, No. 30, from *c*.1134 × 52. See also D. Postles, 'Gifts in Frankalmoin, Warranty of Land, and Feudal Society', *CLJ* 1 (1991), 330–46, who independently reached conclusions compatible with mine.

[184] See Hyams, 'Warranty', 449 and 465 on Stephen's reign; also 475 on express warranty clauses; and Tabuteau, *Transfers of Property*, 198, on 11th-cent. Normandy.

[185] *Ramsey Chronicle*, 275. *Earldom of Gloucester*, No. 186, cited Hyams, 'Warranty', 465 n. 120, is a Norman settlement where the losing party receives less an exchange, more a grant of a life interest.

value and for their warrant, before they are disseised of the said Fifehead'.[186] Now this may be regarded as showing with special precision that exchange was one facet of the warranty procedure, the point here being that the exchange was to be made before disseisin. However, it might also be taken as evidence that warranty and exchange were two promises which at this time might often be linked, but were not yet inextricably so.[187] Warranty might simply be the obligation to support the tenant's claim against a third party. Such an interpretation casts in a slightly different light the charters of St Mary's, York, which deny obligation to provide exchange in event of loss and on which Hyams bases his argument that 'when draftsmen take the trouble to exclude expressly a possible corollary, the existence of the primary obligation is so clear as not to require mention'. Most of the early St Mary's charters do not use warranty language, stating simply that if the tenant should lose the land the house would not give an exchange.[188] Perhaps we have two linked obligations only gradually coming to be combined.[189]

Such exchanges presumably arose when the tenant's land was lost to a third party who henceforth held of the lord. They are thus associated with the so-called 'positive' aspect of warranty. In the wider context of the relationship between lordship and land-holding, it is notable that, according to warranty clauses, it is the tenant

[186] *Chester*, No. 86.

[187] Note that warranty language is not always applied for relevant situations, e.g. *Earldom of Gloucester*, No. 71, *Earldom of Hereford*, No. 30, suggesting that the procedures are still fluid. Note further a problematic passage in *Glanvill*, ix. 4, Hall, 107, saying lords are bound to provide exchange only for lands they themselves had given the tenant, not for the tenant's inheritance. This distinction with reference to inheritance and acquisition does not fit with the picture obtained from charter warranty clauses or early cases. Various explanations are possible, see e.g. Hyams, 'Warranty', 471–2, but none is wholly satisfactory. Perhaps *Glanvill's* views are based on practice in relation to royal warranty. In any case, the passage again suggests a less necessary connection between warranty and exchange.

[188] For St Mary's charters not using warranty language, see *EYC*, i, Nos. 264, 310, 369; ii, No. 1168, all cited by Hyams, 'Warranty', 456 n. 75, in support of the passage quoted above; for St Mary's charters using warranty language, see *EYC*, iii, No. 1303; iv, Nos. 118, 119. Note also from Normandy the Préaux charter cited by Tabuteau, *Transfers of Property*, 199, and her comments.

[189] Note Hyams, 'Warranty', 465, 'the right to escambium *became* an automatic corollary to warranty' (my italics). Hyams gives no chronological suggestions. The final, although not the first or only pressure, may have been the Angevin reforms: in a world without routine royal enforcement, exchange could not always have been enforceable, just as it remained unenforceable in relation to the king. For enforcement of warranty or exchange, see e.g. *Registrum Antiquissimum*, No. 189.

who receives the exchange, the successful claimant who obtains the disputed tenement. Right is here seen to outweigh seignorial acceptance as the best title to a specific piece of land.[190]

Hyams mentions the 'negative' aspect in relation to warranty in its 'developed form', but he is not explicit about when the warranty obligation first included both aspects. Certain arguments might suggest that the link only became tight in the later twelfth century. As we have seen, use of warranty language in vernacular literature emphasized protection against third parties. It is also notable that charters specify warranty 'against all people', again surely meaning third parties; when they direct their warranty clauses against specific people or groups they do not mention the donor.[191] Furthermore, individual charters sometimes differentiate between the obligation to provide exchange arising from the inability to warrant and that deriving from the lord's desire to take the original grant back into his own hand.[192] The need to spell out both situations suggests that they could not both be coped with under the single head of unwillingness or inability to warrant.

In any case, why should a charter, devoted as it was to recording a grant for posterity, need to include an additional way of making it binding upon the lord? The initial granting words in the charter—or in an oral grant—must have been intended to bind the donor and often his heirs into keeping its terms. The lord's promise encapsulated in the warranty clause is not so much that he would not interfere, but that the land was his to give in the first place.[193] Hence the obligation to defend against potential third-party claims—one should not give away what is not one's own to give—and hence the

[190] Note, however, e.g. A. Saltman, *Theobald, Archbishop of Canterbury* (London, 1956), Supplementary Documents B, where the son of a donor to the church, having wrongfully re-acquired the land, gave it to a third party. When persuaded to repent (in 1146), he stated that the land had been alienated thus that in no way could he revoke it. The church agreed to accept an alternative piece of land.

[191] Note that God was sometimes referred to as a warrantor, and the suggestion that God should challenge his own gift would have seemed unlikely; see B. Smalley, *The Study of the Bible in the Middle Ages* (3rd edn., Oxford, 1983), 146 and n. 3, discussed in Hyams, 'Warranty', 444; *Earldom of Hereford*, No. 109, a charter of 1181 × c.1197. For a specific direction in a warranty clause, see e.g. *Mowbray*, No. 250. In addition, some clauses for example laying down that the donor would warrant if need arose or a challenge occurred are hard to see as logically applying if the challenger was the donor: *Northants*, Nos. XXV, XXVI.

[192] e.g. *Earldom of Hereford*, No. 84; see also e.g. *Stoke*, No. 25, for a charter simply providing for an exchange if the lord resumed the grant.

[193] For a late but telling instance, see *Reading*, No. 390.

compatibility with the warranty language concerning chattels where
the vendor was, in part, promising that the chattel was his to sell.[194]
In addition, this emphasis on the positive aspect fits with a view of
pre-Common Law warranty as an active exercise of lordship, backing
up a man inside or outside court.[195] Perhaps the 'negative aspect' of
warranty really emerged when warranty with regard to land came to
be closely associated with homage, which bound the lord to treat the
tenant properly. Then the obligation to allow continuing tenure could
be seen to arise from either or both.

What then of the inclusion of phrases concerning services in
warranty clauses? These could suggest that the warranty did involve a
promise from the donor not to reseise the lands, but only if services
were done. Such is one possible reading, but the clauses could also
be taken as limiting an obligation to warrant against outsiders to those
tenants who were acting properly. Good lordship was a reward for
the good tenant.

Thus it can be argued that at least for much of the period with
which I am concerned, warranty of land was primarily seen as a
means of protecting grants against challenge by a third party. Particularly in times of political strife, this might require very forceful
action.[196] Some warranty clauses even specified protection against
royal violence.[197] In other circumstances, within or without court, the
warrantor may just quietly and forcefully have made the claimant an
offer he could not refuse.

[194] An occasional feature is a chain of warranty, with the grantee's warrantor also
appealing to their own warrantor; see e.g. *Danelaw Documents*, No. 524 (late 12th
cent.), and note *Book of Seals*, No. 194. *Regesta*, iii, No. 579 shows the original holder in
a substitution promising to warrant.

[195] See e.g. *EYC*, v, No. 198; *Ancient Charters Royal and Private Prior to A.D. 1200*,
ed. J. H. Round (PRS, 10; 1888), No. 42, (cited and tr. Pollock and Maitland, i. 307 n.
1), is very significant even though it does not use the term warranty: 'and if any dispute
arise about that church or the possession thereof, I will come to the aid of the monks
to deraign what the church ought to hold, wheresoever it may be needful, to the best of
my power, at their cost and upon a horse of theirs if I have not got my own.' *Book of
Seals*, No. 194, associates warranty with the lord providing aid for the vassal. For
promises to support in court, see e.g. *Rufford Charters*, ed. C. J. Holdsworth (4 vols.;
Thoroton Soc. Rec. Ser. 29, 30, 32, 34; 1972–81), No. 99; cf. a great man taking over
the defence of a lesser in criminal cases, e.g. that concerning the murder of a Jew
recorded in *The Life of St William of Norwich*. Note also warranty by letter, *Monasticon*,
v. 351–2, *EYC*, v, No. 398.

[196] See e.g. Duke Henry's admission that he might be unable to warrant 'because of
war', *Regesta*, iii, No. 81.

[197] See e.g. *Earldom of Hereford*, No. 30, which promised exchange if the donor
could not resist the violence of the king or any other powerful man [*potente*].

CONCLUSIONS

The tenant thus enjoyed considerable security of tenure in his life-time, provided he did not turn against his lord. If not absolutely guaranteed possession of a specific tenement, he was at least to have an alternative holding. Sometimes this would result from an outside challenge, and from the successful claimant's point of view this might involve his own re-establishment of secure tenure. In addition, occasional charters show a lord giving his man's holding to a new beneficiary, whilst offering the vassal an exchange. The pattern of land-holding was thus changed but not the personal relationship of lord and vassal. Whilst it is uncertain how much choice these tenants had concerning such transactions, they do not seem to have been regarded as a threat to security of tenure, and few involve significant vassals as opposed to minor tenants.[198]

As Holt has pointed out, disruption of tenure, at least outside Stephen's reign, seems to have been most common at the top of society. This need not simply result from the prevalence of evidence, but rather from political circumstances, notably when lordship of England and Normandy were separated. Tenants lower down the scale enjoyed greater security, in many instances even surviving the fall of their lords.[199] The impression of common security is re-inforced by the very need on occasion to specify that an estate was only held for a term of years.[200]

---

[198] See e.g. *Northants*, Frontispiece, a charter of William de Roumare, earl of Lincoln, from 1142: since the lands given were not of his demesne, he gave exchanges to those men who held in fee and inheritance. Note that the charter also specifies that *rustici* who wished to remain received exchanges, others received their liberty. See also Stenton, *First Century*, No. 42; *Earldom of Hereford*, Nos. 9, 25. In other instances, the vassal, at least if he were a tenant in chief, might have to pay for the exchange: *PR 31 HI*, 72. Cf. below, p. 228 on forced attornment, the granting of land and vassals to a new lord.

[199] J. C. Holt, 'Politics and Property in Early Medieval England', *P&P* 57 (1972), 30–6, 'Feudal Society and the Family in Early Medieval England: I. The Revolution of 1066', *TRHS*, 5th Ser. 32 (1982), 207–10, 'Introduction of Knight Service'; his explanations include the oaths of loyalty taken by sub-tenants to the king. Such continuity must also have been encouraged by the increasingly strong bond between tenant and land, less affected by lordship, discussed below.

[200] See e.g. *Gesta Abbatum Monasterii Sancti Albani*, ed. H. T. Riley (3 vols.; London, 1867–9), i. 43–4, for a grant for twenty years, at the end of which term problems arose for the granting church; *The Chronicle of Hugh Candidus, a Monk of Peterborough*, ed. W. T. Mellows (London, 1949), 88–9, 99, 111, 123; *Regesta*, ii, No. 1427; iii, No. 675, in which note also the need of the abbot of Reading to have spelt

Such security is also suggested by the quotation from Anselm at the start of this chapter, which pointed out that landed tenants were 'grounded and rooted'. His reservation that they enjoyed their position only so long as they did their lord's will may indeed exaggerate any insecurity, for two reasons. First, we have seen that the room for arbitrary action by the lord could be very limited. Secondly, very often the interests of lord and man were shared. Both benefited from the other's loyalty and aid, and, for example, a lord coming to a tenant's protection against outside claims could often be protecting his own interests too.

Moreover, security in relation to the lord may have increased as time passed, since it would appear that the lordship bond was more important in relation to recent acquisitions than inherited land.[201] This will become apparent when we look further at the inheritance and alienation of land, but is also suggested by a passage of the *Leges Henrici*. In disputes over acquisitions [*de cremento feudi*] a witness had to hold within the same lordship, in disputes about inheritance [*de primo feudi*] any free man or even others could witness.[202] Holding of acquisitions, it would seem, was a matter more internal to the honour than holding of inheritance. Any use of the *Leges*, especially concerning land law, is problematic, but there is no obvious Anglo-Saxon or continental source for these statements. Even if not accepted as an accurate description of regular procedure, they give some indication

out that his officials were to hold not by inheritance but by the will of the abbot and monks. Cf. below, pp. 97–101 on the significance of life-grants.

[201] On the distinction between inheritance and acquisition, the strong form of which may have been a product of the Conquest, see esp. J. C. Holt, 'Politics and Property', 12–19, 41–4; 'The Revolution of 1066', 198–9, 205–6; 'Feudal Society and the Family in Early Mediaeval England: II. Notions of Patrimony', *TRHS*, 5th Ser. 33 (1983), 213–14; S. D. White, 'Politics and Property in Early Mediaeval England: Succession to Fiefs in Early Mediaeval England', *P&P* 65 (1974), 124; and for comparisons, A. Gurevic, 'Représentations et attitudes à l'égard de la propriété pendant le Haut Moyen Âge', *Annales ESC* 27 (1972), 525–6. See also *Leges Henrici*, 70 21, Downer, 224, for its distinction between the 'first fee', which is to pass to the eldest son, and 'purchases and acquisitions', which a man may give to whomsoever he wishes. A similar distinction between inheritance and acquisitions may have existed in the Anglo-Saxon period, see *The Will of Aethelgifu*, ed. and tr. D. Whitelock (Roxburghe Club, 1968), 14, discussed below, p. 206 n. 137. However, the *Leges* statement is based on no written source known to the editors and coincides sufficiently with contemporary practice to be taken as stating custom. In contrast to such emphasis on freedom of alienation of acquisitions, which may well reflect their holders' views, younger sons, and also churches, may have seen themselves having some right to acquisitions.

[202] *Leges Henrici*, 48 10–11, Downer, 160.

of attitudes to land-holding. Taken cautiously, they too suggest that the passage of time increased the feeling, particularly on a vassal's own part, that he was secure in his land, the influence of lordship restricted.[203]

Yet to look simply to post-1066 England may be to miss much. Much remains uncertain about the relationship of lordship and land-holding in Normandy before 1066, but Tabuteau has argued that lordship over land, in legal terms tenure, was growing more important in eleventh-century Normandy, with a consequent decline in allods.[204] However, it is at least arguable that men in their role as tenants retained an aspiration towards the freedom of having land, such as had existed with allods.[205] In twelfth-century England we shall later see an instance where a tenant both ceased to do services to his lord and gave away his holding without seignorial permission.[206] When placed in the context of strong royal power and the possibility of royal protection for land-holding, this aspiration towards holding freely might be seen as a continuing force in the direction of the tenant taking fuller control of the land. Vassals made use of royal actions in order to free themselves from any seignorial discretion. Such may be one element behind the peculiar nature of 'real property' in English Common Law, not allod, but a royally protected form of tenure.

Thus far I have been concerned largely with what vassals regarded as 'good lordship'. On other occasions, we see that the lord's worldly interests caused him to act in a way which his vassals, and indeed at times he himself, might regard as bad lordship. Such, for example, are some of the acts which charters refer to as disinheritances. The

---

[203] Likewise, notions similar to those of canonical prescription strengthened tenure; a charter of Henry II, *CPR, 1408–13*, 301, forbad that Hugh fitzPinchon be placed in plea 'if he and his father have held it for fifty years without challenge'. Note also e.g. the view expressed in the late 13th cent. that men had won their lands by participation at Hastings, as discussed by M. T. Clanchy, *From Memory to Written Record* (London, 1979), 21–4; such a view could encourage a man to feel that land ought to remain securely with him and his descendants. See also Holt, 'Revolution of 1066', 206, concerning Wace's treatment of families who had participated in the Conquest.

[204] Tabuteau, *Transfers of Property*, ch. 5. Cf. Thorne and Milsom, who take the feudal as the original state of land-holding from which property develops.

[205] Latin documentation may hide continuity here, for a mid-11th Norman charter follows the word 'inheritance' with the phrase 'which we call in common parlance allod': Fauroux, No. 93. The word allod was rare in England after 1086; note the unusual usage in *Instituta Cnuti*, III. 46, Liebermann, *Gesetze*, i. 613; ii. 324–5 takes these uses to mean bookland. For a late Norman instance, see *TAC*, lxvi. 2, Tardif, 61.

[206] See below, pp. 215–16.

most famous instances come from a letter which Nigel d'Aubigny, supposing himself to be on his death-bed, wrote to his brother William. He mentioned 'the restorations of the lands which I have made to my men whom I had disinherited'.[207] The letter reveals that these are disinheritances of living tenants rather than the denial of inheritances to heirs. Nigel is admitting to having taken lands without due cause; unfortunately we cannot tell whether he had put forward any justification at the time of the disinheritances. The *Leges Henrici* also note the possibility of bad lordship, and state that 'if a lord deprives his man of his land or his fee by virtue of which he is his man, or he deserts him without cause in his hour of mortal need, he may forfeit his lordship over him'.[208] Bad lordship might also take other forms, such as the enforcement of services upon lands given to the Church in free alms.

Clear instances of 'bad lordship' may not have been very common, and I certainly do not wish to suggest that conflict was the natural state of the relationship between lord and man. Yet the pursuit of their own interests on occasion could require the seeking out of each other's weak spots. The workings of lordship and vassalage led into grey areas whence open disputes could flare up, for example over the proper exaction of services. Another point at which tensions could emerge was the death of a tenant, and it is on to the question of inheritance that I shall now move.

---

[207] *Mowbray*, No. 3, which continues 'and the exchanges for those lands which I have given back to my men to whom I had given them'; the charter lists the restorations and exchanges to be made. Note also Nos. 2–10 for restorations to the Church. Nigel had fairly recently taken over the lordship concerned, and may have been refusing to honour the previous lord's grants, thereby 'disinheriting' sitting tenants. See also Orderic, iv. 106, the famous burial scene of William I where he is accused of having robbed a man of the plot of land in which he is to be buried.

[208] *Leges Henrici*, 43 8; see also 43 9 for the restraint recommended to the vassal; both Downer, 152.

PART II

HERITABILITY

3

The Heritability of Land: I

THE situation following a tenant's death focused attention on the relationship of lord, aspiring vassal, and land. Often the lord would simply want a new tenant, and the dead man's closest relative would be the obvious candidate. The lord might also thereby feel himself to be fulfilling an obligation to his deceased loyal vassal. In addition, acceptance of such claimants was encouraging for other tenants, keen to ensure their families' futures. It was a manifestation of good lordship, and would help to obtain loyal followers. Yet on occasion, a lord might wish to take the land back into his own hand, or give it to someone else whose support he desired, or wished to reward. The dead man's heir might be undesirable, or the lord might feel that his resources would be excessively reduced if he always had to use his demesne lands for new enfeoffments. How much choice, therefore, did a lord have on the death of a tenant? Did, for example, custom, the attitude of his court, or his strength relative to his aspiring vassal constrain him? If his choice was restricted, what could he do when unable to get his own way immediately? What could a man do if he felt his claim to succeed was unjustly rejected? Such questions focus on the development of the heritability of land, a subject much debated in recent decades.[1] Since the discussion has sometimes been rather technical and on occasion at cross-purposes, it is worth considering some of the underlying notions of those involved.

Maitland's has been the classic position on the heritability of land in Anglo-Norman England. With some reserve, he held that 'the followers of the Conqueror who received great gifts of English lands held those lands heritably', and also that 'the *feoda* of the Norman reigns', that is lands held by mesne lords, 'are indubitably hereditary'.[2]

---

[1] J. C. Holt, 'Politics and Property in Early Medieval England', *P&P* 57 (1972), 3–4, notes important views up to 1972. More recently, see esp. S. F. C. Milsom, *The Legal Framework of English Feudalism* (Cambridge, 1976), ch. 5; Holt, 'Notions of Patrimony', *TRHS*, 5th Ser. 33 (1983), 193–220; R. C. Palmer, 'The Origins of Property in England', *L&HR* 3 (1985), 1–50.

[2] Pollock and Maitland, i. 314–16; note ii. 266–7, 309, 312, on suggestions of the division of lands between sons.

The Normans came to England with developing notions of heritability,[3] and no one disputes that after the Conquest at the upper
levels of society lands characteristically passed from father to son,
from ancestor to close heir, and thus that family succession was
normal, often routine. Many take this as sufficient evidence of the
heritability of land, especially when it is supplemented by use of
words such as heir and inheritance, *heres* and *hereditas*.[4] However,
certain writers have argued that these conditions do not establish the
heritability of land in the modern lawyer's sense. Thus Thorne used
the following example to illustrate what he called succession:

> if I hire my gardener's son after his father's death, and my son hires his son
> after him, the place as gardener has descended through three generations of
> the same family. Yet it is obvious that it has come to each by gift, and that the
> son and grandson of my gardener can in no way be said to have inherited it.
> What we have is a fief held by successive tenants in return for service, each
> succeeding by gift.[5]

Thorne stressed that in the early post-Conquest period such 'succession' existed, but no real 'inheritance'. He argued that the lord
had considerable control at the tenant's death. If the heir succeeded,
it was by the lord's gift; 'the tenant's heir had no rights in the land
but merely a claim to succeed his ancestor as the lord's feudal man'.
The tenant of a fee 'held merely an estate for life'. In the early
twelfth century, if the lord died, a new gift was still required if the
tenure was to be re-established. If the tenant owed knight service,
the dead lord's heir was bound to make the gift, but, in Thorne's
words, it was 'a gift nevertheless, for which a relief might legitimately
be asked'. By the second quarter of the century, Thorne asserted,
'holdings devolved according to hereditary right', but they were not
fully heritable, for regrants on the death of a lord or tenant were still
very important. By the third quarter of the century, homage, which
traditionally had 'disappeared with the death of either of the parties
to it, . . . was regarded as continuing for a longer time. It disappeared
only when both were dead, subsisting as long as either survived.' The

[3] E. Z. Tabuteau, *Transfers of Property in Eleventh-Century Norman Law* (Chapel
Hill, NC, 1988), esp. ch. 5; J. C. Holt, 'The Revolution of 1066', *TRHS*, 5th Ser. 32
(1982), 193–212, 'Notions of Patrimony'; for limitations in practice, see 'Revolution of
1066', 204.
[4] e.g. R. H. C. Davis, 'What Happened in Stephen's Reign, 1135–1154', *History*,
49 (1964), 1–12.
[5] S. E. Thorne, 'English Feudalism and Estates in Land', *CLJ* (1959), 196.

personal element in the relationship was thus in decline, a major step towards full heritability of land. Yet a renewal of homage and a regrant were still necessary when both parties had died. By the Assize of *mort d'ancestor* in 1176, however, 'there was no reversion in fact and thus no gift. The way had opened for the idea that an heir inherited directly from his ancestor.'[6] Holdings were fully heritable by *c.*1200.

Thorne unfortunately gave no definition of inheritance, but one can be derived from the related arguments of Milsom: 'When the ancestor dies, the heir is at once entitled under abstract rules of law and enters without anyone's authority'.[7] Such a definition helps to clarify the distinction being drawn between inheritance and succession. First, inheritance involved entry 'without anyone's authority'; succession involved the lord's authority, allowing seignorial discretion. Secondly, inheritance involved 'abstract rules of law'; succession involved no such prescriptive, abstract rules. According to Milsom, each succession was a matter of the establishment of a personal relationship, an isolated instance although tempered by custom. It was binding, at least for the lord and the accepted claimant's lifetimes. If an heir was passed over, and the land given to another, a claim from the disappointed heir would not be entertained by the lord and his court. Earlier decisions were not to be reversed. There could be no binding laws of inheritance which the heir might ask to be applied to the facts of his case.[8] These distinctions need not have had a major influence on the descent of most lands, but in certain fringe yet quite probably important cases the effect would be great.

The distinction between succession and inheritance is an analytical one based on modern legal terms. It focuses attention on certain crucial areas, for example the extent of seignorial power. Within the pre-Common Law world posited by Thorne and Milsom, where the honour was a 'feudal state in miniature', family succession might be usual, indeed supported by custom, but the lord retained discretion as to whether the lands of a deceased tenant should pass to the heir. The heir had only a claim to be seised by the lord. In contrast, they argue, rights can only exist if enforced by a sovereign external authority, and no such regular authority existed until the Angevin

[6] Quotations all from Thorne, 'Estates in Land', 196–7, 195, 199, 198, 200–1, 202 respectively.
[7] Milsom, *Legal Framework*, 154.
[8] Milsom, *Legal Framework*, 41, 60–1, 181.

legal reforms. It was these reforms which transformed succession into strictly defined inheritance.[9] However, useful as it is, the distinction between succession and inheritance can only be used with considerable care. It risks focusing on definitions too specific to one later system of law, and neglecting the terms of thought during the period.

Discussion of the practical aspects of the development of inheritance has primarily concentrated on two closely connected questions: the degree to which the lord is making a new gift and the degree of choice he has as to his new tenant free from outside control. Both bring us face to face with problems of sources and interpretation. Thus we have little evidence for the pattern which events would take following the death of a tenant. In particular, with regard to the question of how far the lord was making a new gift to the heir, we do not know whether the lord would usually take the land back into hand, or what form this action would take. We get only the very occasional glimpse, for example from the honour of Chester in the latter part of Henry I's reign. William fitzNigel, constable of Chester, heard that his tenant Hugh fitzOdard was ill. William, therefore, together with his son and a group of witnesses, visited Hugh, and 'gave back' to Hugh's son his father's land, to hold of William and his son.[10] The succession here seems to have been a simple one, and there is no sign of the lord taking the land into hand. Indeed, the impression is of a lord having to be energetic in the exercise of his lordship.

However, Thorne and Milsom's arguments seem to imply that, prior to the Angevin reforms, the lord could resume sole seisin, whereas following those reforms, according to *Glanvill*, 'although lords may take into their hands the fee with the heir, it ought to be done so gently that they do no disseisin to the heirs'.[11] The basis for views such as Thorne and Milsom's seems to rest on reading later arrangements and statements as relics of the general situation in the period before the Angevin reforms. According to *Glanvill*, 'on the death of any of his chief barons the lord king immediately retains his barony in his own hand until the heir has made satisfaction for the relief, even if the heir is of full age'. Lords other than the king were

[9] Milsom, *Legal Framework*, chs. 2 and 5.

[10] G. Ormerod, *The History of the County Palatine and City of Chester* (3 vols.; London, 1819), i, pt. ii, 690 n.

[11] See Thorne, 'Estates', 196, 198, and esp. 200; also e.g. Milsom *Legal Framework*, 170–1. *Glanvill*, vii. 9, Hall, 82.

only allowed to take the land into hand in this way if, for example, they had doubts as to whether the claimant was the just heir, although according to *Bracton*, some in his day wrongly said that any lord was to have such 'primer seisin' following the death of any tenant.[12] The Assize of Northampton in 1176 provided that 'if any free tenant dies, let his heirs remain in such seisin of his fee as their father had on the day on which he was alive and dead'.[13] I do not see any of these statements as showing clearly that at any earlier time all lords regularly took into hand and enjoyed sole seisin of a dead tenant's lands even if they had thereafter to regrant it to the heir. The royal right which existed in *Glanvill*'s time may have been a peculiar privilege of the king even before the Angevin reforms, or an extension of royal power, either gradually or by Henry II. To read the Assize of Northampton as restricting the lord's power from a once general ability to resume seisin is to take it too much as a statutory-type text concerned with substantive innovation. Much more likely is that it was stating good custom and providing a regular remedy by royal justices.[14] In practice, the lord's decision as to whether he should take the dead tenant's land into hand, and in what way, may have varied with circumstances. Often only some element of ceremony may have asserted the lord's claim. On other occasions, a lord may have simply been glad to accept the tenure of a powerful heir, without any prior show of taking the land into his own hand.[15]

---

[12] *Glanvill*, ix. 6, Hall, 110; *Bracton*, fo. 252b, Thorne, iii. 245–6. See also Pollock and Maitland, i. 310–12.

[13] Assize of Northampton, c. 4, *SSC*, 179. I do not find convincing the arguments of Palmer, 'Origins of Property', 15, that *heredes* should be translated heiresses.

[14] My reading of the Assize is very close to that of Milsom, *Legal Framework*, 164–5, although the wider consequences we draw from such a reading do differ. As to good custom, the Coronation Charter of Henry I might be of some help: a distinction seems to be drawn in ch. 2, Liebermann, *Gesetze*, i. 521, between the heir buying back land, which implies that the king or lord had prime control over it, and the heir 'relieving' the land, which suggests that he was still in prime control. However, the brief statement of the Charter, with its particular vocabulary, cannot give a detailed picture of general practice; for example, 'relieving' the land could be seen as a way of regaining it after it had temporarily been in the lord's hand; on this clause, see also below, p. 129.

[15] Concerning the taking of land into hand, and the whole subject of succession, see also G. S. Garnett, 'Royal Succession in England, 1066–1154', Ph.D. thesis (Cambridge, 1987), esp. ch. 2. Garnett constructs an elegant argument which would suggest that succession, at least for tenants in chief, was less secure than I shall argue. Most notable is his employment of the evidence of royal action during ecclesiastical vacancies and his use of Eadmer, which allow him to put forward a case for William I and II exercising a considerable degree of discretion. I leave him to put forward these

As to outside involvement, debate has tended to identify it with royal enforcement. Yet other types of outside involvement existed. Some scholars write of customary succession whilst emphasizing that succession is a personal relationship between lord and man.[16] This takes custom as a force internal to the relationship of lord and man. Custom can also be seen as an external constraint. At the very least, it existed within the context of the honorial court. This might be taken as part of the personal power relationships of lord and claimant, but this line of argument stretches the meaning of 'personal'. Rather, the intensely personal, formalized relationship manifested in the homage ceremony gained its power not so much by typifying normal life as by contrasting with it: after a difficult negotiation over a claim to succeed, the many supporting actors are expelled into the role of spectators.[17] The inclusion of inheritance language in such ceremonies could have a lasting effect on the relationship of lord, man, and their heirs.

Further external influences existed. A man denied his inheritance might well seek help from his overlord or some other great man of the area. In particular, written records of grants to a man and his heirs acted as an external control of a lord's later actions. For example, a regrant stating that the beneficiary was to hold as witnessed by the charter which he has, suggests that he had brought an earlier charter into court in order to strengthen his claim.[18] However, all these restraints, even the charters, lack the regularity and authority which ultimately came to reside in royal involvement. Hence, rather than establishing a legal rule of inheritance, they produce 'grey areas' between the absolute personality of Thorne's succession of gardeners—a situation which never existed in post-Conquest England—and inheritance as strictly defined by him. It is with these markedly changing shades of grey that I am concerned.

extremely important arguments to a wider audience, and shall just provisionally note that I do not find them wholly convincing. Eadmer had a case to promote, and therefore emphasized arbitrary action. The situation with regard to lay and ecclesiastical honours may have been less similar than Garnett argues. In addition, the position of sub-tenants may have been rather different; as Garnett is the first to recognize, the king was in a peculiar position amongst lords, since he had no worldly superior.

[16] e.g. Palmer, 'Origins of Property', 5.

[17] On the role of baronial counsel in relation to one aspect of succession, see E. Searle, 'Women and the Legitimization of Succession at the Norman Conquest', *A-NS* 3 (1981), esp. 159–60.

[18] e.g. *Regesta*, iii, No. 389.

I shall argue that by the latter part of Henry I's reign, the heir's claim to succeed was considerably stronger than, for example, Thorne allows. External enforcement may have been sufficiently common to force many lords to modify their actions. Under Stephen, the descent of lands was disrupted by political disorder, but notions of succession were not weakened. The first dozen years of Henry II's reign saw at least the restoration of the situation which had existed in the 1120s and 1130s, and the need to settle disputes arising from the previous reign may well have led to considerable royal involvement. A further hardening of inheritance occurred in the last third of the twelfth century.

The limitations of the sources providing statements of custom, for example, and the scarcity particularly of early dispute records is of course a problem in analysing the development of inheritance. Historians have therefore supplemented other arguments by examining certain elements of regular charter phraseology, and it is primarily this approach I adopt for the current chapter. The interest of the language of conveyance to legal historians is obvious, but the commentary offered is inevitably only preliminary to further study of heritability. However wide the sample of documents, analysis of charter language gives only an incomplete picture. For example, if one accepts that a charter recording a grant to 'N. and his heirs' strengthened some heir's claim to succeed, the question arises as to how far this would help a first cousin as opposed to an only son. In this chapter I do touch on such questions as 'Was all property, land held in fee or otherwise, castles, office, title, equally heritable?', and begin to examine disputes with those which demonstrate the practical effect of charter wording. However, other vital questions, such as 'Were all heirs, direct, collateral, immediate or distant, on the same footing?', must be left for the next chapter, where I concentrate on genealogy and the scarce but crucial evidence of cases.[19]

My analysis in this chapter is divided into four main parts. I examine the records of the moment of succession, and ask whether the verbs used to record grants to newly succeeding heirs can help us to assess the strength of the heir's claim and the degree of the lord's discretion. I then turn to the emergence of the use of inheritance language, vocabulary based on the Latin *heres*. Next I look at the increasing precision of such language and its use as a classification of

---

[19] Questions from Holt, 'Politics and Property', 9.

land-holding, and finally I discuss the relevance of grants specifically for life to consideration of the development of inheritance. The analysis therefore begins in substance as an exercise in charter diplomatic, and the establishment of the chronology of charter vocabulary and phraseology is in itself useful. The thrust, though, is legal and, less directly, social and intellectual. I wish to illustrate two main points. First, I suggest that the very existence of written records of grants to a man and his heirs acted as one amongst several external controls of a lord's actions. Secondly, charters can reveal, however indirectly, something of the thought of time.[20] I shall argue that even if succession in the late eleventh and twelfth centuries did not proceed by abstract rules, certain abstract notions of land-holding were developing which affected legal change.

THE LANGUAGE OF REGRANTS

I begin with the aspect of charter language used by Thorne in his seminal article 'English Feudalism and Estates in Land', which did so much to reopen the question of the heritability of land in the twelfth century. Thorne's argument rested partly on the language used to record regrants and confirmations by new lords and to new tenants. Here I shall concentrate on the fundamental issue of regrants to the heirs of dead tenants.[21] Thorne wrote of the early twelfth century that when an heir succeeded to a fief, 'if a charter was drawn the words "*reddo et concedo*", even the words "*do et concedo*" proper to a new and original gift, were quite appropriate'.[22] This phraseology indicates considerable seignorial control and a weak position for the old tenant's heir. In the third quarter of the century,

if a charter were drawn the proper words were '*concedo et confirmo*', denoting an act of confirmation, rather than the '*do et concedo*' which had formerly been appropriate; though not found earlier, charters of this kind have survived in considerable number from the third quarter of the twelfth century.[23]

---

[20] I seek to illustrate this point in my articles 'Milsom's Legal Structure: Interpreting Twelfth-Century Law', *TVR* 59 (1991), 47–66, and 'Life-Grants of Land and the Development of Inheritance in Anglo-Norman England', *A-NS* 12 (1990), esp. 74–7. Holt has done so in exemplary fashion, for example in 'Notions of Patrimony'.

[21] On grants by newly succeeding lords, see below, Ch. 6.

[22] Thorne, 'Estates', 199.

[23] Thorne, 'Estates', 202. Note that he here increased the magnitude of the change by omitting the phrase 'reddo et concedo' included three pages earlier.

This linguistic argument, and its implications for seignorial control of land, are not easy to test. Thorne explicitly presented his view as a hypothesis, based largely on the charters in Stenton's *First Century of English Feudalism* and *Documents Illustrative of the Danelaw* and in *Sir Christopher Hatton's Book of Seals*. I have therefore tested the hypothesis against charters from a much wider range of sources, as Thorne himself intended to do. Even so regrants are often hard to distinguish from, for example, dispute settlements or confirmations made a considerable time after the heir's succession, and the number of relevant documents is small. In addition, an initial identification of a few set phrases for set types of grant, the basis of Thorne's analysis, derives in part from thirteenth-century Common Law, and is too rigid for satisfactory analysis of twelfth-century granting language. Analysis of the meaning of individual words must be made explicit. May one assume, for example, that *confirmare* can happily be identified with the English 'to confirm'? In what other contexts was it used? One word may have several meanings, simultaneously or over a period of time. If so, what do the other meanings tell us of the one that is relevant here? For all these reasons, linguistic analysis must proceed with great care.

I begin by examining the charters Thorne himself cited in support of his statement that in the first part of the twelfth century *reddere et concedere* (to give back and grant) or even *dare et concedere* (to give and grant) were used for regrants. Overall, Thorne's charters do not support his chronology. All but two of his examples come from *c*.1150–75.[24] His only example of the use of *dare* in a probable regrant actually comes from the early thirteenth, not twelfth, century.[25] Few definitely record simple regrants of land at the tenant's death. One involves an exchange, which conceivably arose from a dispute,[26] others may not even come from the time of succession.[27] Another

[24] The two are F. M. Stenton, *The First Century of English Feudalism, 1066–1166* (2nd edn., Oxford, 1961), No. 25; *Sir Christopher Hatton's Book of Seals*, ed. L. C. Loyd and D. M. Stenton (Northants Rec. Soc. and Oxford, 1950), No. 374. Moreover, six of his eight charters come from eastern England: Stenton, *First Century*, Nos. 24–5, *Documents Illustrative of the Social and Economic History of the Danelaw* (London, 1920), Nos. 457, 518, and possibly *Book of Seals*, No. 374, are all from Lincolnshire. The only examples from central English counties are Stenton, *First Century*, No. 43, *Book of Seals*, No. 50.

[25] *Book of Seals*, No. 374.

[26] Stenton, *First Century*, No. 26.

[27] *Danelaw Documents*, Nos. 457, the phraseology of which may suggest that a dispute had occurred or was expected, 518; Stenton, *First Century*, No. 43, probably refers to a grant of a living father's land to his son.

charter, of Rannulf II earl of Chester, may primarily concern the office of cook.[28] It specified that the grantee and his heirs were to have 'his right', which may indicate a disputed succession. Moreover, the situation as to inheritance of office differed from that concerning lands. In the case of a cook, one might expect something closer to Thorne's gardeners. The transmission of skills between generations may have made succession desirable. However, refusal of a cook's claims might not threaten the prospects of succession for the barons of the court: they would have been more interested in the treatment of their peers. The best tentative conclusion to draw from Thorne's charters is that the words *reddere* or *reddere et concedere* were the appropriate ones in the mid-twelfth century and continued in use at least until *c*.1170.[29]

Examination of a broader range of charters supports this conclusion, although unfortunately scarcely any evidence survives from before 1120, when lords may have had greatest control over succession. *Dare* was not usual in private charters and extremely rare in royal ones: perhaps the royal chancery was more careful or regular in its use of words.[30] However, there is no clear decline in the verb's use. Stenton, in the very passage from which Thorne's argument developed, warned that the language 'proper to a new and original

---

[28] Stenton, *First Century*, No. 24 = No. 80 of *The Charters of the Anglo-Norman Earls of Chester, c.1071-1237*, ed. G. Barraclough (Rec. Soc. of Lancs. and Cheshire, 126; 1988); see *Chester*, pp. 397-8, for the suggestion that the grantee was 'actually engaged in the kitchen'. See also *Chester*, No. 92, for the earl alienating the cook's land.

[29] *Book of Seals*, No. 50; Stenton, *First Century*, No. 25, although this does not refer to any of the grantee's predecessors.

[30] Royal uses of *dare et concedere*: *Regesta*, ii, No. 1464, iii, No. 317, neither definitely a regrant of land held heritably; see also iii, No. 277, a note. Early example among private charters, from the later 1130s: Bodleian Library, MS Dugdale 17, p. 60, a charter of Robert earl of Leicester notable for its poor Latin. The witnesses suggest that the charter was given in Normandy. The charter specifies that the son was to hold after his father's death, which may indicate that this was not a regrant but a promise that the son should succeed. Other possibly relevant charters from Stephen's reign use *dare* in combinations not considered by Thorne: e.g. *The Registrum Antiquissimum of the Cathedral Church of Lincoln*, ed. C. W. Foster and K. Major (Lincoln Rec. Soc., 1931-73), No. 1869, 'gave and gave back'; *Charters of the Honour of Mowbray, 1107-1191*, ed. D. E. Greenway (London, 1972), No. 383, 'gave back, gave, and granted'; however, this may concern the settlement of a dispute, see *Mowbray*, p. 115, note on No. 150. See also *Chester*, Nos. 40, 73, although in each case special factors may lie behind the use of *dare et reddere*—see J. G. H. Hudson, 'Diplomatic and Legal Aspects of the Charters', in A. T. Thacker (ed.), *The Earldom of Chester and its Charters* (Journal of the Chester Arch. Soc. 71; 1991), 164.

'gift', *dare et concedere*, sometimes occurred in regrants during the third quarter of the twelfth century.[31] His example, concerning lands held in fee and inheritance for knight service, can be supplemented by a few others.[32] Exceptionally, the charters recording regrants of Earl Hugh II of Chester use *dare* proportionately more frequently than had those of his predecessor.[33]

So there are problems with Thorne's chronology of the use of *dare*. Moreover, when writers of charters used *dare*, were they really treating regrants like new gifts? Or could *dare* be used, heard, and read in various ways according to circumstances? The phrase *dare et reddere* does not seem to have been considered inconsistent for regrants.[34] Contemporaries no doubt knew what *dare* meant in each case, and, in difficulties, witnesses to the grant could testify to the charter's meaning.[35]

At least until 1154, royal and private charters recording regrants most often used *reddere* or *reddere et concedere*, for both military and non-military tenures.[36] The only two possibly relevant examples from before 1130 in my selection of private charters both use *reddere*.[37] The first definite royal regrant, from the second decade of Henry I's reign, used *reddidisse et concessisse*.[38] Even during the third quarter of the century, *reddere* remained frequent, and indeed was the most common verb used to describe regrants, both of land and office, in

[31] Stenton, *First Century*, 162 and n. 2.

[32] See e.g. an early charter of Henry II, *Cartae Antiquae, Rolls 1–10*, ed. L. Landor (PRS, NS 17; 1939), No. 200.

[33] *Chester*, Nos. 150—made at the request of the heir's father—171, 195–an urban grant; no other probable regrants of Earl Hugh survive. For a discussion of the possible reasons for such usage, see Hudson, 'Chester Charters', 164–5.

[34] See above, p. 74 n. 30.

[35] By the time all the witnesses had died, the land was likely to have descended in the family and thus their right become still more established.

[36] Royal: *Regesta*, ii, Nos. 1552, 1556, 1563, 1639, 1710, 1760, 1809, 1934; iii, Nos. 41, 129, 312, 577, 634–5, 911. Private: *The Cartulary of the Priory of St Denys near Southampton*, ed. E. O. Blake (2 vols.; Southampton Rec. Soc. 24, 25; 1981), No. 66; *Mowbray*, No. 374; *EYC*, iv. 102 only survives as a note, but suggests that the original charter used *reddere* to record a regrant; *EYC*, iv, no. 26—a dispute had existed concerning the service of this land, but seems to have been settled long before this grant: on the background, see *EYC*, v. 242, *Domesday*, i, fo. 347a, *The Lincolnshire Domesday and the Lindsey Survey*, ed. C. W. Foster and T. Longley (Lincoln Rec. Soc. 19; 1924), 242.

[37] *Earldom of Gloucester Charters*, ed. R. B. Patterson (Oxford, 1973), No. 152; *Beauchamp Cartulary: Charters 1100–1268*, ed. E. Mason (PRS, NS 43; 1980), No. 355, which may concern a dispute, see p. 140.

[38] T. Foulds, 'The Lindsey Survey and an Unknown Precept of King Henry I', *BIHR* 59 (1986), 212–15.

private charters.[39] Sometimes it appeared with *confirmare* in phrases such as 'to give back and grant and by this my present charter confirm'.[40]

Concedere was occasionally used alone to describe regrants, perhaps particularly those to lesser men.[41] Only one of Henry I's and none of Stephen's regrants used *confirmare*.[42] In private charters, the phrase *concedere et confirmare* probably appeared before 1150, and became increasingly frequent thereafter.[43] Although Henry II's charters show continuing diversity, they do contain signs that the formula *concedere et confirmare* was becoming more common for regrants of land.[44] However, it did not become the sole 'proper words' for regrants in the third quarter of the century, and even its increased use after 1154 hardly proves a development towards automatic confirmations. Before and after 1154, *confirmare* was generally used to show not that the lord was simply confirming to an heir his father's lands but rather that he was strengthening his grant by the use of writing. This was also its common use in other granting contexts throughout the period.[45]

[39] Royal examples include *Book of Seals*, No. 280, the note to which on p. 193 states that *concedere et reddere* was 'the correct technical term for the admission to an inherited office of this kind', i.e. of marshal; see also next footnote. Private: e.g. *EYC*, iv, No. 47; Bodleian Library, MS Dugdale 13, p. 35; 'Mordak Charters in possession of Lord Willoughby de Broke', *Miscellanea Genealogica et Heraldica*, 5th. Ser. 6 (1926), 97–8. The dating is from *PR 21 HII*, 94, which mentions Roger Murdac.

[40] e.g. *Regesta*, ii, No. 1524; HMC, *Report on the Manuscripts of Lord Middleton* (London, 1911), 2–3.

[41] e.g. *Earldom of Gloucester*, No. 75, *Early Charters of the Cathedral Church of St Paul, London*, ed. M. Gibbs (Camden Soc., 3rd Ser. 58; 1939), No. 214. Apart from the charter cited at n. 38 above, Henry I's remaining two possible regrants from the 1110s simply use *concedere*. One concerns land held at farm, the other may refer to the dower of the dead man's widow: *Regesta*, ii, Nos. 1226, 1151 respectively; on the latter, see also No. 1446.

[42] *Regesta*, ii, No. 1524.

[43] Pre-1150: *EYC*, iv, No. 19, although there are peculiarities in the circumstances of this grant. Post-1150: e.g. 'Charters of the Earldom of Hereford, 1095–1201', ed. D. Walker, in *Camden Miscellany*, xxii (Camden Soc., 4th Ser. 1; 1964), No. 122, datable only to 1165 × *c*.1197, which probably does record a normal regrant.

[44] e.g. *Beauchamp*, No. 176; Cartae Antiquae, Roll 28, m. 1d, No. 20 (photo courtesy of Professor Holt); *Ancient Charters Royal and Private Prior to A.D. 1200*, ed. J. H. Round (PRS 10; 1888), No. 39; the charter seems to be a regrant, since it is datable to 1163 × 6, whilst the decedent appears regularly in the Pipe Rolls until 1165–6 and never thereafter. On the continuing variety, especially in the first half of the reign, e.g. *Book of Seals*, No. 280, HMC, *Middleton*, 2–3; note also *Formulare Anglicanum*, ed. T. Madox (London, 1702), No. DVIII.

[45] e.g. Stenton, *First Century*, Nos. 3, 9, 15. See also Bracton, fo. 34b, Thorne, ii. 111.

Variations even in royal use of language suggest that the granting verbs still were not technical terms of art, applied automatically by chancery clerks for specific situations. It is notable that royal confirmations of regrants by other lords do not automatically use *concedere et confirmare*, even when that formula was becoming common in royal regrants; rather, they tend to use the formulae of the lords' own charters. This surely indicates that the royal clerks did not see phrases such as *reddere et concedere* as incompatible with regrants.[46] Nor is there any sign of clear change following Henry II's reforms.

Thus changes in the wording of regrants do not support Thorne's chronology for the development of inheritance. As soon as charters survive, contemporaries are seen generally to distinguish between regrants and new gifts, primarily through the use of *reddere*. Let us therefore examine *reddere* more closely. To seek to clarify one meaning of a word by its other uses, though not conclusive, is illuminating. Thus *reddere* was used for the payment of rents, of dues. In this, there is no sense of choice. *Reddere* was also used in settlements: land to which a man had proved his right would be 'given back' to him.[47] It was a new grant in the sense that homage might well be taken, and one must not underestimate the importance of such ceremonies. However, in the terms of the time, the tenant had far more than a claim; he had proved his right, or at least his *maius ius*, to hold the land. Anglo-Norman vernacular literature from the mid-twelfth century shows the verb *rendre* being used in the same way.[48] If *reddere* has similar implications of right when used in regrants, the heir's position was considerably stronger by Henry I's reign than Thorne would allow.

INHERITANCE LANGUAGE IN CHARTERS

Do other aspects of charter language support this conclusion? I begin by simply examining the frequency of charter use of inheritance language, by which I mean in this first instance words based on the

[46] Cf. below, p. 90, on royal clerks 'correcting' charter language in another context.
[47] See e.g. *Regesta*, i, No. 423, CMA, ii. 129.
[48] For restoration of inheritance, see e.g. Wace, *Le Roman de Brut*, ed. I. O. Arnold (2 vols.; Société des Anciens Textes Français, Paris, 1938–40), ll. 9613–6; Gaimar, *L'Estoire des Engleis*, ed. A. Bell (Anglo-Norman Texts Society, 14–16, 1960), l. 3920; see also l. 2681 for a man 'giving back' his homage to a lord whom he is defying.

Latin *heres*, heir. Whilst Holt and others have looked at the emergence of such language, private documents have not been analysed in large numbers, and in addition some fine-tuning of chronology is possible: hence the need below to run somewhat laboriously through the charters of *c.*1100–35. Later I shall look at the various meanings of a wider range of words and phrases and at their changing implications.

Few charters recording grants to laymen survive from before 1100, and a large proportion of these record grants by churches for limited periods of lives.[49] Explicit statements with which future heirs could support their claims are very rare. On the other hand, many men certainly did succeed to their family's lands. Ignorance of inheritance language cannot explain its absence from charters, as the Normans came to England familiar with it.[50] Several charters state that the Conqueror came to the realm 'by hereditary right'.[51] In 1067, William I's charter to the citizens of London clearly recognized the practice of succession in the city: 'and I will that every child shall be his father's heir (*yrfnume*) after his father's day.'[52] Moreover, inheritance language is not wholly absent from early post-Conquest charters in favour of individual laymen. Notably, two royal charters use inheritance language in their efforts to prevent succession.[53] At the end of the eleventh century or the beginning of the twelfth, an agreement between Pleines of Slepe, together with his sons William and Richard, and the abbot and convent of Ramsey, allowed Pleines to possess one hide 'by hereditary right'. This does not indicate the routine heritability by the eldest son, for the agreement went on that after Pleines's death, the son whom he had chosen as his heir was to possess the land, without any relief. Still, whichever son was chosen as heir might use this charter to support his claim.[54]

The brevity of some early charters to laymen may be one reason for the absence of inheritance language. Also, writers of charters may not have thought of including statements of heritability: if the grantee had a son it might be assumed that he would succeed, unless special

---

[49] e.g. J. A. Robinson, *Gilbert Crispin, Abbot of Westminster* (Cambridge, 1911), 38; V. H. Galbraith, 'An Episcopal Land-Grant of 1085', *EHR*, 44 (1929), 371–2.

[50] Holt, 'Notions of Patrimony', 199–205. See also e.g. William of Poitiers, *Histoire de Guillaume le Conquérant*, ed. and tr. R. Foreville (Paris, 1952), 30, 88, 100.

[51] e.g. *Regesta*, i, Nos. 231, 272.

[52] *Regesta*, i, No. 15.

[53] *Regesta*, i, Nos. 270, 466. Such a use is also prominent in the first decade of Henry I's reign: *Regesta*, ii, Nos. 966–7.

[54] *Chronicon Abbatiae Rameseiensis*, ed. W. D. Macray (London, 1886), 235–6.

reasons existed to the contrary. Sometimes a statement that the grantee was 'to hold as N. had held' might sufficiently define the conditions of holding.

Henry I's Coronation Charter used words such as heir in a way not dissimilar to later usage, and his grants to laymen used inheritance language increasingly frequently.[55] Only one of nine royal charters recording gifts of land made to laymen between 1100 and *c.*1110 uses inheritance language.[56] Such language would be inappropriate for some,[57] but would later have been expected in others. Two of the five charters recording gifts which survive from *c.*1110–20 use inheritance language,[58] as do two of the four charters where it might be appropriate during the 1120s.[59] A third is to a man and his son, and the mention of the latter could support later succession.[60] It is in Henry's last five years that inheritance language becomes usual in royal charters. It appears in the only gift by subinfeudation where it might be expected, and also in all three surviving charters wherein laymen granted land to the king who then granted it to other laymen.[61] In addition, other types of royal grant, for example confirmations that lands be held as originally given, suggest a similar pattern.[62] Thus by 1130–5, inheritance language was very common in royal charters.

[55] Liebermann, *Gesetze*, i. 521–2; Holt, 'Politics and Property', 39. The *Leges Henrici*'s language is idiosyncratic; see e.g. below, p. 123.

[56] *Regesta*, ii, Nos. 519, 661, 707, 818a—a charter of Queen Matilda—848–9, 998, 1120 do not use inheritance language, No. 793 does. Some of the Latin of No. 793 is unclear; probably the 17th-cent. transcript is inaccurate. I take this as a new gift, despite the use of *concedere*, which may be used because of the money rent, or just be casual drafting.

[57] e.g. *Regesta*, ii, No. 661 is a temporary grant.

[58] *Regesta*, ii, Nos. 987, 992—a grant in fee farm—use inheritance language, Nos. 1062, 1119, 1357 do not; see also No. 1163, which uses inheritance language for a rather different form of gift.

[59] *Regesta*, ii, Nos. 1256, 1395; No. 1279 does not use inheritance language.

[60] *Regesta*, ii, No. 1560. On grants to a man and his son or a man and his heir, see below, n. 154.

[61] *Regesta*, ii, Nos. 1723, 1607, 1668, 1719.

[62] e.g. *Regesta*, ii, No. 911. From after 1120 survive several confirmations of other lord's gifts to laymen, and they frequently include inheritance language; e.g. *Regesta*, ii, Nos. 1268, 1603, 1722, 1758, 1778; No. 1498 is an exception. Likely regrants, excluding brief orders to hold as father held: 1100–10: *Regesta*, ii, No. 843, although not a standard regrant, uses inheritance language and, unusually, refers to itself as a *hereditamentum*; 1110–20: Foulds, 'Lindsey Survey', 212, definitely a regrant, and *Regesta*, ii, Nos. 1151, 1226, possibly regrants, did not use inheritance language; 1120–30: Nos. 1446, 1524 use inheritance language; Nos. 1552, 1639, probable regrants, and Nos. 1556, 1563, 1809, possible regrants, do not use inheritance language; 1130–5: nos 1710, 1760 include inheritance language, No. 1934 does not. On the absence of inheritance language, see below, p. 82.

During Henry's reign, the number of surviving private charters to laymen increases, probably reflecting the number written. Inheritance language begins to appear quite frequently amongst the few surviving examples between 1100 and 1120. Two charters of Ralph de Tosny from 1102 × 26 use inheritance language,[63] as did all of Rannulf Flambard's surviving charters as bishop of Durham recording his gifts to laymen.[64] That these early charters employ inheritance language suggests that such language had previously been used in oral grants.

From 1122 × 37 comes the first large group of private charters in my selection recording grants to laymen from a single donor, St Mary's, York. Ten survive, all using inheritance language. For example, Abbot Geoffrey and the chapter 'granted' one carucate to Richard son of Godive 'in fee heritably', as freely as the monastery's other free tenants held.[65] Although St Mary's charters share certain features which amount to a house style,[66] they are not atypical in the frequency of their use of inheritance language.[67] Lay grantors also regularly used inheritance language in their charters, as soon as we have surviving examples.[68] There is no indication of significant honorial variation in the emergence of inheritance language.

Thus, perhaps surprisingly, inheritance language seems to have been rather more common in private than in royal charters during the period 1100–*c*.1130. Is this the result of the production or survival of charters, or does it reflect a real difference in the nature of grants? Perhaps private grantors, particularly lay ones, were less likely to produce charters for anything but long-term grants, but we have seen that a large proportion of ecclesiastical documents before 1100 were specifically intended to enforce short-term grants. Perhaps the pre-

---

[63] *Beauchamp*, Nos. 355, 356. See also *EYC*, i, No. 25, a gift to a layman and his son *in feudum*. On mention of disinheritance in *Mowbray*, No. 3, see above, p. 62.

[64] *Durham Episcopal Charters, 1071–1152*, ed. H. S. Offler (Surtees Soc. 179; 1968), Nos. 11–13, 19, 22, 23—the last being a dubious document.

[65] *EYC*, iii, No. 1303; see also i, Nos. 310–12, 340, 460, 637; iv, No. 105; ix, Nos. 134–5.

[66] See also above, p. 56; P. R. Hyams, 'Warranty and Good Lordship in Twelfth Century England', *L&HR* 5 (1987), 456.

[67] See e.g. the thirteen Bury grants broadly datable 1121 × 48, *Feudal Documents from the Abbey of Bury St Edmunds*, ed. D. C. Douglas (London, 1932), Nos. 115–27; only three do not use inheritance language, No. 116 being a grant 'in feudum perpetuum', Nos. 115, 120 concerning restorations, regrants, or confirmations of lands a predecessor had held.

[68] e.g. Stenton, *First Century*, No. 29.

servation of royal charters was particularly desirable, whatever the nature of the grant and even if they did not use inheritance language. Yet the pattern may not just be determined by the surviving evidence. Conceivably the king was in a stronger position than some lords to refuse to make grants explicitly mentioning the grantee's heirs, or perhaps for political reasons he was unwilling to do so. Although a growing proportion of Henry I's charters mention inheritance, in the 1120s a significant number still lack such language where it would later have been used. In the 1130s, such language becomes usual, and although charters are few, the change seems to have come by 1135. It is arguable that this in part may reflect concessions by Henry I to his barons. Increased use of writing, 'advances' in charter wording, need not always indicate strong government, as seems sometimes to be assumed. Although the chronology is problematic, one possibility is that by the 1130s Henry was conceding promises as he sought to reinforce his plans for the royal succession, and that these promises included mentions of the grantees' heirs in royal charters.[69]

From the 1130s and thereafter, private charters to laymen become more common, and the prevalence of inheritance language continues.[70] Similarly, almost all of Stephen's charters recording gifts of land to laymen use inheritance language, and in one of the two exceptions such language would not be appropriate.[71] His opponents used inheritance language equally frequently for gifts.[72] Henry II's

[69] Such a situation might fit, for example, with the possible suspension of the Danegeld recorded by John of Worcester, *Chronicle*, ed. J. R. H. Weaver (Anecdota Oxoniensia, 13; 1908), 33–4; his concessions to the Beaumonts and the disgrace of Geoffrey de Clinton discussed by D. B. Crouch, 'Geoffrey de Clinton and Roger, Earl of Warwick: New Men and Magnates in the Reign of Henry I', *BIHR* 55 (1982), 113–24; and the concession to William de Roumare concerning his mother's inheritance, discussed below, p. 146.

[70] All such charters in the appendix of Stenton, *First Century*, include inheritance language if it would be appropriate, e.g. Nos. 3, 26, 28; so do those of William, earl of Warwick, 1153–84, e.g. Bodleian Library, MS Dugdale 13, p. 35. The only exception amongst the abbot's charters in *Feudal Documents*, where inheritance language might have been expected is No. 136, a regrant mentioning the grantee's father. For gifts by laymen of less than comital rank, see e.g. *EYC*, v, Nos. 181, 191, 196, 267. For the regular use of inheritance vocabulary in the charters of the earls of Chester, see Hudson, 'Chester Charters', 165–6.

[71] *Regesta*, iii, Nos. 174–7, 276, 319, 493–4 use inheritance language. The exceptions are Nos. 179, 201.

[72] *Regesta*, iii, Nos. 111, 180, 274–5, 316a, 393, 438–9, 634–5 use inheritance language, No. 320 does not. Other types of grant: present in e.g. *Regesta*, iii, Nos. 41,

charters as king recording gifts and confirmations to laymen almost invariably include inheritance language where appropriate.[73]

What then of charters from *c*.1130 onwards where inheritance language did not appear when it might have been appropriate? Many are restorations, regrants, or confirmations of land held by a predecessor. These probably omitted inheritance language because mention of the grantee's predecessor, by establishing the heir's claim to succeed, rendered inheritance language unnecessary.[74] This was particularly so if the heir had a charter in favour of his predecessor which stated that the land was to be held heritably.[75] Elsewhere, the absence may be explained by the nature of the grant or of the document.[76] Only very rarely can no reason be suggested for the absence of inheritance language.

So far I have concentrated on grants of land; what of charters concerning grants to laymen of office and, for example, castles?[77] Among the few private examples, usage resembles that concerning grants of land, except that the relevant charters only become at all numerous from *c*.1135. Thereafter inheritance language is commonly included where it might be expected.[78] Likewise, the pattern in royal

---

43, 129, 166, 307, 312, 317, 386–7, 581, 634–5, 911–12; absent from e.g. Nos. 413, 577.

[73] Present in e.g. *CChR*, ii. 34; iii. 477–8; iv. 83, Round, *Ancient Charters*, No. 40, *Beauchamp*, No. 176; absent from e.g. *EYC*, i, No. 286.

[74] A possible example from earlier in Henry I's reign is Foulds, 'Lindsey Survey', 212. Note the scarcity of inheritance language in Henry II's regrants, e.g. *EYC*, ii, No. 1240, *CChR*, ii. 137 (2), *Cartae Antiquae, 11–20*, ed. J. C. Davis (PRS, NS 33; 1960), No. 535. Some of Henry's regrants do use inheritance language, e.g. *Beauchamp*, No. 176.

[75] See e.g. Henry I's regrant to Alan son of Reginald Belet, *Regesta*, ii, No. 1809, and the charter in favour of his father, No. 992.

[76] e.g. *Beauchamp*, No. 358, where the brevity of the document, its function, and the existence of a longer charter, No. 357, confirming to the grantee his father's lands, explain why it did not use inheritance language.

[77] See Holt, 'Politics and Property', 25–30; J. A. Green, *The Government of England under Henry I* (Cambridge, 1986), 163–6; J. O. Prestwich, 'The Treason of Geoffrey de Mandeville', *EHR* 103 (1988), 306–9. Also above, p. 74, for the verbs used in regrants of offices.

[78] Possible instance from 1114 × 19, *Feudal Documents*, No. 108, which exists in various versions, only the latest cartulary copy including inheritance language. From Stephen's reign, e.g. *Beauchamp*, No. 285 concerning the shrievalty of Warwickshire; *Chester*, No. 55; *Durham*, No. 41; Stenton, *First Century*, Nos. 24, 47 and 48—the latter two concerning a castle, on which see E. King, 'Mountsorel and its Region in King Stephen's Reign', *Huntington Library Quarterly*, 44 (1980), 1–10; an exception is *Feudal Documents*, No. 136, a regrant. After 1154, e.g. *EYC*, iv, No. 47, *Feudal Documents*, No. 166; *Earldom of Gloucester*, No. 48 all use inheritance language. Pre-

charters suggests an emergence of inheritance language quite similar to that in grants of land.[79] Equally notable, however, is the absence of charters granting certain types of office, for example shrievalties, except in Stephen's reign.[80] The existence of such charters, containing inheritance language, from a period of royal weakness is a sign of the desirability of such language to the grantee.[81] Charters for these offices may once also have existed from the late years of Henry I and from Henry II's reign, their failure to survive perhaps explicable by the temporary nature of their grants. Alternatively, charters may not have been so necessary for non-heritable grants. Either explanation would fit the argument that Henry I and II sought to prevent family succession to such offices, and reveals an awareness of the importance of charters including inheritance language.[82]

sumably few private charters recording grants of office were ever written. Lords knew their officers personally. Grants of office were peculiarly internal to the honour; in contrast with grants of land, no one could challenge a grant by claiming to hold it of another lord. Charters were therefore not needed as defences against outsiders.

[79] Henry I: e.g. *Regesta*, ii, Nos. 543 and 1524, grants to father and son from 1101 and 1116 × 27 respectively; only the second used inheritance language. All three of Henry's grants of office in England from after 1120 use inheritance language: Nos. 1749, 1777, 1835; see also No. 1947, the pantry in Normandy. Henry II: e.g. *Cartae Antiquae, 1–10*, No. 277, *Cartae Antiquae, 11–20*, No. 553. Some of Henry II's charters concerning office did not use inheritance language, but these record regrants or restorations, and emphasize the tenure of an ancestor of the grantee; e.g. *Book of Seals*, No. 280.

[80] All six charters from the reign recording grants of shrievalties were explicitly heritable: *Regesta*, iii, Nos. 68, 274–6, 386, 388; see also Holt, 'Politics and Property', 28. Similarly, great offices: Nos. 68, 111, 438–9, 582, 634. Earldoms: *Regesta*, iii, Nos. 273–4, 393, 634; on earldom as an office, see Holt, 'Politics and Property', 29. Grants of the 'whole county': *Regesta*, iii, Nos. 180, 437 use inheritance language, No. 272, the Treaty of Westminster granting Norfolk to William son of King Stephen, does not. On such grants, see P. Latimer, 'Grants of "Totus Comitatus" in Twelfth-Century England: their Origins and Meaning', *BIHR*, 59 (1986), 137–45. *Regesta*, iii, Nos. 274–6 are the only grants of local justiciarships, all to Geoffrey de Mandeville and all apparently heritable. Forest: *Regesta*, iii, Nos. 68, 391. Eleven charters use inheritance language concerning castles or their custody (on the limits of the distinction between which, see Holt, 'Politics and Property', 25): *Regesta*, iii, Nos. 68, 180, 274–6, 387–8, 391, 393–4, 437; the one exception is No. 494, wherein Stephen gave William de Roumare, earl of Lincoln, Gainsborough castle with all the free customs with which any earl could hold his castle. See also Nos. 178, 430, 959.

[81] The majority of the charters were to earls, who were probably particularly capable of demanding great concessions. Twenty-four relevant charters: thirteen to earls, *Regesta*, iii, Nos. 180, 273–6, 393–4, 437–9, 494, 634–5; four to Miles of Gloucester before he became an earl, Nos. 386–8, 391; seven to others, Nos. 23, 41, 68, 111, 129, 433, 582.

[82] On Henry II, see Holt, 'Politics and Property', 28–9. A most notable exception is Round, *Ancient Charters*, No. 36: at the very time at which he was seeking to reassert

Having thus surveyed the use of inheritance language in charters, I do not wish to imply that its notable frequency proves that land was heritable in the lawyer's strict sense. A dead tenant's son stood in a different position to the lord in 1189 from in 1066, even though at both times he would have been referred to as heir. Nevertheless, the use of inheritance language is significant. First, its early appearance notably in private charters strongly suggests that it had previously been used in oral ceremonies which were not recorded in writing. Such ceremonies, and the memory of them, restricted the lord's right to deny an heir his claim. Secondly, the appearance of such language in charters shows concern with preserving promises of benefits to heirs, with reinforcing custom, and perhaps with the classification of land-holding. The preservation of such promises could further reinforce the heir's position. Take the following case. A tenant died, leaving a son. Usually his lord would have accepted the son as the dead tenant's heir and his new tenant. Sometimes, however, the lord might have wished to give the land to some other applicant, or keep it in demesne. This was not customary, but a truly sovereign lord would have been free to do so, and certainly to reserve his position in this regard. The decedent's son then produced a charter stating that the land had been given to his father and his heirs. The lord might not have felt bound to accept the claimant just because of this charter, and an ecclesiastic, for example, might appeal to the higher authority of Canon Law.[83] Yet its very existence must have affected his decision if he desired to appear a good lord. He would not wish to seem perfidious, or disrespectful of his ancestor's gift. The barons of his court would fear lest their own charters from the lord be rendered worthless. A charter recording a lord's gift to a man and his heirs therefore was in a sense an external authority, restricting the lord's freedom of choice. Henry II admitted the binding force of a genuine charter of his grandfather when he remarked 'By God's eyes, if you could prove this charter false, you would make me a profit of a thousand pounds in England.'[84] In addition, before royal involvement

royal rights over castles, in 1155 × 8, Henry 'gave back and granted' to Richard de la Haye in fee and inheritance the custody of the king's castle at Lincoln. This contrasts with Stephen's attempts to keep at least some control over Lincoln castle. For later examples of heritable grants, see J. C. Holt, *The Northerners* (Oxford, 1961), 221, Prestwich, 'Geoffrey de Mandeville', 309.

[83] See esp. A. Saltman, *Theobald, Archbishop of Canterbury* (London, 1956), No. 103.
[84] *The Chronicle of Battle Abbey*, ed. and tr. E. Searle (Oxford, 1980), 216.

in succession cases became routine, a convincing charter may have been an important aid in getting royal help.[85] Thus the use of inheritance language not merely in ceremonies but also preserved in charters marks a stage in strengthening the right of a dead tenant's heir.

THE CLASSIFICATION OF LAND-HOLDING

Thus far I have only assessed the frequency with which inheritance language was used. I now analyse its meaning more closely and discuss its increasing precision and abstraction. I assess the distinction between language based on *heres* and on *successor*, particularly with regard to the differentiation of laymen and clerics.[86] I then examine the use of alms and inheritance language as classifications of land-holding, that is of how lands are held, with implications for the future and possibly the past. I do not wish to suggest that a fixed set of classifications, equivalent to those of the later Common Law, existed during this period. Nor do I mean that men throughout the period distinguished between the concrete and the abstract in the same way as we do today, or did in *Bracton*'s time, or even *Glanvill*'s. Yet some men at least considered land-holding in certain abstract ways, and this influenced the development of land law.

Uses of *successor* and *heres* reveal careful discrimination. For laymen, *successor* was usually only employed in very particular contexts. Many grants to the Church contain clauses stating that they were made 'for the soul' of the grantor and his kin, and throughout the period such clauses account for most charter references to laymen's

---

[85] See e.g. *EYC*, iv, No. 47; v, No. 178, where the existence of an earlier charter may well have helped a man get royal support against his lord early in Henry II's reign. See below, p. 152, on the importance of royal confirmations.

[86] I concentrate on the noun form, *successor*, since in the very notable absence of a common verb related to *heres* and meaning 'to inherit', *succedere* was widely used in combination with inheritance language: men might 'succeed by hereditary right': e.g. *Registrum Antiquissimum*, No. 907; *Leges Henrici*, 70 20a, Downer, 224, from *Lex Ribuaria*, 56 3. See also *Durham*, No. 12, a grant to a man and his heirs 'per hereditariam successionem successuris'. *Hereditare* generally meant 'to create an heir', see below, p. 122, although occasionally it could mean 'to inherit', e.g. the *Quadripartitus* version of *Ine* 53 1, Liebermann, *Gesetze*, i. 113; HMC, *Ninth Report, Appendix* (London, 1883), 65, 'Sanctus Paulus hereditare debuit'.

successores.[87] Amongst them are charters which elsewhere use *heres.*[88]
The great majority of remaining uses of *successor*, be it the grantor's
own or some other lay person's successors, also concerned gifts of
alms to churches. The donor's successors, or heirs and successors,
were to preserve the gift, or not to impede it. Or it was ordered that
the gift be held freely of the donor's successors.[89] Other uses, for
example charters addressed to the grantor's successors, or referring
to addressees' successors, are extremely uncommon.[90] Thus *successor*
was largely confined to situations particularly concerned with the
spiritual welfare of those denoted and their relationship to churches.
The word's use may reflect ecclesiastical views, although it is not
peculiarly common in beneficiary-drafted documents. Its continuing
appearance in *pro anima* clauses almost certainly owes much to its
symmetry with the word *antecessor*, which it in nearly all instances
accompanies.[91]

For grants to clerics, a distinction between succession and inheritance language existed throughout the period. Under the influence
of the reform movement clerics were seeking to define, limit, and
sometimes avoid use of *heres* with its connotations of blood relationship. Clerics could of course be heirs to family lands, and Canon

[87] e.g. *Earldom of Hereford*, Nos. 23, 25, 47–8; Nos. 94–5 use *heres*; *Earldom of Gloucester*, e.g. Nos. 68, 84, 86, 156, 177. *Successor* was not more common than *heres* in the *pro anima* clauses of charters of all lay families, see e.g. *Mowbray*, Nos. 210, 216, 220, 264.

[88] e.g. *Earldom of Gloucester*, No. 156. *Regesta*, ii, No. 1014 recorded a grant made for the souls of all the king's successors and heirs, this surely being rhetorical emphasis, not an attempt to cover all eventualities.

[89] e.g. *EYC*, v, No. 222; British Library, MS Harley 3650, fos. 21ᵛ–22; *Book of Seals*, No. 287; *Danelaw Documents*, No. 522; *Regesta*, ii, Nos. 822, 1751, 1969; *Earldom of Gloucester*, Nos. 5, 169, both of which use heirs and successors; *Chester*, No. 144. Note also *The Cartulary of Shrewsbury Abbey*, ed. U. Rees (2 vols.; Aberystwyth, 1975), No. 15. Royal charters show a marked decline in use of *successor* after 1135; only a group of three of Stephen's charters, all written at York in Feb. 1136, possibly all by a single scribe, use *successor* where *heres* might be expected; *Regesta*, iii, Nos. 335, 716, 919. Explanations of the unusual wordings are possible, see Hudson, 'Seignorial Control of Land', 81–2. For an exception amongst Henry II's charters, *CChR*, ii. 351–2, a confirmation to the burgesses of Maldon and their successors.

[90] e.g. *The Cartulary of Worcester Cathedral Priory*, ed. R. R. Darlington (PRS, NS 38, 1968), No. 117, *Earldom of Hereford*, No. 17 respectively; see also *Regesta*, ii, No. 886. In Henry I's charters, *successor* sometimes clearly referred to office-holding; e.g. *Regesta*, ii, No. 1377. However, any hint that succession language might come to be used of office-holding does not develop.

[91] In some instances it instead accompanies *predecessor*, e.g. *Earldom of Gloucester*, No. 86, *Mowbray*, No. 13.

Law refers to them having lands 'by hereditary succession'.[92] They might also have heirs for such lands, although under restrictions not applying to laymen. In addition, clerics held lands which belonged to their church, not their family, and to these kinship brought no automatic claim to succeed. Such distinctions were reflected in charter wording. Charters very rarely used inheritance language of great clerics,[93] although occasional grants for canons to hold 'by hereditary right' survive.[94] In most of the few surviving charters using inheritance language for a lesser churchman, he is referred to either as *clericus* or *capellanus*, very rarely as, say, *presbyter* or *persona*.[95] Often they were men with a close connection to the donor or his household.[96] It may well be that use of inheritance language was generally limited to clerics still in sufficiently low orders to marry and have children.[97] In contrast, the word *successor* was free of inheritance language's connotations of a genealogical claim. Throughout the period, some surviving charters recording grants to bishops and abbots mentioned their successors,[98] and after 1100 a few charters

[92] e.g. Gratian, *Decretum*, C. xii, q. v, c. iv.

[93] The first royal charter example is *Regesta*, ii, No. 1283; this may be an unusual instance referring specifically to the bishop's illegitimate son. *Regesta*, iii, No. 980 refers to a grant to an archbishop 'in fee and inheritance'.

[94] e.g. *Registrum Antiquissimum*, Nos. 914–15.

[95] Post-1135 royal examples: e.g. *Regesta*, iii, Nos. 15, 897; PRO, DD 664/1, Henry II to William clerk of Holm. *Regesta*, iii, p. xi: 'the two terms "clerk" and "chaplain" of the king seem to have been used synonymously'.

[96] e.g. *Regesta*, ii, No. 1502, a grant to William, archdeacon of Ely and the king's chaplain, to be held by hereditary right. Although archdeacons were frequently exhorted to enforce clerical celibacy, William, like some others, was married and produced a son; see M. Brett, *The English Church under Henry I* (Oxford, 1975), 203; E. Miller, *The Abbey and Bishopric of Ely* (Cambridge, 1951), 168–9. See also e.g. *Regesta*, ii, No. 1872. Henry I's only charter using inheritance language for a lesser cleric not closely attached to the household is *Regesta*, ii, No. 1709; on this land see also *Regesta*, iii, No. 793, *The Register of St Osmund*, ed. W. H. Rich Jones (2 vols.; London, 1883–4), i. 337. Amongst private charters, see e.g. *Registrum Antiquissimum*, No. 614, for a gift to a cleric with a known close connection to the donor, e.g. *Registrum Antiquissimum*, No. 1295, *EYC*, iv, No. 57, for clerics with no such clear connection.

[97] See C. N. L. Brooke, 'Gregorian Reform in Action: Clerical Marriage in England, 1050–1200', *CHJ* 12 (1956), 1–21; Brett, *English Church*, 219–20; C. R. Cheney, *From Becket to Langton* (Manchester, 1956), 137–8; B. R. Kemp, 'Hereditary Benefices in the Medieval English Church: A Hereford Example', *BIHR* 43 (1970), 1–15. For an instance where the beneficiary was a priest, see *Facsimiles of Early Charters in Oxford Muniment Rooms*, ed. H. E. Salter (Oxford, 1929), No. 77 and note.

[98] e.g. *Regesta*, i, Nos. 272, 288e, 326, 337; ii, Nos. 864, 1093, 1475; iii, Nos. 4, 142; *CMA*, ii. 217, 220, *Registrum Antiquissimum*, No. 136; *Book of Seals*, No. 431. Also Henry I's Coronation Charter, c. 1, Liebermann, *Gesetze*, i. 521.

recording grants to the canons of a church do likewise.[99] Only rarely did grants to heads of lesser churches and to lesser clerics use *successor*. Such usage tended to be for office-holders,[100] and this might also fit with mentions of greater clerics' successors, since they too could be seen as ecclesiastical office-holders.

Occasionally, individual charters illustrate men distinguishing between where inheritance and where succession language should be used. When Henry I gave Calne church *in prebendam* to the church of Salisbury and Nigel of Calne the royal chaplain and his successors, he also gave various lands *in prebendam* to Salisbury and to a layman Arnold the Falconer and his heirs.[101] Then probably in the 1150s, a charter of the chapter of Lincoln distinguished between the succession language used for canons of a church and the inheritance language which might be appropriate for a lesser clerk; they granted two bovates in Bishop Norton to Miles the clerk of Norton and his heirs 'to hold of us and our successors'.[102]

Bearing in mind this capacity of twelfth-century draftsmen to distinguish the appropriateness of various forms for certain situations, let us turn to the classification of land-holding. I begin with the Church, for which evidence is relatively plentiful, and which, I shall argue, played an important part in the process of classification. According to Holt, in Normandy, 'the whole language of inheritance was first generated' in the records of endowments of churches and monasteries. A grant to a church, he argues, was a transfer of the donor's right, and a man could only give what he held by hereditary right. Words such as *hereditas* were 'part of the common jargon of conveyancing. They were shared with the Anglo-Saxon *landbocs* and Carolingian *diplomata*.'[103]

Both the diploma and the use of inheritance language for churches were declining forms in Anglo-Norman England. Three of the Conqueror's four charters which record grants in England and use inheritance language in favour of churches are diplomas.[104] Thereafter,

[99] e.g. *Regesta*, ii, No. 1343; *Registrum Antiquissimum*, Nos. 118–19, 122.

[100] e.g. *St Paul's*, No. 273. See also e.g. *Regesta*, ii, No. 1164 to a royal chaplain. Also e.g. *Regesta*, i, No. 361, for Rannulf Flambard, perhaps in his office of dean of the church concerned.

[101] *Regesta*, ii, Nos. 1163–4; see Brett, *English Church*, 188–9.

[102] *Registrum Antiquissimum*, No. 1191.

[103] Holt, 'Notions of Patrimony', 199–200.

[104] *Regesta*, i, No. 8 (despite the comment of *Regesta*, i. 3, the charter is very suspicious in its current form. referring to 'suprascripti reges', which must mean kings

the use of inheritance language in royal charters for churches is very rare, and confined to diplomas or mixed-style documents, generally beneficiary-drafted and often dubious.[105] The lack of early private charters may hide uses of inheritance language; in the 1090s Hemming employed such language in his narrative on the unjust losses incurred by Worcester.[106] However, as in royal documents, inheritance language rarely appeared in twelfth-century private charters to describe church land-holding, although it was occasionally still used after 1150.[107]

What caused the decline in the use of inheritance language for churches, which is clear at least in royal documents? The replacement of diplomas by writ-charters was important, but cannot fully explain developments in terminology. There seems no intrinsic reason why writ-charters should not use inheritance language for charters; one of William I's and some private charters did so.[108] The developments also reflect deeper intellectual changes. The aspirations of the Church reformers discouraged the use of inheritance language to classify

mentioned earlier in the cartulary); No. 28, on which see F. M. Stenton, *Latin Charters of the Anglo-Saxon Period* (Oxford, 1955), 87–8; No. 135, from the queen. Charter with letter-style address etc.: No. 160.

[105] Copying formulae from earlier documents may explain the persistence of such language in beneficiary-drafted documents, trustworthy and suspect. The only surviving example from Rufus's reign is a diploma for St-Pierre-au-Mont-Blondin at Ghent, possibly copied from forged diplomas of the Confessor and Conqueror; *Regesta*, i, No. 323; the Conqueror's charter is No. 141. Cf. Henry I's confirmation by writ, *Regesta*, ii, No. 1148, which did not use inheritance language for the Church. A surviving charter in the Confessor's name is *Cartae Antiquae, 11–20*, No. 581 (= Sawyer, No. 1002); however, P. Chaplais, in *A Medieval Miscellany for Doris Mary Stenton* (PRS, NS 36; 1960), 92, takes this as the work of Osbert de Clare, probably after Henry I's reign, whereas Henry I's writ also mentions a charter of the Confessor. Perhaps the surviving document is an 'improved' version. See also *Regesta*, ii, Nos. 988, 1391; iii, No. 284, based on ii, No. 1391, very dubious; No. 718, based on ii, No. 636, a mixed-style document written by a Rochester or Canterbury scribe, which iii. 265 notes that Chaplais considers genuine.

[106] *Hemmingi Chartularium Ecclesie Wigorniensis*, ed. T. Hearne (2 vols.; Oxford, 1723), i. 250, 263. For a case record from Henry I's reign ending with a restoration to a church 'hereditario jure', see *An Eleventh-Century Inquisition of St Augustine's, Canterbury*, ed. A Ballard (London, 1920), 22.

[107] e.g. *Chester*, No. 116; *EYC*, iv, No. 81 is unique in this respect amongst 12th-cent. charters of the earls of Richmond. Note also H. G. Richardson and G. O. Sayles, *The Governance of Medieval England from the Conquest to Magna Carta* (Edinburgh, 1966), 277, a letter to the king's justices which mentions the church holding in fee and inheritance.

[108] See above, p. 82; on the absence of inheritance language, note also Holt, 'Notions of Patrimony', 214.

ecclesiastical land-holding. As suggested above, their fight against clerical marriage and nepotism militated against ideas of inheritance.

Yet it is the beneficiary-drafted documents of Henry I and Stephen which tend to mention inheritance. The same impulses that made churchmen use such language in documents they drafted as beneficiaries might have made them demand it of charters produced in the royal chancery. Did the chancery resist? Perhaps the frequency with which royal scribes wrote charters was already producing standardization. Perhaps they, even more than some churchmen, were sensitive to the importance of different classifications of land-holding. If an overall policy decision seems unlikely, numerous individual decisions must have been taken in the chancery. In this context, certain groups of charters from Stephen's reign are especially notable. Take one example. Probably in the 1130s, Rainald de 'Chukes' gave 'his vill' of Yanworth to St Peter's, Gloucester, in fee and inheritance to hold by perpetual right and inheritance. However, Stephen and Duke Henry's confirmations refer to the church holding 'in alms'.[109] As we have seen there were other circumstances, such as the confirmation of regrants, when royal clerks did not change the grantor's language. Here they did. This is the strongest possible evidence that, by 1150 at the very latest, royal authority saw inheritance language as inappropriate for grants to churches. Classification of land-holding was hardening.

When royal clerks 'corrected' the wording of these charters, they replaced the mention of inheritance with the words *in elemosinam*, 'in alms'.[110] More broadly, this term, which had been known but unusual in England and Normandy before 1066, replaced inheritance language as it disappeared from grants to the Church.[111] The change surely reflects the influence of the ecclesiastical reform movement. Just enough charters survive from the late eleventh century to show how *elemosina* came to be used not only to describe the nature

---

[109] *Historia et Cartularium Monasterii Sancti Petri Gloucestriae*, ed. W. H. Hart (London, 1863–7), No. DCCXXV and the chronicle entry at i. 90, which suggests the 1130s as the date for the gift; see also DCCXXVIII; *Regesta*, iii, Nos. 361–2; Henry's confirmation as king, No. DCCXXX, is almost identical to that he granted as duke. Note further No. DCCXXVI, which used *in elemosinam*. See also *Earldom of Gloucester*, No. 5, 'in elemosinam et feodo', cf. Duke Henry's confirmation *Regesta*, iii, No. 49, 'in elemosinam perpetuam'.

[110] For a fuller discussion, see Hudson, 'Seignorial Control of Land', 85–90.

[111] e.g. England: *Anglo-Saxon Charters*, ed. and tr. A. J. Robertson (2nd edn., Cambridge, 1956), No. XXIII. Normandy, Fauroux, Nos. 208, 218.

of certain gifts or to specify certain of a church's lands, but also through the phrase *in elemosina(m)* as a classification of land-holding. This last usage was still new in Normandy at the time of the Conquest, and in William I's charters concerning England, the phrase *in elemosinam* was used only once, markedly less than inheritance language for churches.[112] The Domesday survey, which used the phrase much more often, may have stimulated such classification of land-holding.[113] In Rufus's charters, and particularly from *c*.1093, *in elemosinam* was used much more frequently than in his father's.[114] In the twelfth century, the phrase *in elemosina(m)* is by far the most common use of alms language in private and royal charters.[115] Adjectives were added to emphasize the freedom, purity, and perpetuity of such grants, contrasting them with lay land-holding. However, although ecclesiastical land-holding continued to develop and grow more defined, there was no further major shift in vocabulary such as that from inheritance to alms language which had taken place in the late eleventh century.

Like alms language with reference to church lands, inheritance language might be used in several ways with reference to lay ones. For example, *hereditas*, inheritance, could mean the lands a man's ancestors had held and he hoped his descendants would hold, and also the actual inheriting or right to inherit.[116] Such language could be used simply to describe land which had been or was now being inherited, or to express intent that the land should be inherited. However, it is often difficult to place uses of inheritance language into either category.[117] When the Anglo-Norman kings used the

---

[112] J. Yver, 'Une boutade de Guillaume le Conquérant: Note sur la genèse de la tenure en aumône', in *Études d'histoire du droit canonique, dédiées à Gabriel le Bras* (2 vols.; Paris, 1965), i. 784–6. *Regesta*, i, No. 200; *elemosina* is also used in e.g. Nos. 58, 140, 232, but not in this phrase.

[113] e.g. *Domesday*, i, fos. 22a, 58a, 63b, 214b. Note, however, that some Domesday uses differ from later ones; Hudson, 'Seignorial Control of Land', 87–8.

[114] *Regesta*, i, Nos. 228—ii. 396 on dating—301, 326, 338a, 361, 421. Amongst private charters, *EYC*, i, No. 41, in 1070 × 81 did not use *in elemosina*, but in 1078 × *c*.1087 the phrase was included in *EYC*, i, No. 42 recording a gift of the same and other lands. *Select Documents of the English Lands of the Abbey of Bec*, ed. M. Chibnall (Camden Soc., 3rd Ser. 73; 1951), No. XL, supposedly uses 'in perpetual and free and pure alms' before 1086, No. XXXIX before 1090; however, the editor, p. x, calls into doubt the authenticity of the wording.

[115] e.g. *Regesta*, ii, Nos. 571, 602, 674, 679, 742, 996.

[116] Note also the *Quadripartitus* translates *bocland* in *I Cnut*, 11 as 'in hereditate sua terram habeat', Liebermann, *Gesetze*, i. 294.

[117] Holt, 'Politics and Property', 40, 'Notions of Patrimony', esp. 204; Holt's notion

phrase *iure hereditario*, by hereditary right, to emphasize the legitimacy
of their succession in the past, they were also implying that their heirs
should succeed to the throne 'by hereditary right', since their position
was just.[118] Past facts legitimated future intent. From an early date at
least some of the inheritance terms were used as classifications of
land-holding, of how land was now held, with implications for the
future and sometimes the past.

To test these ideas, I now examine the words which constituted
inheritance language, in itself a valuable exercise. Sometimes a grant
was simply described as to a man and his heirs. Sometimes an
adverb, 'heritably' or 'hereditarily', was added, often a phrase, 'by
hereditary right' or 'in fee and inheritance'. With the exception of the
last phrase, most of the vocabulary was old. It probably originally
entered charters from Roman Law, but was also familiar notably from
the Bible.[119]

One must not assume the degree of precision of these words.
Chance and fashion must have influenced which formulae caught on.
'By hereditary right' seems to have had a burst of popularity in royal
charters late in Henry I's reign before a relative decline.[120] Individual
benefactors favoured certain words.[121] Phrases were sometimes piled
up for rhetorical effect.[122] And sometimes a variety of formulae
appears within one document. A charter of Christmas 1141 records
various grants by Stephen to Geoffrey de Mandeville: some were in
fee and inheritance, some simply to him and his heirs, and some used
no inheritance language, although mentioning that his grandfather

of intent is in fact in many ways similar to my 'classifications of land-holding', with
implications for the present holding of the land, although Holt emphasizes the future
element. See also Holt, 'Revolution of 1066', 203–5, esp. at 203 where he writes of
the conversion of 'fact into title'.

[118] See *Regesta*, i, Nos. 21, 231, 272; ii, No. 919; also ii, No. 544; G. S. Garnett,
'Coronation and Propaganda: Some Implications of the Norman Claim to the Throne
of England in 1066', *TRHS*, 5th Ser. 36 (1986), 91–116.

[119] Holt, 'Notions of Patrimony', 198 and n. 28. *Iure hereditario*, e.g. *Institutes*, ii.
xviii; *hereditarie*, *Code*, 3. 20. 1. *Hereditarie*: Ezekiel, 46: 16; *hereditario iure*: Leviticus
25: 46; in addition there are references to lands given *in hereditatem*, e.g. Leviticus 20:
24, Ezekiel 25: 4, and 36 *passim*. From such biblical and Roman Law sources the
phrases passed into Canon Law.

[120] *Regesta*, ii, Nos. 1502 and 1709 (to clerics), 1607, 1719, 1722–3, 1758, 1760,
1777; iii, Nos. 43–4, 68, 273, 925; see also No. 272, the Treaty of Westminster;
Henry II, e.g. Cartae Antiquae, Roll 24, m. 2, No. 15. (Photo courtesy of Professor
Holt.)

[121] e.g. the prevalence of *iure hereditario* in *Worcester*, e.g. Nos. 179, 439, 488.

[122] e.g. *Regesta*, iii, No. 312.

had held them. A clause at the end of the charter stated that all the above were granted 'in fee and inheritance from me and my heirs for him and his heirs for his service'.[123] The exact wording of each grant does not seem to have been vital.

'Heritably' and 'hereditarily', *hereditabiliter* and *hereditarie*, seem not to have differed greatly in meaning from one another. The charters of honours which frequently used one rarely used the other.[124] 'Heritably' would seem most obviously to refer to the future, to land which could be inherited. 'Hereditarily' is peculiarly common in royal grants of office, sometimes combined with lands,[125] but there is no such association of the word with office in private charters. Usually 'hereditarily' can best be taken as a classification of land-holding. Thus the Empress Matilda's second charter to Geoffrey de Mandeville stated that William of Eu was to have Lavendon 'hereditarily as his right'.[126] This stresses William's hereditary claim, as well as promising that he should hold 'hereditarily'.

'By hereditary right', *hereditario iure*, was a broadly applicable phrase. No king would say that he held 'in fee and inheritance', which might imply dependence, but he could easily use 'by hereditary right'. It could clearly refer to claims based on the past; men described themselves as having 'succeeded by hereditary right'.[127] However, when the words first appear, soon after 1100 in royal charters referring to grants to lay persons and before 1120 in my selection of private charters, they were also used in new gifts, where 'hereditary right' cannot refer to the past.[128] In these, and elsewhere, the easiest and most obvious reading is to take the phrase as a classification of land-holding, with possible implications for past, present, and future.[129]

---

[123] *Regesta*, iii, No. 276.

[124] For example, Bury charters use *hereditarie* several times, e.g. *Feudal Documents*, Nos. 142, 148–9, but never *hereditabiliter*. *Hereditabiliter* was an uncommon word in charters, e.g. *EYC*, iii, No. 1303, *Regesta*, ii, No. 1607; see also No. 1946, a charter concerning Normandy; iii, Nos. 15, 274–5, 897. *Regesta*, iii, Nos. 15, 897 were to clerics, but private charters give no further evidence of such specialization of usage. However, *Glanvill* frequently used it, e.g. vii. 1, Hall, 71–3.

[125] Three of the four instances in Henry I's charters 1130–5 were regrants or restorations which included offices; *Regesta*, ii, Nos. 1710, 1749, 1835.

[126] *Regesta*, iii, No. 275.

[127] See above, pp. 91–2, on royal usage.

[128] *Regesta*, ii, No. 793 uses *ius hereditarium*, *Durham*, No. 11 uses *iure hereditario*. The phrase is used earlier, but not in the context of a normal grant to a layman; *Regesta*, i, Nos. 21, 135.

[129] See e.g. *Registrum Antiquissimum*, No. 611, *Worcester*, No. 439, *Durham*, No.

'In fee and inheritance', *in feudo et hereditate*, was the phrase which
came to predominate for military tenure. It emerged slowly. The
word *feudum*, according to Tabuteau, came into use in Normandy in
the mid-eleventh century, her first example being from 1031 × 40,
whilst *in feudo* only appeared in ducal charters just before 1066.[130]
The phrase was not used in William I's extant charters concerning
England. Domesday did use 'in fee', but only rarely, the *Domesday
Monachorum* of *c.*1090 rather more frequently.[131] The first trace in a
royal charter comes when Rufus made a grant to Peter de Valognes
'in fee'.[132] From 1106 comes Henry I's grant to Hardulf 'in fee and
hereditary right', and then in 1107 × 16, he gave lands in Berkshire
to Robert Achard and his heirs 'in fee and inheritance'.[133] The
phrase only became at all common in royal charters from the 1120s,
and appears in private charters as soon as written grants to laymen
survive in any numbers.[134] Amongst most of the sets of private
charters which I have examined, for example those of Bury, Richmond, and the earls of Hereford, the majority of charters using
inheritance language specify 'in fee and inheritance'.[135] Only occasionally do a smaller proportion use the phrase, as in the case of the
charters of Lincoln Cathedral.[136] Amongst Stephen and Henry II's
charters, on the other hand, fewer than half of those which include
inheritance language use 'in fee and inheritance'.[137]

26e; *Regesta*, ii, Nos. 1502, 1723, 1758, 1760; iii, Nos. 44, 925. On the changing
frequency of the use of the phrase, see above, p. 92.

[130] *Feudum*: R. Carabie, *La Propriété foncière dans le très ancien droit normand, i. La
Propriété domaniale* (Caen, 1943), 245–54, Tabuteau, *Transfers of Property*, 51–65,
297–8, M. Chibnall, 'Military Service in Normandy before 1066', *A-NS* 5 (1983),
66–7; see also e.g. Fauroux, Nos. 120, 183, 213. *In feudo*: Fauroux, Nos. 165, 229.

[131] See below, nn. 139–40; *The Domesday Monachorum of Christ Church Canterbury*,
ed. D. C. Douglas (London, 1944), 82, 84, 93.

[132] *Regesta*, i, No. 346; despite the use of *concedere* in the charter, this was almost
certainly a new gift, for the king held the lands in 1086, *Domesday*, i, fo. 133a.

[133] *Regesta*, ii, Nos. 793, 1134 respectively.

[134] *Regesta*, ii, Nos. 1256, 1314, 1326, 1395, 1446, 1719, 1723, 1778, 1872, 1913,
1984; see also No. 1369 'in feodo'. Private charters: e.g. *Feudal Documents*, No. 119,
EYC, i, No. 340, Stenton, *First Century*, No. 29, *Book of Seals*, No. 528.

[135] *Feudal Documents*, Nos. 118–19, 121, 123–5, 129–32, 134, 139, 141, 143–4,
147, 152, 155–6, 161; see also Nos. 108–9. Counts and earls of Richmond: *EYC*, iv,
Nos. 9, 14, 22, 47, 52, 65. Other Richmond charters: *EYC*, iv, Nos. 87–8, 106,
118–19; v, Nos. 181, 189, 196, 267, 281, 331. *Earldom of Hereford*, Nos. 7, 45, 53, 64.
See also Hudson, 'Chester Charters', 165–6.

[136] See *Registrum Antiquissimum*, No. 1295.

[137] Stephen: e.g. *Regesta*, iii, Nos, 177, 316, 319; Henry II: e.g. *Cartae Antiquae,
1–10*, Nos. 141, 293, *CChR*, iv. 83, 257. For a fuller description of the emergence of

Did the phrase establish a special class of land-holding?[138] Having already considered the senses of *hereditas*, let us look more closely at the first element of the phrase. Domesday uses *feudum* for large holdings, notably lands formerly held by Odo of Bayeux.[139] However, the entry for Starston, Norfolk, stated that Roger Bigot claimed the land as the holding [*feudum*] of his free men.[140] A similar use appears in the charter of the Conqueror's reign concerning the enfeoffment of a knight, Peter, with possessions of the abbey of Bury, which specifies the fees given, for example 'the land of Edric the blind with fourteen freemen and as many peasants . . .'.[141] Here fee is used of land and minor men.

Thorne argued that by the mid-twelfth century 'lords had come to regard their fiefs as divided into two clearly distinguished portions: lands subinfeudated to others for military service and lands not so subinfeudated, *feudum* and *dominium*.'[142] The evidence is far from conclusive. For example, one of the most common uses in charters was when the lord, 'of whose fee' the land was, confirmed his vassal's gift. 'Fee' here could refer just to the land the lord had subinfeudated, but could equally well mean his entire holding.[143] Presumably the word could be used in both ways.

'Fee' had connotations of lasting tenure, be it the occasional references to a church's fee,[144] or the much more common ones to lands held in fee by laymen.[145] An agreement preserved in the *Abingdon*

the phrase, see Hudson, 'Seignorial Control of Land', 99–100. I found no relation between any type of grant and the use of the accusative or ablative case in the phrase *in feud/um*, *-o et hereditat/em*, *-e*. There are changes in the relative frequency of the phrases 'to give in fee and inheritance' and 'to hold in fee and inheritance', but it is unclear whether such changes had much significance.

[138] On fee, see also S. M. G. Reynolds, 'Bookland, Folkland, and Fiefs', *A-NS* 14 (1992), 211–27.

[139] e.g. *Domesday*, i, fo. 143a; ii, fo. 55b; Odo of Bayeux's fee: i, fos. 10b, 11a, 16a, 62b, 63b, 199a, 220a; ii. 17b, 26a.

[140] *Domesday*, ii, fo. 186a.

[141] *Feudal Documents*, No. 168. On this text, see Holt, 'Notions of Patrimony', 219–20.

[142] Thorne, 'Estates', 200.

[143] e.g. *Regesta*, ii, Nos. 1681, 1738; iii, No. 40. See also the *Leges Willelmi*, 2 4, Liebermann, *Gesetze*, i. 495; Constitutions of Clarendon, c. 2, *SSC*, 164.

[144] e.g. from Henry I's reign, *EYC*, iii, No. 1622; *Feudal Documents*, No. 114. These grants show no association of fee with military or any other particular kind of service.

[145] Pollock and Maitland, i. 67–8; F. W. Maitland, *Domesday Book and Beyond* (Cambridge, 1897), 152–4; Holt, 'Politics and Property', 6–7. The *Quadripartitus* used it to translate *bocland*, *II Edgar*, 2, Liebermann, *Gesetze*, i. 197. See also Reynolds, 'Bookland, Folkland, and Fiefs', 226. Note that lands to be held by a man and his heirs

Chronicle refers to land granted to a man to hold 'in fee, that is for himself and his heirs after him'.[146] However, some grants of fee farm were only for periods of lives.[147] Generally 'fee' also implied that the holding owed temporal, often military, service.[148] As early as the 1080s in Normandy, holding in alms and holding in fee could be tersely and explicitly contrasted with one another.[149] In England in Rufus's reign, lands which a bishop had held in fee were given so that he and his successors could have them in alms.[150] The implication seems to be that the lands would no longer owe secular service. However, a few charters refer to lands held in fee and alms.[151] This apparent contradiction suggests that the temporal connotations of *feudum* were not always overwhelming. According to *Glanvill*, the assize *utrum*, in deciding whether certain lands were the free alms of a church, asked whether they were 'lay fee or church fee'.[152]

These meanings of *feudum* suggest that the phrase 'in fee and inheritance' was most appropriate for heritable grants by secular, and often military, service. Within these limits, 'in fee and inheritance' acted as a classification of land-holding probably with the same

for a fixed money rent were sometimes referred to as held 'in fee farm', sometimes as 'in fee and inheritance'. Here fee seems to be used to emphasize the durability of the grant rather than the nature of the service: e.g. *Regesta*, iii, No. 319.

[146] *CMA*, ii. 167.

[147] R. V. Lennard, *Rural England, 1086–1135* (Oxford, 1959), 111–12, giving examples including a charter of 1153 × 68.

[148] Amongst the few royal charters detailing services from grants 'in fee and inheritance' a greater proportion of Henry II's than of his predecessors' specify military service: e.g. *Cartae Antiquae, 1–10*, No. 293, *Recueil*, No. CCCXI. This may suggest a narrowing of the phrase's use, although the spread of military tenure ensured that it was used of small holdings and minor men. However, it may simply reflect an increasing tendency to specify services. Pollock and Maitland, i. 234–5, suggested that fee may for a short time after 1066 have had connotations of military tenure, but soon came to imply no more than heritability.

[149] Yver, 'La Tenure en aumône', i. 788.

[150] *Regesta*, i, No. 338a; see also No. 372c. Note also on bishops' fees, J. C. Holt, 'The Introduction of Knight Service in England', *A-NS* 6 (1984), 102–3; B. Dodwell, 'The Honour of the Bishop of Thetford/Norwich in the Late Eleventh and Early Twelfth Centuries', *Norfolk Archaeology*, 33/2 (1963), 186–8.

[151] e.g. *Regesta*, iii, No. 34, *Earldom of Gloucester*, No. 5, *EYC*, v, No. 156 *Book of Seals*, No. 197.

[152] *Glanvill*, xiii. 2, 24, Hall, 149, 163. However, the Constitutions of Clarendon, c. 9, *SSC*, 166, simply contrast 'elemosinam' and 'laicum feudum', and the distinction is between free alms and lay fee in the writs contained in *Early Registers of Writs*, ed. E. de Haas and G. D. G. Hall (Selden Soc. 87; 1970), Hib. 21, CA 49, CC 52 and 54, R 96–8.

implications for heritability as the more widely applicable 'by hereditary right'. As noted above, wording often varied within individual charters. A charter recording the grant of Brompton in Pickering Lyth to Eustace fitzJohn 'in fee and inheritance' also granted him a mill 'in fee and by hereditary right' as Rabel de Tancarville had given it to him.[153] The two were surely synonymous in their ultimate effect, yet the existence of the narrower term suggests that men did take care to classify land-holding with some precision.

GRANTS FOR LIFE AND THE HERITABILITY OF LAND

Such classification helps to reveal the distancing of family succession from the field of purely personal relationships. Milsom emphasizes the importance of the relationship between man and lord, plays down that between man and land. The increase in abstract thought concerning land-holding weakens this argument. When a succession dispute arose, the lord was restricted not only by custom and the desire to appear a good lord, but also by the classification of the decedent's hold on the land. This becomes clear when one considers the effect of charter wording on disputes. A tenant has died and the lord is now faced by one or more claimants. Their claim might turn on the grant to the decedent, and the first question raised, therefore, could be 'Did the grant to the decedent permit succession?' A grant, be it recorded in a charter or not, might be expressly to a man and his heirs, for a specific limited period, or neither.[154] If the grant mentioned the grantee's heirs, or stated, for example, that the land

---

[153] *Regesta*, ii, No. 1722. The different wording may reflect the donors' charters, which do not survive.

[154] I concentrate on life-grants, but other types of grant such as those for terms of years could of course prevent succession. More problematic are grants to a man and his heir. J. H. Round, 'The Burton Abbey Surveys', *EHR* 20 (1905), 279, and S. D. White, 'Succession to Fiefs in Early Medieval England', *P&P* 65 (1974), 119–20, argued that such grants were only for two lives. However, the absence of reversion clauses and their varying use with regard to the number of the noun *heres* suggest strongly that they were intended to reinforce continuing succession rather than being carefully drafted attempts to limit succession to one heir only; see Lennard, *Rural England*, 173–4, J. C. Holt, 'Politics and Property in Early Medieval England: a Rejoinder', *P&P* 65 (1974), 130–2, Hudson, 'Seignorial Control of Land', 118–19 and references at pp. 121–2. In addition, other grants such as prebends should not pass to lay relatives, e.g. *Regesta*, iii, No. 434.

was to be held hereditarily, the lord could not deny an heir's claim on
the grounds that the grant to the decedent *excluded* succession, except
by claiming that the original grantor had acted wrongly. However, he
might still refuse to regrant the land to the heir on other grounds,
for example because he considered someone else a more suitable
claimant. Such discretion is one element underlying Thorne's statement that, in a lawyer's strict sense, the tenant of a military fief in the
twelfth century had only a life estate.[155]

For contemporaries, a grant for life meant something different, and
this aspect of charter drafting and of the classification of land-holding
is my prime concern for the remainder of the chapter. Charters
record grants specifically for life or lives, and include reversion
clauses and disclaimers of future attempts to succeed. The distinction
is illustrated with particular clarity by settlements which reject a claim
to hold heritably, but permit the unsuccessful claimant to hold for
life, whereafter the land should return to the successful party.

The desire and need to make and record life-grants says much
about the strength of customary pressure for succession. At William
I's request, Bishop Walkelin of Winchester made a life-grant to the
king's cook William Escudet of certain lands in Alton Priors from the
sustenance of the monks of the episcopal church. Domesday simply
records that William held three hides of land in Alton Priors from the
bishop. The land is next mentioned in a royal charter of 1108: Henry
I granted to the prior and monks the land which the Conqueror had
'borrowed [*mutuauit*] from them out of their sustenance for the use of
William Escudet for as long as William lived'. They were to hold
it quit, without any claim of inheritance, as the king's father had
ordered by his writ. Conceivably, a dispute at William Escudet's
death necessitated the second document. Equally possibly, the monks
were simply obtaining a writ to prevent future trouble.[156] Here the
life-grant worked well, yet it is very striking that a powerful ecclesiastical lord looked not exclusively to his seignorial power but also to the
support of specific provision, backed up by royal charter, in order to
prevent succession.

---

[155] Thorne, 'Estates', 195.

[156] *Regesta*, i, No. 270—one of the two royal charters pre-1100 using inheritance
language for specific laymen—*Domesday*, i, fo. 65b, *Regesta*, ii, No. 884; VCH, *Wiltshire*, xi. 192. See also J. H. Round, *The King's Serjeants and Officers of State* (London,
1911), 10–11. Note how Domesday may hide holdings for life—see also Lennard,
Rural England, 175.

In other instances, these late eleventh-century life-grants resulted in great difficulties for the ecclesiastical grantors and sometimes in lasting alienation from the church's demesne. Cases arising from such grants appear in charters and feature prominently in monastic chronicles.[157] A dispute which kept re-emerging for a century and a half illustrates the extent of troubles a grant for lives might cause. In 1088 the abbot of Ramsey granted that William Pecche, for his own and the abbey's profit, might have under his custody the land of Over in Cambridgeshire. He, and his wife if she outlived him, were to hold for life, whereafter the land was to return to the abbot's hand. An initial dispute after William's death was settled in Henry I's court in favour of the abbey. However, at some point, the abbey regranted the land to William's son Hamo for life, at the king's request, since Hamo was a royal favourite. The abbey was unhappy with the arrangement, and throughout Stephen's reign and beyond sought papal help in regaining the land. Hamo was able to enfeoff his own younger son with the land, and the dispute was only finally concluded under Henry III.[158] The case is notable with regard to heritability in four main respects. It shows the pressure on churches, and perhaps other lords, to allow succession. The later Pecches possibly saw themselves as pressing a valid claim, for the land certainly had been in their family for a considerable time. The power of charter language was not absolute. Secondly, it is at least very likely that the value of the land increased during the period of the dispute, making it particularly undesirable for Ramsey that the Pecches hold it heritably for an unchanging rent.[159] For once the economic circumstances of a land dispute are apparent, and such a desire to exploit any increases in value surely inspired other short-term grants. Thirdly,

[157] e.g. Eadmer, *Historia Nouorum in Anglia*, ed. M. Rule (London, 1884), 219; F. R. H. Du Boulay, *The Lordship of Canterbury* (London, 1966), Ch. 3. On the case of Walter de Lacy and Holme Lacy, see Galbraith, 'Episcopal Land-Grant', H. M. Colvin, 'Holme Lacy: An Episcopal Manor and its Tenants in the Twelfth and Thirteenth Centuries', in V. Ruffer and A. J. Taylar (edd.), *Medieval Studies Presented to Rose Graham* (Oxford, 1950), 15–40. See also the cases discussed below, pp. 132, 134, and e.g. *Shrewsbury*, No. 1. The Treaty of Westminster, aided by the rapid demise of the life-tenant Stephen, was an unusually successful example of a settlement involving a life-grant to the losing party; *Regesta*, iii, No. 272.

[158] *Ramsey Chronicle*, 233, *Regesta*, ii, No. 1629, *Cartularium Monasterii de Rameseia*, ed. W. H. Hart and P. A. Lyons (3 vols.; London, 1884–93), Nos. xxx–xxxiva. For a full discussion of the case, and references down to the time of Henry III, see J. G. H. Hudson, 'Life-Grants of Land and the Development of Inheritance in Anglo-Norman England', *A-NS* 12 (1990), 67–80.

[159] See Hudson, 'Life-Grants', 70.

we see the church, and perhaps the Pecches, looking for outside help, taking matters of succession outside the honour. One might have expected the initial case to be one for the honour court, yet it was in fact heard by Henry I. Fourthly, such disputes must have stimulated the classifying of land-holding; Ramsey had to emphasize the restriction to a life-grant, and this must at least implicitly have been contrasted with grants 'to a man and his heirs'.

The number of charters recording life-grants by churches during the late eleventh century is striking, especially when compared with the total number of surviving charters. Initially, the prevalence of life-grants may in part reflect a conservative retention of pre-Conquest practice,[160] but such grants continued during the twelfth century. Charters of lay grantors provide little evidence of grants for life or lives. Most notable is a surrender of land by Ralph fitzPichard to Margaret de Bohun, daughter and heiress of Miles of Gloucester.[161] The charter states that, following Ralph's exile from Winchester in which he lost his houses and chattels, Miles granted him for life all the lands which Ralph held there as sustenance for himself and his family. Ralph swore that he would never attempt any trick by which the land he had received would be alienated from Miles's heirs. Mindful of this kindness and his oath, he now recognized Margaret's right and gave back the lands of his own free will, setting aside all claim from himself or his relatives. He requested that she grant the lands to the canons of Llanthony.

The preponderance of ecclesiastical life-grants may just result from the production and survival of charters.[162] Lay lords may often have made grants for life, as Miles did to Ralph. Their relatively short-term nature perhaps decreased the chance of their being recorded in writing. Or lay lords may have relied on grants for terms of years. Alternatively, lay lords really did have more discretion following the death of a tenant, and hence had less need to make specific life-grants. However, I argue in my next chapter that if a close relative

---

[160] Galbraith, 'Episcopal Land-Grant', 354, 367–8; Lennard, *Rural England*, 159–70.

[161] D. Walker, 'Ralph son of Pichard', *BIHR* 33 (1960), 201. See R. Fleming, *Kings and Lords in Conquest England* (Cambridge, 1991), 130–1 on pre-Conquest leases by laymen continuing to have an effect after 1066. Also Jordan Fantosme, *Chronicle*, ed. and tr. R. C. Johnston (Oxford, 1981), l. 1103 for William king of Scots offering Earl David of Huntingdon a life tenancy of all Lennox.

[162] See also Lennard, *Rural England*, 166 n. 1 for comment on the Anglo-Saxon situation.

survived, lords rarely exercised such discretion. It seems more likely that what we have is two different perspectives on land-holding. Ecclesiastical lords, in addition perhaps to feeling that their grants were particularly threatened, may have been especially concerned with preventing permanent alienation of lands detailed for their churches' support.[163] Lay lords, on the other hand, may generally have been content to accept succession in a family of loyal vassals.[164] When the two views were brought into contact, notably when a lay family received a series of life-grants from a church, they were likely to come into conflict.[165] One of the by-products of such conflict was the clarification of thought concerning land-holding.

CONCLUSIONS

Thus the wording of grants mattered when heirs sought to succeed, even if persuasion and power might also determine the fate of a claim. I have argued that by *c.*1120 a transformation had taken place in the terms used to refer to land-holding. The language used in later Common Law to describe how land was held by churches and laymen had largely emerged, and by 1135 had come into common use. Certainly many of the elements of the language were very old. However, in its frequent use of 'in alms' and the new phrase 'in fee and inheritance', it differed markedly from that employed in Normandy and England in the first half of the eleventh century. Such a shift surely suggests an interest in the classification of land-holding which must have been bound up with changes in land law. Thereafter, it

[163] It is notable that where Domesday specifies that land was held for life or lives, the lord was ecclesiastical; Lennard, *Rural England*, 159–75 gives a wide range of examples. See below, Ch. 8, for the Canon Law restrictions on the Church, and also general ecclesiastical concern about alienation of land.

[164] Note that *Facsimiles of Early Charters from Northamptonshire Collections*, ed. F. M. Stenton (Northants Rec. Soc. 4; 1930), Frontispiece, providing for exchanges for land given away by the lord, divides tenants into *rustici* and those holding in fee and inheritance; see also above, Ch. 2, n. 198. This may mean that these were the sole categories the lord had. Alternatively it may mean that others held for shorter terms or at the lord's will and received no exchange, but the inclusion of *rustici* amongst those receiving exchange may render this explanation the less likely.

[165] See also J. Biancalana, 'For Want of Justice: Legal Reforms of Henry II', *Columbia Law Review*, 88 (1988), 500. Note also the jury decision in the Cockfield case; *The Chronicle of Jocelin of Brakelond*, ed. and tr. H. E. Butler (London, 1949), 58–9, 123–4, 138–9; *CRR*, i. 430; *The Kalendar of Abbot Samson of Bury St Edmunds and Related Documents*, ed. R. H. C. Davis (Camden Soc., 3rd Ser. 84; 1954), No. 90.

was in part the continuing increase in precision and abstraction
that changed the connotations of words and phrases. There was
no parallel generation of new vocabulary arising from the Angevin
reforms.[166]

I have concentrated on charters, but other sources do not use
a markedly different vocabulary. Take chronicles. They too generally avoid inheritance language for clerics and churches.[167] Often,
although not exclusively, they use 'by hereditary right' to refer to the
past,[168] but this may reflect less the essential meaning of the phrase
than the chroniclers' own interests. They were rarely concerned with
new grants, much more often with, for example, succession disputes
or the descent of lands of great men. This concern probably also
explains their frequent use of 'to disinherit' and 'patrimony'.[169] It
further helps to explain the absence from chronicles of the phrase 'in
fee and inheritance', although 'in fee' does occasionally appear.[170]
Glanvill too preferred the form 'in fee'. Perhaps these differing
usages indicate an awareness on the part of charter draftsmen that
they had to close potential loopholes, and therefore include both
terms. *Glanvill* and probably the chroniclers would have been aware
of charter usage, but could adopt shorter forms for their different
purposes. The French vocabulary of mid-twelfth-century literature is
similar to that of chronicles. 'Eir', 'eritage', 'deseritez', 'fieu', and

[166] Some other terms did emerge gradually, such as assigns and fee simple, see e.g.
Pollock and Maitland, ii. 14, A. W. B. Simpson, *A History of Land Law* (Oxford, 1986),
56 respectively; but these do not mark the same sort of fundamental shift as occurred
in the latter half of the 11th and the early 12th cents.

[167] For exceptions, note Hugh the Chantor, *The History of the Church of York,
1066–1127*, ed. and tr. C. Johnson (Edinburgh, 1961), 15, on the passing of the
archbishopric of York from uncle to nephew; 'quasi iure hereditario proxime successit';
also *The Life of Christina of Markyate, a Twelfth-Century Recluse*, ed. and tr. C. H.
Talbot (Oxford, 1959), 110. For chronicle references to a man making the Church his
heir, see *CMA*, ii. 205, *Battle Chronicle*, 256.

[168] e.g. Eadmer, *Historia Nouorum*, 25.

[169] *Exheredare*: Henry of Huntingdon, *Historia Anglorum*, ed. T. Arnold (London,
1879), 235, 237; William of Malmesbury, *De Gestis Regum Anglorum Libri Quinque*, ed.
W. Stubbs (2 vols.; London, 1887–9), ii. 331; also Geoffrey of Monmouth, *The
Historia Regum*, ed. N. Wright (Cambridge, 1985), 51. *Patrimonium*: e.g. Eadmer, *Vita
Anselmi*, 11; William of Malmesbury, *Gesta Regum*, ii. 337. More generally, see also
Holt, 'Notions of Patrimony', 215–16 on Orderic's language.

[170] e.g. *Liber Eliensis*, ed. E. O. Blake (Camden Soc., 3rd Ser. 92; 1962), 217; see
also the interesting use in Walter Espec's address to the troops at the Battle of the
Standard, *Chronicles of the Reigns of Stephen, Henry II, and Richard I*, ed. R. Howlett (4
vols.; London, 1884–9), iii. 185. Note also the use of *in hereditate*, Orderic Vitalis, *The
Ecclesiastical History*, ed. and tr. M. Chibnall (6 vols.; Oxford, 1969–80), v. 286.

their variants are all quite frequent.[171] Very occasionally a phrase such as 'claiment en eritage' appears,[172] as does 'en fieu'.[173]

What explanations can then be given for the increasing appearance of inheritance language in charters? Various causes can be mentioned. Political disturbance would make a written promise to the heirs desirable. That inheritance language has come into general use by 1135 rebuts suggestions that the troubles of 1135–54 caused its regular use.[174] However, earlier doubts about the royal succession, perhaps from *c*.1086 and certainly from 1120 may have encouraged men to demand written promises of inheritance from the king. And problems about the royal succession may well have provoked more general discussion of succession.[175]

However, the simplest cause is probably the most fundamental. Men recognized the usefulness of a mention of their heirs in the gift ceremony. As they began to obtain documents to record the grants, they had their heirs written into the charters. Lords too might be willing to speak in these terms—grants were after all intended to promote loyalty from the vassal, and the lord therefore had an interest in making the grant desirable. Once negotiations and court hearings revealed that these mentions increased the security of a disposition, all grantees would desire such passages in their charters. By *Bracton*'s time, a grant needed to be explicitly to 'N. and his heirs' to ensure its heritability.[176] Earlier, the situation was less clear. A grant just to 'N.' did not necessarily prevent the heir from succeeding to the land. From the mid-twelfth century, charters stating not only that grants are for life but that they are not by hereditary right or not in fee and inheritance hint at requirements for stricter wording.[177]

---

[171] e.g. 'Eir' etc.: Gaimar, *L'Estoire des Engleis*, ll. 68, 2513, 4759; Wace, *Brut*, ll. 7565, 8343, 8955. 'Eritage' etc.: Wace, *Brut*, ll. 6512, 13191; Jordan Fantosme, *Chronicle*, ll. 50, 134. 'Deseritez' etc.: Wace, *Brut*, l. 9613, Jordan Fantosme, *Chronicle*, l. 1388. 'Fieu' etc.: Wace, *Roman de Rou*, ed. A. J. Holden (3 vols.; Société des Anciens Textes Français, Paris, 1970–3), iii, ll. 1040, 2253, 2774, 3240; Gaimar, *L'Estoire des Engleis*, l. 1350.

[172] Gaimar, *L'Estoire des Engleis*, l. 13; see also l. 3475, Wace, *Rou*, ii, l. 2495.

[173] Wace, *Rou*, ii, l. 2493; iii, ll. 657 (with reference to the kingdom of France), 3413, 8553. On English words, see A. Williams, 'The Knights of Shaftesbury Abbey', *A-NS* 8 (1986), 215, 233–7.

[174] Davis, 'What Happened in Stephen's Reign', esp. 12.

[175] See below, p. 111, for a discussion between Brian fitzCount and Gilbert Foliot concerning the Empress Matilda's hereditary claims.

[176] Pollock and Maitland, i, 308, citing *BNB*, pl. 964, 1235, 1811.

[177] *EYC*, i, No. 414; from Canterbury, *Regesta*, iii, No. 148, Saltman, *Theobald*, No. 44, discussed below, p. 144. See also e.g. Madox, *Formulare Anglicanum*, No. CXCV, a

A similar concern with precise wording is revealed by a case recorded in a charter of Archbishop Theobald, from 1154 × 61.[178] A dispute had arisen between a certain Peter and the canons of St Paul's concerning possession of lands pertaining to the archbishop's manor of Wimbledon and Barnes. A royal order laid down that the case be settled in the archbishop's court. Peter demanded the land since his father, so he said, had possessed it at the death of Henry I and his mother had had the same possession until she had been violently ejected. However, there was no mention of inheritance or fee, and the canons denied that his father and mother's possession was such that succession was owed to him or anyone. Since Peter could produce no documents or witnesses as proof, the judgment went against him, saving the question of right. Here the key phrase seems to have been missing from Peter's claim, or perhaps from the original gift, rather than from a charter. However, such strict construction of wording is also notable for charters and the development of inheritance, for it increased in particular the power of charters as external authorities determining the relationship of claimant and lord. Once lords took the absence of inheritance language to give them an explicit right to deny succession, the presence of inheritance language surely strengthened still more the heir's claim to succeed. Meanwhile, some sub-tenants were obtaining royal confirmations using inheritance language. These are especially significant, as they might be deemed promises of outside enforcement for future succession.[179] In both these ways, by introducing a check on lords' discretion and extending external control, the very proliferation of charters using inheritance language can be seen as strengthening the potential heir's position.

As for the refinement of classifications of land-holding, let us look first to pre-1066 Normandy, from where the Anglo-Norman aristocracy brought their ideas. Changes in family structure and a greater emphasis growing upon lordship over land, might make new, perhaps clearer, classifications of land-holding desirable. It is notable

grant by the prior and convent of Christ Church Canterbury to a widow, dating from *c*.1175.

[178] *St Paul's*, No. 163.
[179] See below, p. 152. *Leges Henrici*, 10 1, Downer, 108, suggests various grounds on which the king might claim to hear a case concerning disregard of a royal confirmation, for example 'plea of contempt of his writs and orders', and perhaps 'breach of the king's peace given by his hand or seal'.

therefore that soon after these changes concerning lordship of land, the phrases 'in alms' and 'in fee' started to come into common use, helping to clarify the division of interests between parties.[180]

The refinement of such classifications must have been a gradual process, linked to wider intellectual change and increasing education.[181] The role of the Church may have been an important factor, somewhat neglected by historians. Following the Conquest, churches may have been particularly aware of the contrast between old and new forms of land-holding, and this may have encouraged definition and abstraction. At the same time, Church reformers emphasized the special characteristics of ecclesiastical land-holding. This would also have had a wider effect; church land-holding provided a contrast with lay, which must in turn have stimulated more abstract thought about the latter. There was no lack of channels whereby reform ideas might penetrate the circles which helped to determine the terms of lay land-holding. Churchmen figured prominently amongst lords and royal advisers and officials. Laymen attended great trials, such as that of William of St Calais at which land-holding was discussed.

Nor were laymen necessarily incapable of abstract thought, particularly thought affecting a subject like land-holding.[182] Among laymen as well as ecclesiastics, thought about and classification of landholding may well have been encouraged by the settlement of England, and the need to work out the terms on which their new lands were held. They too were confronted with different systems of landholding, most clearly, for example, in the Domesday survey. The

[180] On family structure, see below, p. 151. On lordship, see Tabuteau, *Transfers of Property*, ch. 5; also D. Bates, *Normandy before 1066* (London, 1982), 102, 122–4, noting the discussion of allods. NB *Regesta*, i, No. 171, a grant by William I to St Stephen's, Caen, including all the land which Gerald the Marshal held of him 'in territorio Cadomi, tam in alodio quam in foedio'; see also the examples cited by Holt, 'Notions of Patrimony', 199–200, and C. H. Haskins, *Norman Institutions* (New York, 1918), 21–2, for an agreement of 1070 × 81 which mentions holding 'in parage'.

[181] On the growth of schools early in this period, see R. W. Southern, *Medieval Humanism and Other Studies* (Oxford, 1970), 163–4, and 175 on the learning of secular government and in particular legal learning with reference to the *Leges Henrici*. On Anglo-Norman involvement in the study of the learned laws, see e.g. R. C. van Caenegem, *The Birth of the English Common Law* (2nd edn., Cambridge, 1988), 91, 100. From Henry II's reign comes Peter of Blois's famous statement that 'with the king of England it is school every day, constant conversation of the best scholars and discussion of problems', *Epistolae*, No. LXVI (*PL*, 207), i. 198. On the gradual classification of land-holding, see also Lennard, *Rural England*, 106.

[182] On the learning of laymen, see Richardson and Sayles, *Governance*, ch. XV; they particularly emphasized developments under Henry II, but their arguments do span the whole 12th cent.

terms of the Inquest did not specifically ask 'How are the lands held?'
but such a question must have arisen. Other developments such
as the introduction of knight service may also have had a similar
effect. Meanwhile, throughout the period, disputes and no doubt
negotiations before grants forced people to establish how lands were
held, and as these terms were increasingly written down, again precision may have increased.[183] We must now, therefore, supplement the
study of charter diplomatic with the crucial analysis of genealogy and
succession disputes.

[183] See Holt, 'Notions of Patrimony', esp. 193, 199; Hudson, 'Life-Grants', 75–6.

4

The Heritability of Land: II

As my analysis of life-grants demonstrated, it is records of disputes which most clearly reveal the interaction of the principles and norms affecting heritability with the workings of power.[1] Moreover, it was at least partly within disputes that such principles and norms were developed and clarified. Sometimes they acted as important constraints on the arguments which participants put forward, sometimes they were made explicit, examined, contrasted. Within a single case, the different parties might view the situation in opposing ways, and implicitly or explicitly appeal to different norms in support of their position. In this chapter I look at a wider range of such cases. Whilst my main concern is with the situation involving land immediately following the death of a lay tenant, in the latter stages of the chapter I also consider longer-running disputes and claims arising from earlier succession decisions.

Following the death of a tenant, various situations might arise. Unless he wished to defy the lord, an heir had to obtain seignorial acceptance, whether or not he was in physical possession of the land. The heir might offer homage and relief. Generally the lord would accept the heir if he was closely related to the dead man. However, he might reserve judgment, possibly doubtful of the claim's validity, or seek to deny the heir's claim and retain the land in demesne, possibly later to grant it to another party. He might be faced with rival claimants, and have to decide between them or arrange a compromise. Or he might use such a dispute as an excuse for at least temporarily retaining the possession himself. In the century following the Conquest, three questions may often have arisen when the claim was made. The first—was the grant to the predecessor such as to

---

[1] For a rather similar approach, based on French material but drawing conclusions for England, see S. D. White, 'Inheritances and Legal Arguments in Western France, 1050–1150', *Traditio*, 43 (1987), 55–103. Again my concern is with the higher levels of society; for the possible insecurity of succession at the lowest levels, see e.g. *CMA*, ii. 25.

permit succession—I have already discussed. The second—was the claimant the closest heir—and the third—was there some other reason why the claimant should succeed—form the major concern of the early parts of this chapter, in which I also ask in what circumstances succession tended to be disputed. Finally I examine the actions taken, the strategies adopted, by the disputing parties, concentrating on cases within honours rather than those between king and tenant in chief.

CLAIMS TO BE THE CLOSEST HEIR

If the grant to the claimant's predecessor permitted succession, the claimant would usually have sought to prove that he was the closest heir.[2] Often this would have been a matter of common knowledge, particularly if there were a son. But who else might be termed heir? Presumably men carried in their heads certain views of the priority and acceptability of heirs. Contemporary written guidelines varied. The *Leges Henrici* stated that the closest relative up to the fifth joint might succeed 'by hereditary right'.[3] The passage is based on the seventh-century *Lex Ribuaria*, and I have found no other contemporaries using such terminology. *Glanvill* distinguished between the 'closest' and 'more distant' heirs:

Closest heirs: sons and daughters.

More distant heirs, in order of decreasing proximity:
  (i) grandchildren and their descendants;
  (ii) brothers and sisters, and their descendants;
  (iii) paternal and maternal uncles, similarly aunts, and their descendants.[4]

---

[2] Useful discussions of the subject with regard to the Continent occur in M. Bloch, *Feudal Society*, tr. L. A. Manyon (2 vols.; London, 1961), i. 199–205, and J. Martindale, 'Succession and Politics in the Romance-Speaking World, *c*.1000–1140', in M. Jones and M. G. A. Vale, *England and her Neighbours, 1066–1453. Essays in Honour of Pierre Chaplais* (London, 1989), 19–41.

[3] *Leges Henrici*, 70 20a, Downer, 224; the source is *Lex Ribuaria*, 56 3. On counting by digits, see Pollock and Maitland, ii. 307.

[4] *Glanvill*, vii. 3, Hall, 75; on the weaker position of more distant heirs, see also vii. 1, p. 71, and below, Ch. 6, p. 194.

A passage closely following suggests that yet more distant heirs would not be considered; listing possible heirs, it concludes 'lastly aunts and their children'.[5]

I now examine the position of the various relations who might be heirs. In order to assemble sufficient genealogical evidence, especially for the early part of the period, I have had to rely considerably on the descents of tenancies in chief, but these do seem consistent with the mesne tenancies which I have also been able to trace. A further problem is our lack of biographical knowledge of even some fairly important men. Thus what may look like the disinheritance of an heir after his predecessor's death may actually involve events in the-predecessor's lifetime. I argue that lords rarely denied legitimate sons or daughters their inheritances. Nor was their claim to be the closest heir often contested by a rival. Grandchildren, brothers, and sisters also generally succeeded, but the claims of more distant relatives were less certain of undisputed acceptance.

The strength of customary succession by the eldest son to the bulk of the patrimony in the century after 1066 is generally recognized.[6] Although some of the patrimony might have been granted to younger sons during the father's lifetime, radical departures from the above pattern are rare. Occasional divisions of land held by military tenure

---

[5] *Glanvill*, vii. 4, Hall, 79. Note also the phrase *sanguinis heres* used in Richard Fitz Nigel, *Dialogus de Scaccario*, ed. and tr. C. Johnson, rev. F. E. L. Carter and D. E. Greenway (Oxford, 1983), 94. On the limits of inheritance, see also Pollock and Maitland, ii. 307–8.

[6] On occasion, a son might succeed his father but only as sub-tenant of a new lord who had been given his father's lands; e.g. the case of Siward of Arden who succeeded his father but only as sub-tenant of the earl of Warwick. Charters sometimes refer to the eldest son as 'heir' in distinction from other 'sons', e.g. *Documents Illustrative of the Social and Economic History of the Danelaw*, ed. F. M. Stenton (London, 1920), No. 103 witness list, sometimes as heir whilst also mentioning other heirs, e.g. No. 203. Chroniclers sometimes wrote as if the word *heres* was only proper for a son: e.g. *Chronicles of the Reigns of Stephen, Henry II, and Richard I*, ed. R. Howlett (4 vols.; London, 1884–9), iii. 183; iv. 308; see also Martindale, 'Succession and Politics', 26–7. *Raoul of Cambrai*, ed. and tr. S. Kay (Oxford, 1992), ll. 525–6, states that 'Everybody knows that a father's fief ought in all justice to pass on to his son' ['l'onnor del pere, ce sevent li auqant, | doit tot par droit revenir a l'esfant']. Henry II's circle knew of the legend, and quite probably of the poem, of Raoul; see Walter Map, *De Nugis Curialium*, ed. and tr. M. R. James, rev. C. N. L. Brooke and R. A. B. Mynors (Oxford, 1983), 441, Gerald of Wales, *Opera*, ed. J. S. Brewer, J. F. Dimock, and G. F. Warner (8 vols.; London, 1861–91), viii. 258. I concentrate in this first section upon heirs who were of age; I comment on the position of minors below, pp. 113, 116.

did occur,[7] but Holt rightly argues that such subdivision 'was unusual even in the generation immediately following the Conquest and later examples are exceptional'. He also mentions the percentage of parents who would have twins, and notes that 'it may simply be coincidental that this matches the known cases of partition'.[8] Moreover, most such divisions seem to have involved lands acquired rather than inherited by the father. The eldest son's claim to these following his father's death, as during his father's lifetime, may have been less strong than to the father's inheritance. Alternatively, what seem like divisions after the father's death may in fact stem from otherwise unknown dispositions during his lifetime.[9] In Kent, land held for military service and that held in gavelkind may sometimes have grown confused, but it was never considered that lands held for military service should, *per se*, be divided.[10] Even groups such as the Bretons, who came from areas where division of the patrimony may have been common, generally practised primogeniture in England.[11]

[7] The descent of the lands of Siward of Arden, son of Turkill, may be one such case, Siward's lands being divided between his three sons, Hugh, Henry, and Osbert; certainly in the early 13th cent., *CRR*, v. 241, it was stated that part of Siward's inheritance 'descended' to Henry. Other evidence shows that he was not the eldest brother; PRO, E 13/76, m. 71, transcript courtesy of Dr Crouch. Other examples all concerning acquisitions include I. J. Sanders, *English Baronies: A Study of their Origin and Descent* (Oxford, 1960), Caxton, Skirpenbeck; C. T. Clay and D. E. Greenway (edd.), *Early Yorkshire Families* (Yorks. Arch. Soc. Rec. Ser. 135; 1973), 92, cf. p. 55 not concerning acquisitions. Sanders, *Baronies*, Rayne concerns inherited land. The division of the inheritance of William Paynel, *EYC*, vi. 6–7, 18–19, 31–3, seems to stem partly from political event, partly perhaps from William's dispositions in his lifetime, and perhaps by grants at the marriages of his daughter by his second marriage. For a bestiary text, originating in the 5th cent. but circulating in early 12th-cent. England, which criticizes man for concentrating his fortunes on one son, whereas the crow takes care of all its offspring, see *The Book of Beasts*, tr. T. H. White (London, 1954), 142–3. *Leges Willelmi*, 34, Liebermann, *Gesetze*, i. 514, specifies that if the *pater familias* died intestate, his sons were to divide the paternal inheritance equally between them. Use of *paterfamilias*, mention of testamentary disposition, and the fact that the clause appears in a section largely derived from the Digest, suggests strong Roman influence.

[8] J. C. Holt, 'Politics and Property in Early Medieval England', *P&P* 57 (1972), 11 and n. 49.

[9] The provision for the division of lands between the Beaumont twins, *Regesta*, ii, No. 843, is a rare case where we do know of such provisions because they survive in writing. See also the discussion of forisfamiliation in *Glanvill*, vii. 3, Hall, 78.

[10] F. R. H. Du Boulay, *The Lordship of Canterbury* (London, 1966), 67–75. On gavelkind, see e.g. Pollock and Maitland, ii. 271–3.

[11] M. Jones, *The Creation of Brittany* (London, 1988), 84–6. The discussion by S. Painter, 'The Family and the Feudal System in Twelfth-Century England', *Speculum*, 35 (1960), 2–3, ignores the fact that the cases he cites concern acquisitions. For

Did lords ever seek to prevent sons from succeeding, except on the grounds that their fathers had held specifically for life? Unfortunately the evidence before 1100 is very sparse. However, although Henry I of course did disinherit disloyal vassals, he did not retain baronies when a son survived a baron who died seised.[12] When other lords denied eldest sons their inheritances, the sources usually give specific reasons for their unusual action.[13]

In the 1160s, both parties to the Anstey case accepted that 'a daughter is to be preferred to a nephew in inheritance from the father'.[14] Heiresses seem to have been considerably more important during this period than previously, both in England and on the Continent,[15] and in the absence of sons, daughters in England appear to have enjoyed a fair security of succession.[16] Theoretical justification of female inheritance appears outside law books. In 1143 × 4 Gilbert Foliot wrote to Brian fitzCount, setting down the Empress Matilda's claims.[17] He stated that Robert earl of Gloucester—who had himself

Count Geoffrey's decree of 1186 ending division in Brittany, see M. Planiol, *La Très Ancien Coutume de Bretagne* (Rennes, 1886), 319–25.

[12] Cf. C. A. Newman, *The Anglo-Norman Nobility in the Reign of Henry I* (Philadelphia, 1988), 119 on the failure of William fitzBaderon's barony of Much Marcle to pass to his son; William held not a barony but half a hide there; *Domesday*, i, fos. 179b, 185b. We cannot be sure that even this failure to succeed did not result from some form of tenurial rearrangement rather than disinheritance.

[13] See below, pp. 125–8.

[14] *The Letters of John of Salisbury*, ed. W. J. Millor, H. E. Butler, C. N. L. Brooke (2 vols.; Edinburgh and Oxford, 1955–79), i, No. 131, p. 227.

[15] See Martindale, 'Succession and Politics', 32–9; J. Gillingham, 'Love, Marriage and Politics in the Twelfth Century', *Forum for Modern Language Studies*, 25 (1989), 295–6; J. C. Holt, 'Feudal Society and the Family in Early Medieval England: IV. The Heiress and the Alien', TRHS, 5th Ser. 35 (1985), 5.

[16] Holt, 'Heiress and Alien', 5, and the examples cited there. On female succession generally, see esp. *Glanvill*, vii. 12, Hall, 85–6; Holt, 'Heiress and Alien'; S. F. C. Milsom, 'Inheritance by Women in the Twelfth and Early Thirteenth Centuries', in M. S. Arnold, *et al.* (edd.), *Essays in Honor of S. E. Thorne* (Chapel Hill, NC, 1981), 60–89; also E. Searle, 'Women and the Legitimization of Succession at the Norman Conquest', *A-NS* 3 (1981); S. L. Waugh, 'Women's Inheritance and the Growth of Bureaucratic Monarchy in Twelfth- and Thirteenth-Century England', *Nottingham Mediaeval Studies*, 34 (1990), 71–92. On occasion an heiress may have had to give up some of her inheritance when she remarried, see below, p. 115.

[17] *The Letters and Charters of Gilbert Foliot*, ed. A. Morey and C. N. L. Brooke (London, 1967), No. 26. Also A. Morey and C. N. L. Brooke, *Gilbert Foliot and his Letters* (Cambridge, 1965), ch. 7, esp. p. 117; D. B. Crouch, 'Robert, Earl of Gloucester and the Daughter of Zelophehad', *JMedH* 11 (1985), 227–43; M. Chibnall, *The Empress Matilda* (Oxford, 1991), 85, who questions whether Robert earl of Gloucester would have known the continuation of the passage concerning marriage outside the tribe.

obtained the barony of Gloucester through marriage to Mabel, heiress of Robert fitzHamo—was fond of quoting the last chapter of the Book of Numbers in the following way:

The man Zelophehad was a Jew of the tribe of Manasseh; he had only daughters and no son. It seemed to certain people that the daughters, because of the imbecillity of their sex, should not be admitted to the father's goods. Asked about this, the Lord promulgated a law, that everything possessed by their father should be yielded entire to the daughters of Zelophehad.

In fact the biblical passage does not question women's right to succeed, but concerns the marriage of daughters outside the tribe, another subject relevant to the empress. Even so the version in the letter remains very significant: there were norms, at least inside people's heads, which would help to decide each case, having regard for the particular facts.

Henry I's Coronation Charter promised that if one of his barons or other men died, leaving a daughter as heiress, he would give her with her land, by the counsel of his barons.[18] As Milsom has pointed out, the nature of the heiress's hold on the inheritance differed from that of a son.[19] Control of her inheritance, except perhaps during widowhood, rested in varying degrees and at different times with her lord, her husband, and her children. Thus if a married heiress succeeded to her father's lands, it would be her husband's homage which cemented the lord's acceptance of her claim. A woman's claim to inherit thus rested on an acceptable marriage. Holt has clarified the meaning of a *statutum decretum* in the 1130s providing for the division of land between coheiresses.[20] The latter arrangement may have caused some

---

[18] Coronation Charter, c. 3; Liebermann, *Gesetze*, i. 521.

[19] Milsom, 'Inheritance by Women', 64, 89 speaks of women as 'transmitting' inheritances; see also Holt, 'Heiress and Alien', 3. Note Holt, 'Heiress and Alien', 4 on widowhood.

[20] Holt, 'Heiress and Alien', 8–21; pp. 8–9, may be overemphatic in suggesting that division between heiresses did not take place before the *statutum decretum*. There are possible instances; thus a considerably later dispute, *Placitorum in Domo Capitulari Westmonasterii Asservatorum Abbreviatio: Richard I–Edward II* (Record Commission, 1811), 79b, recalls a division between heiresses sometime in Henry I's reign, although it may concern acquisitions. The *statutum* might be better seen as deciding between two possible customs rather than effecting a complete change. See also Geoffrey of Monmouth, *Historia Regum*, ed. N. Wright (Cambridge, 1985), 19, for King Leir and his three daughters; note, however, that Geoffrey also on occasion had Britain divided between sons, e.g. p. 15; cf. primogeniture at p. 32.

problems, but otherwise there is no sign that their successions were particularly marked by disputes in times of political stability.[21]

A few grants, generally family arrangements, restricted succession to heirs of the grantee's body, sometimes further limited to the children of a particular wife. In 1123, a marriage settlement involving Robert Ridel and a granddaughter of Ralph Basset restricted succession to the children of the specified wife, and laid down what was to happen in the absence of such heirs.[22] However, a few examples were not family settlements. In Henry II's reign William de Roumare gave Reinold de Neufmarché two bovates 'to be held of me and my heirs in fee and inheritance if he has an heir from the wife he has married [*de uxore desponsata*]'. If he had no such heir before he died, the land was to return to William's demesne.[23] I have found no disputes arising from such grants, and they were not widely adopted by lords to preserve any discretion once enjoyed. Usually they were employed by families in order to control the descent of their lands.[24]

I turn now from *Glanvill*'s 'closest heirs', sons and daughters, to those he termed 'more distant heirs'. First came grandsons and granddaughters. When Henry I took into his hand the lands of Eudo dapifer, who had drowned with the White Ship, he may have disinherited two grandsons in the female line, who would still have been minors.[25] Generally, however, grandchildren's claims appear to have been accepted. For example, the barony of Stainton le Vale passed

---

[21] Holt, 'Heiress and Alien', 16–17; also 15 on the effect of political interests on divisions between tenants in chief. P. A. Brand, 'New Light on the Anstey Case', *Essex Archaeology and History*, 15 (1983), 68–83, suggests that a dispute over the division of lands between heiresses arose after the settlement of the Anstey case; below, p. 117 on the Beauchamp inheritance in Stephen's reign, p. 115, on the lands of the Countess Lucy. See also Milsom, 'Inheritance by Women', on problems such as the place *maritagium* was to take in any division. See e.g. Sanders, *Baronies*, Folkestone, for a barony passing twice in succession through inheritance by daughters.

[22] *Regesta*, ii, No. 1389. Note also the agreement between Rufus and Robert Curthose in 1091, *ASC*, 169.

[23] *Danelaw Documents*, No. 519; see No. 514 from late in Henry II's reign. See further e.g. J. Nichols, *The History and Antiquities of the County of Leicester* (4 vols. in 8; London, 1795–1815), iv, pt. 2, 645.

[24] Note also *Chronicon Abbatiae Rameseiensis*, ed. W. D. Macray (London, 1886), 295; a tenant of Ramsey, about to depart for Jerusalem, agrees that if he died without children from his lawful wife, the church should be made heir of his lands.

[25] J. A. Green, *The Government of England under Henry I* (Cambridge, 1986), 179, R. DeAragon, 'The Growth of Secure Inheritance in Anglo-Norman England', *JMedH* 8 (1982), 384; on the complexities of the political and kin relationships, see also C. W. Hollister, 'The Misfortunes of the Mandevilles', *History*, 58 (1973), 18–28.

from Ralph de Criol to his granddaughter Bertha.[26] However, their position could be weak if a younger brother of their deceased father survived. This is the *casus regis*, which I discuss later in this section.

After lineal descendants, according to *Glanvill*, came brothers and sisters. Again there are many examples of peaceful succession by mesne tenants and tenants in chief.[27] I have found very few cases where the king denied succession to a brother's lands.[28] When Walter succeeded his brother Roger earl of Hereford in 1155, although he lost the county of Hereford and the city of Gloucester, he did receive the whole paternal inheritance of lands. These later passed in turn to his brothers, Henry and Mahel, and to his sister, Margaret.[29]

Nephews and nieces often succeeded to their uncles' lands as heirs.[30] However, this may be the stage where succession became less secure.[31] In Stephen's reign, William II Peverel and Walchelin Maminot shared the inheritance of their uncle, Hamo Peverel, who died probably in 1139. However, Henry II never recognized Walchelin's claim to the Peverel lands.[32] Succession by uncles, aunts, and their

[26] Sanders, *Baronies*, Stainton le Vale. Note also J. H. Round, 'Bernard, the King's Scribe', *EHR* 14 (1899), 422, No. 16, for Bernard regaining land which had belonged to his grandfather. It cannot be told, for example, whether grandchildren through the female line were in a weaker position than those through the male. Note also the exclusion of grandchildren from *mort d'ancestor* by the time of *Bracton*: fo. 261b, Thorne, iii. 269; see also *Early Registers of Writs*, ed. E. de Haas and G. D. G. Hall (Selden Soc. 87; 1970), Hib. 8, CA 16. D. M. Stenton, *English Justice between the Norman Conquest and the Great Charter 1066–1215* (Philadelphia, 1964), 44, points to an assize concerning a grandmother's land; the reference, *PR 26 HII*, 41, states only that Henry fitzMargaret owes 3m. for a recognition about the death of his grandmother, so the case need not necessarily have involved *mort d'ancestor*.

[27] e.g. *HKF*, iii. 35, 66 by brothers, ii. 193, iii. 405, 424 by sisters; Sanders, *Baronies*, Beckley, Clare, Hook Norton, Okehampton by brothers, Belvoir, Bourn, by sisters. See also Martindale, 'Succession and Politics', 29 on fraternal succession.

[28] Sanders, *Baronies*, Bradninch seems to be an example under Henry I, but we cannot be certain on what grounds it returned to the king's hand.

[29] 'Charters of the Earldom of Hereford, 1095–1201', ed. D. Walker, in *Camden Miscellany*, xxii (Camden. Soc., 4th Ser. 1; 1964), 9–10.

[30] e.g. Sanders, *Baronies*, Bourn, Ellingham, Wrinstead. Cf. the problematic descent of the honour of Tickhill, mentioned below, n. 129, and discussed by Holt, 'Politics and Property', 52.

[31] Note also in this context the *Relatio de Standard* on Walter Espec: although he had nephews, he lacked children as heirs, and he therefore made Christ heir of his best possessions; *Chronicles Stephen, Henry II, Richard I*, iii. 183. The implication seems to be that Walter's nephews, his sister's sons, had less of a claim to inherit all his lands than his children would have done, had he had any; see also below, p. 194 n. 94. In fact, his lands were divided between the heirs of his sisters, Sanders, *Baronies*, Helmsley, Old Wardon. The partition proved problematic, see e.g. *PR 4 HII*, 140, 146.

[32] *The Cartulary of Shrewsbury Abbey*, ed. U. Rees (2 vols.; Aberystwyth, 1975), i. 43b.

descendants was uncommon,[33] probably because they were rarely the closest heirs, but also because lords did not accept their claims. Robert of Torigny wrote that Walter Giffard died heirless in 1164, but by *Glanvill*'s standards Walter did have heirs, for his aunt, Rohese, had descendants. Nevertheless, Walter's English earldom and Norman lands returned to Henry II's demesne, and his heirs only obtained their potential inheritance at the beginning of the next reign.[34] Too few instances survive to tell whether aunts were in a weaker position than uncles. In 1120, Rannulf le Meschin succeeded his cousin Richard as earl of Chester.[35] However, he had to pay a very heavy relief and surrender his rights to his wife's inheritance. Lords exploited the weakness of the more distant claims, even if they did not refuse to regrant the land. As in the case of Chester, a compromise, or indeed over time a series of compromises, might be the result.

Lastly comes the question of parents 'succeeding' to their children's lands. Beyond the statement of the *Leges Henrici*, derived from the *Lex Ribuaria*, that 'if anyone dies without children his father or mother shall succeed to the inheritance', I have found no evidence for succession by ascendants.[36] Such occasions would be very hard to trace genealogically, unless there were specific reference to the child's holding in the parent's lifetime. If lands did pass from child to parent, it might appear to us, and have appeared to people at the time, as a reversion similar to that to a lord, rather than as a form of succession.

Thus succession by the more remote relatives could be vulnerable. Towards the closer end it was generally secure and followed a consistent pattern. Disputes concerning the closer heirs generally arose in two situations. In the first, the heir was clear, but in a peculiarly weak position, personally or politically; in the second, there were problems deciding who was the closest heir. The youth or absence of an heir might cause problems. Heirs might be conceived

---

[33] For an example of an aunt succeeding in *c.*1190, Sanders, *Baronies*, West Greenwich. See also *Gesta Stephani*, ed. K. R. Potter, intro. R. H. C. Davis (Oxford, 1976), 200–2, for Earl Gilbert of Pembroke claiming that the castles which Stephen had confiscated from his nephew, Gilbert fitzRichard earl of Hertford, should be his 'by hereditary right', even though Gilbert fitzRichard was still alive.

[34] *Chronicles Stephen, Henry II, Richard I*, iv. 222; Sanders, *Baronies*, Long Crendon; *CP*, ii. 386–7.

[35] Holt, 'Politics and Property', 51–2.

[36] *Leges Henrici*, 70 20, Downer, 224. A parent might conceivably have succeeded to their child's acquisition.

but not yet born when their fathers died, as with Henry II's ill-fated grandson, Arthur son of Geoffrey of Brittany.[37] Succession by minors was common, but could have been the more threatened the less close the kinship of heir to decedent, and was also at particular risk during political strife.[38] Sometimes the closest heir must have been of age but absent, even perhaps his existence unknown. Although I have found no disputes arising from a man's claim that he had been passed over in this way, the accessions of Henry I and Stephen showed the advantages of swiftly pressing a claim when their rivals were absent.[39]

The personal situation which has left most evidence of causing disputes is that of the heir whose mother remarried. One such dispute stretched through the twelfth century, and concerns the honour of Huntingdon and the descendants of Waltheof and William the Conqueror's niece, Judith.[40]

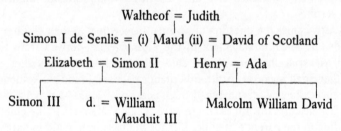

---

[37] The fictional Raoul de Cambrai found himself in this situation as he relaxed in his mother's womb; *Raoul*, laisses III and IV. From the 13th cent., see e.g. the case recorded in *CRR*, x. 305, and the writ 'De ventre inspiciendo', *Early Registers of Writs*, CC 139, R 752. *The Registrum Antiquissimum of the Cathedral Church of Lincoln*, ed. C. W. Foster and K. Major (10 vols.; Lincoln Rec. Soc., 1931–73), No. 953 stated that if Fulk Basset died before his wife had conceived, the lands which the bishop of Lincoln had granted him were to pass to his brother Thomas.

[38] For a minor son losing his inheritance in Stephen's reign, see *RCR*, i. 440–1. Note also the difficult descent of the lands of Geoffrey fitzPain, which may involve a minor losing lands; *EYC*, x. 1–6. See also the case of the Clintons, D. B. Crouch, 'Geoffrey de Clinton and Roger, Earl of Warwick', *BIHR* 55 (1982), 120. Note, however, that often we do not know the age of the heir, and to assume that an easy succession indicates that the heir was of age can lead to an underestimating of the security of succession at least by closely related minors.

[39] White, 'Inheritances and Legal Arguments', 100–1, suggests that *Earldom of Gloucester Charters*, ed. R. B. Patterson (Oxford, 1973), No. 186 is one such case from Normandy. *CMA*, ii. 206 reveals a potential heir living overseas.

[40] For this case, see K. J. Stringer, 'A Cistercian Archive: The Earliest Charters of Sawtry abbey', *JSA* 6 (1980), 326–30, on which I primarily rely; *CP*, vi. 640–7; Sanders, *Baronies*, Fotheringay; *HKF*, ii. 296–9. For the sake of clarity, the family tree in the text includes only the main characters. For another instance, see Holt, 'Politics and Property', 48–9, on the Bigod succession dispute of 1177.

Earl Waltheof married Countess Judith and they produced a daughter, Maud. In *c*.1090 she married Simon I de Senlis who died in 1111 × 13, leaving a son Simon II. Maud then married David of Scotland, and Simon, still a minor, became his stepfather's ward. It is unclear whether David established his hold on the lands as Simon's guardian or by right of his wife.[41] In 1124 David became king of Scots and Simon passed into the wardship of his great uncle, Stephen count of Aumale. Maud died in 1130/1 and David held her lands, possibly by the widower's right of curtesy, until he resigned their custody to his son Henry in 1136.[42] The political desirability of an alliance with the Scots led Henry I and Stephen in the early years of his reign to turn down Simon's repeated requests for his inheritance, even though he was now of age. However, the collapse of Stephen's relationship with the Scots led him finally to restore the inheritance to his supporter Simon. When Simon died in 1153, his son Simon III was a minor and soon lost control of the honour of Huntingdon; Henry II gave it to the king of Scots, now Malcolm, who held them until he died childless in 1165. They then passed to his younger brother William the Lion, but he forfeited them after his invasion of England in 1174. They were granted to Simon III but he too died childless in 1184 and the lands returned to William the Lion in 1185. The original remarriage, the succession of minors and the deaths of holders without children ensured an unstable descent for these lands.

The turn the dispute took under Stephen also reveals how politics could affect a succession. Daughters were supposed to inherit before nephews, but early in Stephen's reign a dispute arose between the daughter and heiress of Simon de Beauchamp and his nephews. Miles, the most prominent, was castellan of Bedford, and, with his brothers, resisted royal demands for the surrender of the castle. According to the *Gesta Stephani*, Miles claimed that the castle was owed to him 'from paternal right'. Orderic gives a rather different explanation:

It was not that they intended to withhold the obedience and service due to their lord, but having heard that he had given the daughter of Simon de Beauchamp in marriage to Hugh le Poer with her father's honour, and fearing to lose their whole inheritance, they had taken the advice of friends to put up a stout opposition.[43]

---

[41] *HKF*, ii. 296 suggests the latter.
[42] On curtesy, see Pollock and Maitland, ii. 414–20.
[43] *Gesta Stephani*, 46–50: it is unclear whether 'ex paterno iure' means anything

According to Orderic, the bishop of Winchester persuaded Miles to surrender the castle. However, Hugh le Poer and his wife only enjoyed it until the empress's period of dominance in 1141. The *Gesta Stephani* records that

Hugh, surnamed the Poor, who by the king's permission had obtained the earldom of Bedford when Miles de Beauchamp was dislodged, behaving carelessly and slackly (for he was a dissolute and effeminate man) willy-nilly handed over the castle to Miles, and by a just judgment of God became in a short time a knight instead of an earl and instead of a knight a very poor man.[44]

Further instances will be considered below, in relation to heirs seeking to persuade their lords to accept them because of the political advantage which would result.[45]

In addition to cases where the heir was clear but circumstances produced a dispute, it was sometimes unclear who was the closest heir. For example, in the thirteenth century, difficulties could still arise if a man left off-spring from two marriages.[46] The most famous instance of dispute arising from lack of clear norms of inheritance is the *casus regis*, summarized by *Glanvill* in the following way:

When ... anyone dies leaving a younger son or daughter, and a grandson born of an eldest son already dead, a great legal problem arises [*magna ... iuris dubitatio solet esse*] as to which is to be preferred to the other in that succession ... Some have sought to say that the younger son is more rightly heir [*rectiorem esse heredem*] than such a grandson, on the ground that since the eldest son did not survive until the death of his father he did not survive until he was his heir; and therefore, so they say, since the younger son survived both father and brother, he rightly succeeds to his father. Others, however, have taken the view that such a grandson ought in law to be preferred to his uncle; for, since that grandson was born to the eldest son and was heir of his body, he ought to succeed to his father in all the rights which his father would have if still alive.[47]

other than 'by hereditary right'; Orderic Vitalis, *The Ecclesiastical History*, ed. and tr. M. Chibnall (6 vols.; Oxford, 1969–80), vi. 510; F. M. Stenton, *The First Century of English Feudalism, 1066–1166* (2nd edn., Oxford, 1961), 237–8.

[44] *Gesta Stephani*, 116.
[45] See below, pp. 127–8.
[46] Pollock and Maitland, ii. 302–5; *Bracton*, fos. 65–65b, Thorne ii. 190–1.
[47] *Glanvill*, vii. 3, Hall, 77–8; Pollock and Maitland, ii. 283–6; J. C. Holt, 'The *Casus Regis*: The Law and Politics of Succession in the Plantagenet Dominions 1185–1247', in E. B. King and S. J. Ridyard (edd.), *Law in Mediaeval Life and Thought*

Unless it could be proved that the deceased son had done homage to the chief lord, 'the position at the present day as between uncle and grandson is that the party in possession will prevail.' I have found no such cases between 1066 and 1166; maybe disputes did occur, but left no trace, or maybe succession was peaceful, settled by individual decisions and honorial custom. Alternatively, the royal house's problems of the late twelfth century may not have been the product of doubts about custom but have produced those very doubts. If so, it reveals how custom could still change, despite the hardening of inheritance rules.

The heir might also be in doubt when the validity of the decedent's marriage was disputed. Such was the situation in the Anstey case, much cited as evidence of the tardiness and expense of medieval justice, but strangely ignored in discussions of inheritance.[48] The dispute was between William de Sackville's daughter Mabel de Francheville, and his sister's son, Richard de Anstey, who left a memorandum of the case.

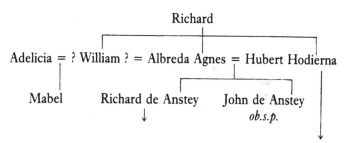

The case turned on the validity of William's marriage to Mabel's mother, Adelicia. William died between *c.*1149 and 1153, and the dispute over the lands went to the court of Theobald, count of Blois, who at least in France appears to have been lord of the Sackvilles 'by

(Sewanee, 1990), who at pp. 23–6 deals with the circumstances in which the quotation was written. Holt, p. 26, suggests that the Beauchamp family dispute over Bedford castle in Stephen's reign may have arisen from such an inheritance problem, but the Beauchamp genealogy is unclear, and Stenton, *First Century*, 237 n. 1, seems to be a better interpretation: 'behind this dispute there lay the difficult question whether a barony should descend through the daughter of its last possessor or pass to a collateral kinsman descended in the male line from a common ancestor.' See Orderic, vi. 430 for a *casus regis* situation in the descent of Burgundy in the 11th cent.

[48] P. M. Barnes, 'The Anstey Case', in P. M. Barnes and C. F. Slade (edd.), *Stenton Miscellany* (PRS, NS 36; 1960), 1–2 and notes. On the case generally, see also Brand, 'Anstey'; C. N. L. Brooke, *The Medieval Idea of Marriage* (Oxford, 1989), pp. 149–52.

right of fee'. Theobald recognized William and Adelicia's children as legitimate heirs, but thereafter the case continued in the courts of the king, Theobald archbishop of Canterbury, papal judges delegate, and the Pope himself.[49]

A surviving letter, datable to late 1160, from Theobald to Pope Alexander III outlines the parties' versions of the events and the positions upon which they based their claims.[50] Richard asserted that William had contracted to marry Albreda de Tresgoz but broke his promise and deserted her. He proceeded to take to wife Adelicia, daughter of Amfrid the sheriff, who bore Mabel and other children. The couple went through a form of marriage, despite Albreda's protests during the ceremony. According to Mabel, the agreement to marry Albreda did not constitute marriage and had been annulled by mutual consent. The dowry had been refunded, as witnesses would establish, and Albreda's father had approved the marriage to Adelicia, which was duly consummated. However, according to Richard, Albreda then persuaded the papal legate, Henry bishop of Winchester, to order William to return to her. The Pope confirmed this decision, and 'from that date to the last days of his life William abandoned the adulteress and clove to his former wife.' Mabel denied that a proper divorce had taken place. Only after Adelicia had been violently ejected from the house, and the bishop of Winchester bribed, were William and Albreda married in church. On his death-bed, according to Mabel, William repented that he had agreed to such fraud.

Thus Richard stressed the validity of William and Albreda's marriage based on the consent of the parties, the authority of the divorce from Adelicia, and produced witnesses who stated that 'he had been appointed as heir by his uncle William, while the others had been disinherited as bastards.'[51] Mabel claimed, among various pleas, that consent was not enough to establish marriage, that the divorce was not valid, and especially that her father's last will and the judgment of Count Theobald established her right.[52] The case only came to its long-awaited end in July 1163 with the parties appearing before the king at Woodstock. Richard's account puts it thus: 'And at last, by

[49] Brand, 'Anstey', 72; Barnes, 'Anstey'; L. Voss, *Heinrich von Blois, Bischof von Winchester, 1129–1171* (Berlin, 1932), 167–8.

[50] The remainder of this paragraph is based on *Letters of John of Salisbury*, i, No. 131; see also Voss, *Heinrich von Blois*, 166–8.

[51] *Letters of John of Salisbury*, i, No. 131, pp. 228–30, 234.

[52] *Letters of John of Salisbury*, i, No. 131, pp. 230–7.

the grace of God and the king, my uncle's land was adjudged to me by the judgment of the king's court, and there I expended £7 12s.'[53]

The Anstey case again puts the development of inheritance into a wider context of changing ideas. Strict legal rules of inheritance required not only regular enforcement by lay authority, but also the definition of issues in which the Church was intimately involved. The Popes, and notably Alexander III, were grappling with a complex and developing law of marriage.[54] The Anstey case was particularly difficult, but the more general question of succession by bastards must have been settled by a mixture of lay and ecclesiastical attitudes. In 1035 William the Bastard succeeded in Normandy. According to Orderic, in 1103 the Normans chose to accept William de Breteuil's illegitimate son Eustace as his successor, rather than his legitimate heirs who were a Breton and a Burgundian.[55] However, in 1091 William Rufus and Robert made each other their heir in the absence of any legitimate child.[56] In 1135 Robert of Gloucester was not seriously considered as a contender to the throne.[57] In the Anstey dispute, Mabel stressed her legitimacy, never a right to succeed despite illegitimacy. *Glanvill* included an exception of bastardy in his discussion of *mort d'ancestor*.[58] Whilst pre-Conquest English custom may have treated bastards more harshly than did continental, after 1066 the teachings of the reform movement on proper marriage clearly had an important effect.[59]

Increased definition of marriage could strengthen a lord's position. The tale of Raoul de Cambrai suggests a tension in lay attitudes to succession by bastards. Ybert de Ribemont, count of Vermandois,

[53] Barnes, 'Anstey', 21.

[54] Brooke, *Mediaeval Idea of Marriage*, 152, 169–72, 265–6, replaces the more schematic treatment of Alexander's views in *Letters of John of Salisbury*, i. 267–71. See also C. Donahue, 'The Policy of Alexander III's Consent Theory on Marriage', in *Proceedings of the Fourth International Congress of Medieval Canon Law*, ed. S. Kuttner (Vatican City, 1976), 251–81.

[55] Orderic, vi. 40.

[56] ASC, 169.

[57] See also C. W. Hollister, 'The Anglo-Norman Succession Debate of 1126: Prelude to Stephen's Anarchy', *JMedH* 1 (1975), 24. Note also John of Salisbury, *Historia Pontificalis*, ed. and tr. M. Chibnall (Oxford, 1986), 83, on Matilda's birth.

[58] *Glanvill*, xiii. 11, Hall, 154. However, note also *Glanvill*, vi. 17, Hall, 68, on the situation following divorce for consanguineity; the woman is to have no dower, 'and yet her children can be heirs and by the law of the realm succeed to their father by hereditary right'.

[59] On bastardy and succession, note the dispute in Geoffrey of Monmouth, 3. On bastardy generally, see Newman, *Anglo-Norman Nobility*, 197–201.

produced a son, Bernier, by an illicit liaison. Although Ybert had brothers, the mother told Bernier concerning his father's patrimony that 'he has no other heirs, you cannot lose it.' Ybert gave his lands to Bernier, leading the king to complain that he had done so without royal agreement and to ask 'Ought now a bastard hold an honour?'[60] From the king, and any other lord's point of view, to deny a bastard's right to succeed was to increase his own seignorial discretion and the likelihood of escheat.

Thus the Church and lay society narrowed the definition of an heir. Yet difficult cases remained, even in the next century. Theobald's letter to Alexander III stated that

> There are occasions when the clemency of the law spares those who, though debarred from marriage by reason of their kinship, have married in ignorance, and frees from infamy and the loss of their inheritance the children of those who have been wrongfully joined together in ignorance by the Church.[61]

Although the reference is to the clemency of Canon Law, this clearly affected lay succession, and the canonical position remained unchanged in the thirteenth century. The increase in abstraction and definition which was an important element in the development of inheritance was a gradual process. The Anstey case provides a notable illustration of how far it had gone by *c.*1166.

OTHER CLAIMS TO SUCCEED

Not all claims to succeed to land were based on genealogical proximity.[62] An heir might claim to have been designated. Although bequests of land by written will were disappearing, there is some evidence in this period for men creating heirs. Various charters use the verb *hereditare*, 'to make an heir'.[63] The *Leges Henrici* state

---

[60] *Raoul*, ll. 1200, 6265–7 ['Doit dont bastars nulle honor maintenir'] respectively.

[61] *Letters of John of Salisbury*, i, No. 131, p. 235. Note that the passage preceding the quotation suggests that the decision in the Anstey case might have been different had it concerned a mother's inheritance rather than a father's; again the impression is given that in such circumstances there need not have been one single correct outcome.

[62] Claims to succeed to office were open to a wider range of possibilities, as is most obviously the case with the succession to kingdoms; see e.g. John of Salisbury, *Historia Pontificalis*, 84.

[63] e.g. Stenton, *First Century*, No. 7. See also e.g. *Chronicon Abbatiae de Evesham ad annum 1418*, ed. W. D. Macray (London, 1863), 98.

If anyone abandons his father or relative in mortal need or illness or poverty without due cause, and any relative or outsider [*extraneus*] helps the person in such necessity of his life, and he at the end makes him his heir and constitutes him son for his fee or his acquisition, before witnesses, this is to be settled between the claimants [*heredipetas*] by judgment of wise men, accordir.̣ to the circumstances.[64]

No obvious written source exists for the statement, and it may reflect current opinion,[65] but creation of heirs at the expense of genealogically closer relatives was not common. There was, perhaps, a feeling that men should not interfere with such weighty matters. *Glanvill*'s statement that a man 'cannot make another his heir, whether a [religious] community or a man; for only God, not man, can make an heir' has precedents stretching back into the eleventh century.[66]

The Treaty of Westminster of 1153 also gives the impression that the creation of heirs was unfamiliar and a situation for which there was no readily acceptable vocabulary. Henry of Huntingdon wrote that 'the king took Henry as his adoptive son and constituted him heir of the realm.' Henry had probably grasped a Roman Law term, *adoptiuus*, then in circulation, but did not use it technically.[67] The Treaty itself used neither *adoptiuus* nor a word such as *hereditare*:

I King Stephen have constituted Henry duke of Normandy successor of the realm of England and my heir by hereditary right after me, and thus I have given and confirmed the realm of England to him and his heirs . . . Also I

---

[64] *Leges Henrici*, 88 15, Downer, 274–6.

[65] Cf. this emphasis on personal loyalty with the preference for the 'hearth-heir' in cases arising from the *casus regis*; Pollock and Maitland, ii. 285, and also *Glanvill*, vii. 3, Hall, 78, with its comments on forisfamiliation. R. J. Faith, 'Peasant Families and Inheritance Customs in Medieval England', *Agricultural History Review*, 14 (1966), 83–4 provides a link to Borough English, the custom of succession by the youngest son.

[66] *Glanvill*, vii. 1, Hall, 71. *Glanvill*'s statement is similar to that of an 11th-cent. tract on succession to kingdoms, *De Unitate Ecclesiae*, c. 13, in MGH, *Libelli de Lite* (3 vols.; Hanover, 1891–7), ii. 204; see also Fauroux, No. 93; references from J. Biancalana, 'For Want of Justice: Legal Reforms of Henry II', *Columbia Law Review*, 88 (1988), 512 n. 423. Note also *The Cartulary of Tutbury Priory*, ed. A. Saltman (HMSO, 1962), No. 103. *Glanvill*'s phrase may only mean that all is uncertain until the hour of a man's death, which only God knows. A son, by God's will, might predecease his father.

[67] Henry of Huntingdon, *Historia Anglorum*, ed. T. Arnold (London, 1879), 289. Henry also used *adoptiuus* of the agreement between Edmund Ironside and Cnut in 1016, p. 185. See also *Regesta*, iii, No. 929, a Westminster charter forged between 1138 and 1157, using *adoptiuus* of the relationship of the Norman kings to the Confessor. On adoption in Roman Law, see e.g. *Institutes*, Bk. I, Title XI.

have given security to the duke by oath that . . . I will maintain him as my son and heir [*sicut filium et heredem*] in all things as I am able and guard him against all whom I can.[68]

The impression is of a struggle with language. Stephen avoided calling Henry simply *filius*, whereas he referred to his own son William as *filius* but never *heres*. Yet the analogy of kinship was still introduced: 'as my son and heir'. Stephen made Henry 'successor of the realm of England' but also stated that he had 'given' Henry the kingdom. The parties could not turn to contemporary practice, or to Roman Law, for a brief formula to cover the situation.

In most lay cases, the heir 'created' was in fact the genealogically closest. For example, in the late eleventh century, Geoffrey de Mandeville with his wife made a grant to Westminster Abbey 'by grant of my son William whom I have arranged to make my heir'. William was Geoffrey's eldest son.[69] There are only very occasional suggestions of laymen choosing heirs other than the genealogically closest. For example, Henry II granted Hugh of Hanslope one hundred acres of assarts, 'and that he may make whomsoever he wishes heir thereto'.[70] Such grants coincide with the first mentions of assigns in charters.[71] However, cases from the fifty years after 1166 indicate that lords still retained some control over these arrangements.[72] There is no sign during the century after the Conquest that the designation of an heir was being widely used to evade the normal patterns of succession.

If 'creating' an heir generally involved only the special nomination of one likely to succeed anyway, it resembles other methods of ensuring the heir's succession. The very few surviving examples of bequests of land by will were to heirs who had a strong claim to

[68] *Regesta*, iii, No. 272.

[69] *Westminster Abbey Charters, 1066–c.1214*, ed. E. Mason (London Rec. Soc. 25; 1988), No. 436. See also e.g. *Charters of the Honour of Mowbray, 1107–1191*, ed. D. E. Greenway (London, 1972), No. 3; *HKF*, i. 1. Note the parallel to the Capetian and Norman rulers having their successors recognized, sometimes even crowned, during their own lifetimes.

[70] *Cartae Antiquae, 11–20*, ed. J. C. Davis (PRS, NS 33; 1960), No. 411. Note also *Feudal Documents from the Abbey of Bury St Edmunds*, ed. D. C. Douglas (London, 1932), No. 129, from the second quarter of the 12th cent., which records that Oswald of Barton 'hereditauit' Adam of Cockfield and his wife and heirs. The transaction is a complex one, and the relationship of Oswald and Adam cannot be fully uncovered.

[71] e.g. *EYC*, i, No. 422, *Danelaw Documents*, No. 175.

[72] S. F. C. Milsom, *The Legal Framework of English Feudalism* (Cambridge, 1976), 104, 107–9, 146–53; see also below, Ch. 7 on substitution.

succeed.[73] An heir might also be presented to his lord for acceptance during his father's lifetime, a process Milsom calls 'accelerated inheritance'. Thus a charter of Hugh of Bolbec opens 'Know that I have given back to Robert of "Broch" all his father's land, of Chesham and "Broch", and for this received homage from him and he gave me his relief, at the request of his father—and other friends—who presented him to me as his son and heir.'[74] Such a grant might well be desired to give the son wealth and independence from his father, sometimes perhaps on his marriage, to provide additional assurance of his position for his new wife and her kin.[75]

In the majority of these cases of the nomination of an heir, or the reinforcement of an heir's claim, the lands concerned were acquisitions. Given that the beneficiary was usually the genealogically closest heir, such practices may have been intended to prevent later challenges by others, notably younger sons, who saw themselves as having a strong claim to receive the decedent's acquisitions.

Did these practices restrict seignorial control? If the nomination were made without the lord's consent, it certainly did not bind him, but the additional publicity for the heir, together with a possibly solemn ceremony of nomination, must have reinforced opinion in favour of the custom of succession. In practice, such arrangements may often have been made in potentially complex situations, such as succession by twins. Lords may happily have consented to or even promoted these, sometimes no doubt encouraged by a sweetener from the current tenant.

A man might also claim that, if not the closest heir, he was the most suitable. A very unusual written agreement records Robert count of Meulan's provision that his lands be divided between his twin sons, Robert and Waleran: 'if the said Robert dies or is such as to be not suitable for controlling land, I grant that same inheritance to his

---

[73] e.g. *Regesta*, ii, No. 843; *EYC*, ii, No. 778. See also below, pp. 133–5, for the case of Modbert and North Stoke; despite mention of the decedent's 'testamentum' and 'nouissima uerba', there is no sign in the case of a written will. On bequest of land by will, see J. C. Holt, 'The Revolution of 1066', *TRHS*, 5th Ser. 32 (1982), 196–8; M. M. Sheehan, *The Will in Medieval England* (Toronto, 1963), 107–19.

[74] Stenton, *First Century*, No. 43; Milsom, *Legal Framework*, 147. See also e.g. Warwick Record Office, MS CR 26/1(i)/Box 1/W2 (transcript courtesy of Dr Crouch).

[75] The son's position could also be strengthened by granting him a charter when his father was enfeoffed; *Registrum Antiquissimum*, Nos. 952 and 953 may well be an example of this, although it cannot be proved that the charters are contemporaneous.

brother Waleran, and equally if Waleran dies, or is not suitable for possessing land, I grant this to Robert with the fee in Normandy.'[76] A case probably of 1199 records that Bernard le Franceis, who died in the time of Henry I, had two sons, the elder named Osmund, the younger John. 'By the feebleness [*per inpotentia*]' of Osmund, John possessed the inheritance, by the grant of the lords of the fee to whom he did service.[77] The 1208 Pipe Roll recalls that Henry I 'by will [*per uoluntatem*]' enfeoffed the son of a second marriage with the barony of Marshwood because he was a better knight than the son of the first.[78] Such cases suggest that where the lord chose a suitable heir rather than the closest, personal capacity to serve clearly was important.

Yet it is questionable how frequent such cases were. Certainly we only know of these because the elder line later claimed the holding, and many an unsuitable heir—whatever the form of their *inpotentia* —may have had few marriage prospects and produced no children. However, the Marshwood case notably involves a second marriage, a situation which as we have seen affected inheritance claims. It may be that unsuitability generally had to be severe, for example serious mental handicap, if the heir was to be denied the inheritance. In clear instances of unsuitability, preference for the younger line would have been popular both with the lord and with the family, who wished the inheritance to be held by a man who could maintain it. Only when unsuitability was questionable were disputes likely to arise between claimants and lord, and within the family.

A question which may be linked to that of suitability arose when aspiring heirs claimed inheritances because of their faithful past service to the decedent's lord, despite the existence of closer heirs. A certain Robert, *nepos comitisse*, appears to have done outstanding service to Lucy, mother of William I de Roumare. In *c*.1135, William granted him the land of his uncles Ivo and Colsuen, to hold in fee and inheritance, 'for the service which Robert did to my mother'. Most unusually for a grant to a layman, the charter specifies that the gift was for Lucy's soul. Later evidence reveals that at least Ivo had a child, whose claim was passed over because of Robert's service to

---

[76] *Regesta*, ii, No. 843.
[77] *RCR*, i. 360. Note the statement that John held 'ut purchacium suum'.
[78] *PR 10 J*, 113 n. 8.

Lucy; around 1200 Ivo's grandson Alan regained the lands through a writ of right in the court of the earl of Chester at Bolingbroke.[79]

Gilbert I de l'Aigle received various lands in England and Normandy after William count of Mortain's forfeiture in 1106. Possibly just before Gilbert's death in 1114 × 18, his eldest son Richer rebelled with William Clito against Henry I. Henry denied Richer's claim to his father's lands in England, 'saying that Geoffrey and Engenulf his brothers were serving in the king's household and confidently expecting the same honour by hereditary right'. Richer's repeated requests ended with Henry refusing outright, and Richer turned to Louis VI of France for help. However, Richer's uncle, Rotrou count of Perche, persuaded Henry to regrant to Richer all he sought. Richer was delighted, but now found himself at loggerheads with Louis. After further difficulties, Richer finally acquired all his father's lands in England and Normandy. Thus the dispute reveals both the possibility of a claim based on loyal service and the strength of the claim of the closest heir, even when his loyalty was in doubt.[80]

Faithful service can be linked to political considerations which played a particularly notable part during the mid-twelfth century. Take the inheritance which the Treaty of Westminster granted William the king's son, consisting of all the lands Stephen had held before he became king and further extensive holdings. In 1159 Henry took advantage of William's childless death on the Toulouse campaign. Henry's wish to control Boulogne, which was held of the king of France, made desirable the continuing support of the family. William's sister and closest heir Mary abbess of Romsey was extracted from the cloister to marry Matthew of Flanders. Henry retained most of the family's English lands, compensating Matthew with money. Despite further concessions in 1167, Matthew died a rebel in 1173, and his death marked the effective end of the honour of Boulogne in England.[81]

Did such political considerations affect succession lower in society? Service and patronage must have influenced regrants and settlements. Yet it was the divided royal succession which produced the forfeitures of

---

[79] *Danelaw Documents*, No. 507, 510, *The Charters of the Anglo-Norman Earls of Chester*, ed. G. Barraclough (Rec. Soc. of Lancs. and Cheshire, 126; 1988), No. 302; see also *Danelaw Documents*, Nos. 508–9, 511.

[80] Sanders, *Baronies*, Pevensey; Orderic, vi. 188, 196–8, 250; Green, *Government*, 179–80. Cf. above, Ch. 2 on forfeiture.

[81] J. H. Round, *Studies in Peerage and Family History* (Westminster, 1901), 168–80.

the late eleventh and early twelfth centuries and which ensured that in the mid-twelfth century two parties were bidding for support with grants of lost inheritances.[82] Lengthy succession disputes producing similar violence seem not to have occurred at the baronial level, except perhaps under Stephen. Then parties may have built up within honours, backing the disputing lords. This would have produced rival grants of lands and have left multiple claims to inherit. Within honours, the compromises of early in Henry II's reign must have reflected honorial politics as lords sought to establish peace, and in some cases to reassert their authority. In the Mowbray honour, a certain Aldelin had held Winterburn in 1135. However, when Roger de Mowbray regranted to Ralph fitzAldelin his father's lands, Winterburn was not amongst those named, and Stephen's reign left it in the possession of William Graindorge. When Roger granted Furness Abbey the service of half a knight in Winterburn, Ralph also issued a quitclaim in favour of the abbey. It seems that the claimants and their lord managed to arrange a settlement which left all parties sufficiently satisfied to prevent any later succession claims.[83]

All these claims—nomination, suitability, service, political advantage —would have been helped by proffers of gifts and money. So too must have been claims based on being the closest heir, especially if the claimant were one of the more remote relatives. Proffers might also persuade a lord to regrant land which the claimant's ancestor had held only for life.[84]

Such payments raise the question of the significance of reliefs for the development of inheritance. Indeed, gifts and proffers might be seen to merge into reliefs, especially if the latter were not simply payments by an accepted tenant but also bids to be accepted. According

---

[82] Holt, 'Politics and Property', 36. See e.g. the dispute over the Huntingdon inheritance, above, p. 117.

[83] *Mowbray*, Nos. 383, 150 respectively. Roger's charter provided that 'preterea si Willelmus Graindorge in aliquibus forisfecerit elemosina ista prenominata in pace quieta sine omni uexatione erit.' This may imply the possibility of William forfeiting, quite probably arising from Ralph fitzAldelin's claim to the land. Alternatively, however, 'forisfecerit' may just mean 'commit wrong'. Cf. the case of Stephen Dammartin and Pitley, below, p. 144; see also generally, R. C. Palmer, 'The Origins of Property in England', *L&HR* 3 (1985), 8–13.

[84] V. H. Galbraith, 'An Episcopal Land-Grant of 1085', *EHR* 44 (1929), 372. I take the reference to payments for the inheritances of others in Henry I Coronation Charter c. 6, Liebermann, *Gesetze*, i. 522, to mean payments for lands which had escheated, rather than the out-bidding of heirs at the time of succession; cf. G. S. Garnett, 'Royal Succession in England, 1066–1154', Ph.D. thesis (Cambridge, 1987), 76–9.

to Richard fitzNigel, children should not be denied their inheritances because of failure to pay relief. Presumably this means that homage had to be taken, and only thereafter might the relief be exacted by distraint. In addition heirs might have been allowed to pay their relief by instalment. However, Richard also recorded, and rejected, another opinion, 'that those who owe reliefs to the king and fail to pay on summons . . . shall not receive their grants'.[85]

It is possible that such was an earlier view of relief, emphasizing the lord's control of succession.[86] However, earlier evidence suggests restriction of seignorial discretion. At least since Cnut's time men had sought to set down in writing what they considered reasonable heriots, and Anglo-Norman writers of *Leges* translated these as reliefs. The *Leges Willelmi*, dated by Liebermann to approximately Henry I's reign, mention 100 shillings as an acceptable monetary relief for a knight, and the same figure per knight's fee continued to appear in the *Dialogus*, *Glanvill*, and, as a maximum, in Magna Carta.[87] The existence of such a notion of correct relief, even though it was far from prescriptive, is significant, particularly when taken alongside Henry I's Coronation Charter. Henry criticized Rufus for forcing heirs to buy back their fathers' lands:

If any of my barons, earls, or others who hold of me, should die, his heir will not buy back [*redimet*] his land as he did in my brother's time, but will relieve it by a lawful and just relief. Likewise my baron's men will relieve their lands from their lords by lawful and just relief.[88]

'Buy back his land' implies that if payment were not made, the land was not restored; the payment constituted almost a new purchase, and hence the grant approached a new gift. If other lords acted thus, succession was less secure in the late eleventh century than it was soon to become, but there is little evidence either way, and it is notable that such demands were already regarded as an abuse in

---

[85] *Dialogus*, 121. Cf. *Glanvill*, ix. 4, Hall, 108, which allows an heir to remain in his inheritance 'provided he offers his homage and reasonable relief to his lord in the presence of reputable men, as he is bound to do', and ix. 6, p. 110, which lays down that following the death of a chief baron, 'the lord king immediately retains his barony in his own hand until the heir has made satisfaction for relief'.

[86] See e.g. Garnett, 'Royal Succession', 87–9; cf. my comments above, p. 69 n. 15.

[87] *Leges Willelmi*, 20 2a, Liebermann, *Gesetze*, i. 506–7; *Dialogus*, 96–7, 120–1, *Glanvill*, ix. 4, Hall, 108, *Magna Carta*, c.2. On reliefs, see S. Painter, *Studies in the History of the English Feudal Barony* (Baltimore, 1943), 56–64, 146–8; Stenton, *First Century*, 22–3, 163–4.

[88] Liebermann, *Gesetze*, i. 521; see also above, p. 69 n. 14.

1100. Henry I charged high reliefs, particularly of more distant heirs, but apparently allowed sufficient time for payment that inheritances were not lost through lack of money. However, a late twelfth-century case shows that even then money might be vital in complicated disputes. The Mandeville family in 1189 was faced with a situation similar to that of the royal house ten years later. Geoffrey fitzPeter claimed the inheritance as husband of the granddaughter of William de Say and Beatrice de Mandeville and representative of the elder line. Geoffrey de Say claimed as William and Beatrice's surviving son. Geoffrey de Say outbid Geoffrey fitzPeter for the inheritance but failed to fulfil his payments and the lands passed to Geoffrey fitzPeter.[89]

The Mandeville case provides a good point at which to conclude this section of analysis. It reveals the problems which might arise when there was not a single clear heir. In such hard cases, although not necessarily in simpler ones, the lord might have considerable discretion. The more complicated the situation, the more it came to rest on the power relations of the parties, on politics rather than custom. However, what is striking even earlier in the twelfth century is the apparent lack of honorial variation in custom and the rarity and lack of success of claims other than being the closest heir, especially in time of peace. Very few, if any, examples survive of eldest sons passed over in favour of another heir, on grounds, for example, of being 'a scoundrel'.[90]

It must be emphasized that custom and the lord's interest were usually congruent, and the eldest son would usually have been a suitable tenant. To this, I would add the effect of outside influences, such as the existence of charters. These reasons must explain the consistency with which the king followed custom, a consistency particularly notable in cases such as that of Richer de l'Aigle, where the claimant hardly appears desirable to the king. Further explanations

---

[89] Holt, '*Casus Regis*', esp. 29; *CP*, v. 120–4. See also the Bigod dispute in 1177, Holt, 'Politics and Property', 48.

[90] The proposition to the contrary is made by Palmer, 'Origins of Property', 6 n. 20. The passing over of Geoffrey de Mandeville II's eldest son, Ernulf, in favour of his next son, Geoffrey, might be seen as one such instance. However, the case against Ernulf was not simply that he was a 'scoundrel'—however much he may have been! He was probably illegitimate, see Chibnall, *Empress Matilda*, 110 n. 74. In addition he had rebelled against Stephen, which was surely grounds for disinheritance. He was exiled and also excommunicated. See J. H. Round, *Geoffrey de Mandeville* (London, 1892), ch. 10. On a later attempt by Geoffrey III to control Ernulf, see below, p. 220.

are also possible. One is the complexity of land-holding in England.[91] Another is that at least Henry I was sufficiently involved in seignorial affairs not only to affect individual cases, but to force lords to take the possibility of royal involvement into account in their regular dealings with their tenants.

THE CONDUCT OF SUCCESSION DISPUTES

I now, therefore, concentrate on the strategies employed during succession disputes. Some of these merge with the types of claim already discussed, most notably the influence of service or political considerations, and the use of money, whilst others have been revealed in the cases analysed. Disputes could involve one claimant and the lord. Or they might involve several claimants, in which case the lord might feel strongly committed to one party, or might perhaps feel no strong attachment. The outcome in the former situation would be strongly indicative of seignorial power, in the latter less so, provided the lord retained control over the tenement. Even so, the lord might well desire that his court be the one in which the dispute was settled. Again my primary interest is in cases arising at or soon after the death of a tenant. However, I also bring into consideration cases stemming from problems of succession, but only arising long after the death of the claimant from whom the claim was derived. I am concerned not only with actions in court but also other strategies employed, noting, for example, the ways in which claimants might exploit temporary seignorial weakness and the forms which settlements took. Various important questions will recur: What authorities were invoked? How autonomous was the honour? When did the king start to be significantly and regularly involved in disputes within honours?

Succession disputes must often have been dealt with in lords' courts. For example, the lord might take the lands into his own hand. The aspiring heirs would bring their claims to his court. Succession

---

[91] See 'Epistulae Fiscannenses: Lettres d'amitié, de gouvernement et d'affaires', ed. J. Laporte, *Revue Mabillon*, 43 (1953), 29–31, esp. 30 for the description of England: 'locus iste autem tot dominis subiacet quot uicinis'; see also J. Boussard, *Le Gouvernement d'Henri II Plantagenêt* (Paris, 1956), 33–62, and for comparison with the simpler Norman situation D. B. Crouch, *The Beaumont Twins* (Cambridge, 1986), 131–2, 138, J. A. Green, 'Unity and Disunity in the Anglo-Norman State', *Historical Research*, 62 (1989), 132.

would then depend on the acceptance of one party by lord and court. Before *mort d'ancestor*, writs rather similar to the later *breue de recto* must often have concerned succession disputes. It is therefore indicative of the lord's court's control of succession that some such writs were addressed to the lord.[92]

Unfortunately, the only seignorial court that can be watched in detail is that of the king dealing with his tenants in chief, be they great men or fairly minor royal servants. Evidence is very sparse concerning courts of other lords, especially those not of ecclesiastics or the greatest laymen. Even for such lords examples are few from before the end of Henry I's reign. A charter of 1133 records a claimant winning his case in the chapter of Hereford Cathedral to hold of the chapter as his father had.[93] Unusually this charter also reveals something of procedure; the claimant deraigned the land 'by the oath of twelve honest men and the judgment of that court', and was seised and invested of it 'as the neighbours and those who knew that land had perambulated all around it'. In addition, charters recording regrants may well hide judgments in seignorial courts, and the first royal court rolls recall some otherwise unknown settlements in honorial courts.[94] Occasionally a chronicle reveals a lord's court hearing a case following a tenant's death. Vincent abbot of Abingdon had granted land to a certain Roger for life. During Stephen's reign, Roger's son Robert retained it by force, with the help of his friends.[95] With much trouble Abbot Ingulf got Robert into his court, where Robert and his heir quitclaimed the land. Money was useful in preventing as well as obtaining succession and Robert was given twenty shillings lest he feel harmed or renew his evil deeds.

As for cases resulting from earlier successions, a charter of 1158 × 65 records that the abbot of Reading had 'seised Roger of Letton of land at Hurstley which his grandfather had held and which he had deraigned against Robert of Brobury in our court at Reading'. The

---

[92] e.g. *Royal Writs in England from the Conquest to Glanvill*, ed. R. C. van Caenegem (Selden Soc. 77; 1958–9), Nos. 19, 25, see also Nos. 11, 16 (= *Regesta*, ii, Nos. 1201, 1685a); cf. *Glanvill*, xii. 8, Hall, 140. See Milsom, *Legal Framework*, 80–5. However, it is notable that some precursors of the writ *de recto* included the sheriff in their address, suggesting at least some supervision of the seignorial court; e.g. Van Caenegem, *Writs*, No. 6 (= *Regesta*, ii, No. 654), and also below, p. 279.

[93] D. Walker, 'Some Charters relating to St Peter's Abbey, Gloucester' in P. M. Barnes and C. F. Slade (edd.), *Stenton Miscellany* (PRS, NS 36; 1960), 259.

[94] See above, p. 73 on charters; for court rolls, e.g. *RCR*, i. 440–1.

[95] *CMA*, ii. 202.

case is particularly notable since Robert seems to have been the accepted tenant of the abbey for this land, possibly despite having taken the land from Roger's predecessor during Stephen's reign; the charter specifies that Roger is to hold for the same service as Robert was accustomed to render. The case thus shows that a lord was not irrevocably bound to his tenant against an outsider with a succession claim; there were other bases to title.[96]

However, in many of the recorded cases in lords' courts, the aspiring heir brought not simply a claim but a royal order to his lord. This preponderance may result partly from the nature of the sources: the production of a writ greatly increases the chance of our knowing of the case, be it through the writ itself or through other sources, notably chronicles, which drew on such documents. Very little can be said of the frequency of the use of such writs in the period before 1100, but some striking evidence comes from Henry I's reign. A case between Modbert and the priory of Bath concerning North Stoke surely could have been dealt with solely by a seignorial court. The claimant Modbert's case rested on his disputed nomination as heir by the previous tenant, Grenta. One might have expected that even if he was already in physical possession of the land, Modbert should have gone to his lord and requested his predecessor's lands. The lord would have refused the claim on the grounds that Grenta had not held hereditarily, and that would have been the end of the matter. In fact, the claimant looked to an outside authority and obtained a royal writ to Bishop John of Bath, as lord of the abbey's lands: 'I order that you seise Modbert justly of the land which Grenta of Stoke held, as he made him his heir during his life.' According to the Bath cartulary account, the bishop's court immediately latched on to the word

---

[96] *Reading Abbey Cartularies*, ed. B. R. Kemp (2 vols.; Camden Soc., 4th Ser. 31, 33; 1986, 1987), No. 349; see also from the first years of Henry II's reign e.g. *Charters and Documents illustrating the History of the Cathedral, City, and Diocese of Salisbury in the Twelfth and Thirteenth Centuries*, selected W. Rich Jones, ed. W. D. Macray (London, 1891), No. XX. In neither case is there evidence of the plaintiff bringing a royal writ, although in the second case note the royal confirmation, *Sarum Charters*, No. XXIX. Note further *Earldom of Hereford*, No. 15 (= Z. N. and C. N. L. Brooke, 'Hereford Cathedral Dignitaries in the Twelfth Century; Supplement', *CHJ* 8 (1944–6), 185), an agreement between Earl Roger of Hereford and his brother-in-law, William de Braose, datable to 1148 × 55. This contains a provision concerning claims quite possibly based on inheritance being made in a seignorial court. It seems to make a distinction between procedure in clear and in hard cases; in the former 'evident justice by testimony of my barons' led to automatic restoration, in the latter a more formal court hearing was required [*rectum ei . . . in curia mea tenebo*].

'justly'. The bishop told the court that he would obey the order, if the court decided it was just.[97]

The convent's case did not centre on the possibility of creating an heir to heritable lands, but on whether Grenta's tenure permitted succession. The prior held counsel with the monks and then addressed the court. The lands had been given to the monks' own use. Grenta, when dying, had refused advice to set an heir in his place by a testament, and the prior put a speech into Grenta's mouth: 'this is the inheritance of the servants of the Lord which I was allowed to hold in the manner of a stipend [*uice stipendii*] not by law of inheritance as long as I lived. Now dying, I leave myself with the land to the brothers to whom it rightly belongs.' Those who had witnessed these statements confirmed the prior's case. A charter of King Cynewulf was also produced and read out, complete with impressive witness list and awe-inspiring anathema clause.[98] This left the court divided and Modbert again claimed that he was Grenta's heir. He had married Grenta's daughter and been adopted [*adoptatus*] during Grenta's life as his son. He should inherit because Grenta had held not in farm but hereditarily.[99] The bishop asked those who were followers of neither party to decide the case. The men greater by birth or more experienced in law reached a decision and gave their judgment: he who called himself heir by right was to prove this claim by at least two witnesses, free and law-worthy men of the *familia* of the church, to be named on that day and produced in a week's time, or/and [*uel*] by a cirograph. If he failed to do either, 'let him not be heard further'. All agreed. The claimant was silent. The prior and the monks won their victory.

Overall, the case is a fascinating one for the history of inheritance. It involves not only the issue of the creation of an heir, but also—according to the successful party—a man seeking to turn a life-grant

[97] *Two Chartularies of the Priory of St Peter at Bath*, ed. W. Hunt (Somerset Rec. Soc. 7; 1893), Nos. 49–50; also *Regesta*, iii, No. 47; see also Van Caenegem, *Writs*, 274. Unfortunately it cannot be told how long the dispute had been running before Modbert brought the writ.

[98] Sawyer, No. 265. The charter is probably genuine.

[99] Had just the royal writ survived, we might have thought that Grenta had no heirs, or at least no children, and had therefore created an heir from outside his family. In fact we have a son-in-law claiming that he had been adopted. Did Grenta have other children, whom he was passing over in favour of Modbert? There is no evidence of this and *hereditare* again seems only to mean the special nomination of one who would have been heir anyway.

into hereditary tenure, and suggests considerable royal involvement even in minor disputes as early as the 1120s. Though an isolated example in our records, little else suggests that Modbert's case is exceptional. There is no sign that Modbert had any special link to the royal household or was a particularly rich or powerful man. There is no mention of extraordinary difficulties before he turned to the king, nor in obtaining a writ. The cost of the writs in the 1130 Pipe Roll is high compared with the later years of Henry II's reign, but this one must have been sufficiently cheap to be worth paying for in order to obtain the land. Modbert seems to have acted rather as a man might have sixty years later: when denied his claim, he sought a royal writ. The 1130 Pipe Roll, and other evidence, likewise shows Henry I involved in various kinds of disputes within honours. Thus Walter fitzOdo rendered account of £21 13s. 4d. 'for justice concerning his inheritance from the countess of Chester'.[100]

The situation under Stephen is unclear, but from 1153 or 1154, the need to settle disputes seems to have stimulated demand for writs and moved Henry II towards regular involvement in land cases.[101] Thus the case between Peter and the canons of St Paul's concerning lands pertaining to the manor of Wimbledon and Barnes saw the plaintiff bring a royal order to the lord's court.[102] The impetus need not all have been from the consumers: the king as supplier had advertised his promise that the disinherited should be restored, an invitation to request royal help.[103]

---

[100] *PR 31 HI*, 114; p. 88 also concerns inheritance within the honour, e.g. p. 33 may do so. For other interventions in the honour, see e.g. pp. 85, 123.

[101] *Ramsey Chronicle*, 273, a charter of 1134 × 60, takes into account the possibility of future royal action compelling a hearing in the abbot's court. No earlier Ramsey charter contains such a clause. Unfortunately one cannot be certain that the charter comes from Stephen's reign. For Stephen issuing a writ at the end of his reign, the case later going to the shire by royal order, see *CMA*, ii. 184.

[102] *Early Charters of the Cathedral Church of St Paul, London*, ed. M. Gibbs (Camden Soc., 3rd Ser. 58; 1939), No. 163; the word for order is *preceptum* which probably means writ. For another instance, this time between two related lay claimants, *Sarum Charters*, No. XXI.

[103] On the provision of the 1153 settlement laying down that the disinherited were to receive back their right, *Gesta Stephani*, 240; *Chronicles Stephen, Henry II, Richard I*, iv. 177; Palmer, 'Origins of Property', 8–13; P. R. Hyams, 'Warranty and Good Lordship in Twelfth Century England', *L&HR* 5 (1987), 497–503. Palmer, 'Origins of Property', 9, argues that the existing tenant was to hold for life, but at his death 'his heir would be denied in favor of an outside claimant whose ancestor had been tenant in fee in 1135 such that, in the normal course of things, he would have been regarded as heir'. However, the chronicles cited simply specify the restoration of the disinherited On the court roll evidence cited by Palmer, see Biancalana, 'Legal Reforms of Henry

A further form of royal involvement was the presence of not only a royal writ but also royal officials in the lord's court. No doubt benefiting from his connections, Bernard the king's scribe enjoyed the presence of royal justices in the court of the bishop of Exeter when in *c.*1121 × 30 he successfully

deraigned the land of Trecharl against the son of Elwius Gold to whom the bishop had given the land and who restored it to the bishop by the judgment of the bishop's court, and the bishop gave it to Bernard as his inheritance for a relief of four marks of silver.[104]

Other land cases also reveal that men other than the lord and barons might be present in a seignorial court.[105]

Royal involvement at the claimant's request could also take the form of the case being heard before a royal official, for example the sheriff in the county court, or in the king's court itself. Before 1100, the evidence concerning such hearings is again minimal. The Domesday inquest took place before many genealogical succession claims could arise.[106] Henry I, however, was considerably involved in succession disputes, at least in ecclesiastical honours. The king might become involved in the case at various stages, including after an initial judgment of the lord's court. Mary Cheney argues that 'in Henry I's time, there existed a customary procedure by which a case could be transferred from a lord's court to the jurisdiction of the king or a higher lord, upon a complaint of defect of justice, and also on complaint by a challenge (*wemming*) to unjust judgement', and Palmer agrees that there is much evidence of this practice 'when the lord held the land after the death of a tenant'.[107] The *Leges Henrici*

II', 469 n. 169. See also G. J. White, 'The Restoration of Order in England, 1153–65', Ph.D. thesis (Cambridge, 1974), esp. 79–89, 296–302.

[104] Round, 'Bernard, the King's Scribe', 421, No. 15. Mention of relief encourages me in taking such cases as explicitly concerning succession.

[105] See below, p. 279.

[106] One possible case is recorded in *Domesday*, i, fo. 373b. Note also the Domesday pleas based on the claim that an English *antecessor* had held; see esp. P. R. Hyams, '"No Register of Title": The Domesday Inquest and Land Adjudication', *A-NS* 9 (1987); G. S. Garnett, 'Coronation and Propaganda: Some Implications of the Norman Claim to the Throne of England in 1066'; *TRHS*, 5th Ser. 36 (1986). Such pleas often occurred in the shire court, before the royal commissioners.

[107] M. Cheney, 'A Decree of Henry II on Defect of Justice', in D. E. Greenway, C. Holdsworth, and J. Sayers (edd.), *Tradition and Change: Essays in Honour of Marjorie Chibnall* (Cambridge, 1985), 192: note that she seems to avoid the word tolt in her own discussion, although this discussion follows her summary of other historians' use of the word for pre-Henry II procedure; cf. Biancalana, 'Legal Reforms of Henry II',

reveal transfers of cases because of delay or denial of justice.[108]

The large number of Henry's servants must have stimulated royal involvement in land cases. Bernard the king's scribe had another of his claims to his grandfather's land heard in the county court of Devon.[109] Royal officials might enjoy special access to the king's support, whilst their opponents would often need royal help in order to restrain the official from perpetuating the case. A further Abingdon case illustrates Henry being drawn into a dispute because one party was a royal servant who turned to him in a matter otherwise internal to the honour.[110] Following a dispute, Abbot Reginald's son William had been permitted to keep the church of Marcham and some land at Garsington for life. When, a few years later, William felt himself close to death, he gave back the church and the land, and became a monk of Abingdon. However, in the vacancy following Abbot Faritius's, death in 1117, Simon the dispenser of Henry I took his claim to the king in Normandy. Simon suggested that, since he was a relation of William, the church of Marcham and the lands which William had had by Abbot Reginald's gift pertained to himself by hereditary right—this despite William's holding being limited to life and his subsequent quitclaim. According to the chronicler, Simon's sister was Reginald's niece. If she and Simon were full siblings, Simon was William's cousin. The chronicle does not specify this, if anything trying to make the relationship sound somewhat tenuous. We have already seen that lords did not always accept the claims of such distant heirs even when the predecessor had not held specifically for life. However, perhaps because of the vacancy, no one resisted the claim, and by the king's order Simon gained seisin of the land and church, and held them until Vincent became abbot in 1121.

459–61, P. A. Brand, '"Multis Vigiliis Excogitatam et Inventam": Henry II and the Creation of the English Common Law', *Haskins Society Journal*, 2 (1990), 218. The fact of the possibility of transfer seems more important than whether procedure in Henry I's reign was, or closely resembled, tolt. See also R. C. Palmer, *The County Courts of Medieval England, 1150–1350* (Princeton, NJ, 1982), 137, 144–5, 156, 298–9, cf. Palmer, 'The Feudal Framework of English Law', *Michigan Law Review*, 79 (1981), 1141–2.

[108] *Leges Henrici*, 9 4, 4a, 5; 10 1; 33; 59 19; Downer, 104–8, 136, 188. On removal of cases under Henry I, see also Biancalana, 'Legal Reforms of Henry II', 452–60.

[109] Round, 'Bernard, the King's Scribe', 422, No. 16; see also R. W. Southern, 'King Henry I', in his *Medieval Humanism and Other Studies* (Oxford, 1970), esp. pp. 226–7. On the number of royal servants, see Green, *Government*, esp. the biographical appendix.

[110] *CMA*, ii. 37, 130–1, 166–9.

Whether Simon had obtained any acceptance from the abbey and its tenants is uncertain. Vincent moved his claim in the king's court. This may suggest that Simon had turned to Henry for a royal favour, rather than simply as lord *in loco abbatis* during the vacancy. Otherwise the honour court might have dealt with the matter. Alternatively, the parties may have worked out a deal before coming to the royal court. Certainly there is no sign of a judgment and the two sides came to an agreement, described by the chronicler as a fine. Simon quitclaimed everything which he had held of the abbey's possessions before Vincent became abbot. The abbot, wishing to keep Simon, 'a good and prudent man', in his service, granted him the land in Garsington which he had held, 'in fee, that is to him and his heirs after him', and also the manor of Tadmarton in fee farm. Thus, even though the case originally concerned preventing succession, the abbot was prepared to make a hereditary grant in order to keep his tenant. Still, the abbot's control over the new grant was emphasized. It was laid down by common decree that if Simon or his heirs failed to pay the farm, the abbey could take back Tadmarton into demesne with no appeal allowed. Further ceremonies followed, including Simon's homage.

The 1130 Pipe Roll provides particularly significant evidence since it reveals the king involved in the affairs of a lay honour. William de Hotot owed twenty marks for justice [*pro recto*] concerning his father's lands from William d'Aubigny Brito, who was his lord.[111] Whether the payment was for a writ or for justice in a royal court is not clear. However, an ecclesiastical honour provides the strongest evidence for the regularity of Henry I's involvement. Many charters of St Mary's, York, state that the abbey would not provide exchanges in the event of the loss of the lands granted. In 1122 × *c*.1137, the abbey granted a messuage in Fossgate, which Richard Tortus had held of them, to Ougrim of 'Frisemareis' and his heirs to hold in fee: 'if any heir of Richard Tortus can acquire that messuage of land from the king or deraign it against us or the said Ougrim and his heirs, we will not give exchange.'[112] Charters, chronicles, and the Pipe Roll show us individual instances of claimants obtaining Henry's help. This charter suggests that lords expected disappointed claimants to do so, and modified their actions accordingly.

Evidence of Stephen or the empress and her son hearing succession

---

[111] *PR 31 HI*, 88.
[112] *EYC*, i, No. 310.

cases is much scarcer.[113] Certainly Stephen's court did hear cases of various sorts concerned with the internal affairs of honours, but the impression of reduced royal involvement during the troubles of his reign will be confirmed later in this section when we look at the other methods men used to regain their inheritances.

Royal hearing of cases revived under Henry II. For example, one of the final stages of the long-running dispute between Abingdon and the son and grandson of Henry I's dispenser was a judgment of Henry's court in favour of the abbey.[114] In addition, as Mary Cheney has shown, Henry II made it easier for claimants disappointed in their lords' courts to obtain a royal hearing.[115] According to Guernes's *Life of St Thomas*, a recent royal enactment laid down that:

If anyone pleads about land in the court of his lord, he should come with his supporters on the first appointed day, and if there is any delay in the case, he should go to the justice and make his complaint. Then he shall return to the lord's court with two oath helpers, and swear three-handed that the court has delayed in doing him full justice. By means of that oath, whether it is false or true, he shall be able to go to the court of the next higher lord, until he comes to the court of the king [*segnur suverain*].[116]

Lords, as well as claimants, requested royal help. In the case of Abingdon and Simon the dispenser, the claimant's turning to the king forced the lord to do likewise, in that of the Ramsey lands of Over, the lord may well have been the first to seek royal aid.[117] That

[113] *EYC*, iv, No. 118, another charter of St Mary's, York, this time of *c.*1137 × 61, specifies that no exchange will be given if the land is lost 'by force or by royal justice'. Even if the document is of Stephen's reign, it is less notable than the earlier example, since it may result from the reproduction of stock phrases.

[114] *CMA*, ii. 186–7; the case previously went to the shire by Henry's order.

[115] Cheney, 'Decree of Henry II', 'The Litigation between John Marshal and Archbishop Thomas Becket in 1164: A Pointer to the Origin of Novel Disseisin?', in J. A. Guy and H. G. Beale (edd.), *Law and Social Change in British History* (London, 1984), 9–26. The case between John Marshal and Becket which she discusses may have concerned inheritance. Howden alone states that John claimed it 'by hereditary right', which might indicate that John's father had held it, but the silence of the other writers may reflect their desire to show John's case as weak; *Chronica Magistri Rogeri de Hovedene*, ed. W. Stubbs (4 vols.; London, 1868–71), i. 224. Although John is not a typical tenant, being marshal in the royal household, the story does well illustrate the problems that could be caused for any lord by a man who could look to the king for justice.

[116] M. Cheney translation of Guernes de Pont-Sainte-Maxence, *La Vie de Saint Thomas Becket*, ed. E. Walberg (Paris, 1936), ll. 1401–10. On the enactment being recent, see *MTB*, iv. 40–1. See also Biancalana, 'Legal Reforms of Henry II', 460–5.

[117] See above, pp. 138, 99 respectively. Also e.g. *PR 31 HI*, 53, concerning Hasculf de Tany may involve a lord seeking royal support in a succession dispute. Writs for the

a lord turned to the king suggests that he needed help in controlling his honour, and such practices were almost certainly not restricted to churches. Royal involvement was a matter of power as well as of jurisdiction or the logic of land-holding.

Kings were thus extensively and influentially involved in succession cases. Nevertheless, it must still be remembered that even under Henry I and Henry II, royal involvement might be of limited effect. Henry I adjudged and later confirmed Over to Ramsey Abbey, but it passed from their demesne again, possibly before his death and by his influence. Nor did Henry II's involvement bring a decisive end to the dispute. During periods of extensive royal involvement, lords had to take the king very much into consideration in their actions, but having done so, they might still seek their own ends even against the royal will.

Cases were sometimes taken to courts other than those of the king or the lord of whom the claim was being made. Overlords might become involved either from the start of a dispute, or following what the claimant saw as default of justice in the court of his immediate lord. The possible need for such intervention may be one reason why some donees obtained confirmations of their lands from their overlords.[118] Early evidence is scarce, but a Tosny charter probably of 1102 × 26 suggests that hearings in overlords' courts did occur: 'in my presence [*coram me*], Richard of Porton gave back to Richard of Necton the land which was Bunde his grandfather's and Adam his father's, for him and his heirs ... by hereditary right [*hereditarie iure*].'[119] Perhaps the regrant was a simple one, although notably in the overlord's presence. Richard of Porton may have had no court and hence sought the publicity provided by his overlord's. However, the production of a charter for a simple regrant would be surprising at this early date. Perhaps Richard of Necton had looked to Ralph for justice against Richard of Porton. A royal charter worded in a similar fashion and emphasizing that the transaction occurred *coram me* would suggest just such a resort to higher authority by the claimant. If this argument is acceptable, evidence for overlords' courts is more plentiful than some have thought. It may well be that a lord's court

resumption of their demesnes helped churches to reclaim lands originally granted for life but which had been retained by the grantees' heirs; see below, Ch. 8.

[118] See below, Ch. 7.

[119] *Beauchamp Cartulary: Charters 1100–1268*, ed. E. Mason (PRS, NS 43; 1980), No. 355.

sometimes dealt with business not just between himself and his vassals but also between his vassals and their tenants.[120] *Glanvill*'s express prohibition against writs of right being addressed to the overlord, rather than the lord of whom the demandant claimed to hold, surely indicates that overlords were in fact becoming involved in cases, at royal command, during the reign of Henry II.[121]

As for requests that overlords hear claims that an intermediate lord's court had failed to do justice, the 'constitution' on the transfer of cases early in Henry II's reign certainly allowed overlords' courts to such hear cases.[122] Probably in 1162 × 3, John of Burgh brought a writ to the court of John de St Clair, a tenant of the archbishop of Canterbury, seeking a hide of land in Burgh against Gilbert of Preston. He then went to the county court and stated that John de St Clair's court had failed to do him justice. The archbishop's seneschal also arrived, and sought the case for his master's court. There, the parties prepared for a duel concerning that hide and another in the vill of Preston, but before they could fight, they were brought to agreement through the licence of the court. Gilbert recognized both hides to be John's right and inheritance. John granted him the hide in Burgh for life and gave him twenty marks.[123]

In France, locally dominant magnates were crucially involved in succession cases.[124] One notable piece of evidence suggests that they had some part to play in England too, at least in the late eleventh century. The first witnesses of a *priuilegium* by which Roger de Lacy received Holme Lacy were the earl of Shrewsbury, his sons Hugh

---

[120] See also above, n. 98, where the earl of Hereford seems to be offering justice to William de Braose's men. See above, pp. 35–6, for further comments on overlords' involvement in disputes.

[121] *Glanvill*, xii. 8, Hall, 140. See N. Hurnard, 'Magna Carta, Clause 34', in R. W. Hunt *et al.*, *Studies in Medieval History Presented to F. M. Powicke* (Oxford, 1948), 160–1.

[122] See above, p. 139.

[123] *CRR*, iv. 264–5. Hurnard, 'MC 34', 162, argued that the actions of the archbishops of Canterbury may have been exceptional, and certainly similar procedure was later seen as the result of franchisal privileges which gave the archbishop full power to hear cases which would otherwise have gone to the county. However, for this period, she did not take into account either the 'constitution' on default of justice, or some of the earlier evidence for the actions of overlords' courts.

[124] See e.g. G. Duby, 'The Evolution of Judicial Institutions', in his *The Chivalrous Society*, tr. C. Postan (London, 1977), 15–58; F. L. Cheyette, 'Suum Cuique Tribuere', *French Historical Studies*, 6 (1970), esp. 291–3; White, 'Inheritances and Legal Arguments', 67.

and Everard, and his countess, Adeliza.[125] There followed some of
the earl's men, including his sheriff and constable. Roger de Lacy
was one of the earl's vassals, and perhaps the earl had been the most
powerful of the 'friends' who persuaded the bishop to make the grant
to Roger. Probably, though, the earl witnessed as the dominant lord
of the area. Possibly the settlement was made in the earl's court. At
the very least, his witnessing must have constituted a promise to help
enforce the agreement. His or his descendants' power was likely to
influence any dispute arising from the grant. On other occasions, the
court of a locally prestigious lord may have been the place for
mediation.[126]

Under Stephen, churchmen increasingly turned to ecclesiastical
authorities instead of the king during succession disputes. Most
importantly churches turned to the Pope. The abbot of Ramsey's
attempts to regain Over had rested on the king until Henry I's death,
but thereafter he looked to the Pope.[127] This reflected not only royal
weakness but also increasing papal influence. It is therefore unsur-
prising that churches continued to look to the Pope under Henry II,
especially when the king was not showing them favour. Matthew
Paris preserved a plausible account of a dispute early in the reign.[128]
It again starts with a life-grant, by Abbot Paul of St Albans to Peter
de Valognes, in 1077 × 93. The wood concerned, Northaw, was later
given in turn to Peter's son and grandson for life. The grandson,
Peter II, confessed as he was dying that his predecessors had not held
hereditarily, and at his death Abbot Robert repossessed the wood.
However, some men believed that Peter's brother and heir Robert
had a hereditary right to the land. Robert's claim was repeatedly
refused by the abbot, so he obtained a writ from Henry II, which
prohibited 'that anyone be permitted to take away from him unjustly
anything which Robert's ancestors had possessed hereditarily according to justice'. The abbot refused to answer in person before the
justiciar and Robert was given possession. The abbot then obtained

---

[125] Galbraith, 'Episcopal Land-Grant', 359–60, 372.
[126] *Stoke by Clare Cartulary*, ed. C. Harper-Bill and R. Mortimer (3 vols.; Suffolk
Charters, 4–6; 1982–4), No. 165 may be one such instance from the late 12th cent.
[127] See above, pp. 99–100; also M. G. Cheney, 'The Compromise of Avranches of
1172 and the Spread of Canon Law in England', *EHR* 56 (1941), 177–80.
[128] The story is printed in *Gesta Abbatum Monasterii Sancti Albani*, ed. H. T. Riley
(3 vols.; London, 1867–9), i. 63, 159–66; *CRR*, i. 116, 178, 291, record a later
dispute concerning the wood. On Matthew's 12th-cent. source, see R. Vaughan,
Matthew Paris (Cambridge, 1958), 182–3.

letters from Queen Eleanor and the Pope. The latter stated that Robert held the wood 'against justice' and ordered his excommunication. However, the prelates addressed feared to offend the king by excommunicating a tenant in chief, and the abbot had to turn again to Henry before at last getting a royal judgment in the abbey's favour. The case thus shows that if the Pope originally became involved in succession cases as a substitute for the king under Stephen, he remained involved as an additional weapon under Henry II. Again one can see the variety of strategies open to parties in disputes at any one time.

Scholars writing on the development of inheritance have generally concentrated on the role of the honorial and royal courts. I have just examined the part other lords' courts and the Pope might play, but in addition much business took place outside courts. Some campaigned at length to regain their inheritances. When we turn from successions following soon after the death of a vassal to restorations resulting from longer running disputes and claims, we again see good service being used to back claims, and also the effect of more general political considerations. Some had their inheritances restored in reward for loyal service,[129] and indeed on occasion such restoration seems to have been the specific aim of the one serving. Thus whilst his particular concern was heirs seeking to get back lands their parents had forfeited, it is notable that St Anselm when preaching used the image of princes having at their courts soldiers 'who labour with unbroken fortitude to obey his will for the sake of receiving back again an inheritance of which they bewail the loss . . .'.[130]

---

[129] e.g. following the death of Roger de Bully at the end of the 11th cent., the honour of Tickhill remained in royal hands until Stephen accepted John count of Eu's claim to it, doubtless because the count was a valuable supporter; Holt, 'Politics and Property', 52. In 1140, anxious to pressure his enemies in the Marches, Stephen granted Robert earl of Leicester the earldom of Hereford, Robert's wife being the great niece of Roger earl of Hereford who had forfeited in 1075; Holt, 'Politics and Property', 22 n. 99; Crouch, *Beaumont Twins*, 48–9, 87. See also e.g. Hollister, 'Misfortunes of the Mandevilles'. For a debate on the importance of the succession claims behind such grants, see E. King, 'The Tenurial Crisis of the Early Twelfth Century', *P&P* 65 (1974), 110–17, and Holt, 'Politics and Property in Early Medieval England: A Rejoinder', *P&P* 65 (1974), 127–8.

[130] Eadmer, *Vita Anselmi*, ed. and tr. R. W. Southern (2nd edn., Oxford, 1972), 94; see also p. 95. On such 'feudal imagery', see Southern, *Saint Anselm: A Portrait in a Landscape* (Cambridge, 1990), 221–7. For the effect of politics and good service on a dispute where one party was seeking to regain lands forfeited by a predecessor, the other to maintain a claim based on the subsequent grant of the lands to their

The threat or use of force was a further option. This might occur
between claimant and lord. Often an aspiring heir would already have
had effective control of the land, and would refuse to surrender it if
his claim was refused. This occurred in the disputes over the lands
which Robert fitzRoger held of Abingdon and over the barony and
castle of Bedford early in Stephen's reign.[131] Or an heir might take
advantage of a period of weak lordship, for example a vacancy in a
church lordship, to seize the land from his lord.[132] In other disputes,
a man with a relatively weak claim could enter the land and seek to
maintain his hold on it against a rival claimant rather than against the
lord. A royal plea roll case of 1208 tells of how, during Stephen's
reign, sometime after the death of Osbert son of Colegrim, Osbert's
younger son John intruded himself into all the lands which rightly
belonged to the elder son, Alexander.[133] Here we have trouble within
a family, but on occasion an heir might lose out to the violence of one
with little if any genealogical claim to the land. Probably in the mid-
1170s, Richard de Clare wrote to six of his beloved men who had
been ordered to swear before the king's justices that they had seen
Stephen Dammartin seised of the land of Pitley as of fee and inheritance. He informed them that he had learnt the truth about this
matter from older men. Stephen, while he was steward and master of
all Earl Gilbert's lands, had occupied 'unjustly and against reason'
the land which had belonged to William the reeve of Bardfield and
his heirs. He had cruelly and unjustly had one of William's sons
killed since he knew him to be 'closer . . . to his father's inheritance
with regard to possessing that land'.[134] In this case, notably, the lord

predecessor, see the long-running conflict between Robert de Stuteville III and Roger
de Mowbray during the mid-12th cent.; *Monasticon Anglicanum*, ed. W. Dugdale (6
vols. in 8; London, 1817–30), v. 351b–352a—discussed by A. Gransden, *Historical
Writing in England c.550 to c.1307* (London, 1974), 290–1, *Mowbray*, pp. xx, xxviii–
xxxi, *EYC*, ix, Nos. 19, 42–4, *Red Book*, i. 419–20; Hudson, 'Legal Aspects of
Seignorial Control of Land in the Century after the Norman Conquest', D.Phil. thesis
(Oxford, 1988), 144–6.

[131] See above, pp. 132, 117.

[132] A. Saltman, *Theobald, Archbishop of Canterbury* (London, 1956), No. 44; despite
the next archbishop's efforts and royal intervention, the claimant's family were to
regain control of the lands and hold them for the next two and a half centuries: A. E.
Conway, 'The Owners of Allington Castle, Maidstone (1086–1279)', *Archaeologia
Cantiana*, 29 (1911), 12–13.

[133] *CRR*, v. 181–2, vi. 17–18; *EYC*, v. 256–7; for the identification of the family,
see also Clay and Greenway (edd.), *Early Yorkshire Families*, 46–7. See also below, n.
146, for a later stage of the dispute.

[134] *Stoke*, No. 50 (= Stenton, *First Century*, No. 21); see Stenton, *First Century*,

may well initially have benefited from the use of violence by one of his men.

An heir might also turn to others to support his claim. Such help might involve peaceful urging of the lord and his court. A charter of *c.*1160 × 70 records that William son of Siward and his heirs granted William son of Swetin the lands his father had held in Henry I's time and after. This was done 'by the request and grant of William fitzRalph'. Swetin had probably been a moneyer and a William fitzRalph certainly was, so William son of Swetin appears to have profited through the professional or amicable connection.[135] At other times the urging was less peaceful. When the father of Robert, the knight of Abingdon mentioned above, died, Abbot Ingulf had seized certain lands he had held for life. However, Ingulf kept them for only four years before, worn down by the demands of Robert and his friends and afraid of their strength in war, he leased them to Robert.[136] This case comes from Stephen's reign, in which we see other men seeking help simply to seize their inheritances. This is one major concern of the treaties between magnates. In 1141 × 3, Robert earl of Gloucester promised Miles earl of Hereford aid in maintaining his current possessions and dues of all kinds 'and in acquiring his inheritances which he does not now have'.[137] Nor was it only the greatest magnates who made such agreements. Roger of Benniworth and Peter of Goxhill joined to seek the inheritance which had been Odo of Benniworth's.[138] There is no sign that Peter had any hereditary claim to a share in the fee, and Roger apparently was offering land in return for money and physical support.

Were such alliances, together with violence, used in England to any significant extent only under Stephen? The scarcity of evidence before 1100 and the comparative abundance from the mid-twelfth century may exaggerate the relative level of disorder under Stephen. The written treaties provide a unique kind of record, while similar

82–3. *Stoke*, Nos. 538 and 539 record Gilbert son of Stephen Dammartin's grant of the land to Stoke, No. 540 a quitclaim by a surviving son of William of his inheritance of Pitley which Gilbert had given to Stoke.

[135] *Facsimiles of Early Charters in Oxford Muniment Rooms*, ed. H. E. Salter (Oxford, 1929), No. 84. See also e.g. Galbraith, 'Episcopal Land-Grant', 372, where the claimant came to the lord's court accompanied by his friends.

[136] *CMA*, ii. 200–1; see above, p. 132.

[137] *Earldom of Gloucester*, No. 95.

[138] Stenton, *First Century*, No. 6. *Danelaw Documents*, No. 474 has Roger and Peter as joint addressees.

oral agreements could have been common earlier. Perhaps Hamo Pecche with the help of his friends forcibly resisted the abbot of Ramsey's attempts to repossess Over late in Henry I's reign.[139] However, Orderic's anecdotes strongly suggest that violence and alliances were a more regular part of continental succession disputes early in the twelfth century than of English ones. Most notable is the strategy adopted against Henry I by William de Roumare following the rejection of his claim to what he regarded as his inheritance in Normandy and England. According to Orderic, when William made his initial request,

the king, far from acceding to the petition, gave him a scornful answer. The young man therefore immediately crossed to Normandy in anger and, seizing a favourable moment, withdrew from his allegiance to the king and waged a bitter war against the Normans, relying on the help of many men from Neufmarché.[140]

From England, we have no such evidence of revolt and alliance designed to obtain an inheritance from Henry I. The very conditions of the civil war of Stephen's reign created the need for such alliances. Under Henry I, a Roger of Benniworth might have been able to regain his inheritance by other means, be it through the king or the peaceful help of others. At least as far as the twelfth century is concerned, Stephen's reign was unusual in the importance of physical threat and action in disputes.

In addition to these still visible types of action, there must have been much negotiation, both within and outside court, which is now hidden from us. Such negotiation might lead to an agreement. Rearrangements of inheritances occasionally occurred in a seignorial court, for example the famous instance involving Henry and Sewall sons of Fulcher in the court of William, earl Ferrers.[141] Some agreements might prove at least temporarily more satisfactory for the immediate parties than for others closely involved. The Countess Lucy's surrender of her inheritance to Henry I when she married the earl of Chester resulted in the rebellion of her son by a previous marriage, William de Roumare. Other agreements arose directly

---

[139] See above, p. 99.

[140] Orderic, vi. 332–4; for private war not existing in England, vi. 18.

[141] Stenton, *First Century*, No. 7, and pp. 51–3; note the importance of this case and Stenton's conclusions for Milsom's view of the seignorial world, e.g. *Legal Framework*, 107 n. 3.

from disputes, and it is notable that several of the cases which I have considered ended with some sort of compromise, rather than a decision entirely in favour of one side. A disappointed party might receive an exchange, or at least a payment; the disputed lands might be shared; or they might eventually be given to a church.[142]

Compromises resulted in part from an ideal commitment to settlement by 'Love' rather than 'Law'.[143] In addition, some must have been caused by the relative power of the parties concerned. Were they also the result of the nature of judicial authority and of the norms which affected succession? From French evidence it has been argued that compromises were very frequent and stemmed in part from the weakness of judicial authority.[144] Conclusions are necessarily impressionistic, the evidence unsatisfactory, but quite clear-cut decisions seem rather more usual in England. One cause may be the range of authorities to whom disputes in England might be brought. As for the effect of the nature of succession norms, different types of compromise need to be distinguished. In some, for example, they simply provide limited compensation for the disappointed, and need not imply any ambiguity in succession norms. However, there were also those which stemmed from hard cases. Thus there is no sign that the death of a tenant with a son as clear heir was often followed by compromise. In contrast, the case of a woman's inheritance might become very complicated if she married several times, and such cases did produce agreements and rearrangements of lands.[145] Similarly, the practical difficulties of settling some of the mass of complex cases

---

[142] See above, pp. 132, 114, 128 respectively.

[143] See e.g. *Leges Henrici*, 49 5a, Downer, 164; M. T. Clanchy, 'Law and Love in the Middle Ages', in J. Bossy (ed.), *Disputes and Settlements: Law and Human Relations in the West* (Cambridge, 1983), 47–67. See *Mowbray*, No. 109 for a settlement of a case with a long history which emphasizes the concord of the parties. Note also *English Lawsuits from William I to Richard I*, ed. R. C. van Caenegem (2 vols.; Selden Soc. 106, 107; 1990–1), No. 423, for two ex-parte accounts of a settlement of a long-running dispute—not concerning inheritance—each of which presents their party as the more successful.

[144] See e.g. S. D. White, '"Pactum . . . Legem Vincit et Amor Iudicium": The Settlement of Disputes by Compromise in Eleventh-Century Western France', *AJLegH* 22 (1978), 281–308, 'Inheritances and Legal Arguments', esp. 69 n. 82.

[145] e.g. see Sanders, *Baronies*, Bolingbroke, *CP*, vii. 667–75, 743–6 on the Countess Lucy's inheritance; also *CP*, ix. 578 n. c, for a marriage which 'may have been arranged to settle rival claims'. Note also the use of marriage as a way of legitimizing succession after a break in the descent through the male line of the woman's family: Holt, 'Politics and Property', 22 nn. 99, 31, 'Heiress', 4 n. 7; Searle, 'Women'.

arising from Stephen's reign produced compromises.[146] In all such cases, political and other considerations might become important. Again we must conclude that norms were clear for many cases, but that in some areas the norms were not sufficiently strong to produce decisive and consistent results.

CONCLUSIONS

It is now time to draw general conclusions. Throughout the century after the Conquest, at least lay lords and tenants were generally content to accept succession particularly of eldest sons. Moreover, I have also argued that the position of the heir clarified and strengthened during this period. One element was increased royal involvement in succession disputes, not simply in order to make the feudal courts work within their own terms, but in order to maintain the peace and also to extend royal power.[147] However, other factors were also involved. I have examined both the language of charters and the practice of succession in order to map these developments. I have found that, outside periods of political disturbance and perhaps the initial settlement of the country, succession was normal for the closer heirs. Whilst descent norms also favoured the succession of more distant heirs, their position was more likely to be influenced by other factors. There is little sign of familial, regional, or honorial variation in succession norms. In addition to the complexity of land distribution, this can be explained by the variety of external influences which could affect succession cases. Such influences also helped to ensure that a disappointed claimant might reverse a lord's decision. An heir was seen as having a certain right to the land; the personal relationship of lord and tenant was not the sole element in landholding.

As for a more precise chronology, all conclusions for the period before 1100 must be very tentative, but the conquerors of England in 1066 were familiar with customary succession. The emphasis which churches in their charters laid upon life-grants reveals that they feared succession would normally take place. Moreover, whatever its

---

[146] The case cited above, n. 133, ended in compromise in the court of Richmond at Boston. One party quitclaimed the disputed land to the other, and received lands in exchange.
[147] Cf. Milsom, *Legal Framework*, esp. pp. 1–8, 183–6.

precise purposes, it seems most unlikely that the compilation of Domesday Book would have been considered worth while if lordly discretion, from the king downwards, was likely soon to render its list of land-holders obsolete. Turning to royal enforcement, the regimes of William I and II clearly were capable of extraordinary exertions. Whether they were regularly involved in the affairs of honours is unclear. The *priuilegium* concerning Holme Lacy suggests that men in certain areas sometimes looked to the greatest figures of the region rather than the king. Henry I's Coronation Charter suggests that Rufus and probably other lords had been using discretion with regard to succession, and that such activity might be considered wrong.

If one concludes that until 1100 the situation may have involved elements of flexibility and lordly discretion, by the end of Henry I's reign a significant shift had occurred. Already the language recording regrants of a decedent's lands to his heir does not suggest that the grant amounted to a new gift. By the 1130s, an increasing proportion of the growing number of charters recording grants to laymen use inheritance language. This reflects partly an increased use of writing, partly a greater concern with succession. At the same time, notions of land-holding were growing more precise and more abstract. Such circumstances limited a lord's discretion at the death of a tenant, and may also have increased the chances of a disappointed claimant or his heirs later remedying a past decision.[148]

There is sufficient evidence to suggest that cases were often heard in an honorial court during Henry's reign, whether that of the lord immediately concerned or of an overlord. However, the evidence for extensive royal involvement is also quite strong, particularly in the latter years of the reign and for ecclesiastical honours. The king was not always impartial, not an automatic 'external enforcement agency'. He could support men, for example his officials, who were making claims of their lords which he might well have rejected had they been made concerning lands held directly of him. However, royal involvement overall almost certainly did work towards conformity. Those who felt that they had suffered injustice turned to the king and his officials, as did some lords when faced with difficult vassals. Men with fairly minor claims obtained royal writs. Henry I was sufficiently involved in the internal affairs of at least ecclesiastical honours for

---

[148] See above, p. 8 n. 28, on law and fact; also White, 'Inheritances and Legal Arguments', 100–1.

some lords to modify their actions. If this does not constitute a
regular external enforcement authority, it still creates a situation far
from purely personal politics within autonomous honours.

Such a chronology restricts the importance of Stephen's reign in
the development of inheritance. Certainly political struggle threatened
the practice of succession. At least for extensive periods and in
many regions, royal authority was less effective than under Henry I.
Churches which had previously relied on the king turned to the Pope.
The sources may distort the level of violence compared with other
reigns, but men do seem to have relied on force far more than
in Henry I's England. However, there is no sign that notions of
the correctness of succession declined. Political uncertainty could
encourage men to obtain written promises that grants were heritable.

Under Henry II, the practice of succession became more stable
again, and royal power was reasserted. The problem of sorting out
disputes from Stephen's reign produced royal involvement on a probably unprecedented scale.[149] The settlement of disputes thereafter
must have given potential claimants a growing impression that unfavourable events or decisions affecting succession were remediable,
often through royal action.

Given this chronology, why did such developments occur? The
conclusions necessarily resemble those already given concerning
security of tenure. First, there are the notions of secure succession
brought by the Normans to England. Indeed, Holt has suggested that
whereas succession in early Anglo-Norman England may have been
viewed as a seignorial concession, in pre-Conquest Normandy 'it was
more like a primordial right over which, in time, the dukes came to
exercise superiority'.[150] It is arguable that the stronger view of the
right to succeed continued, perhaps in modified form, as one of those
held by aspiring heirs as opposed to lords. However, here it must
again be asserted that the interests of lord and heir often coincided,
and the lord would be very willing to accept his new vassal. Had
every succession been a struggle, the development of inheritance
would have been much more difficult.

Secondly, as the Normans remained in England, the cumulative
effects of lasting tenure of pieces of land became important. Land-
holding was not regarded as being based solely on a relationship

---

[149] Whether the restoration of order began before Henry II's accession remains a
moot point; for one case datable precisely to 1153 × 4, see *Regesta*, iii, Nos. 129–31.
[150] J. C. Holt, 'Notions of Patrimony', *TRHS*, 5th Ser. 33 (1983), 199.

between lord and man. Families felt considerable attachment to 'their' land, and such attachment no doubt grew with time.[151] It is reflected most clearly in the widespread and increasing use of toponymic surnames.[152] There are also a few instances where inheritance language is applied to the land itself, rather than to the relation of grantee and heirs to lord and heirs.[153] Moreover, a tenant's control of his inheritance was stronger *vis-à-vis* his lord than was his control of his acquisitions.[154] Each succession would strengthen future heirs' claims. The connotations of the very word *hereditas* were forward- as well as backward-looking. The attitudes expressed in these various ways would not have been ignored by courts. They must greatly have reinforced the family's current and future hold on the land.

Thirdly, I have also argued that other changes in thought encouraged the development of inheritance. Ways of land-holding were contrasted with one another. For lay land-holding, the important contrast in terms of permanence was between life-grants and those which were potentially heritable. If the 'abstract rules of law' which later governed Common Law inheritance were not yet fully in existence, there certainly were norms of land-holding which affected all successions and disputes.

A further stimulus for thought concerning land-holding may have been the very Conquest and settlement, and these also help to explain the strength within the family of the lineal descendants' claims, particularly those of the eldest son. This linearity of the family in part derives from patterns which had developed in pre-Conquest Normandy.[155] However, in England after 1066, the colonial situation, where individuals had received new lands in return for their help in Conquest, where acquisitions continued to make it relatively easy for younger sons to establish junior lines, favoured the development of the linear family. Lineal descendants and siblings were also those

---

[151] See A. Gurevic, 'Représentations et attitudes à l'égard de la propriété pendant le Haut Moyen Âge', *Annales ESC* 27 (1972). Cf. Milsom, *Legal Framework*, 37, on the lack of relevance of possessives; see also above, p. 60.

[152] J. C. Holt, *What's in a Name? Family Nomenclature and the Norman Conquest* (University of Reading, 1982).

[153] e.g. Orderic, ii. 260; *Ramsey Chronicle*, 262–3; *Sir Christopher Hatton's Book of Seals*, ed. L. C. Loyd and D. M. Stenton (Northants Rec. Soc. and Oxford, 1950), No. 50; also William of Malmesbury, *De Gestis Regum Anglorum*, ed. W. Stubbs (2 vols.; London, 1887–9), ii. 294 on Count Alan of Brittany.

[154] See above, p. 60, below, p. 209.

[155] D. Bates, *Normandy Before 1066* (London, 1982), 111–21.

most likely to participate in transfers of land, and such too were the
strongest bonds in political relationships.[156]

Fourthly, there is the relative power of lord and vassal. When faced
with an heir unwilling to leave his predecessor's land for which his
claim had been rejected, the threat of exerting physical power must
have been a vital weapon. The same threat might also have deterred
the claimant who considered seeking outside, perhaps royal, help.
However, by 1135, the king was certainly involved in succession
cases within ecclesiastical honours. This perhaps reflects ecclesiastical
lords' unwillingness and inability to enforce their will physically upon
recalcitrant claimants. Ecclesiastical lords were not necessarily pacific
men, much evidence exists to the contrary, but they may have been
more reluctant than laymen to use force and not have maintained the
large military household which a lay lord would have seen as a vital
sign of his power. Nevertheless, the relative strength of lord and
vassal varied not only according to whether the lord was a cleric or a
layman. We have seen claimants benefit from their position as royal
office-holders. A claimant with a royal confirmation of a grant to his
ancestor and the ancestor's heirs was surely in a good position to
obtain royal support, and at least written confirmations of this type
were growing increasingly common under Henry I and II.[157] Or the
claimant might have another powerful lord who would support him in
a dispute. Weak lords, or ones facing particularly powerful vassals,
might also turn to the king. And if they acted thus, might not any lord
do likewise, if he felt he could rely on royal favour, and wished to
bring every possible force into winning a succession dispute?[158] In
addition, as I have already suggested, social change may have shifted

---

[156] See Holt, 'Revolution of 1066', 'Patronage and Politics', *TRHS*, 5th Ser. 34
(1984), *What's in a Name?*; below, Ch. 6.

[157] See e.g. *Regesta*, ii, Nos. 1268, 1603, 1722, 1758, 1778; iii, Nos. 412–41; Henry
II: *Cartae Antiquae, 1–10*, ed. L. Landor (PRS, NS 17; 1939), No. 141, Cartae
Antiquae, Roll 29, m. 1, No. 15 (photo courtesy Prof. Holt), *CPR, 1354–8*, 316,
1461–7, 306, *Recueil*, Nos. CLXIV, CCLXXIII, *CChR*, ii. 137, Staffs. Record Office,
D. 986/16 (photo courtesy Prof. Holt), Bodleian Library, MS Dugdale 12, p. 133;
Henry II's confirmation to Lewin chamberlain of the earl of Gloucester ended that no
one was to harm him 'since he and his heirs and all his lands and possessions are in my
own custody and protection', *The Great Chartulary of Glastonbury*, ed. A. Watkin (3
vols.; Somerset Rec. Soc. 59, 63, 64; 1947–56), ii. 551–2. Note the stimulating ideas
of A. Harding, 'Medieval Brieves of Protection and the Development of the Common
Law', *Juridical Review*, NS 11 (1966), 115–49.

[158] See e.g. *PR 31 HI*, 29 for an entry which might well concern a lord seeking help
against tenants claiming land by hereditary right.

the balance of power towards the tenant: by weakening seignorial control, it may have furthered the move towards inheritance.

Historians agree that in terms of the descent of lands, customary succession patterns in the eleventh and twelfth centuries may not have differed greatly from those under Common Law in the thirteenth. However, the phrase 'customary succession' can give too static a view of the situation before the Angevin reforms. If it took regular royal enforcement finally to bring into existence inheritance according to strict rules, various forces, including royal involvement, were already working in the same direction during the century after 1066. Areas of uncertainty remained, but succession in many circumstances was not only normal but liable to be enforced. The change thereafter is better seen as a mental and practical process of extension and hardening, rather than as a transformation.

PART III

ALIENABILITY

5

The Securing of Grants

THE previous two chapters analysed the strategies which donors and donees adopted to ensure or prevent succession. They illustrated one of the major problems facing land-holders: how to make a grant secure and lasting, despite death inevitably preventing continued personal involvement. I now examine further aspects of this problem. I shall concentrate in following chapters upon participation in alienation, upon consent and confirmation by heirs—succeeding, expectant, or potential—, lords, and ecclesiastical chapters. First, however, I briefly examine some other, often related, modes of assuring the security of grants. As ever, one is faced with limited materials which need not give a typical, let alone a complete set of transactions and ceremonies, and which provide only a much processed view of procedures.[1] Yet despite the problems of evidence, one can make certain general points about these various modes of assurance. By providing publicity, they sought to prevent challenges to the grant, by the immediate parties, their heirs, other successors, or outsiders, who might claim either that no gift had been made, or that it was not binding upon them. In addition, whilst I concentrate on their importance with regard to land-holding, it must be remembered that the modes of assurance were concerned not only with legal control of land or with economic transactions, but also with social and spiritual relations. Giving and receiving might establish, define, reinforce relationships between all the parties involved in the grant: grantor, grantee, kin present, past, and future, and—in the case of gifts to the Church—God and saints.

In this chapter, I look at witnessing, ceremonies, countergifts, and penalties for infringement of the grant. This list is not exhaustive.

---

[1] Cf. analysis based upon longer, less formulaic, French documents: e.g. the accumulation of ceremonies listed by S. D. White, *Custom, Kinship, and Gifts to Saints* (Chapel Hill, NC, 1988), 31–2, or E. Z. Tabuteau, *Transfers of Property in Eleventh-Century Norman Law* (Chapel Hill, NC, 1988), 135–40 on oaths and speeches. In a few cases, other evidence allows us to see that a charter has excluded a relevant point; see below, n. 42.

For example, occasionally, indeed rarely compared with some areas of the Continent, sureties or pledges were given for the fulfilment of the terms.[2] More importantly, negotiations before a grant was finally made, the *prelocutio*, could be of considerable consequence.[3] In *c.*1145 Roger de Valognes confirmed a gift by his kinsman Walter to Binham Priory. His charter stated that

I have done this at the advice and with the approval of many wise men, moved especially by the exhortation, prayers, and counsel of the lord Theobald, archbishop of Canterbury and primate of all England, who showed me by most reasonable and unanswerable arguments that a noble and generous man who has the fee of six knights should give not only the third part of a knight's land to God and the Holy Church for the health of his and his kin's souls, but the whole of a knight's land or more . . .[4]

Unfortunately most charters are uninterested in recording such negotiations.

Men also made speeches announcing the reasons for their gifts, and demanding their future maintenance.[5] They often swore on holy books to maintain their grants.[6] On occasion, they pledged their faith in the presence of a third party, a ceremony which is most commonly mentioned by charters from eastern England.[7] In addition, donors'

---

[2] e.g. *Formulare Anglicanum*, ed. T. Madox (London, 1702), No. II, *Regesta*, iii, Nos. 491, 492; see also *EYC*, v, No. 228. Note hostages as guarantees in the treaties and in other grants during Stephen's reign; F. M. Stenton, *The First Century of English Feudalism, 1066–1166* (2nd edn., Oxford, 1961), No. 48, *Regesta*, iii, Nos. 275, 634. The prevalence of these practices in Stephen's reign may suggest a breakdown in the otherwise more usual ways of assuring gifts. For the Continent, see Tabuteau, *Transfers of Property*, 163–9; White, *Gifts to Saints*, 36; W. Davies, 'Suretyship in the *Cartulaire de Redon*', in T. M. Charles-Edwards, M. E. Owen, and D. B. Walters (edd.), *Lawyers and Laymen: Studies in the History of Law presented to Professor Dafydd Jenkins* (Cardiff, 1986), 72–91.

[3] See e.g. Stenton, *First Century*, No. 42. Note also passages about grantees seeking a gift, e.g. *The Chronicle of Battle Abbey*, ed. and tr. E. Searle (Oxford, 1980), 256.

[4] Stenton, *First Century*, No. 5; see below, p. 189, for the continuation of this passage.

[5] Note M. T. Clanchy, *From Memory to Written Record* (London, 1979), 205, *The Guthlac Roll*, ed. G. F. Warner (Roxburghe Club, Oxford, 1928), plate xviii. *Arengae* perhaps give some idea of the motives which churchmen would have liked the laity to express, see e.g. *Regesta*, i, No. 28. Note also other charter passages, e.g. P. M. Barnes and C. F. Slade (edd.), *A Medieval Miscellany for Doris Mary Stenton* (PRS, NS 36; 1960), 107–8, *Sir Christopher Hatton's Book of Seals*, ed. L. C. Loyd and D. M. Stenton (Northants Rec. Soc. and Oxford, 1950), No. 287.

[6] e.g. *EYC*, v, No. 195 for an oath on the missal, in the presence of the *parochia* of the church.

[7] See *Transcripts of Charters Relating to the Gilbertine Houses of Sixle, Ormsby, Catley, Bullington and Alvingham*, ed. F. M. Stenton (Lincoln Rec. Soc. 18; 1922), p. xxix and

names and sometimes their grants might be recorded in the recipient church's memorial book.[8]

The obtaining of publicity is most obvious in the witnessing of a transaction.[9] Witnesses should testify for the rest of their lives that the transaction had taken place. The later testimony would generally be oral, but occasionally written.[10] There should preferably be large numbers of witnesses, trustworthy people and some at least of relatively high status. The witnessing of his grants was one of the major functions of a man's court,[11] and we also sometimes see his grants being made in his lord's or a local court.[12] Wide attendance might be encouraged by holding the ceremony on an especially appropriate day. Thus in *c.*1130 × 40 Hugh Bigod confirmed William de Burnville and his sons' and daughter's gifts to Thetford Priory made on All Saints' Day.[13] Some of those witnessing might take a particularly active part and perambulate the land given, thus checking and establishing the bounds of the grant and thereby, it would be hoped,

refs.; also e.g. *Formulare Anglicanum*, No. II. A narrative passage in the *Liber Eliensis*, ed. E. O. Blake (Camden Soc., 3rd Ser. 92; 1962), 335 mentions a ceremony not included in the charter which follows it, pp. 336–7. One who broke an oath or pledge of faith had obviously committed a spiritual offence, and could be considered liable to a spiritual penalty; on such penalties, see below, pp. 167–71.

[8] e.g. *The Charters of the Anglo-Norman Earls of Chester*, ed. G. Barraclough (Rec. Soc. of Lancs. and Cheshire, 126; 1988), No. 2.

[9] Note D. Postles, 'Choosing Witnesses in Twelfth-Century England', *Irish Jurist*, NS 23 (1988), 330–46. Postles argues that witnessing grew less important from the second half of the 12th cent., being superseded by other modes of assurance. As usual, the fine-tuning of the relationship between legal and diplomatic change is very difficult. On pp. 345–6, Postles discusses the witnessing of the making of the charter, as opposed to the livery of the gift.

[10] e.g. *Rufford Charters*, ed. C. J. Holdsworth (4 vols.; Thoroton Soc. Rec. Ser. 29, 30, 32, 34; 1972–81), No. 758.

[11] See also Postles, 'Witnesses', 337; see also P. A. Brand and P. R. Hyams, 'Seignurial Control of Women's Marriage', *P&P* 99 (1983), 125. Explicit references to grants *in curia mea* may be fairly few since this was assumed to be the place that a grant was made, and the names of the witnesses also made this obvious.

[12] Donor's lord's court: e.g. Stenton, *First Century*, No. 41; *Book of Seals*, No. 146; *Earldom of Gloucester Charters*, ed. R. B. Patterson (Oxford, 1973), No. 151, and below, p. 208. Local court: e.g. *Facsimiles of Early Charters in Oxford Muniment Rooms*, ed. H. E. Salter (Oxford, 1929), No. 77. For a grant at least confirmed and perhaps made in the court of the Rape of Bramber which was under the donor's lord's control, *Oxford Charters*, No. 9, one of a group of charters cited below, p. 208 n. 2. Such grants in local courts became more common towards the end of the 12th cent., e.g. *Beauchamp Cartulary: Charters 1100–1268*, ed. E. Mason (PRS, NS 43; 1980), No. 219; *Early Charters of the Cathedral Church of St Paul, London*, ed. M. Gibbs (Camden Soc., 3rd Ser. 58; 1939), No. 262.

[13] *Book of Seals*, No. 284.

helping to prevent future disputes.[14] At his death-bed, a donor might
be surrounded by prominent clerics who would witness his gifts.[15]
Further, lasting publicity would be provided by issuing a charter
recording the grant. Not only did this record the grant, provisions for
its security, and the names of the witnesses, but it also ensured that
all who saw the charter thereby became in a sense witnesses to the
grant. Specific addressees, such as bishops, were no doubt meant
particularly to lend their weight to the maintenance of the gift.[16]

What of the actual ceremonies of giving? All gifts presumably
should have involved some clear act, but its nature and the degree of
formality might vary. Occasionally a very spectacular act publicized
a grant. One Abingdon example illustrates the desirability of an
especially memorable action in order to secure a troubled grant.
Giralmus de Curzun had granted and added to his relatives' gift of
tithes to the abbey. None the less, he still came to withhold the tithe.
Eventually, persuaded of his wrong by the sacrist, he demonstrated
his restoration of the tithe by breaking the bolts of his barn with his
own hands, and confirmed by an oath that such an offence would not
happen again.[17]

In thirteenth-century Common Law, livery of seisin on the land
was necessary for the transfer of property.[18] Thorne argued that such
livery on the land had not been necessary in the Anglo-Norman
period or early in Henry II's reign, and I have found no reason to
contradict him.[19] Nevertheless, some act of investiture seems to
have been a common part of transfer, even if it was not identical
with thirteenth-century livery of seisin.[20] Domesday Book records

---

[14] See e.g. *Durham Episcopal Charters, 1071–1152*, ed. H. S. Offler (Surtees Soc.
179; 1968), No. 42; also *Register of Abbey of St Benet of Holme*, ed. J. R. West (2 vols.;
Norfolk Rec. Soc. 2, 3; 1932), No. 139. S. E. Thorne, 'Livery of Seisin', *LQR* 52
(1936) 351, suggests that surveying of the land's boundaries would generally have
occurred earlier, during the negotiation of the gift.

[15] e.g. *Chester*, No. 117.

[16] e.g. *Chester*, No. 96, *Documents Illustrative of the Social and Economic History of the
Danelaw*, ed. F. M. Stenton (London, 1920), No. 516.

[17] *CMA*, ii. 203.

[18] Thorne, 'Livery', 345; see e.g. *Bracton*, fos. 38b, 39b–40, Thorne, ii. 121,
124–6. Pollock and Maitland, ii. 84, note that the transfer was fulfilled by a real
quitting of possession by the grantor, for example the removal of chattels, and a
concomitant acquiring of seisin by the grantee.

[19] Thorne, 'Livery', esp. 353–5.

[20] Pollock and Maitland, ii, 32–3, reassure me that occasional uses of 'vested and
seised', e.g. *Glanvill*, vi. 8, Hall, 62, do not refer to two separate ceremonies. On the
13th cent., see Thorne, 'Livery', 361. On continental rituals of investiture with land,

production of a man who has seised the claimant as one way of establishing title to land.[21] Examples of ceremonies described as seising can be found in Anglo-Norman England, with reference to grants to laymen, clerics, and churches. Thus a cartulary note records that 'by this rod William son of Reginald son of the earl seised Walter the constable, son of Earl Miles, of Alvington, without any future claim by him or his heirs.'[22] In 1139 × 40 King Stephen wrote to the bishop of Lincoln, arranging for his church to have £14 per annum of the tithe of his farm of the city, for a prebend for the use of Baldric de Sigillo. He asked the bishop to send one of his canons, 'who may receive the investiture of that prebend from my hand, and take [*deferat*] seisin for the church by my ring, at the same time as my charter, and who on behalf of you and your chapter may invest that Baldric of the said things'.[23] As this example shows, it was quite often not the donor him or herself who delivered seisin. The donor might instead send his steward or chaplain.[24]

Probably 'seising' was one of various, perhaps not always wholly distinguishable, ceremonies which could take place. Throughout the period, the act of giving may sometimes have been simple, sometimes more spectacular and involving several occasions. A late eleventh-century charter records a gift by Geoffrey de Mandeville I to Westminster Abbey in the following terms:

With my wife Lesceline, and by concession of my son William whom I have arranged to make my heir, both of whom I wish to share in this alms in everything, I placed this gift to God and St Peter on the altar of the said apostle Peter in the presence of Abbot Gilbert and of the monks and many of

see e.g. J. Le Goff, 'Symbolic Ritual', *Time, Work and Culture in the Middle Ages*, tr. A. Goldhammer (Chicago, 1980). On the Norman situation, see Tabuteau, *Transfers of Property*, 119–33.

[21] See e.g. *Domesday*, i, fos. 62a, 148b. Thorne, 'Livery', unfortunately did not discuss the Domesday evidence.

[22] 'Charters of the Earldom of Hereford, 1095–1201', ed. D. Walker, in *Camden Miscellany*, xxii (Camden Soc., 4th Ser. 1; 1964), No. 71, datable 1155 × c.1160. Note also *Book of Seals*, No. 301. Charters recording sales also occasionally mention livery of seisin; e.g. *Chronicon Abbatiae Rameseiensis*, ed. W. D. Macray (London, 1886), 249.

[23] *Regesta*, iii, No. 478, an early use of the noun form *saisina*. See also *The Cartulary of Worcester Cathedral Priory*, ed. R. R. Darlington (PRS, NS 38; 1968), No. 252, a document of 1139 × 48 laying considerable emphasis on seisin before war broke out, and No. 253.

[24] e.g. *CMA*, ii. 53, 96, 107; see also *Gesta Abbatum Monasterii Sancti Albani*, ed. H. T. Riley (3 vols.; London, 1867–9), i. 113.

my and their knights. And to continue I made St Peter be seised of the said manor by [*per*] Ralph de Hairun.[25]

The charter thus distinguishes between Geoffrey's personal placing of the gift on the altar, and his making the church be seised through Ralph. In grants to the laity, the taking of homage may have become part of the various ceremonies involved in the transaction.[26] It reinforced any submission implied by the vassal having to travel to the lord's court in order to receive the gift, and made firm and public the relationship of donor and donee.

Objects were often used in ceremonies.[27] As is so often the case, the clearest evidence comes from grants to the Church. We have seen above a son confirming his father's gift by placing it on the altar.[28] As with livery of seisin, this act was sometimes performed by proxy. Thus in 1106 × 7 Miles Crispin sent his steward with his chaplain to Abingdon, ordering that by their hand his gift be placed on the altar in the presence of the abbot and the whole convent.[29] However, use of proxies in such ceremonies seems to have been less usual than in livery of seisin. The grantors, and anyone else involved in the gift, for example those consenting, wished to be seen to be sharing in the gift ceremony. They had already demonstrated their devotion to the church by travelling there. The gift ceremony now took them out of the nave, the lay space of the church, to the altar, the most spiritual space.

Money gifts were sometimes physically placed on the altar. Thus Robert d'Oilly offered more than £100 on the altar at Abingdon.[30]

---

[25] *Westminster Abbey Charters, 1066–c.1214*, ed. E. Mason (London Rec. Soc. 25; 1988), No. 467. See also e.g. *English Lawsuits from William I to Richard I*, ed. R. C. van Caenegem (2 vols.; Selden Soc. 106, 107; 1990–1), No. 348, a quitclaim; *Gilbertines*, p. xxx; 'Charters relating to the Priory of Sempringham', ed. E. M. Poynton, *Genealogist*, NS 15 (1899), 222; White, *Gifts to Saints*, 31–2.

[26] P. R. Hyams, 'Warranty and Good Lordship in Twelfth Century England', *L&HR* 5 (1987), 447–8.

[27] In addition to the examples cited below, see also *Regesta*, ii, No. 1030: following the witness list is added 'per tres parmenos quos ego ei dedi apud Tromplinton'. Clanchy, *Memory to Written Record*, 23–4, a gift ceremony in front of the altar involving the cutting of hairs from the heads of the donor and his brother, and the passing of possession by these hairs; p. 24 on items that might themselves have intrinsic value being used in gift ceremonies; p. 25, a man, on becoming a monk, offers an estate and symbolizes his change of life by placing his sword on the monastery's altar.

[28] Above, p. 161.

[29] *CMA*, ii. 97. See also e.g. *Stenton Miscellany*, 107.

[30] *CMA*, ii. 14. See *Earldom of Gloucester*, No. 69, for the placing of a regular payment on the altar.

When the grant was of land, however, clearly the placing had to be symbolic. The object used might be a turf, twig, or rod from the land, or any turf, twig, or rod. Thus the Ramsey chronicler, writing in Henry II's reign, recorded that the abbey still had a staff cut from the land given to Ramsey in 1121 × 2 by a certain Wulfget.[31] Also used were knives, perhaps themselves used for or symbolic of the cutting of the turf, twig, or rod. A famous story recalls the Conqueror giving land in England to Holy Trinity, Rouen. William made the gift to the abbot by [*per*] a knife, pretending jokingly to stab the abbot's palm, whilst saying 'thus should land be given'.[32] Other more peaceful examples are quite frequent.[33] Some churches had their own customs. Stoke by Clare charters record several gifts made by the placing of a candlestick on the altar. The practice may well go back to the mother church at Bec, but in England probably stemmed from the founder's act in 1090 of placing a candlestick on the altar in token of his own gifts.[34] Whether the monks kept a single candlestick for such ceremonies, or whether each donor gave one is unclear.

Gospel books were sometimes used. In 1153 Ralph de Sancto Audoeno gave a saltpan to St Peter's Priory, Sele, Sussex, by the text of the Holy Gospel upon the altar of St Peter, with many seeing and hearing.[35] Another form of writing employed was the charter. Thus in 1130 × 2 Nicholas fitzRobert and Robert his first-born and heir confirmed various gifts to the prior and canons of Kenilworth. The document closed with the statement that 'we confirmed this charter and placed it on the altar in the church of Stone'.[36] The charter was

---

[31] *Ramsey Chronicle*, 246. See also Pollock and Maitland, ii. 87–8; *Cartularium Abbathiae de Whiteby*, ed. J. C. Atkinson (2 vols.; Surtees Soc. 69, 72; 1879, 1881), i, No. XCIII.

[32] *Regesta*, i, No. 29.

[33] e.g. *EYC*, iv, No. 11; *Feudal Documents from the Abbey of Bury St Edmunds*, ed. D. C. Douglas (London, 1932), Nos. 172, 173; *Historia et Cartularium Monasterii Sancti Petri Gloucestriae*, ed. W. H. Hart (3 vols.; London, 1863–7), No. DCCV; *St Benet of Holme*, No. 139; A. Saltman, *Theobald, Archbishop of Canterbury* (London, 1956), Supplementary Documents B. See the note to *EYC*, v, No. 162, on a 14th-cent. statement that a manor was given to Selby in the reign of Henry I by the handle of a chisel; also Clanchy, *Memory to Written Record*, 24–5.

[34] *Stoke*, Nos. 21, 137 (ii, xxvii), 318, 335, 532; see also iii. 48.

[35] *Oxford Charters*, No. 9; Clanchy, *Memory to Written Record*, 205. See also *Earldom of Hereford*, No. 90. If the donor also swore an oath, it presumably may well have been on the same gospel book as was placed upon the altar.

[36] *Book of Seals*, No. 130. Common at Gloucester; *Gloucester Cartulary*, i. 106, Nos. CCCXLIX, CCCCLXVII, DVIII. *Guthlac Roll*, plate xviii, shows benefactors of Crowland approaching the altar with scrolls, presumably recording their gifts.

thus not just a document, but also a symbolic—if not a religious—object.[37] The link between the use of documents and other objects is further brought home by the fact that some symbolic objects bore writing, be it as parchment attached to the object, or engraving on the object itself.[38] All these objects provided the focus for the ceremony and a monument for both ceremony and grant. They could be of great use to the church as a guarantee that a promised gift would actually be fulfilled. Kept in an archive, amongst a church's treasures, they might be produced in any future dispute.[39]

Such focusing on an object provides clear parallels to another mode of assurance, the countergift, a material gift made by the main grantee to anyone participating in the grant. Were these simply concealed purchase payments or the buying off of possible claims?[40] Some transactions are described as gifts in return for money by one charter, as sales by another.[41] Certainly churches were sometimes extremely keen to conceal the fact that they were receiving lands other than by free gift. They might do so by simply not recording payment in a charter.[42] However, this desire to suppress mention of

[37] See Clanchy, *Memory to Written Record*, 207, 244–8, on seals.
[38] Clanchy, *Memory to Written Record*, 24–5, 127, 206–7. *Danelaw Documents*, No. 157 uses the phrase 'confirming by a knife', reminiscent of the common forms such as 'confirming by my charter'; as well as suggesting that the knife took the place of the charter, it could be seen as evidence that charters took the place of symbolic objects.
[39] Clanchy, *Memory to Written Record*, 127; *The Chronicle of Jocelin of Brakelond*, ed. and tr. H. E. Butler (London, 1949), 2 on a seal hanging from the feretory at Bury; also William of Malmesbury, *De Gestis Pontificum Anglorum*, ed. N. Hamilton (London, 1870), 80, and Eadmer, *Historia Nouorum in Anglia*, ed. M. Rule (London, 1884), 31, on Rufus placing a gage on the altar in support of his promise that he would, for example, fill ecclesiastical vacancies.
[40] This problem confronts historians in various contexts; see e.g. J. Campbell, 'The Sale of Land and the Economics of Power in England: Problems and Possibilities', *Haskins Society Journal*, 1 (1989), 23–8. Unfortunately because charters at best give the sizes of land given, and not, for example, any indication of their productivity, we cannot show whether or not there was commonly any relationship between the size of countergift and the value of the land given. Some discussing grants to the Church have written of spiritual countergifts, such as admission to the fraternity of the church to which the main grant was made or the provision of prayers for the salvation of grantor and his kin's souls; e.g. Tabuteau, *Transfers of Property*, 115; White, *Gifts to Saints*, 111, 245 n. 54. Yet many such agreed spiritual returns for gifts seem more closely equivalent to the services promised by a lay grantee: they were the primary purpose for the gift. Countergifts, on the other hand, were represented as a secondary return.
[41] e.g. compare *Earldom of Gloucester*, No. 5, with Henry II's confirmations, *Regesta*, iii, No. 49, *Two Chartularies of the Priory of St Peter at Bath*, ed. W. Hunt (Somerset Rec. Soc. 7; 1893), No. 68.
[42] e.g. at *CMA*, ii. 26–7 compare narrative and charter (= *Regesta*, i, No. 359).

purchase at the same time as recording the return made to the grantors surely suggests conscious differentiation between sales and countergifts. Similarly, trouble was sometimes taken to make clear that even before the donee of his own accord offered a countergift, the donor was already set upon making the gift for no monetary return.[43] Moreover, the stress which some charters lay upon the charity of the provider of the countergift cannot wholly be ignored. Words such as *de caritate sua* emphasize that countergifts were presented voluntarily, not as a purchase price.[44]

Countergifts, of course, could be materially very welcome to the recipient, perhaps on account of his financial need. When Robert Borne granted a right of way to the monks of Battle, 'the monks gave him, both as payment for the kindness and as future evidence, 6s. and iron leg-pieces, by some properly called greaves, so that he might get a place for one of his brothers in the army.'[45] However, the nature of some countergifts takes them outside the area of normal economic exchange. There are a perhaps surprising number of countergifts which included gold coins, and also frequent were gold rings.[46] A certain Roger, granting his father's gift to Battle, received a dog for which he had been asking.[47] In return for a charter recording a gift, Regnerus the painter gave Hugh de Camville a chess-board and his wife some veils.[48]

What then was the purpose of the countergift? It re-emphasized

---

[43] See below, p. 166.

[44] e.g. *Book of Seals*, Nos. 197, 221, 334; *Stoke by Clare Cartulary*, ed. C. Harper-Bill and R. Mortimer (3 vols.; Suffolk Charters, 4–6; 1982–4), No. 309. In addition to sales and countergifts, payments 'in return for' land might also be taken to include reliefs, which add a further nuance to the complicated thought concerning payment for land grants; see the distinction drawn in Stenton, *First Century*, No. 41. It is perhaps best to see purchases and countergifts as ends of a scale. At one end is payment in anonymous cash, readily disposable. At the other is the countergift, which had much wider purposes. People may, in differing circumstances and over the period, have chosen to see the division at different points on the scale but differentiate they certainly did.

[45] *Battle Chronicle*, 254–6.

[46] *First Century*, No. 33, *Earldom of Hereford*, No. 39, *Danelaw Documents*, Nos. 205, 556, *Earldom of Gloucester*, No. 29. Cf. White, *Gifts to Saints*, 167 on coin and countergifts. Rings: e.g. *Charters of the Honour of Mowbray, 1107–1191*, ed. D. E. Greenway (London, 1972), No. 331, *Facsimiles of Early Charters from Northamptonshire Collections*, ed. F. M. Stenton (Northants Rec. Soc. 4; 1930), No. XXXVa, *Book of Seals*, No. 48.

[47] *Battle Chronicle*, 120.

[48] *Oxford Charters*, No. 54.

the mutuality of the relationship between the parties.[49] Secondly, it could later provide evidence of the main grant. Another passage from the *Battle Chronicle* illustrates both these points. Abbot Walter persuaded Robert Borne and his son Ralph to give a piece of land to the abbey:

When they both, with full consent, had made him heir to the land before the altar in St Martin's monastery, the abbot determined not to take it entirely free, but rather he made to be given to the father ten shillings, to the son one gold piece, both as an exchange [*pro mutua uicissitudine*] between them and as evidence for the future.[50]

A countergift to the donor put pressure on his heirs to continue the gift. Thus a charter of Conan duke of Brittany and earl of Richmond stated: 'and so that my heirs may firmly keep this, let it be known that I accepted fifty marks of silver from the monks for making this confirmation and warranting my gift.'[51] For similar purposes countergifts could be made to those consenting to or confirming the grant.[52] Countergifts also concerned the social relations of those receiving them. They could establish the recipient as one of a close-knit social group, and, for example, re-emphasize the position of the donor's eldest son as his heir.

Ceremonies and countergifts emphasized the mutual obligations of the parties, but people still disputed the terms of grants. Those helping to maintain grants were sometimes explicitly promised a blessing.[53] Those harming them could face spiritual or worldly penalties. Spiritual penalties protected church lands, which had been given for the benefit of the donors' souls. Some charters spoke of the act of harming the grant, others the intention of doing so. Thus a

---

[49] See also White, *Gifts to Saints*, 166. In *EYC*, v, No. 187, the donor or his heirs' failure to warrant was to result in the return of the countergift.

[50] *Battle Chronicle*, 256.

[51] *EYC*, iv, No. 56.

[52] e.g. *Stoke*, No. 335; also D. Postles, 'Securing the Gift in Oxfordshire Charters in the Twelfth and Early Thirteenth Centuries', *Archives*, 19 (1990), 187. See *Stoke*, No. 264, *Ramsey Cartulary*, Nos. LVIII, LXXII for countergifts to sons, without specific mention of their consent, the last being to an infant whom his mother was holding at the ceremony; *CMA*, ii. 202, a countergift to a son swearing to observe the settlement of a dispute. See also Tabuteau, *Transfers of Property*, 178, White, *Gifts to Saints*, 47, 53—on relatives who only gave up claims on receiving a countergift, 80. Note that the range of relatives receiving countergifts was smaller in England than, for example, in the areas of western France studied by White, pp. 111–13; White, p. 47, also found *donors* in western France giving countergifts to those consenting.

[53] e.g. Stenton, *First Century*, No. 5, *Worcester*, No. 392.

charter to Abingdon specified that whoever wished to change the gift recorded therein was not to have a share in the realm of God or Christ.[54] However, the distinction, although showing the complexities of thought, may be more a matter of wording than substance.[55]

Penalty clauses generally came towards the end of charters. Their form varied, and each could contain several elements. Some specified that those harming the grant were to share the fate of some particularly notorious sinner, such as Dathan and Abiron, Pilate and Herod, but most commonly Judas.[56] Further, the malediction of God, and sometimes a saint or two, could be called down on the offender. Thus William de Curci's confirmation of his father's gift to Abingdon ended 'Whoever will violate this restoration or gift by deed or counsel shall undergo the curse of God and his Mother Mary.'[57] The malediction might also be directed against specified potential offenders, for example the donor's heirs.[58]

Most common, however, were anathemas and excommunications. The difference between these may have been limited, although anathema was seen as a severe type of excommunication.[59] The two words do appear separately,[60] but are often combined, as in the following impressive excommunication recorded not in a charter but a monastic chronicle:

[54] *CMA*, ii. 74. Cf. also e.g. *Oxford Charters*, No. 52, emphasizing intention, with e.g. *Liber Eliensis*, 362; *Feudal Documents*, Nos. 106, 112; *Oxford Charters*, No. 5, concentrating on the act. Note also the scribe's curse at the end of *Northants*, No. XVIII.

[55] Tabuteau, *Transfers of Property*, 206, lays greater emphasis on Norman charters' statements concerning intention of harming. The long procedure for excommunication might make sure that any intentions were fairly manifest.

[56] *Regesta*, i, No. 26; Stenton, *First Century*, No. 5; *CMA*, ii. 39; *Regesta*, ii, No. 1489; *Monasticon Anglicanum*, ed. W. Dugdale (6 vols. in 8; London, 1817–30), iv. 149. Dathan and Abiram revolted against Moses, and as a consequence were swallowed by an earthquake; Num. 16: 1–35. Judas was particularly appropriate as one whose word could not be trusted. See also White, *Gifts to Saints*, 36, and 208–9 for a French curse from *c.*1040.

[57] *CMA*, ii. 55. Mary was here asked to look after her own, since Abingdon was dedicated to her; see e.g. *CMA*, ii. 13–14 for her miraculous intervention in a land dispute.

[58] e.g. *Liber Eliensis*, 388. See also *EYC*, iv, No. 8; note that this charter mentions neither the consent nor the witness of the heirs; the curse seems to have been considered sufficient protection against future challenge.

[59] L. K. Little, 'La Morphologie des malédictions monastiques', *Annales ESC* 34 (1979), 50; E. Vodola, *Excommunication in the Middle Ages* (Berkeley, Calif., 1986), 29; on excommunication and its procedure, see also J. Goebel, *Felony and Misdemeanour* (New York, 1937), 263–5, 308 and n. 81.

[60] Excommunication e.g. *Oxford Charters*, No. 52, *Stoke*, No. 71; anathema e.g. *Feudal Documents*, Nos. 103, 105–6, 112, *Oxford Charters*, Nos. 27, 79.

I Reginald abbot and the whole convent of the church of Abingdon, from the authority of God the omnipotent father, and of the Son, and of the Holy Spirit, and of the most holy Virgin Mary Mother of God, and of all of God's Saints, excommunicate and anathematize and exclude from the doorways of the Holy Mother Church all whether men or women who act in deed or counsel that the vill called Leckhamstead be taken from the demesne of the same church by any scheme or agreement; and whoever act thus are to be perpetually damned with Judas the Lord's betrayer and Pilate and Herod, unless they repent and reach satisfaction.[61]

Again the penalty could be directed against specific potential infringers.[62]

It is possible that some at least of these passages attempt to represent words used in the actual ceremony. That some charters ended 'fiat, fiat' or 'Amen, Amen' suggests that they may have been read out and assented to by all.[63] The *Battle Chronicle* lists certain assignations made by Abbot Walter to the sacristy, and to the food allowances of the monks:

And lest any of his successors should dare in the future to lessen his decree, or to oppose him by any change in it, before the brothers in chapter he put on his stole and took a lighted candle, and commanded each of the brothers who were priests or deacons to take up stoles and lighted candles, while those who were of inferior grade and the lay brothers had lighted candles alone. Then in the presence and with the consent of all, he pronounced a perpetual and irrevocable anathema on all violators of his decree.[64]

However, charter and chronicle entries may be very abbreviated forms of the words used. Churches kept suitable texts in their records. These could combine damnation with sinners, malediction, and anathema. Most famous, largely thanks to Laurence Sterne, is that of Ernulf bishop of Rochester, preserved in the *Textus Roffensis*:

We excommunicate, and anathematize him, and from the thresholds of the holy Church of God Almighty we sequester him, that he may be tormented, disposed and delivered over with *Dathan* and *Abiram*. May he be damned wherever he be,—whether in the house or the stables, the garden or the field, or the highway, or in the path, or in the wood, or in the water, or in the church. . . . May he be cursed in eating and drinking, in being hungry, in

---

[61] *CMA*, ii. 39.
[62] See e.g. *CMA*, ii. 147, for an abbot directing an anathema against his successors.
[63] e.g. *Feudal Documents*, No. 103.
[64] *Battle Chronicle*, 252–4; see also *Gesta Abbatum Monasterii Sancti Albani*, i. 76.

being thirsty, in fasting, in sleeping, in slumbering, in walking, in standing, in sitting, in lying, in working, in resting, in pissing, in shitting, and in blood-letting.[65]

Perhaps not surprisingly, spiritual penalties tended to be used by churchmen more than laymen.[66] Except for resort to lay authority, the Church had few weapons with which to fight force. Not only individual charters but Church councils therefore looked to anathema as a way of protecting church lands.[67] Churches felt greatest need of such penalties in time of strife, when their rights were particularly threatened and the option of royal support was reduced. Various monastic chronicles record the use of ecclesiastical penalties during Stephen's reign.[68] The reign also coincided with increased papal emphasis upon excommunication for offences against the Church, and these circumstances combined to produce such legislation as that of the legatine council at Westminster in December 1138 which laid down that 'if anyone presumes to seize violently the moveable or immoveable possessions of churches, unless he makes amends following canonical summons, we order him to be excommunicated'.[69]

During our period, a decreasing proportion of charters recording lay grants to churches directly prescribed spiritual penalties. This may in part reflect an attempt by the Church to make such penalties its special preserve, but changes in drafting practices were at least equally important. Take royal charters as the largest, and in this case a representative, sample. These clearly reveal a decline in the inclusion of spiritual penalties but this can very largely be explained

---

[65] *Tristram Shandy*, vol. 3, ch. 11; Liebermann, *Gesetze*, i. 439–40. See *CMA*, ii. 39, on the anathema quoted above, p. 168, being written down in a gospel book.

[66] Monastic charters were presumably often written out in the *scriptorium*, and the ambience of such a location fits with the emphasis on elaborately worded spiritual penalties.

[67] The legatine council at Windsor in May 1070 may have pronounced anathema a suitable penalty for anyone invading ecclesiastical goods; *Councils and Synods*, i, ed. D. Whitelock *et al.* (2 vols.; Oxford, 1981), ii. 581.

[68] e.g. *Chronicon Abbatiae de Evesham ad annum 1418*, ed. W. D. Macray (London, 1863), 100. See *Charters and Documents illustrating the History of the Cathedral, City, and Diocese of Salisbury*, ed. W. D. Macray (London, 1891), No. XXV, for an agreement in 1152 between Duke Henry and the bishop of Salisbury. The archbishop of Canterbury granted that if either withdrew from the agreement, he would be coerced by canonical justice.

[69] *Councils and Synods*, *i*, ii. 777. See also Henry of Huntingdon, *Historia Anglorum*, ed. T. Arnold (London, 1879), 276; Orderic, Vitalis, *The Ecclesiastical History*, ed. and tr. M. Chibnall (6 vols.; Oxford, 1969–80), vi. 276. On the papal background, see Vodola, *Excommunication*, 28.

by the decline of old-style charters and diplomas, which had habitu-
ally included such penalties. Furthermore such documents may often
have been drafted by the beneficiary. The inclusion of a spiritual
penalty does not therefore indicate that the layman was claiming the
right to give spiritual sentences, but rather that the beneficiary was
seeking to protect the gift by every possible means.

Increasingly, as the writ-charter took over, and perhaps as lay
lords' own scribes became responsible for writing charters, lay grantors including the king looked to churchmen to impose the spiritual
penalty. Thus the witness list of a charter of William Rufus in favour
of Christ Church, Twynham, dating from 1093 × 4, opened 'Anselm
archbishop of Canterbury, who at my prayer gave his and God's
malediction to all who henceforth impede or unjustly go against my
gift.'[70] When in 1160 × 70, Gilbert de Monte granted twenty-three
acres to the hospital of Brackley, he laid down that anyone infringing
was to be excommunicated by episcopal authority.[71]

How effective were such penalties? The fear of hell could be very
real.[72] Moreover, excommunication could bring worldly problems.
Canonists held that vassals were freed from their oaths of fealty
whilst their lords were excommunicate.[73] Yet we know that some
lords, most famously Geoffrey de Mandeville, went to their death
still excommunicate. Other sources also point to the ineffectiveness
of spiritual penalties. The *Anglo-Saxon Chronicle*, during its famous
entry *s.a.* 1137 stated that 'the bishops and learned men were always
excommunicating [those harming the Church], but they thought
nothing of it, because they were utterly accursed and perjured and
doomed to perdition.' Abbot Reginald's impressive excommunication
concerning Leckhamstead, cited above, had only a limited success.[74]
Should one therefore conclude that spiritual penalties had little sway?[75]
The monastic chronicles present some contrary evidence. Sometimes
they simply link divine intervention to the fact that a man was

---

[70] See above, n. 54, on a scribe being responsible for proclaiming the sentence on
those harming his charter. *Regesta*, i, No. 361; cf. *Chester*, No. 78.

[71] *Oxford Charters*, No. 52.

[72] See e.g. C. Harper-Bill, 'The Piety of the Anglo-Norman Knightly Class', *A-NS*
2 (1980), 63–4; White, *Gifts to Saints*, 76.

[73] Vodola, *Excommunication*, 23. In a period such as Stephen's reign, with many
lords excommunicate, such might have been the source of anarchy indeed.

[74] *ASC*, 199; *CMA*, ii. 39–40, 43.

[75] See also Tabuteau, *Transfers of Property*, 207 on Normandy.

excommunicate or cursed.[76] However, the *Ramsey Chronicle* records the case of Robert de 'Broi', who had unjustly occupied some land of the church, but having been bound by the chain of anathema, restored it to the abbey.[77] Only by arguing that medieval people did not really believe in the threats of hell can one firmly argue that the chronicler was pretending that a purely temporal link between anathema and restoration was in fact a causal one. In each case, a variety of factors, including not only the past history of the land and the relative power of the parties, but also piety of the individual, would have helped to determine the effectiveness of spiritual penalties.

Worldly penalties can be dealt with much more briefly. Divine maledictions were sometimes accompanied by curses in the grantors' own name.[78] Royal charters sometimes specified that no one was to harm their grants 'on my love', or at the risk of losing the king's friendship,[79] and occasionally infringers were threatened with the penalty of royal vengeance.[80] Other lords might similarly threaten worldly ill-favour or worse: 'if anyone henceforth tries to break my gift he will be opposed to me and all my predecessors and all my friends.'[81] In other cases the lord in whose court a grant was made might promise to enforce it.[82]

However, the most common type of worldly penalty clause was rarely concerned with the preservation of land grants. The £10 penalty prescribed by numerous royal charters was primarily concerned with grants of privileges, such as warren, tolls, and judicial

[76] e.g. *CMA*, ii. 231; William of Malmesbury, *Gesta Pontificum*, 253, concerning Urse d'Abetot. The *Liber Eliensis*, 202–3, records that Earl William de Warenne died a miserable death whilst still retaining some of Ely's lands. He was damned, until the abbot one night heard a voice crying 'Lord take pity, Lord take pity'.

[77] *Ramsey Chronicle*, p. 308 (= *English Episcopal Acta, I. Lincoln 1067–1185*, ed. D. M. Smith (London, 1980), No. 225). See also e.g. Saltman, *Theobald*, Supplementary Documents B, *The Domesday Monachorum of Christ Church Canterbury*, ed. D. C. Douglas (London, 1944), 108–10.

[78] See e.g. *EYC*, v, No. 201, 228 (both to Easby Abbey, suggesting beneficiary influence on drafting), *The Cartulary of Shrewsbury Abbey*, ed. U. Rees (2 vols.; Aberystwyth, 1975), No. 294, a restoration of land unjustly held; also William of Malmesbury, *Gesta Pontificum*, 253.

[78] e.g. *Regesta*, ii, Nos. 817, 840, 1055, 1388, 1867.

[80] *Regesta*, ii, No. 1338, no one to violate the charter 'ne lese magestatis ulcionem experiatur'; No. 1068, anyone harming 'corporis sui membrorumque suorum dampnum sustineat'. See also *Liber Eliensis*, 378.

[81] *Stoke*, No. 144; see also *Mowbray*, Nos. 313, 351.

[82] Stenton, *First Century*, No. 7. Cf. above, p. 142, on the grant of Holme Lacy.

rights, and this was also true of the undifferentiated royal statements that infringement of a privilege would be 'on my forfeiture [*super forisfacturam meam*]'.[83] However, such penalties were sometimes included in charters concerning lands.[84] By the 1130s, lay lords were occasionally using similar language.[85]

All the acts I have just considered were means of assuring the continuance of a grant. In addition, with the partial exception of some of the worldly penalties, they were social transactions. The participants need not always have been consciously aware of this, for such ceremonies were a common, if special, part of medieval life, but they created, reinforced, and at times weakened or denied social links. In this, as in much else, they resembled and were connected to participation in alienation, and on to this subject I now move.

[83] Note that monetary and spiritual penalties were occasionally combined, e.g. *Regesta*, ii, No. 1591, which specified that if anyone harmed Henry I's gift to the church, 'he is now to pay one hundred pounds of silver to the royal fisc, and in future not escape divine judgment'.

[84] e.g. *Regesta*, ii, No. 1173.

[85] e.g. *Book of Seals*, No. 130; for lay lords forbidding infringement of privileges concerning tolls 'on my forfeiture', see e.g. *Earldom of Gloucester*, Nos. 71, 110, 111, 127; for a £10 penalty for molestation contrary to grants both of lands and quittance from toll, e.g. Nos. 68, 89. I have found no English penalty clauses specifying the 'unbelievably large, uncollectible, but still fearsome fines' which appear in some French charters; White, *Gifts to Saints*, 36; see also Fauroux, No. 188, from pre-1066 Normandy.

6

Heirs and Grants: Participation and Challenges

We, my wife Sibyl and my sons Roger, Walter, and Henry, made this gift in the church of the canons at Gloucester thus that Roger, now a knight and married, swore on the altar of Mary and on the four gospels that he would never thenceforth do wrong, or seek harm, or any diminution to the canons in anything concerning that manor, neither through his own deed or another's; my son Walter also swore the same.

> Miles of Gloucester's foundation charter for
> Llanthony Secunda[1]

PARTICIPATION, counsel, and consent figured prominently in many spheres of eleventh- and twelfth-century life. When describing Anselm's youthful contemplation of his future, Eadmer paraphrased Ecclesiasticus 32: 24: 'Do everything by counsel and you will not repent after the event.'[2] In vernacular literature, consent was sought for numerous purposes. In Chrétien de Troyes's *Cligés*, from the 1170s, we hear of Alexander, son of the king of the Greeks. He had learnt of the deeds of Arthur and desired to join him, but had to obtain his father's permission before proceeding to Britain and Cornwall. He married Soredamors with the approval and permission of her brother Gawain and of Arthur. Having returned to the East, he died, begging his son to heed his counsel and follow in his footsteps to Arthur's court.[3] Participation in land grants was thus one

---

[1] 'Charters of the Earldom of Hereford, 1095–1201', ed. D. Walker, in *Camden Miscellany*, xxii (Camden Soc., 4th Ser. 1; 1964), No. 2. This is a composite document, recording gifts made on more than one occasion.

[2] Eadmer, *Vita Anselmi*, ed. and tr. R. W. Southern (2nd edn., Oxford, 1972), 10. The Vulgate reads 'Fili, sine consilio nihil facias, et post factum non poenitebis.'

[3] Chrétien de Troyes, *Cligés*, ed. W. Foerster (Halle, 1884), ll. 78–80, 2350–3, 2603–18. Cf. *Leges Henrici*, 43 2, Downer, 152 on leaving a lord without permission. Record evidence and chronicles also show that marriage was of crucial concern to the lords of the marriageable and to their families.

manifestation of a network of obligations and interests. Examination of such participation is of great interest in revealing the land-holder's power and obligations in relation to others, and also more generally the social aspects of land-holding.

The Normans came to England experienced in such participation. Pre-1066 Norman evidence records kin—and others including lords —consenting to land grants.[4] Occasional Anglo-Saxon examples also show that kin felt they had an interest in some lands held, and possibly granted, by their relatives, but the kin's consent to alienation was not a feature of Anglo-Saxon charters.[5]

Before presenting my own analysis of heirs' participation in alienation in England, it is again useful to examine other historians' main arguments on the subject. First, however, one must recall the main forms of alienation. Subinfeudation involved a gift by the donor directly to the donee who, if a layman, thus became tenant of the donor. By substitution, the donor surrendered the land to his lord, who then gave it to the donee who had been designated by the original donor. Thus the donor's right in the land was extinguished, and a lay donee would become the tenant of the donor's lord.

Continental historians have examined participation in alienation more fully than have English.[6] They have disagreed, in particular, as to whether the kin's consent, the *laudatio parentum*, was in some sense mandatory, a lasting gift impossible without it. Beneath their disputes lies a wider disagreement over the definitions of 'rule'.[7] Is it just a strong custom? Or must it be strictly enforced? My own analysis

---

[4] e.g. Fauroux, Nos. 122, 206, 229; Orderic Vitalis, *The Ecclesiastical History*, ed. and tr. M. Chibnall (6 vols.; Oxford, 1969–80), ii. 132; E. Z. Tabuteau, *Transfers of Property in Eleventh-Century Norman Law* (Chapel Hill, NC, 1988), ch. 8.

[5] *Alfred*, 41, Liebermann, *Gesetze*, i. 74, restricts alienation of bookland outside the kin. For a challenge by kin to a grant by will, see *The Will of Aethelgifu*, ed. and tr. D. Whitelock (Roxburghe Club, 1968), discussed below, p. 206 n. 137. On the absence of consents: Pollock and Maitland, ii. 251, 255. C. Hart, *The Early Charters of Eastern England* (Leicester, 1966), 253, notes a lost charter of King Ethelred to Cranborne Abbey confirming a grant by a widow made with the consent of her son. (I would like to thank Eric Hemming for this reference.)

[6] e.g. F. Olivier-Martin, *Histoire du droit Français des origines à la Révolution* (Paris, 1951), 271; M. Bloch, *Feudal Society*, tr. L. A. Manyon (2 vols.; London 1961), i. 130–3; G. Duby, *La Société aux xi⁰ et xii⁰ siècles dans la région Mâconnaise* (2nd edn., Paris, 1971), 221–4, 366–8; R. Fossier, *La Terre et les hommes en Picardie jusqu'à la fin du xiii⁰ siècle* (2 vols.; Paris, 1968), i. 263–5.

[7] See S. D. White, *Custom, Kinship, and Gifts to Saints* (Chapel Hill, NC, 1988), esp. ch. 2.

rests on the framework of principles, norms, and rules outlined in Chapter 1.

What then of historians of English land law? Their concern has partly arisen from the importance participation has for legal definition, especially in two respects. First, freedom of alienation is integral to some Common Law definitions of ownership. Secondly, freedom to alienate without the heir's consent is sometimes seen as necessary for inheritance to exist in its strictest sense.[8] The need for such consent may indicate that a gift 'to N. and his heirs' entitles the heirs to the entire gift: the gift is 'to N. and to his heirs'. Inheritance according to some strict definitions only exists when the gift gives nothing to the heirs, and they succeed by hereditary right only to what is left at the ancestor's death.

Maitland wrote that

Down to the end of the twelfth century the tenant in fee who wished to alienate had very commonly to seek the consent of his apparent or presumptive heirs. While this was so, it mattered not very greatly whether this restraint was found in some common-law rule forbidding disherison, or in the form of a gift which seemed to declare that after the donee's death the land was to be enjoyed by his heir and by none other. But early in the next century this restraint silently disappeared.[9]

Maitland regarded consent as having two main purposes. For the donee, it was to ensure the security and permanence of the gift; for the donor's heirs, it was to prevent their disinheritance and to ensure an equal division of lands between them, in his view the correct inheritance pattern in the century after 1066.[10]

Thorne argued that Maitland was wrong since he treated the tenant as an owner.[11] In the early twelfth century he was far from being one, since alienation of land beyond his death 'apparently required the consent of his expectant heirs'. The vassal was only a

[8] See S. E. Thorne, 'English Feudalism and Estates in Land', *CLJ* (1959), 193–209; S. D. White, 'Politics and Property in Early Medieval England: Succession to Fiefs', *P&P* 65 (1974), 122–3.

[9] Pollock and Maitland, ii. 13. Like Maitland, I use the word 'heirs' to indicate both actual and potential heirs. Maitland did not make clear whether he saw consent as an absolute requirement, although he did refer to 'the necessity for the heir's concurrence': ii. 309; see also ii. 248, 250 on birthrights. Maitland overestimated the proportion of Anglo-Norman charters which mentioned the consent of the heir; ii. 255; see also *Transcripts of Charters Relating to the Gilbertine Houses*, ed. F. M. Stenton (Lincoln Rec. Soc. 18; 1922), p. xix.

[10] Pollock and Maitland, ii. 309–12.

[11] For this paragraph, see Thorne, 'Estates', esp. 194, 202, 205–8.

life-tenant, and his heir did not inherit but succeeded by a new gift from the lord; the heir therefore received the land free of his ancestor's alienations.[12] After *c*.1150 succession by hereditary right grew stronger so that a man's heirs succeeded to his life-estate after him 'no longer by successive gifts and homages renewed but by force of the original gift made to him and his heirs and the original homage'. However, consent was still required, since the original gift in its entirety had been promised to the donee's heirs. On succession, the heir had to consider which gifts to renew. According to Thorne, he was required to continue those for military service since they were for the defence of the realm. Gifts to churches were prima facie reasonable and hence often confirmed. However, the prudent donor would make his heir either join in the gift as co-donor, or consent to, or at least witness it. After the third quarter of the twelfth century, according to Thorne, the charters which heirs issued for their late ancestors' beneficiaries came to record more of a confirmation, less of a new gift. They used *confirmare* instead of *concedere*. At the same time consent clauses were disappearing. By *c*.1200 the tenant was *uerus dominus*, the true owner, and free to dispose of his land as he wished.

Milsom's discussion of subinfeudation concentrates on the areas concerning which he finds 'detailed rules' in *Glanvill*, and which, he suggests, are entirely concerned with gifts free of service.[13] The framework in which *Glanvill*'s rules make sense is one where

there was no ownership to pass or not by a valid or invalid grant. The ancestor made an allocation from his inheritance, and undertook as a matter of obligation that he and his heirs would maintain it. When he died, his heir had to decide whether to honour that obligation, or rather his court had to

[12] The discontinuation or renewal of a gift need not have been an arbitrary action. New lords would have held enquiries into the standing of their predecessors' tenants before deciding which grants to continue; S. F. C. Milsom, *The Legal Framework of English Feudalism* (Cambridge, 1976), 45–7; P. R. Hyams, 'Warranty and Good Lordship in Twelfth Century England', *L&HR* 5 (1987), 460–3. Henry of Blois's description of his administration of Glastonbury Abbey is largely concerned with cases arising from such enquiries: Adam of Domerham, *Historia de Rebus Gestis Glastoniensibus*, ed. T. Hearne (2 vols.; Oxford, 1727), ii. 305–15.

[13] The following paragraph is based on Milsom, *Legal Framework*, 121–32, reference to detailed rules at p. 121, to gifts free of service, p. 122. Unfortunately, his concentration on *Glanvill*'s discussion means that he does not examine in depth subjects such as alienation to churches. On substitution, Milsom, *Legal Framework*, 109, argues that only the emergence of royal interference 'subjected it to the will of the natural heir as well as of the lord'.

decide whether the circumstances were such that he was not bound to honour it.[14]

Glanvill summarizes the customs governing the heir's decision, and includes 'a procedural discussion showing how they are brought to bear. It is very short: the heirs of donors are bound to warrant gifts rightly made.'[15] Milsom concludes that *Glanvill*'s rules perished because they could not well be enforced in the king's court. Instead, the royal court came to force the heir to warrant his ancestor's gifts and therefore to accept the sitting tenants.

The implication of the arguments put forward in particular by Thorne is that before the Angevin reforms lasting alienation from a man's inheritance was impossible without the kin's or at least the heir's consent and later confirmation. This situation stemmed not from a royally enforced legal rule but from the very nature of land-holding and succession. Such would be one explanation for the participation of heirs, but how convincing is it? Some possible objections are not necessarily compelling. Whilst records of consent are irregular, it might be argued that the very impossibility of lasting alienation without the heir's consent explains this irregularity: the giving of consent was simply assumed. The absence of any explicit statement of the requirement of the heir's consent within, for example, charters or dispute records is not definitive evidence against the existence of such a norm. Very few such general statements exist. In England evidence is lacking for heirs pleading that discontinuance of a gift was just since they had never consented to it, whereas such arguments were put forward for instance in western France,[16] but this could result from the noteworthy fact that English documents generally give fewer details of disputes. Ecclesiastics anyway wished to record their own strongest arguments, not those of their opponents. A similar explanation could be given for the prevalence of unfavourable settlements against kin challenging their relatives' gifts.[17] Yet if these

---

[14] Milsom, *Legal Framework*, 131; see also p. 90.

[15] Milsom, *Legal Framework*, 131.

[16] See White, *Gifts to Saints*, 48–51, 61–2, 77–8. See below, n. 34 for Normandy.

[17] See below, p. 206. See also e.g. *CMA*, ii. 205–6; note ii. 206, the unsuccessful claim by a canon, returning from abroad, to houses given to the church by his father's widow. Why he failed is unclear, for it may be doubted that a widow could usually give lands without the heir's participation. Perhaps absence, at least for an extended period, prevented successful claims; or perhaps the canon was not the widow's son, and the houses were her own. Nevertheless, the return of absent heirs may have been a repeated source of trouble.

objections can be rejected individually, their cumulative weight is suggestive.[18]

Moreover, there are other grounds for criticizing such arguments as Thorne's. In the first place, they rest heavily on the premise of a structure, not necessarily perceptible to men of the time, of land-holding based on successive life-tenures. I have argued that this premise is flawed: not only did men perceive of lands as descending in families, but outside forces strengthened the claim to succeed. It is anyway dangerous to explain the *laudatio parentum* without considering contemporary views of land-holding. Were all land-holding temporary in the minds of men of the time, it is hard to believe that the *laudatio parentum* would have existed: those consenting would only have had a claim to participate based on another future claim to succeed. In addition, their long-term interests would not have been so threatened by grants which lasted only as long as donor and donee both survived. But men did not see all their lands as held merely for life. If one thing is certain, it is that the alienability of land held heritably in twelfth-century terms, was greater than that of land which, in the same terms, was held only for life.

In addition, the evidence for the necessity of renewal of gifts by the heir is weak. Occasional charters suggest that heirs were not seen as succeeding to the entirety of the predecessor's possessions, irrespective of dispositions made during the ancestor's lifetime. Thus in 1137 Stephen's regrant to Roger fitzMiles and his wife Cecily, daughter of Payn fitzJohn, gave them not all the lands which Payn had ever held, free of alienations, but only those which he had on the day when he was alive and dead.[19] Furthermore, the granting language of charters

---

[18] Moreover, the arguments that consent was necessary because of the nature of land-holding and succession fail, for example, to explain why consent was not equally necessary for the alienation of acquisitions, if the heir was entitled to the entirety of the gift to his predecessor and if consent was in a sense the waiving of this entitlement; see above, p. 176, below, p. 183.

[19] *Regesta*, iii, No. 312. On 'alive and dead', see G. S. Garnett, 'Royal Succession in England, 1066–1154', Ph.D. thesis (Cambridge, 1987), esp. chs. 1 and 2. Cf. the problem concerning whether dower constituted one-third of the husband's lands at the time of marriage, or one-third of his lands in his lifetime; Pollock and Maitland, ii. 420–1, J. Biancalana, 'Widows at Common Law: The Development of Common Law Dower', *Irish Jurist*, NS 23 (1988), 255–329. Thorne, 'Estates', 197, seems to imply that in the early 12th cent. a new lord would take his predecessor's tenants' lands into hand. The cases of existing tenants retaining lands whilst refusing homage to a new lord, above, Ch. 2, show that this was not always the case.

clearly distinguishes between the original gift and the heir's confirmation. *Concedere* was often used, whereas *dare* very rarely appears in confirmations to churches.[20] Certainly a significant proportion of charters recording renewals to laymen use the verb *dare*, suggesting some equation with new gifts.[21] However, the rarity of such renewals suggests that they, like charters concerning regrants on the succession of a tenant, often record abnormal instances. *Confirmare*, although not by itself, appears from the late eleventh century and in the majority of such grants during the first three-quarters of the twelfth.[22] The language of heirs' confirmations only reveals that such grants did not amount to new gifts, and does not imply a power to discontinue a predecessor's gift.

The argument from the nature of land-holding would also appear to allow each successive heir equal discretion over past gifts. In fact, the grantee's long tenure had an effect. Most specific confirmations of predecessors' gifts are by immediate heirs; later heirs' confirmations are usually more general, perhaps suggesting that they did not really consider discontinuing each individual gift.[23] Certainly grandsons occasionally went back on their grandfather's gifts,[24] but the nature of land-holding need not have entitled them to do so. Moreover, if a real renewal were needed with each generation, one

[20] *Concedere*: e.g. F. M. Stenton, *The First Century of English Feudalism* (2nd edn., Oxford, 1961), No. 5; *Documents Illustrative of the Social and Economic History of the Danelaw*, ed. F. M. Stenton (London, 1920), Nos. 19, 94; *Earldom of Hereford*, Nos. 1, 11, 49, 81, 82, 101; *EYC*, iii, No. 1484, viii, No. 7. *Dare*: e.g. *EYC*, v, Nos. 280, 399; it continues occasionally to appear in the late 12th cent.; *Earldom of Hereford*, Nos. 75, 86 (*dono*), *The Registrum Antiquissimum of the Cathedral Church of Lincoln*, ed. C. W. Foster and K. Major (10 vols.; Lincoln Rec. Soc., 1931–73), No. 1936; *Stoke by Clare Cartulary*, ed. C. Harper-Bill and R. Mortimer (3 vols.; Suffolk Charters, 4–6; 1982–4), No. 316. See also Hudson, 'Chester Charters', 163–4. See above, Ch. 3, on granting language in regrants to heirs.
[21] e.g. *Earldom of Hereford*, Nos. 45, 54; 'Mordak Charters', *Misc. Genealogica et Heraldica*, 5th Ser. 6 (1926), 97; Stenton, *First Century*, No. 31; see also *Feudal Documents from the Abbey of Bury St Edmunds*, ed. D. C. Douglas (London, 1932), No. 103.
[22] *Confirmare* in late 11th cent.: *Regesta*, i, No. 314a; *EYC*, iii, No. 1484. 12th cent.: e.g. *Sir Christopher Hatton's Book of Seals*, ed. L. C. Loyd and D. M. Stenton (Northants Rec. Soc. and Oxford, 1950), No. 507; *Earldom of Hereford*, Nos. 1, 6, 11, 44, 46, 69, 75, 76, 81, 82.
[23] Specific confirmation of a grandfather's gifts: *Stoke*, No. 36; No. 29 includes a general confirmation of predecessors' gifts, together with some specific confirmations.
[24] See e.g. *English Episcopal Acta, II. Canterbury, 1162–90*, edd. C. R. Cheney and B. E. A. Jones (London, 1986), 197.

would also expect such renewals to include the heir's consent as often as do original gifts. They do not.[25] In addition, had this necessity existed, one might have expected a donee to be obliged to pay a relief on the succession of the donor's heir, but this was not so. As Holt has argued, the confirmations which donors' heirs issued were no doubt granted at a price, but 'such payments arose from the exercise of the new lord's will rather than the terms on which his predecessors had enfeoffed their tenants'. For their money, the tenants may have been seeking 'the convenience of a primitive form of warranty in a world in which actions of right were determined in feudal courts'.[26] Similarly, the act of confirming seems to have been clearly distinguished from that of giving. Heirs' confirmations do not mention ceremonies of seisin. Had heirs on their succession resumed seisin of their predecessors' gifts in any meaningful way, one would surely expect at least rare mentions of reseisin. Thus succession did not necessarily bring into question all the decedent's gifts.

One may anyway ask whether any rule preventing lasting gifts without the heir's participation really could have existed when there was such ideological pressure for the maintenance of gifts. An heir seeking to discontinue a gift to the Church confronted well-organized pressures and arguments. When Walter of Hereford confirmed his predecessors' grants to Llanthony Secunda, the charter stated that 'sons rightly succeed to their fathers in inheritance in this way, when they maintain and increase their alms as much as they can'.[27] Gifts to churches were intended to be perpetual. Charters from both before and after 1066 which might play a part in disputes stressed such perpetuity, sometimes adding anathemas or threats of eternal punishment to protect the gifts from infringement by heirs or others.[28] If

---

[25] For an exceptional case, see *Charters of the Honour of Mowbray*, ed. D. E. Greenway (London, 1972), No. 390. According to the Thorne model, one might also expect the lord's kin to consent to confirmations, but again instances are very rare; see *Earldom of Hereford*, No. 82; also *Danelaw Documents*, No. 244, *Monasticon Anglicanum*, ed. W. Dugdale (6 vols. in 8; London, 1817–30), vi. 865.

[26] J. C. Holt, 'Politics and Property in Early Medieval England: A Rejoinder', *P&P* 65 (1974), 133–5; cf. Garnett, 'Royal Succession', 72, who emphasizes the significance of William II's writ demanding a relief from the tenants of the vacant bishopric of Worcester, *Regesta*, i, No. 387. See also above, p. 69, on the taking of lands into hand and the receiving of homage.

[27] *Earldom of Hereford*, No. 69; maintain [*manutenere*] probably meant that the heir should not only continue the gift but also protect it.

[28] For post-1066 examples, see above, p. 168; for pre-1066, see e.g. *CMA*, i. 279–80, *Anglo-Saxon Charters*, ed. and tr. A. J. Robertson (2nd edn., Cambridge,

the gift was of long standing, the challenger also faced the canonical doctrine of prescription.[29] This laid down that churches were entitled to possessions which they had held securely, for a period generally of thirty years. This rule affected tithe litigation, a matter for church courts, and was probably also raised in land disputes.[30] Obviously we know most about moral and other pressures from the Church, and there were counter-pressures. Yet as we have seen earlier, there were also considerable pressures for the continuation of many gifts to laymen. Heirs felt bound by their predecessors' word, notably as recorded in charters. Moreover, donees, ecclesiastical or lay, did not simply rely on the good faith of heirs, backed up by moral pressure and spiritual penalties: rather they could look to others—for example the king or the donor's lord—to maintain their gift.[31] Even in an instance when a son succeeded in reclaiming his father's gift for 'certain and reasonable causes', he had to come to a compromise.[32]

Heirs' participation in grants was not a necessity, its absence automatically preventing a permanent grant. Simple legal explanations do not suffice; rather, participation was the product of a variety of social and religious obligations, some but not all of which may be referred to as legal. The views of all the parties must be taken into consideration, and it must be remembered that even an individual's view of proper practice might differ in each particular instance according to whether he was donor, donor's heir, or donee.

The grantor and the grantee both wished the grant to be as secure as possible, so that it fulfilled its intended function, and the *laudatio* was one way in which prudent donors and donees ensured this.[33] The donor's heirs might desire this, but also feel that their other interests were threatened. Participation was intended to reconcile

1956), No. CXX (= Sawyer, Nos. 732, 1032). For a pre-Conquest charter playing a part in a post-Conquest dispute, see *CMA*, ii. 35.

[29] See *Collectio Lanfranci*, Trinity College Cambridge, MS B 16 44, pp. 246, 323, Hinschius, 286, 369; Gratian, *Decretum*, C. xvi, q. iii.

[30] See e.g. *EYC*, xii, No. 76 for use concerning the donor's tenure of land he was giving to the Church. On prescription and its possible influence on vaguer lay ideas that long tenure strengthened the holder's title, see also above, p. 61 n. 203.

[31] See also Chs. 2, 7, 8. For royal protection, e.g. *Royal Writs in England from the Conquest to Glanvill*, ed. R. C. van Caenegem, (Selden Soc. 77; 1958–9), Nos. 47, 47a.

[32] *EYC*, iv, No. 105.

[33] A. Murray, *Reason and Society in the Middle Ages* (Oxford, 1978), 132–6, illuminates the two connotations of prudence in the period: it was a Christian virtue, but could also mean worldly-wise, possessing foresight. Clearly both meanings are relevant in this context of gifts to churches and their preservation.

these possible tensions. Some consent clauses must hide tough negotiation. The rejection of the idea that the *laudatio* stems from a
rule does not exclude the possibility that decisive arguments of a
legal nature sometimes could be based on participation. The heir's
previous consent might provide such an argument for a grantee
seeking that the heir continue his predecessor's gift. In unusual
circumstances, such as death-bed gifts, the absence of consent might
decisively invalidate the grant. However, in each instance the relative
importance of the norms and obligations would be affected by the
particular power circumstances.

This conclusion is backed up by Tabuteau's detailed study of the
custom which the Normans brought with them to England,[34] and also
by the nature of the treatment of alienability in twelfth-century law
books, particularly *Glanvill*.[35] *Glanvill*'s basic premiss is that a man
can give 'a certain part of his free tenement to whom he pleases in
recompense of his service, or to a religious place in alms', or as a
marriage portion.[36] Unless seisin follows the gift, nothing can effec-
tively be sought against the heir, since according to the interpretation
customary in the realm such is a naked promise rather than a true
gift. If seisin does follow 'that land will remain forever with the donee
and his heirs, if it was given to them by hereditary right.'

Having discussed death-bed gifts, *Glanvill* considers how much of
his land a man might alienate.[37] He draws in the distinction between
inheritance and acquisition. If a man has only inherited land, he can
give a certain part of it to any stranger he wishes. However, grants to

[34] Tabuteau, *Transfers of Property*, ch. 8, esp. 172–3, 175–9, 194. From Normandy,
unlike England, there survive instances of heirs pleading that the absence of their
consent entitled them to discontinue predecessors' gifts. Note e.g. the case recorded in
Orderic, iii. 186–8, where an heir challenges a gift on these grounds, although the
case is complicated by his additional claim that the land had previously been given to
him by his father. According to Orderic, the claimant had in fact previously consented
to his father's alienation, and the case ended in compromise. *Regesta*, ii, No. 1921,
confirms a gift by William Peverel 'save however the right [*rectitudine*] of William's
relatives, if they have any in it'. This suggests that relatives did not automatically have
any right in lands given away. It may be that particular circumstances here made a
challenge likely.

[35] The *Leges Henrici*'s treatment of alienation is brief, and cannot be seen as
recording generally applicable rules concerning alienation; see above, p. 60 on
inheritance and acquisition, below, p. 204 on the *retrait lignager*. The remainder of
its treatment rests heavily on *Alfred*, 41, and cannot be taken as reflecting 12th-cent.
reality; *Leges Henrici*, 70 21a, 88 14a, Downer, 224, 274.

[36] *Glanvill*, vii. 1, Hall, 69.

[37] *Glanvill*, vii. 1, Hall, 70–1; the passage is followed by a shorter discussion of
socage.

younger sons cannot easily be made, 'except with the consent of the heir'. If a man has only acquisitions, he can give some to whomever he wishes, but should not disinherit any child he may have by giving away all his acquisitions. In the absence of children, remoter heirs are no bar to complete alienation of acquisitions. If he has both inheritance and acquisition, he can give a large part or all of the acquisition to whomever he wishes and also reasonably give from his inheritance, as described above.

Glanvill's language is far from that of detailed mandatory rules. He invokes principles, for example against unreasonable acts caused by excessive emotional attachment, in a discussion of norms which generally or customarily hold true. He states that a man cannot 'easily' give 'as much as he likes' to his younger son, despite his emotional inclination so to do; 'generally a person may freely give during his life a reasonable part of his land according to his will to whomsoever he wishes.'[38] *Glanvill*'s emphasis on reasonableness resembles the moral principles sometimes put forward in the preambles to charters: 'What is reasonably done by fathers is rightly to be preserved as settled by sons who succeed them in all their possessions [*in uniuersitate possessionis*].'[39] No specific amounts are defined, whereas the later portion of the Norman *Très Ancien Coutumier* in 1218 × 23 was to specify one-third as a reasonable part.[40] Yet meanwhile the royal power which *Glanvill* describes, and the intellectual changes of which his very work is a major sign, were helping to transform his norms into more rigid legal rules.

GIFTS TO CHURCHES

I shall look first at gifts to churches, next at those to laymen other than kin, and finally at those within the family. Let us begin by simply analysing the frequency of heirs' participation in gifts to churches as recorded in charters. Unfortunately, the words denoting assent give little indication of the form, or necessity, of participation.[41] The

[38] All from *Glanvill*, vii. 1, Hall, 69–74. See P. R. Hyams, 'The Common Law and the French Connection', *A-NS* 4 (1982), esp. 81–4.

[39] *Registrum Antiquissimum*, No. 328.

[40] *TAC*, lxxxix, Tardif, 99–100.

[41] The most common words are *consensu, assensu,* and *concessu/concessione/concedente*. Slightly less frequent are *annuente* and *consilio,* and further variations exist such as *per*

forms of participation varied, from witnessing, through the consent clause, to the joint grant, and their relative significance is hard to uncover. Especially amongst lesser families, few have left many charters, and in these cases one beneficiary often dominates, so the charters may well reflect that beneficiary's drafting practice. When more than one record of a gift survives, it becomes clear that charters cannot be relied on to mention assent actually given.[42] Obviously these are major problems, and my figures cited in the text are only indications of approximate proportions of charters recording the heirs' participation, and cannot by themselves be taken as a straightforward measure of its importance.

It is, however, clear that even amongst charters recording gifts from the donor's inheritance, many do not include consent clauses. Few charters recording royal gifts mention the *laudatio*, the kin's consent. Most examples of royal family participation from before 1100 are *signa* in diploma or mixed-style documents.[43] Henry I only had a legitimate son until 1120, and William's participation is mentioned very rarely indeed.[44] Even though he was often away from the king, it is perhaps surprising that he witnessed only five of Henry's surviving charters, the first in 1115, and his *signa* appeared on two others.[45] No potential successor was singled out late in the reign through involvement in grants. Few of Stephen's charters refer to Eustace's consent, although Eustace did witness several of his father's charters, all to the Church, and in some cases issued his own

bonam uoluntatem. No word or phrase seems to be linked to a particular set of circumstances, and combinations occur.

[42] e.g. cf. *The Cartulary of Worcester Cathedral Priory*, ed. R. R. Darlington (PRS, NS 38; 1968), Nos. 116 and 117. In addition, it is often impossible to discover whether a gift was from the donor's inheritance or acquisitions. Similarly, it is often impossible to identify relationships to witnesses in lesser families, and many charters only survive in cartulary copies without witnesses. On heirs witnessing, see also D. Postles, 'Choosing Witnesses in Twelfth-Century England', *Irish Jurist*, NS 23 (1988), 336–7. Because of all these difficulties, the small numbers of charters, and the problems of dating, I do not represent the figures graphically.

[43] Robert, Rufus, and Henry appear approximately equally in their father's grants of lands and rights in England; *Regesta*, i, Nos. 105, 149 include Robert's *signum*; Nos. 105, 149, 192, 206, 232, 237a Rufus's; 135, 149, 232, 237a Henry's. Of these, No. 105 is an untrustworthy document, No. 135 a charter of the queen, and No. 149 a joint grant by the king and queen. Mention of the king's son as witness in a writ charter is extremely rare; No. 247. In Rufus's grants, the *signa* of his brother Henry appear very rarely, in mixed-style documents; *Regesta*, i, Nos. 301, 398.

[44] See *Regesta*, ii, Nos. 1091, 1223.

[45] *Regesta*, ii, Nos. 1092, 1098a, 1102, 1131, 1204, 1224; he also witnessed No. 1108, a charter of his mother's. See also No. 1015a.

charter of confirmation.[46] Several joint grants of the empress and Duke Henry survive. In part, this may reflect Angevin practice: the counts' charters record the participation of their kin much more often than do those of the kings of England. However, it is notable that when Henry appears in charters with the empress, even in his father's lifetime, he is described not as consenting but as joint grantor. Henry was not simply heir to Geoffrey and the empress. In the 1140s and early 1150s he was claimant to the throne. Joint grants advertised his claim, even at a very young age.[47] Moreover, grantees desired his name on their charters for future security. Thereafter, amongst Henry's charters as king, only very occasionally did one of his legitimate sons act as witness.[48]

The participation of heirs is also rare in great laymen's charters, particularly after 1100. Of the two eleventh-century Mandeville charters concerned with English gifts to the Church, one records the consent of the donor's son and heir, the other threatens with divine judgment any heirs who harmed the gift.[49] The donor was Geoffrey I, the first member of the family to hold lands in England, so both gifts consisted of acquisitions. However, no Mandeville charters in the period 1100–66 mention the heir's consent even to gifts from the inheritance.[50] Of the gifts to the Church by Henry and Roger, earls of Warwick from 1088 to 1153, only one mentions his son and heir's consent.[51] The charters of most other families show similarly few

---

[46] e.g. *Regesta*, iii, No. 694, Eustace's own charter of confirmation No. 694a; see also e.g. Nos. 327, 551.

[47] *Regesta*, iii, Nos. 88, 372, 836; in addition, Nos. 705, 708 recall joint grants now lost. On Henry as claimant, see W. L. Warren, *Henry II* (London, 1973), 32, 38; M. Chibnall, *The Empress Matilda* (Oxford, 1991), 112, 115, 143–59. Angevin practice: e.g. two of Count Geoffrey's three grants to the cathedral of Angers mention his sons' participation: *Cartulaire noir de la cathédrale d'Angers*, ed. C. Urseau (Paris and Angers, 1908), Nos. CXXXVIII, CCX; the exception is No. CCXI. None of these is a standard gift of land. See also *Regesta*, iii, Nos. 19–21.

[48] Early in his reign, Henry's brothers sometimes witness: e.g. *Ancient Charters Royal and Private Prior to A.D. 1200*, ed. J. H. Round (PRS 10; 1888), Nos. 34, 36, 38. Henry the young king witnessing: see 'The Staffordshire Chartulary', ed. R. W. Eyton and G. Wrottesley, *William Salt Arch. Soc.* 3 (1882), 226. John witnessing in the decade after 1175: e.g. *Cartae Antiquae, 11–20*, ed. J. C. Davis (PRS, NS 33; 1960), No. 518.

[49] *Westminster Abbey Charters, 1066–c.1214*, ed. E. Mason (London Rec. Soc. 25; 1988), No. 436; P. M. Barnes and C. F. Slade (edd.), *Stenton Miscellany* (PRS, NS 36; 1960), 107–8.

[50] *Monasticon*, iv. 148–9, the foundation charter of Walden Abbey, from 1140 × 4, curses anyone interfering with the gift.

[51] Bodleian Library, MS Dugdale 12, p. 267.

mentions of the heirs' participation.[52] A possible exception may be the charters of Earl Robert of Leicester, if one takes witnessing to amount to consent. Although only two of his relevant charters mention the assent of Robert his son, another three are witnessed by him.[53]

As for lesser families, of the charters of the Honour of Richmond besides those of the earl, only one of the nine from the 1120s mentions assent, and this for a gift of an acquisition,[54] but thereafter until the 1170s about half do so.[55] In the last quarter of the century, participation becomes rarer.[56] Turning to grants to individual beneficiaries, the picture is varied. Oseney charters often mention the *laudatio* even into the thirteenth century, whereas it is less common in Eynsham ones.[57] The latter pattern seems the more widespread.

---

[52] (a) *Earldom of Gloucester Charters*, ed. R. B. Patterson (Oxford, 1973): no examples of *laudatio* for male donor; a gift of Countess Mabel, No. 167, mentions her heir's participation; son witnesses No. 34. (b) *Earldom of Hereford*: gifts with *laudatio*, Nos. 2, 3, 82 (inheritance, see VCH, *Wiltshire*, x. 62), 99, all to Llanthony Secunda; No. 62 to St Peter's, Gloucester. It is unlikely that any of these lands were Earl Roger's acquisitions. Gifts certainly from inheritance without *laudatio*, Nos. 90, 94, 119; in addition other gifts made without the *laudatio* may well be from the inheritance although this cannot be proved. (c) Charters of earls of Richmond: no examples of *laudatio* for gifts. Examples of gifts certainly from the inheritance without *laudatio*: e.g. *EYC*, iv, Nos. 3, 13. (d) See also Hudson, 'Chester Charters', 171. Occasionally charters may have included other devices which rendered heirs' consent irrelevant; e.g. *EYC*, iv, No. 11 addressed to sons, No. 8 anathema against heirs violating gift. On the other hand, an anathema against the heirs might be a sign that they had refused to consent.

[53] Consent: PRO, C 146/C 6859 (at least in part from the inheritance; transcript courtesy of Dr Crouch); J. Nichols, *The History and Antiquities of the County of Leicester* (4 vols. in 8; London, 1795–1815), iii, pt. 2, 814. Witnessing: Nichols, *Leicester*, iii, pt. 2, 814; British Library, Add. Chart. 47384; D. B. Crouch, 'The Foundation of Leicester Abbey', *Midland History*, 12 (1987), 9. In addition, Robert's foundation of Luffield Priory in 1124 almost certainly took place before his son's birth, and was done by the counsel of the earl de Warenne, Nigel d'Aubigny and Waleran de Meulan, Robert's brother; *Luffield Priory Charters*, ed. G. R. Elvey (2 vols.; Northants Rec. Soc. 22, 26; 1968, 1975), No. 1.

[54] *EYC*, v, No. 358, the last witnesses also being the donor's sons; the charter is the product of slightly peculiar circumstances, and conceivably it records a transaction when the donor knew that death was approaching. The land was an acquisition; *EYC*, v. 297–8.

[55] Gifts probably from inheritance with *laudatio*: *EYC*, v, Nos. 133, 179, 192, 227, 235, 256–7, 367; gifts probably from acquisitions with *laudatio*: Nos. 150, 186, 222, 296. Other gifts with *laudatio*: iv, No. 91; v, Nos. 156, 158, 173, 187, 231, 343, 353, 384. Gifts definitely from inheritance without *laudatio*: e.g. v, Nos. 129, 134. Note that charters from *c*.1130–50 are very scarce.

[56] *EYC*, iv, Nos. 93, 96, 114; v, Nos. 132 (inheritance), 293, 305.

[57] D. Postles, 'Securing the Gift in Oxfordshire Charters', *Archives*, 19 (1990), esp. 186.

Among the gifts of diverse origin to St Mary's, Lincoln, assents remain at a relatively low level throughout the twelfth century, with no sign of major chronological change.[58] Elsewhere, our evidence shows assents as relatively uncommon in gifts to other cathedral churches.[59] Amongst monastic charters there are further signs of decline from *c*.1170 or even earlier. Few charters recording gifts to Stoke by Clare from the early and mid-twelfth century include assent,[60] although the general confirmations to Stoke, notably that by Archbishop Theobald in 1150 × 61, do reveal some instances which might otherwise be unknown.[61] Yet even these confirmations do not suggest that the heir's participation was a feature of all gifts, and thereafter it disappears, apart from very isolated instances in the decades either side of 1200.[62]

Thus clauses recording heirs' participation were more common in lesser men's charters than in those of their superiors. Conceivably different norms might have existed for great men and for lesser, but, apart from the frequency of consent clauses, there is no evidence for this. Certainly *Glanvill* makes no such distinction. Other, probably sufficient, reasons exist for the difference. Consent clauses tend to appear in beneficiary-drafted deeds; these remain more important for lesser grantors than for great. Secondly, lesser families often concentrated their patronage on one church, for example the Kymes on Bullington Priory, and the close bond possibly encouraged participation.[63] Unusually close ties helped to produce the few concentr-

[58] Pre-1160: *Registrum Antiquissimum*, No. 2001; pre-1170: Nos. 1297, 1935, 2065; *c*.1170: No. 1146; later 12th cent.: e.g. Nos. 1111, 1114, 1117, 1144, 1257, 1342 and 1344 (grants by a woman from her dower), 1435. Note a group of three charters of Hugh Malet, datable only to 1154 × 89, all mentioning kin participation: Nos. 1381–3.

[59] e.g. *Worcester*, No. 119; also Nos. 117, 120.

[60] e.g. *Stoke*, Nos. 186, 273, 282, 308, 335, 531, 560; note also No. 264, countergift to heir.

[61] e.g. *Stoke*, No. 137, xxxiv and xxxv, cf. No. 37, x and iii; on No. 137, see *Stoke*, iii. 51–3.

[62] *Stoke*, No. 333 from 1156 × 73, Nos. 158–9, 169, 267 (a quitclaim), 575, 578 from late 12th or early 13th cent. A similar pattern of decline from *c*.1160 is suggested e.g. by the original Kirkstead charters included in *Danelaw Documents*; all four gifts by lesser laymen before 1160 mention assent: Nos. 167, 176, 202 (inheritance—see lvii–lviii), 203. Grants datable to the 1160s are scarce, but fewer than half from the 1170s mention heirs' participation, and thereafter very few do so: Nos. 170, 173, 175, 181, 188–90, 206, 210.

[63] e.g. participation amongst the original charters included in *Danelaw Documents*: gifts definitely from inheritance, Nos. 20, 48, 61; other gifts, Nos. 3, 58, 59, 71, 89; exceptions: Nos. 28, 56 (sons witness), 103 (a temporary gift from acquisitions; sons

ations of consent clauses in grants by greater families, for example
those of the family of Miles of Gloucester to Llanthony Secunda.[64]
Thirdly, families with concentrated lands were more likely to be
present in large numbers at gift ceremonies. Occasionally, as with the
Kymes, the recording of participation may have amounted to a family
custom, although as always the copying of formulae may have had an
effect. However, the inclusion of consent clauses is not standard
practice even in the charters of lesser laymen.[65] I leave my comments
on the limited number of such clauses to the end of the chapter. Now
I ask why did heirs on occasion participate in gifts to the Church?

Donor, donee, and family members themselves might all desire that
the kin be involved in gifts to the Church. The motives were various.
For those consenting, as for the donor, much of the inspiration must
have been religious. The individual participants wished their names
to be recorded so that they might reap due benefit in heaven: they
might also appear in the charters' *pro anima* clauses, which detail
those for whose souls the grants had been made.[66] Donors too
desired the inclusion of kin for their spiritual benefit: 'with my wife
Lesceline and by grant of my son William, . . . whom I wish to share
in these alms in every way, I presented this gift to God and St Peter
on the altar of the said Apostle Peter', declared Geoffrey I de
Mandeville.[67]

witness.) On the early history of the Kymes, see B. Golding, 'Simon of Kyme: The
Making of a Rebel', *Nottingham Medieval Studies*, 27 (1983), 23–6.

[64] *Earldom of Hereford*, Nos. 2, 3, 99.

[65] Bearing in mind that many early post-Conquest grants were likely to concern
acquisitions, note that among the charters from before 1110 in *EYC*, only a few include
the heirs' participation and a few others are witnessed by them: *EYC*, ii, Nos. 855
(witnessed by wife and sons; acquisitions), 856 and 857 (witnessed by brothers; at least
in part inheritance), vi, No. 1 (wife and sons' agreement; acquisitions), xi, No. 3 (joint
gift with brother; acquisitions—wife's *maritagium*, brother probably tenant, see pp. 2,
21), xii, No. 15 (witnessed by son; acquisitions). Note also the relevant charters from
before c.1170 in Stenton's *First Century*, the *Book of Seals*, and *Facsimiles of Early
Charters in Oxford Moniment Rooms*, ed. H. E. Salter (Oxford, 1929). Although few,
these give a reasonable geographical spread. The only charter from before 1130 bears
signa of donor, his wife, and two sons; *Oxford Charters*, No. 14. Thereafter around
one-third mention heir's participation: *Oxford Charters*, Nos. 52, 65 (probably from
inheritance), 83; Stenton, *First Century*, Nos. 38 (inheritance), 46; see also No. 37, wife
as co-donor; *Book of Seals*, Nos. 143 (probably inheritance), 221, 355. Examples of gifts
definitely from inheritance without *laudatio*, *Book of Seals*, Nos. 152, 509; *Oxford
Charters*, No. 76.

[66] e.g. *Registrum Antiquissimum*, No. 1297, *Danelaw Documents*, No. 167.

[67] *Westminster*, No. 436.

Participation also emphasized the religious and emotional tie between family and church. The relationship involved not only the head
of the family, who would be the main donor; other family members
might, for example, be buried at the church. Solidarity would be most
clearly expressed on special, emotional occasions. Thus a charter of
early in Henry II's reign records that Philip of Kyme and his heirs
gave the church of Ingham to Bullington Priory: 'we made this gift to
them in the hand of lord [*domni*] Robert the Second bishop of
Lincoln on the day of the translation of my mother when she was
placed next to my father in the chapter of the nuns, for the souls of
my father and mother and of all the faithful'.[68]

Participation also had more general social aspects. Consent, and
confirmations after the donor's death, expressed family solidarity:

if his heir tries to take away the alms which is interposed as a bridge between
his father and paradise by which his father can cross, the heir is, as far as he
is able, disinheriting his father from the kingdom of heaven, wherefore the
heir will not by right obtain the inheritance which remains, since when he
kills his father he proves himself no son.[69]

The son who did not confirm his father's gift was sinning not only
against God, the saints, and the Church, but also against his father.

Concerns more directly connected to control of land further
encouraged participation in alienation. Even if it was morally wrong
to discontinue any gift which aspired to perpetuity, men certainly did
so in practice.[70] This might be the product of sin, an exertion of
force with no colourable justification, or an assertion of a claim which
the heir, and others, believed justified. He might argue that a closer
but now deceased heir had consented to a gift to which he himself
would not have agreed, or that he had not been born at the time of
the gift.[71] Genuine doubt might also exist over the amount of land

[68] *Danelaw Documents*, No. 58.
[69] Stenton, *First Century*, No. 5. See also above, p. 183, citing *Registrum Antiquissimum*, No. 328; below, p. 223 on Roger of Poitou; also *English Lawsuits from
William I to Richard I*, ed. R. C. van Caenegem (2 vols.; Selden Soc. 106, 107;
1990–1), No. 343 for an heir acting as he should do.
[70] See e.g. *Cartularium Monasterii de Rameseia*, ed. W. H. Hart and P. A. Lyons (3
vols.; London, 1884–93), No. LX; *Textus Roffensis*, ed. T. Hearne (Oxford, 1720),
189–90, where a son makes his claim despite having earlier consented, A. Saltman,
Theobald, Archbishop of Conterbury (London, 1956), Supplementary Documents B.
[71] See also White, 'Succession to Fiefs', 125. *CDF*, No. 320 shows a dispute arising
in Normandy based on a claim through an heir who had not been born at the time of
the gift.

which had been given.[72] Alternatively, the heir might claim that the land still owed service. The church would regard such action as the heir going back on the terms of his ancestor's gift, and in addition if services continued to be refused, the heir might seize back the land.

It was obviously in the interests of the beneficiary that such challenges be prevented or defeated, and there are some signs that the donee provided the main impetus for obtaining consent. The frequency of consent clauses varies between ecclesiastical beneficiaries, suggesting that the church determined their inclusion. Moreover, consent clauses appear most frequently in beneficiary-drafted documents: the draftsman wished to protect his church, and valued the role of carefully phrased writing in so doing.[73]

However, such records were also in the donors' interests, for they too wished their gifts to remain firm.

Herbert fitzHelgot wanted to avoid any claim being made after him concerning the gifts which his father and he had made to [Shrewsbury Abbey] and, although they had been confirmed in a royal charter, he wanted his sons to confirm them by their own grant. He therefore sent them with their pious mother to this church, i.e. Eutropius who was to be the heir after the father and his brothers Nicholas and Herbert, and having prayed in the chapter and granted the donations of their father and their grandfather, they took the text of the gospel into their own hands and offered on the altar of St Peter before many witnesses what had been granted.[74]

An heir's assent to the gift greatly weakened his ability to discontinue it. Consent involved publicity which would later increase at least the moral pressure on him to maintain the grant: men must keep their word. Further publicity and greater moral pressure could be obtained by presenting countergifts to those consenting, and by involving them

[72] An heir who claimed that a beneficiary was holding more than had been given might appear to that beneficiary to be reneging on the initial gift; e.g. *Regesta*, ii, No. 803. A donor might also give the same land to two beneficiaries, one of whom would later accuse the heir of not maintaining the gift; see e.g. *Worcester*, pp. xxxj–xxxiij, Nos. 252–5; *Regesta*, ii, Nos. 1754–5, 1938; *Historia et Cartularium Monasterii Sancti Petri Gloucestriae*, ed. W. H. Hart (3 vols.; London, 1863–7), Nos. CXXX, CXCVIII–CCVII. I do not examine such disputes in depth since they involve not so much the heir as the original donor going back on his gift. See also e.g. HMC, *Ninth Report, Appendix*, 62, where there is a dispute over whether a church had fully paid the purchase price for a piece of land.

[73] See below, p. 205; also Tabuteau, *Transfers of Property*, 179.

[74] *The Cartulary of Shrewsbury Abbey*, ed. U. Rees (2 vols.; Aberystwyth, 1975), No. 1.

in the ceremony of giving.[75] Charters perpetuated such consent and such pressures.[76]

These pressures did not always prevent an heir who had consented from trying to discontinue the gift, but at least in some disputes which ensued, the claimant's earlier consent was decisive. In *c*.1155 × 8 Ralph Carbunel gave the canons of Easby two carucates to hold of him and his heirs in pure and perpetual alms. One and a half were to be held in demesne, the remaining half by Ralph's brother Ernald for an annual service. Ernald solemnly promised that his part, like all the rest, would remain with the church and canons in perpetuity. Soon afterwards, Richard de Rollos confirmed various of his men's gifts to Easby, including Ralph's, and Earl Conan of Richmond quitclaimed the canons of all his services from the lands they held of his men, including these carucates.[77] Yet Ernald still sought to overturn the gift in the court of Richard de Rollos at Richmond, with the help of a royal writ. How far his case went is unclear, but one of the two charters recording the settlement states that Ernald 'gave and granted and by his charter confirmed' to the canons the two carucates which his brother had previously given with his consent. They were to hold free of vexation from him and his heirs. The prominent mention of consent suggests that the canons saw this as their vital argument: consent should prevent future challenge.[78]

The protection provided by participation was also directed against threats other than attempted discontinuation of the gift by the heir.[79] The donor's or his heirs' officials might oppress the beneficiary, against their master's will. Outsiders, with or without a claim, could threaten a gift. Thus Osbert de Wanci made a gift to Biddlesden during Stephen's reign:

I made and granted this gift by the counsel of Alice my wife and Robert my son and heir and my other sons and friends . . . to be defended and

---

[75] See e.g. *Earldom of Hereford*, No. 2; also above, pp. 161, 173.

[76] e.g. in a slightly different context, *EYC*, v, No. 174.

[77] *EYC*, v, Nos. 242, 235; iv, No. 39 respectively.

[78] *EYC*, v, No. 245. The other charter, No. 244, is termed a *conuentio*. There is no information about the nature of the writ. See also *CChR*, v. 57 (10), a dispute stemming from a sale where the heirs had not merely consented but also received money. For later cases, see Milsom, *Legal Framework*, 123 n. 4. From Normandy, see Orderic, vi. 180.

[79] This dual aspect of foreswearing interference and promising protection against others resembles the negative and the positive commitments of the warrantor discussed above, Ch. 2.

maintained free and quit of all secular custom and exaction for me and my
heirs against all who try to bring any claim against the said church.[80]

Such concern with outside challenges also throws a different light on
heirs' charters of confirmation. As well as being renunciations of any
claim the heir might have, they were literally strengthenings of the
gift, promises of help should the church's tenure be threatened.[81]

Thus far I have considered the donor's obligations to the church,
and his heirs' obligations to the donor, the church, and their own
salvation. The donor also had obligations to his heirs, and probably to
the wider kin. If a son acted ill by disinheriting his father of his
heavenly inheritance, his father acted ill by depriving his heir of an
earthly one. He did so if he alienated too much of the family land,
particularly if the gift was made for reduced or no worldly service.
Even a gift requiring the church beneficiary to perform temporal
services could entail a loss of control over the land compared with a
similar gift to a layman. It is notable how few charters to churches
state that the gift was to be held of the donor and his heirs,[82] whereas
most grants to laymen included such a phrase, thus emphasizing the
bond of lordship. Also, distraining churches might involve particular
difficulties.[83] If the gift was made free of temporal service, earthly
disherison was still clearer. Such gifts required care. In *Glanvill*'s
terms, the donor must act reasonably.

Conceivably a standard maximum proportion, say one-third, of a
man's inheritance was customarily alienable in some honours, but
there is more evidence for flexibility.[84] As we have seen, Archbishop
Theobald in 1145 advised Roger de Valognes that a noble and
generous man who had a holding of six knights should give the land
not of a third of a knight but of an entire one or more to the
Church.[85] At Ramsey, it was agreed in one instance that if a man
died without an heir from his wife's body all his land in Huntingdon

[80] Stenton, *First Century*, No. 46.
[81] e.g. *Worcester*, Nos. 146–54, 159, esp. 152. See also below, pp. 196–7.
[82] Specified that church should hold of the donor and his heirs: e.g. *Stoke*, No. 37;
Danelaw Documents, No. 157. An exceptional group are charters to Easby, many of
which contain such references: *EYC*, iv, No. 36; v, Nos. 149–52, 197, 200–1, 211,
213, 235, 242.
[83] See above, Ch. 2.
[84] For suggestions of evidence for a limit to one-third, see J. Biancalana, 'For Want
of Justice: Legal Reforms of Henry II', *Columbia Law Review*, 88 (1988), 493 and n.
321; also above, p. 183, on the *TAC*.
[85] Stenton, *First Century*, No. 5, quoted at greater length above, p. 158.

was to pass to the abbey; if he did have an heir, only half of it was to do so.[86] The reasonableness of each grant was thus determined by negotiation and by particular circumstance.

Throughout the period, such a limitation to reasonable gifts which were not to their own disinheritance must have been the crucial criterion in heirs' decisions whether to consent.[87] Unfortunately, refusals leading to the abandonment or reduction of the proposed gift were unlikely to be recorded; none survive in the evidence which I have examined. Nor have I found cases where the heir attempted to justify his discontinuance of a gift on the grounds that it was to his disinheritance, although such cases probably occurred and Milsom has found some partially hidden in the early plea rolls.[88] However, we do have a general statement of the norm against excessive gifts in a confirmation issued by Archbishop Theobald to Stoke by Clare in 1150 × 61: it records that Gilbert de Clare had ordered his barons to give to the said church as much of their lands, churches, and tithes as they wished, 'without disinheritance of their successors'.[89] This instance is particularly notable for two reasons. First, it shows that the interests of the donor's heir and the donor's lord might be united against excessive alienation free of service. Secondly, it shows at least some acceptance of the norm by the Church, and similar statements appear in canonical collections.[90] These must be taken as a balance to the view, expressed by Orderic, that those who piled up treasures for their heirs were piling up greater evil and wretchedness for themselves.[91] Ecclesiastical views were neither simple, nor universally opposed to lay-generated norms such as this. However, a gift which seemed reasonable to the ecclesiastical beneficiary may often have

---

[86] *Chronicon Abbatiae Rameseiensis*, ed. W. D. Macray (London, 1886), 295. Note also the provision in the spurious foundation charter of St Werburgh's abbey, *The Charters of the Anglo-Norman Earls of Chester*, ed. G. Barraclough (Rec. Soc. of Lancs. and Cheshire, 126; 1988), No. 3. In a Norman charter of 1088, C. H. Haskins, *Norman Institutions* (New York, 1918), 19 n. 60, a man about to enter a monastery states that he was giving 100 vavassours to his sons, but that it was right that he keep one for himself and the monks with whom he would live and die.

[87] See Postles, 'Securing the Gift', 187–8, for the care taken in one 13th-cent. grant which was to the disinheritance of the family. See also White, 'Succession to Fiefs', 124–5 on confirmations.

[88] Milsom, *Legal Framework*, 125–6. On such disputes in western France, see White, *Gifts to Saints*, esp. 76–7, 148–9.

[89] *Stoke*, No. 137 (ii).

[90] e.g. Ivo of Chartres, *Decretum*, pars iii, c.261.

[91] Orderic, iii. 262, see also iii. 152.

seemed unreasonable to the donor's heir. There was plenty of room for dispute.

We have, therefore, different norms and obligations of varying strength. These sometimes helped to persuade men to obtain consent for alienations of acquisitions, more often if they were granting inherited possessions. Besides the amount of land being granted, what else affected the norms' weight? First, one must wonder about the heir's ability to refuse to assent. The younger the heir, the less likely he was to be able to do so.[92] He might later claim the excuse either of his youth or duress, but such were likely to be points of debate rather than knock-down arguments. Documents do not stress that consent should be voluntary, and some record that the father was to make his family assent.[93]

Secondly, the closeness of the heir's kinship to the donor probably affected his say in the gift. As we have already seen, an heir was more secure in his expectation of succeeding if he was a son rather than a distant relative, and records of consents show a similar pattern. Often those consenting are referred to only as heirs, but rarely is any relationship specified except that of son, or more unusually brother. Obligations to other kin may have been weaker, even if they were the closest heir. *Glanvill* made no distinction between children and other heirs for the alienation of inherited land. However, he wrote that if a man held only acquisitions, and had no children of his body, he could give some or all of his acquisitions heritably to whomsoever he wished.[94] Thus the proximity of the heirs affected their control of alienation.

Thirdly, in certain circumstances the desirability of an heir's

[92] See the case discussed by Milsom, *Legal Framework*, 124; for another dispute involving the question of the willingness of the heir's consent, see *CDF*, Nos. 1112–23.

[93] e.g. Stenton, *First Century*, No. 37; *Gloucester Cartulary*, No. DCCXXVIII; Van Caenegem, *Lawsuits*, No. 343. On the other hand, if a father tried to give away land he had already given to his son, the latter might have real choice as to whether to allow the grant; see e.g. *Danelaw Documents*, No. 181. Here, the questions of family and tenant participation become intertwined.

[94] *Glanvill*, vii. 1, Hall, 71. Accounts of Walter Espec's founding of the monastery of Kirkham may suggest a tension in views. The *Relatio de Standard*, cited above Ch. 4 n. 31, stated that Walter made Christ heir of some of his best possessions, since he lacked children as heirs, even though he had 'vigorous nephews'. However, the foundation charter of the abbey stated that he acted 'by the consent of my nephews' and the document was witnessed by the nephews—presumably they participated as his heirs; *Cartularium Abbathiae de Rievalle*, ed. J. C. Atkinson (Surtees Soc. 83; 1889), No. CCCXLVII, see also No. XLII. From pre-1066 Normandy, see Orderic, ii. 132.

consent strengthened towards a requirement, both to prevent unreasonable gifts and to protect those reasonable ones which were
made. The clearest is the death-bed gift.[95] The *Liber Eliensis*
presents a model instance, probably from the 1090s.[96] Harscoit
Musard had always been a friend of St Etheldreda and her monks.
Falling severely ill, he persuaded them to accept him as a monk,
promising to give them a manor together with himself. He was
accepted, and so was his gift. The donor and beneficiary were clearly
determined to show the propriety of the grant for it was sealed in the
sight of clerics and knights, and Harscoit's son Robert quitclaimed
his father's gift from himself and his heirs to the church.

Pressing desire to reach heaven might, however, separate the
interests of a dying man from those of his heir. Previously, both
had earthly interests. Now the dying man might think it perfectly
reasonable to use his possessions to save his soul. To others, such
actions might appear less reasonable, especially if they seemed to
result from excessive clerical pressure.[97] *Glanvill* therefore takes the
death-bed gift as an exception to a person's freedom to give a
reasonable part of his land to whom he pleased. If a dying man acted
contrary to his previous wishes, it was assumed that mental turmoil
was the cause. However, such a gift could be lasting if made with the
heir's consent and confirmed by his consent.[98] The slightly contorted
Latin attempts to cope with a procedural point. A dying man would
have difficulty delivering seisin. Formal livery may not have been
needed earlier in the period, but some ceremony was desirable, and
by performing one an heir might complete his dying relative's gift.
Thus a charter of *c*.1087 records that a certain Swain had given land

[95] On death-bed gifts, Pollock and Maitland, ii. 323–19, M. M. Sheehan, *The Will
in Medieval England* (Toronto, 1963), 115–9, Milsom, *Legal Framework*, 121–2.

[96] *Liber Eliensis*, ed. E. O. Blake (Camden Soc., 3rd Ser. 92; 1962), 277; for the
date, ibid. 207–8, which records the royal confirmation of the gift (= *Regesta*, i, No.
389.)

[97] Sheehan, *The Will*, 270, argues that 'the emphasis on the limitation of ecclesiastical greed is largely based on a text from *Glanvill*'. However, there are other
examples of ecclesiastical pressure: see e.g. the letter 'De Contemptu Mundi' in Henry
of Huntingdon, *Historia Anglorom*, ed. T. Arnold (London, 1879), 307, where the
count of Meulan resists clerical requests to return lands which—according to the
clerics—he had taken by force, rather than to pass them on to his sons. From the
count's point of view, the churchmen's urgings probably sounded like clerical greed.
See also e.g. the 12th-cent. *chanson de geste*, *Garin de Loherain*, where the inability of
the Franks to resist the Vandal invasions is blamed on excessive death-bed gifts to the
Church; White, *Gifts to Saints*, 77.

[98] *Glanvill*, vii. 1, Hall, 70.

at Wheatley to Westminster Abbey, and that Swain's son and wife made the gift on the altar of St Peter on the day that Swain was buried, with their barons watching and in the presence of the abbot and monks.[99]

Nevertheless, disputes arose over death-bed gifts, even when heirs confirmed them. Probably in 1127, the dying Ralph Basset gave Abingdon Abbey four hides in Chaddleworth. The land was seised into the church's demesne, and confirmed by Ralph's sons who were present. However, Ralph's grandson, Richard fitzThurstan, on his succession moved a claim for the lands.[100] He was defeated by the monks through the help of Henry II. Richard's charter recording the settlement acknowledges his father's agreement to the original gift by attributing it to both Ralph and Thurstan.

Assent may have been particularly necessary too if a healthy donor was about to become a monk. Earl Roger of Hereford became a monk in 1155. Although he died within the next nine months, his taking the habit may have resulted from the defeat of his rebellion against the king rather than from ill health. Between 1155 and 1160 his brother and heir Walter granted various lands to St Peter's, Gloucester, in exchange for the 100 solidates which Roger, with Walter's assent, had granted when he became a monk.[101] In addition, the frequency of consent in such circumstances must reflect the presence of relations at a ceremony which had important consequences for the family.

Other circumstances made participation especially desirable. An exceptional series of charters for Easby Abbey shows a donor obliged to obtain the consent both of the heir and of the lord, otherwise the gift would have fallen through. It is the survival of one very unusual document, datable to 1158 × 71, which casts a special light on the case:

I Tiffany daughter of Roald ought to ensure that my heir and my brother and lord Alan the Constable will grant and confirm with their charters, in the

---

[99] *Westminster*, No. 237.

[100] *CMA*, ii. 170–1, 188–90; *Two Cartularies of Abingdon Abbey*, ed. C. F. Slade and G. Lambrick (2 vols.; Oxford Hist. Soc. NS 32, 33; 1990, 1992), ii, No. 294 is a copy of a charter of Ralph recording his grant. The dating, most broadly 1127 × 9, is from the presence of Walter Basset abbot of St Benet of Hulme 1127–34. It is strange that this charter does not appear in the *Chronicle*.

[101] *Earldom of Hereford*, No. 76. See also e.g. *Regesta*, ii, No. 1523; *EYC*, v, No. 296. On the parallel to physical death, see also Van Caenegem, *Writs*, 317 on *mort d'ancestor* applying to descendants of one who had become a monk.

presence of sufficient witnesses, the gift of the land of Warth and my charter which I gave to the church and canons of St Agatha . . . And if I cannot do this, and let that not be the case, I will give back to the canons of St Agatha the twenty marks of silver which they had given me, within a short time just as they please. [Seven men are then listed as sureties.] And that money will be given back to the canons without any trouble if they lose the said land through my heirs. And on top of this, let those who take it away from them have God's and my curse.[102]

The terms of this document are not those of a temporary grant to be extended to permanence by obtaining consent, but of a permanent grant as yet incomplete. Assents were in fact obtained, with the lord promising to warrant the land or give an exchange when the donor's heir came of age, suggesting that the heir would have real discretion over the continuation of the gift on the donor's death. Both the lord's assent and the heir's later confirmation used the verb *dare*, 'to give', to describe their actions. These charters and their exceptional terms may be the product of unusual honorial or family circumstances, or they may result from the donor being a woman. The large proportion of women's grants which record the heir's participation do suggest a special requirement for consent.[103] Again, beneficiaries must have felt it prudent to obtain such consent, perhaps fearing that an heir would claim that the donor, as a woman, had acted unreasonably, probably because they desired male protectors to maintain the gift.

Thus the heirs' participation was most desired when donors themselves were least able to maintain their gifts and to influence the actions of their heirs. Once more we see power and individual circumstances affecting the weight which norms carried. I now go on to analyse the weight and functioning of these and similar norms when gifts were made to laymen.

GIFTS TO UNRELATED LAYMEN

Charters recording gifts to laymen outside the kin mention the *laudatio* much less frequently than do gifts to churches, although again

---

[102] *EYC*, v, No. 228; see also Nos. 227, 229, 230, 237, 239. Possibly the land was Tiffany's *maritagium*. Conceivably some other documents similar to No. 228 were produced concerning other grants, but did not survive because of their irrelevance once the assents were obtained. For a male donor promising to make his lord and kin consent to a gift, see Stenton, *First Century*, No. 37, above, n. 93.

[103] e.g. *Danelaw Documents*, Nos. 113, 210; *Earldom of Gloucester*, No. 167; *EYC*, v, No. 256; also BL MS Harleian 3650, fos. 10ᵛ–11ᵛ. Sons' consents to their mothers' gifts go on well beyond this period; e.g. *Book of Seals*, No. 126 from 1196 × 1213.

there are very occasional exceptions, for example in charters of particular families.[104] Various explanations of the usual pattern are possible. Compared with grants to churches, there was not the same incentive of spiritual reward for participation. The draftsman might have no direct interest in the preservation of the grant and hence have taken less care in recording assents. Perhaps, in the more oral lay world, the act of consent was enough, without it being written down.

Explanations more closely connected to the nature of land-holding are also relevant. Whilst succession generally was secure, there may still be some truth in the idea that consent for grants to laymen was less important because they were less permanent than grants to churches. Charters to laymen generally avoided the perpetuity language which was common for churches.[105] Lay families did die out, and the donor was his lay grantee's *ultimus heres*, his final heir; a church had no *ultimus heres* for it never died.[106] Lay tenants might forfeit for breach of homage, a church would not.

Moreover, for the donor's heir, gifts to laymen did not involve such a loss of worldly resources or control as gifts to the Church, especially those in free alms.[107] Here the interests of the heir were often compatible with those of the donor. His predecessor's gift left a vassal, who would swell his entourage and do services. Whereas some churches enjoyed special protection against distraint, lay tenants were easier to compel to perform service and to answer in court concerning any misdeed.[108] A lay vassal's loyalty might be divided between his various worldly lords, but were not complicated by the other obligations of ecclesiastical tenants.

The lay donee anyway may have been less concerned to obtain the assent of the donor's heir. He might rely more on the support of the seignorial court. On a new lord's succession, all the peers of the court faced a threat to their continuing tenure. Sometimes they may have been happy to see one of their number rejected, but usually they cannot have encouraged seignorial discretion. Some sense of their

[104] See e.g. the charters involving grants to the Galle family from the latter part of the 12th cent.; e.g. *Danelaw Documents*, Nos. 540, 542, 545, 548–9.
[105] Perpetuity language for laymen: e.g. *Regesta*, ii, No. 1562; *Oxford Charters*, No. 49, *Book of Seals*, No. 528, *Feudal Documents*, Nos. 149, 158.
[106] *Glanvill*, vii. 17, Hall, 90. For the feeling that a grant to the Church was lost forever, see also vi. 17, p. 67.
[107] See above, p. 192. It should of course be remembered that a donor's heir might also benefit in many ways from a gift to the Church.
[108] See above, Ch. 2.

common interest would help to pressure the new lord to maintain his father's gift, increase his shame if he sought to break his father's promise that a grant would be heritable. Churches may have been excluded from such solidarity, churchmen socially separated from the barons of the court, and sometimes perhaps resented if they did not contribute to the services owed by the honour.

Given these various reasons for the rarity of charters mentioning the heir's participation in gifts to laymen, it is notable that some of the few which do record consent are for reduced or nominal service. Thus in 1155 × c.65 Richard de Rollos gave forty-six acres to Godric of Skeeby in fee and inheritance, free of all services, in return for one sore sparrow-hawk a year. The gift was made with Richard's son and heir, William, 'granting and witnessing'.[109] In such cases, the obtaining of consent was presumably aimed at preventing a future claim by the heir himself, who might feel that his inheritance had been diminished.

On other occasions, the heir's consent seems rather to be a promise of protection against outsiders. Thus in 1147 × 63 Bertram of Bulmer gave eleven bovates in Flaxton to Asketil son of Gospatric, in exchange for the carucate Asketil held of his fee in Welburn. Bertram's son witnessed and granted the exchange and Bertram promised that he and his heirs would warrant Asketil and his heirs against all whose land it had been and all others.[110] As with grants to the Church, the need for protection against outsiders, claimants, and ex-tenants, also helps to explain heirs' participation in other instances, for example when the donor was a woman.[111]

FAMILY GRANTS

Lastly, I turn to family grants. These might, for example, provide for younger sons who would not inherit lands, or endow daughters before or at marriage. The *Cartae baronum* reveal that such grants were already quite common before 1135, and increasingly so thereafter.[112]

---

[109] *EYC*, v, No. 196.

[110] *EYC*, ii, No. 782.

[111] e.g. *Book of Seals*, No. 145, a gift from dower.

[112] S. Painter, 'The Family and the Feudal System in Twelfth-Century England', *Speculum*, 35 (1960), 10–11; J. C. Holt, 'Politics and Property in Early Medieval England', *P&P* 57 (1972), 43–4. However, as with all grants to laymen, few charters survive.

One might expect the heirs' participation to be mentioned peculiarly frequently in gifts to kin. Consensus was especially needed in family affairs; a conflict within the kin was seen as particularly undesirable. Moreover, as *Glanvill* stressed, the greater emotion involved could lead to unreasonable acts. In his opinion, a gift from inherited lands to a younger son required the heir's consent:

If he had several legitimate sons, he cannot easily give as much as he likes from his inheritance to a younger son without his heir's consent. Since if this were allowed, the disinheritance of eldest sons would often occur because of the greater affection which fathers often have for younger sons.[113]

Although the logic of his norms worried *Glanvill*, since it left the illegitimate younger son better off than the legitimate, he accepted the result.

The heir's consent is common in the few surviving charters for younger sons. The earliest examples I have found both concern substitutions of the donor's acquisitions. Between 1120 and 1140, William d'Anesye 'gave and granted' certain of his acquisitions to his son Richard, 'by grant and will' of William his heir. The charter goes on to describe the form the transaction took. William the elder, by the counsel of his friends and peers, and by the assent of his heir, gave back the fee to his lord, Henry de Port, who then seised Richard and received his homage for the service of one knight, as William had served.[114]

Heirs also participated in subinfeudations of younger sons. In *c.*1160 × 80 Baldwin fitzRalph of Bramhope, by the consent of Ralph his son and heir, gave two bovates to another son, Peter, for his homage and service, to hold in fee and inheritance.[115] The earlier tenurial history of these lands is uncertain, so we cannot know whether they were Baldwin's inheritance. An oddity is the large number of clerics amongst the witnesses: possibly Baldwin was dying.

The practice of obtaining consent for gifts to younger sons extended beyond gifts from the inheritance. Why was the heir's assent obtained for alienation from acquisitions? Substitution may have been felt to extinguish the heir's interests particularly fully: he would not

---

[113] *Glanvill*, vii. 1, Hall, 70–2, quotation at p. 70.
[114] *Book of Seals*, No. 301. See Stenton, *First Century*, No. 41 for a similar instance from *c.*1145. See below, pp. 210–11, for the possible reasons for this prevalence of substitutions.
[115] *EYC*, xi, No. 217.

even receive his brother's homage and services. However, the donor may simply have wished to strengthen his gift by obtaining his heir's consent, even though this was less necessary than for a gift from the inheritance.

Glanvill makes only a general statement about grants to other relatives:

Any free man holding land can give a certain part of the land with his daughter or with any woman as a marriage portion [*in maritagium*], whether he has an heir or not, whether the heir—if he has one—is willing or not, and even if he is opposed to it and protests.[116]

However, as one might expect from a family occasion like marriage, some charters concerning *maritagium* do record participation, particularly when they also mention the actual giving of the daughter. Thus in 1136 × 53 Roger earl of Warwick gave Agnes his daughter as wife to Geoffrey the chamberlain, 'by counsel of the king and the bishop of Winchester and the earl "de Warenne" and Robert my brother and of my other friends and my men, *in maritagium*, and with her the service of ten of the seventeen knights whom he holds of me in fee'.[117] There is no sign of variation in the frequency of consent according to the size of grant, nor of decline during the twelfth century.

A potentially difficult situation was that of an elder brother making a grant to a younger. Sometimes there was no danger of disinheriting sons, living or as yet unborn. The donor might be a priest, unable to have legitimate heirs of the body.[118] Other donors, perhaps close to death, may have been unlikely to produce an heir of the body.[119] However, unusual circumstances cannot explain all such grants to brothers. Unborn sons had no chance to object to the alienation of pieces of their inheritance. Young sons must have had little more choice about consenting to the actions of their elders. Thus a charter

---

[116] *Glanvill*, vii. 1, Hall, 69.

[117] *Beauchamp Cartulary: Charters 1100–1268*, ed. E. Mason (PRS, NS 43; 1980), No. 285; for the reading 'de Warenne', see *English Historical Documents, II. 1042–1189*, ed. D. C. Douglas and G. W. Greenaway (2nd edn., London, 1981), 996 n. 1.

[118] e.g. *Facsimiles of Early Charters from Northamptonshire Collections*, ed. F. M. Stenton (Northants Rec. Soc. 4; 1930), No. XXII.

[119] e.g. *Mowbray*, No. 3, from 1109 × 14; Nigel d'Aubigny constitutes William his brother as his heir. This is a slightly unusual instance in that William was the elder brother who held the family's continental inheritance. In fact Nigel survived until 1129, his lands then passing to his young son Roger, even though William was still alive.

of 1161 × 6 records an elaborate exchange between Henry and
Sewall the sons of Fulcher. Henry, the first born, made Sewall 'lord
and first born'.[120] Fulcher, Henry's son, became Sewall's man. How
willing a party was Fulcher is unclear.

Grants to nephews survive from *c.*1130 onwards and seldom
mention consent.[121] Occasional charters record gifts to sisters. Henry
of Arden gave land to his sister Felicia, 'by grant of Olive my wife
and William my son'.[122] She and her heirs were to hold of him and
his heirs in fee and inheritance. Here the minor service, one sore-
hawk a year, may be the reason for the family's consent, but not all
mentions of consent can be explained as gifts at reduced service.[123]

Thus gifts to kin other than younger sons seem to have needed
family assent no more than did those to other laymen. Sometimes
assent may have been unnecessary because the grant was for full
military service, but in others the freedom of the gift was stressed.
Assent may have been particularly desirable when a likely outside
threat existed, but, overall, family participation was rarely recorded.

CONCLUSIONS

What, then, can we conclude about the purpose of the heir's participation in England, and about its limits? With regard to land-holding,
it was intended to reconcile various potentially conflicting pressures,
notably the donor and donee's desire to ensure the permanence of
the gift with the donor's obligations to maintain his family's lands.
The heir's prior consent greatly weakened his chances of discontinuing the gift. On the other hand, the absence of his consent did
not entitle him to discontinue his predecessor's gift, and he was
under many other pressures to continue it. The weight of the various
norms affecting participation varied. Some, for example the obtaining
of the heir's consent for a lasting death-bed gift, might be almost
mandatory, but even these may have been weaker where, for example, only distant relatives survived. Moreover, the norms were not
mutually exclusive. Obtaining the heir's consent for a gift of acquisi-

---

[120] Stenton, *First Century*, No. 7. The reasons for this peculiar transaction are
unclear.
[121] e.g. Stenton, *First Century*, Nos. 27, 32; *Danelaw Documents*, No. 476.
[122] *Book of Seals*, No. 48.
[123] See e.g. *Book of Seals*, No. 302; *EYC*, xii, No. 21.

tions probably shows the donor's prudence, not the decline of the distinction between inheritance and acquisition. The more norms to which one could appeal, the better.

This balancing of interests, and of norms, is also reflected in the conduct and settlement of disputes arising when heirs sought to discontinue their predecessors' gifts. Here we rely heavily on cases recorded by churches, which suggest that—except very occasionally in particular circumstances—heirs were not to discontinue their predecessors' gifts. Nevertheless, a nuanced reading can give some impression of the lay point of view. In cases where the Church presents the lay claimant as forcibly and unjustly hanging on to the land in question, the lay claimant may well have seen himself as using all justifiable means to maintain his rightful cause, against a gift which seemed to him unreasonable.[124] Likewise, the king and his justices showed some concern with the question of the heir's consent.[125] We know that the king often supported the Church, but he can also be seen providing writs for heirs pursuing claims against the Church.[126] Like others, the king seems to have been guided by some general principles. However, in a wide range of cases there were not agreed and distinct rules which would work irrespective of the power of the parties and their supporters.[127]

Similarly, some settlements show a desire to give something to the defeated party.[128] For example, heirs received gifts or payments for quitclaiming their predecessors' gifts.[129] Unfortunately our knowledge of disputes is limited by the partiality of the records, but it may well be that the return received by the claimant was affected by the strength of his case. For example, if he had not consented to the gift and if it was arguably unreasonable, he might well come away with

[124] See above, pp. 191, 193.
[125] See esp. *Stoke*, No. 275. Note that in other cases concerning alienation in which the king became involved, the question of consent is not recorded.
[126] See e.g. *Ramsey Chronicle*, 247–8, F. M. Stenton, 'The Danes in England', *Proceedings of the British Academy*, 13 (1927), 221–2. None of these claims proved successful—had they, the churches might not have considered them worth recording.
[127] Pollock and Maitland, ii. 311 n. 3, pointed to a late 12th- or early 13th-cent. case where a claim was successfully maintained, and the suffering monks complained that this reflected unjust favour.
[128] I use the words 'defeated party' despite the warnings e.g. of F. L. Cheyette, 'Suum Cuique Tribuere', *French Historical Studies*, 6 (1970), since in many English cases, the result does seem to have been victory for one side, the other at best receiving a sweetener.
[129] e.g. *Shrewsbury*, No. 1; see also e.g. *Textus Roffensis*, 189–90.

more than if his claim had been easily rejected. On some occasions, laymen may have entered into disputes knowing that, although their full claim to the land was unlikely to succeed, their quitclaim had a value. In addition, settlements reveal that unsuccessful claimants might receive the very kind of spiritual benefit for which their predecessor had made the original gift, their relationship with the church thus being clearly reaffirmed.[130]

Comparison with the *laudatio parentum* in France is instructive when considering the importance, inspiration, and functioning of family participation in England. Overall, the *laudatio* seems to have been notably less important in England than in France, although it may also have been less significant in Normandy than in some other regions.[131] It is also notable that family participation was to develop along different lines in England from Normandy and other areas of France. In England, requirements for the heir's consent, and mention of it in charters, disappear from the latter half of the twelfth century. In Normandy, they continued, with the *Très Ancien Coutumier* in 1218 × 23 noting the restriction of gifts in alms or for service to one-third of the donor's free tenement.[132] Moreover, in Normandy there developed the *retrait lignager*, the kin's right to pre-empt any grant by taking it themselves. In England, there is scarcely any evidence for this outside towns.[133]

Certainly the broad social and religious aspects of the *laudatio*, which encouraged a wide range of relatives to participate in alienation in western France, had an effect in England. However, in England

[130] e.g. Saltman, *Theobald*, Supplementary Documents B.

[131] Cf. White, *Gifts to Saints*, esp. 42; above, n. 34, on Normandy; also e.g. Hyams, 'Warranty', 468–9.

[132] *TAC*, lxxxix, Tardif, 99–100.

[133] *Leges Henrici*, 88 14a, Downer, 274 specifies that alienation of the inheritance outside the kin is particularly impermissible if the kin objects to the gift or sale 'and wishes to apply its own money to its acquisition'. Bateson held this to be 'the general English law', which later became limited to boroughs. However, evidence for its existence outside boroughs is extremely scarce whereas it certainly was established in towns in the first half of the 12th cent.; *Borough Customs*, ed. M. Bateson (2 vols.; Selden Soc. 18, 21; 1904, 1906), ii. lxxxvii–xci, quotation at lxxxvii. Town customs including *retrait*: *Earldom of Gloucester*, No. 46, *Feudal Documents*, No. 113. Stenton, *First Century*, No. 7 is a rare, non-urban example of a similar kind of arrangement between brothers. On the possible existence of the *retrait lignager* in Anglo-Saxon England, see J. R. Goody, *The Development of the Family and Marriage in Europe* (Cambridge, 1983), 123. For its possible later existence at lower social levels, see P. R. Hyams, *Kings, Lords, and Peasants in Medieval England* (Oxford, 1980), 79. On the *retrait lignager* in western France, see White, *Gifts to Saints*, ch. 6. Pollock and Maitland, ii. 313 n. 5, noted that 'a right of pre-emption . . . still exists in Montenegro'.

mentions of family consent are fewer, and wide groups of relatives are rarely named, normally only heirs and, for different reasons, wives.[134] This restriction may be taken to emphasize the limits of the importance of the *laudatio* in England, and the strong position of the heir, which I discussed in earlier chapters.

Some of the contrast may derive from the type of evidence. The continuing prevalence of the diploma on the Continent can explain some of the difference. Whereas the earls of Chester's writ-charters very rarely mention the consent to their tenants' alienations by the donors' heirs, such participation is frequently mentioned, for example, in the spurious confirmation charter for St Werburgh's abbey attributed to Rannulf II.[135] This was a beneficiary-drafted document, and the frequent mentions of consent probably reflect the grantee's desire to pile up defences for the gifts. Although writ-charters often were beneficiary-drafted, their model was the royal one, which reflected the views of the royal donor. Perhaps here we have different perceptions of correct practice revealing themselves, the royal coming to predominate over the ecclesiastical. In addition, the royal writ-charter seems to have been influenced by Anglo-Saxon models, and the *laudatio* is not a feature of Anglo-Saxon documents. Yet differences of documentation and diplomatic cannot provide a complete explanation. Had the *laudatio* been extremely important, mention of it could have been included in writ-charters as easily as in diplomas. The Normans developed the Anglo-Saxon writ and were not rigidly bound by its conventions. Nor did the form of the writ-charter provide any necessary limit to the number of consenting relatives recorded.

One further plausible explanation of the relative weakness of the *laudatio* is the Conquest itself. Almost all lands in the first generation after 1066 were acquisitions. The redistribution of lands in the following half-century ensured that a substantial proportion of acquisitions remained. Even when lands were inherited for the first time,

---

[134] For exceptions in England, see e.g. Stenton, *First Century*, No. 37 (will make wife, son, and brothers grant), *Oxford Charters*, No. 65 (sons, wife, brother), *Book of Seals*, No. 214 (wife, sons, brothers, and *nepos*; see also *Formulare Anglicanum*, ed. T. Madox (London, 1702), No. VIII, HMC, *The Manuscripts of his Grace the Duke of Rutland* (4 vols.; London, 1888–1905), iv. 59–60). Cf. Tabuteau, *Transfers of Property*, 175–6 on the importance and variety of kin consents in 11th-cent. Norman charters; however, note the reservations at pp. 177–9, 194, where she emphasizes the links between those recorded as consenting and those likely to succeed the alienor.

[135] *Chester*, No. 28; see also Nos. 3, 8, 13.

alienation may have remained fairly easy. Men are occasionally seen treating their father's acquisitions as more freely alienable than the family's ancient inheritance: a charter of 1174 × 85, containing no mention of family participation, emphasized that the lands which one brother gave the other were 'from my father's acquisition'.[136]

The effect of the Conquest sounds like a sufficient explanation, but the extent of royal power in England was another force for alienability, starting perhaps with alienability to the Church.[137] Royal justice certainly did not pursue a free-market policy, but may well have provided an important extra force for the perpetuation of gifts, particularly those to the Church. The preponderance of ecclesiastical records is one reason why most, although not all, recorded cases show the king supporting the Church against heirs' claims. However, the bias of the evidence may not be the sole explanation for the pattern. The frequent issuing of royal confirmations to churches brought the beneficiaries' land under royal protection. Also, there were many clerics amongst those responsible for royal actions. As well as some bias to the Church, they must have brought canonical ideas to royal justice. Even though notions such as prescription in its Canon Law sense did not become part of the Common Law, this canonical background surely influenced the decision of at least some cases in the century after 1066.[138] Furthermore, although the circumstances of each case would certainly affect the royal attitude, the king had a special duty to protect the Church, expressed, for example, in the Coronation Oath. If a church complained to him that

[136] *Danelaw Documents*, No. 171.

[137] That royal power could be seen as a way of securing gifts is clear from Anglo-Saxon wills, addressed as they so often are to the king and queen; see Sheehan, *The Will*, 43–4, 49; *Anglo-Saxon Wills*, ed. and tr. D. Whitelock (Cambridge, 1930), e.g. Nos. XVI, XXI, XXIX. That the threat often came from family claims in the 11th cent. is clear from *The Will of Aethelgifu*, esp. 14–16. Her husband had bequeathed lands to her 'to give to whom she wished', and she now wished them to be her alms 'because they were her lord's acquisitions'. Even so, the grant was challenged by his kinsmen, but with royal help Aethelgifu was able to defeat the claim. Similarly the extent of ducal power in Normandy might explain any more restricted role for the *laudatio* in Normandy compared with, say, the areas of western France discussed by White, *Gifts to Saints*; on ducal protection for the Church, see e.g. J. Yver, 'Autour de l'absence de l'avouerie en Normandie', *BSAN* 57 (1965), 194–213. Note, however, that ducal or royal power and the *laudatio* could coexist, as nicely illustrated by the charter cited by Tabuteau, *Transfers of Property*, 175, and for England, below, Ch. 7. Cf. Orderic, iv. 146 on men attacking their ancestors' gifts to the Church during Robert's rule.

[138] On prescription, see above, p. 181. Note, however, R. V. Turner, *The English Judiciary in the Age of Glanvill and Bracton, c.1176–1239* (Cambridge, 1985), 291: 'about half of the [royal] judges were laymen ... even as early as the time of Henry II'.

an heir had discontinued a gift made in perpetuity, the king might well grant his support: good men should keep their own, and their fathers', word; gifts to the Church should be lasting.

Thus royal power would protect gifts made to the Church, and thereby help to establish notions of alienability. In addition, certain of the factors which applied to the Church also applied to gifts to laymen. Here too the donor's word was to be observed. Here too written royal confirmations became more common. As with inheritance, royal action had an influence even before it became routine: the possibility of royal maintenance of gifts may have rendered other methods of protection, such as the *laudatio*, not undesirable but less necessary. Seen from a different point of view, the security enjoyed by a tenant and his successors, as described in earlier chapters, is also the security which a donor's gift enjoyed free from challenge by his heirs. In both respects, royal power made an important contribution.

7

Lords and Grants

I NOW turn to the lord's participation in grants. Clearly the degree of
control a lord had over his vassal's grants is a vital indication of his
overall control of their lands and indeed of his seignorial power. We
can learn from charters that some grants were made with the lord's
consent, and that some indeed were made in his court.[1] Sometimes a
charter of the lord would have been the sole written record of a
vassal's gift.[2] Again, however, to think solely in terms of control may
exaggerate any opposition of interests between lord and man. In
many cases a lord would simply have assumed that a vassal, like
himself, would grant away lands, and would be content that he should
do so.

As with the *laudatio parentum*, seignorial participation had many
sides rather than just being the observance of a specific legal rule. It
is noteworthy that the *Leges* and *Glanvill* mention only the underlying
principles of the vassal's obligation to his lord. Thus for example,
according to *Glanvill*, 'the vassal generally cannot, without breach
of the faith of homage, do anything by right which works to the
disinheritance or the bodily dishonour of his lord.'[3] Unfortunately,

---

[1] e.g. F. M. Stenton, *The First Century of English Feudalism* (2nd edn., Oxford,
1961), No. 41; *The Sandford Cartulary*, ed. A. M. Leys (2 vols.; Oxfordshire Rec. Soc.
Rec. Ser. 19, 22; 1938, 1941), No. 432; *Historia et Cartularium Monasterii Sancti Petri
Gloucestriae*, ed. W. H. Hart (London, 1863–7), No. CLXXXIV; *Earldom of Gloucester
Charters*, ed. R. B. Patterson (Oxford, 1973), No. 185; *EYC*, v, Nos. 134, 384. See
also *Facsimiles of Early Charters from Northamptonshire Collections*, ed. F. M. Stenton
(Northants Rec. Soc. 4; 1930), No. XXXb in which the lord states only that he was 'at
that place where' his man made a gift.

[2] One such group survives from the honour of Bramber during the third quarter of
the 12th cent.; see *Facsimiles of Early Charters in Oxford Muniment Rooms*, ed. H. E.
Salter (Oxford, 1929), Nos. 9–11, and notes thereto. See also *EYC*, iv, No. 96, a
charter of 1174 × 81 which records a donor asking his lord to confirm his gift because
he had no seal of his own.

[3] *Glanvill*, ix, 1, Hall, 104. With respect to lords' participation, the *Très Ancien
Coutumier* often provides suggestive material lacking from *Glanvill*; see below, p. 216.
Leges Henrici, esp. 55 3, also 88 14; Downer, 172, 274. On lords' participation on the
Continent, see e.g. S. D. White, *Custom, Kinship, and Gifts to Saints* (Chapel Hill, NC,
1988), 52–3, 137–9.

records of lords' consents are too few to allow even the tentative kind of numerical analysis undertaken in the previous chapter, for example with respect to chronological change. However, careful examination particularly of charters does allow analysis of the practical workings of the general principles.

SUBSTITUTION

All the surviving evidence from this period suggests that the lord's participation was essential for substitutions.[4] Such grants were made by the donor surrendering the land to his lord who then granted it to the donee. The homage ceremony publicized the new tenant's title and made clear who was his lord. Certainly two powerful vassals might force a weak lord to co-operate, but examples are lacking. One may anyway wonder whether men would have thought of, or desired, such transactions, for one of substitution's major attractions was that a beneficiary would generally obtain a more powerful lord and warrantor than by subinfeudation.

Two main types of grant were made by substitution. First, a large proportion concern alienations of acquisitions. The obvious reason is that a tenant's title to his acquisitions was felt to be weaker, *vis-à-vis* the lord and donor, than his title to his inheritance.[5] Just as inherited lands were perceived as more closely attached to the tenant's family, and hence the heir's participation especially desirable for their alienation, so too were acquisitions seen as more closely tied to the lord who had granted them, and hence seignorial participation was especially needed if the tenant wished to alienate them. A charter of

---

[4] Pollock and Maitland, i. 345. Maitland, though, was worried about *Bracton's* statement that the tenant who had done homage might, in Maitland's paraphrase, 'put a new tenant in his place, and the lord must accept him, will he, nill he'; see *Bracton*, fo. 81, Thorne, ii. 235. S. F. C. Milsom, *The Legal Framework of English Feudalism* (Cambridge, 1976), 103–10, 146–53; he seems to place the beginning of the development of 'the possibility of substitution without the lord's consent' around 1200, *Legal Framework*, 152–3, where he also discusses *Bracton's* statement which had troubled Maitland. P. A. Brand, 'Control of Mortmain Alienation in England, 1200–1300', in J. H. Baker (ed.), *Legal Records and the Historian* (London, 1978), 29 n. 4, argues that there is no evidence before 1290 for lords being forced to take the homage of substitute tenants.

[5] Note J. C. Holt, 'Politics and Property in Early Medieval England', *P&P* 57 (1972), 19. See *Glanvill*, ix. 4, Hall, 107, on the differing obligations a lord has with regard to his tenant's acquisitions and inheritance.

Henry I states that Osbert fitzPons had given Longney to the monks of Malvern, in the king's presence. It not only makes clear the common advantage of substitutions, declaring that the king had taken the church 'into the maintenance and defence of his royal power', but also indicates the desirability of substitution for the alienation of acquisitions. So that the grantees possess the land more honourably in future, according to Henry, Osbert

gave back the land into my hand, freed and quit from any claim of his heirs, as [*sicut*] he had held this not by succession from his relatives but by gracious gift of my father. And I gave it to the said monastery and the brothers of the place by my own hand, and confirmed it in perpetual alms by royal authority, so that they may hold it in chief of me and my successors with every freedom and quit of secular service.[6]

Family arrangements constitute the other large group of substitutions recorded in charters.[7] Not all such grants were of acquisitions. A charter of Henry I concerns Ralph Basset's inheritance. Nicholas Basset 'gave back and quitclaimed' to the king all the lands he held in chief and the king 'gave and granted' them to his brother Richard Basset and his heirs to be held in chief. The 1130 Pipe Roll duly records that Richard owed two hundred marks of silver and six destriers for the land which Nicholas held of the king in chief.[8]

Why did family grants take place by substitution? There was some feeling that homage should not enter into family relationships, although in practice it often did so.[9] Revealing evidence comes from

---

[6] *Regesta*, ii, No. 1489. *Charters of the Honour of Mowbray*, ed. D. E. Greenway (London, 1972), No. 290 shows a sale, involving at least some acquisitions, being made by surrender and admittance. Seisin was transferred by a piece of wood from donor to lord to donee. See also *Cartularium Abbathiae de Whiteby*, ed. J. C. Atkinson (2 vols.; Surtees Soc. 69, 72, 1879, 1881), Nos. I (p. 6), CCLXXXIII, CCLXXXIV, CCLXXXVI. A late 12th-cent. substitution explicitly involving acquisitions is *Formulare Anglicanum*, ed. T. Madox (London, 1702), No. C. For other instances of sale through surrender and admittance, see *Documents Illustrative of the Social and Economic History of the Danelaw*, ed. F. M. Stenton (London, 1920), l–li.

[7] See also above, Ch. 6. Unfortunately the proportion of family gifts made by substitution cannot be discovered, nor any chronological change in that proportion. The *Cartae baronum* shows relatives being enfeoffed, e.g. *Red Book*, i. 256, 286, 297, 302.

[8] *Regesta*, ii, No. 1668; *PR 31 HI*, 82.

[9] See Milsom, *Legal Framework*, 151. Note also *Glanvill*'s discussion of forisfamiliation, which seems to imply that a gift to a son at his request with seisin and quite possibly homage could be incompatible with a full familial relationship: the son was to be satisfied with that land, and no longer be an heir or pass a hereditary claim; *Glanvill*, vii. 3, Hall, 78.

relations within the royal family in 1183, when, according to Ralph of Diceto, Richard refused to submit thus to Henry the Young King, on the grounds that it was wrong that there should be subjection between the children of the same parents.[10]

By *Glanvill*'s time there was a more specific, although connected, reason for the use of substitution in family gifts: 'generally it is true according to the law of the realm that no-one can simultaneously be heir and lord of the same tenement'.[11] Take the following example. An older brother enfeoffed a younger. The older is succeeded by his son. The younger then dies childless. The older brother's son might seem the obvious heir but is barred by the above norm. Had the alienation been by substitution, the older brother's son would not have been lord, and so could be heir. Can this norm explain some of the family substitutions we have seen taking place from the earlier twelfth century? Perhaps, but I have found no evidence to allow me to go beyond the usual, rather vague, attribution of the emergence of the norm to Henry II's reign.[12]

SUBINFEUDATION

Now let us move on to subinfeudation, including grants by the donor directly to the Church. Writers again have dealt with seignorial participation largely in legal terms. According to Maitland, lords sometimes contested grants made without their assent. This was not because of a threat to services, for

> nothing that the tenant can do without his lord's concurrence will remove from the land the burden of that service which is due to his lord from him and from it. The tenement itself owes the service; the 'reality', if we may so speak, of the burden can be brought home by means of distress to any one into whose hands the land may come.

A grant might nevertheless harm a lord, for example threatening the incidents due to him.[13] Maitland hesitated as to whether there was a

---

[10] Ralph de Diceto, *Opera Historica*, ed. W. Stubbs (2 vols.; London, 1876), ii. 18–19; W. L. Warren, *Henry II* (London, 1973), 588.

[11] *Glanvill*, vii. 1, Hall, 72; see also xiii. 11, p. 155.

[12] e.g. A. W. B. Simpson, *The History of Land Law* (Oxford, 1986), 57, Milsom, *Legal Framework*, 139–40.

[13] Pollock and Maitland, i. 330, where Maitland also noted that substitution might, for example, leave the lord with an enemy as a vassal, and that it anyway enfeebled the 'solemn bond of homage'.

rule against alienation without seignorial consent, but concluded that
the situation was not clear-cut:

> The tenant may lawfully do anything that does not seriously damage the
> interests of his lord. He may make reasonable gifts, but not unreasonable.
> The reasonableness of the gift would be a matter for the lord's court; the
> tenant would be entitled to the judgment of his peers.[14]

Thus Maitland presented seignorial consent as an important condition
for a vassal's gift, but distinguished the lord's and the vassal's roles in
a grant.

Thorne and Milsom have criticized such arguments, which tend to
separate giving and consenting. For Thorne, in the early twelfth
century the real owner of the land was not the tenant but the lord,
who was thus also the real donor.[15] Later, as customary succession
hardened, ownership was divided between lord and tenant, and so
the lord must still join in the gift. A grant for full service caused no
difficulty, but the tenant had to ensure that any gift free of services
was reasonable if the lord's co-operation were to be gained. This
needed a judgment by the lord and his court that sufficient lands
remained for the tenant to fulfil his services. By the late twelfth
century, *Glanvill*'s silence reveals that the lord's consent was no
longer necessary. Whereas the lord's interest had been evident so
long as the vassal could be regarded only as a life-tenant, royally
enforced inheritance ended this. By *Bracton*'s time, the lord's interest
was only incorporeal, and he was seised of homage and services, not
in demesne. The tenant was *uerus dominus* of the land.

For Milsom, twelfth-century land-holding was a matter not of
ownership—divided or otherwise—but of personal relationship.[16]

Before royal control, and in particular before mort d'ancestor allowed an heir
to feel that he entered in his own right rather than under a grant to himself
from the lord, no tenant could think he had something which he could by
himself give for ever to an institution which would last for ever: of course the
lord must join in. His confirmation would not just add some marginal
advantage to a self-sufficient gift. The gift was unthinkable without it.

---

[14] Pollock and Maitland, i. 343.

[15] For this paragraph, see S. E. Thorne, 'English Feudalism and Estates in Land',
CLJ (1959), 205, 208–9.

[16] For this paragraph, see Milsom, *Legal Framework*, 120–1; according to Milsom,
Glanvill does not consider seignorial assent because it was not a problem at the time he
wrote, certainly not a problem for the king's court.

However, the shift of control changed the situation. A lord previously had only a life-tenant, who could therefore give only for life. His son might renew the gift but had also to consider his other obligations, especially the 'overriding' one to his lord. From Henry II's time, royal control produced a title for the tenant which he could transfer as his own, although perhaps with some marginal loss to the lord. The royal court would also make the donor's son honour the grant even if it left him too little in demesne to support his lord's services. 'Royal control is creating a sort of ownership, which in this as in every other respect is incompatible with a system of truly dependent tenures.'

Such arguments as Thorne's and Milsom's indicate that the underlying structure of land-holding made alienation impossible without the lord's participation; the tenant's and lord's actions were inextricably linked. However, again the arguments would seem to be flawed. I have already challenged key premisses, for example that vassals saw themselves only as tenants for life, incapable of making lasting alienations.[17] Moreover, the granting language of lords' confirmations does not signify that the lord was seen at the time as the real or even the co-donor of all gifts his tenant might make. The verb *dare*, which might suggest that the lord played an essential part in giving, rarely appears.[18] The type of transactions referred to by the unusual relatively frequent use of *dare* in the charters of Roger earl of Warwick refine rather than contradict the general pattern: they record grants by his valet; by an Englishman; and by his wife, a man,

[17] Note also that if the need for consent arose from land-holding being based on successive life relationships of lord and man, one would expect the *laudatio* to appear in lords' confirmations; in fact instances are rare, e.g. 'The Staffordshire Chartulary', ed. R. W. Eyton, *William Salt Arch. Soc.* 2 (1881), 247–8.

[18] No instances in the charters of William I or Rufus, and very few amongst those of Henry I, Stephen, or Henry II: *Regesta*, ii, Nos. 706, 714, 784, 1249, 1327, 1399; iii, Nos. 203, 247, 586 a gift by an archdeacon, 699, 864; see also No. 116a; Henry II: *Cartae Antiquae, 11–20*, ed. J. C. Davis (PRS, NS 33; 1960), No. 452, a gift by an archdeacon. That a small group of Henry I's and Stephen's charters for Tynemouth used *dare* suggests either an unusual drafting custom of one beneficiary or the copying of a formula from one unusual charter; *Regesta*, ii, No. 1170; iii, No. 905, see also No. 906. See also e.g. *Regesta*, ii, No. 1012, a diploma of Henry I, which displays many unusual features in its drafting; see e.g. *Earldom of Gloucester*, Nos. 156–7; Hudson, 'Diplomatic and Legal Aspects of the Charters', in A. T. Thacker (ed.), *The Earldom of Chester and its Charters* (Jnl. of Chester Arch. Soc. 71; 1991), 162–3. Even some charters using *dare* in one passage omit it elsewhere; e.g. *Stoke by Clare Cartulary*, ed. C. Harper-Bill and R. Mortimer (Suffolk Charters, 4–6; 1982–4), No. 23. Again, one is warned against taking granting verbs as precisely used terms of art from which significant conclusions can be drawn directly.

and some rustics.[19] Usually charters, whether to laymen, ecclesiastics, or churches, refer to the tenant as 'giving', the lord as 'granting' or 'confirming', and this was so even when the lord joined in the gift ceremony.[20] The main twelfth-century change was the increasing use of *confirmare*, often with connotations of writing, to supplement *concedere* in describing the lord's part.[21] Clause seven of Henry I's Coronation Charter, concerned with death-bed distribution of chattels [*pecunia*], makes the evidence of granting language particularly striking: 'And if any of my barons or men will be ill, I will grant that his chattels be given, just as he will give them or dispose to give them.'[22] The same distinction in granting language is thus made both for confirmation of gifts of chattels, over which men certainly had freedom of disposal, and of land.

Of course, even if Thorne and Milsom's particular arguments are rejected, there remains the possibility that contemporaries viewed the lord's consent or confirmation for a gift as necessary. The overall scarcity of charters which mention seignorial consent to gifts may simply result from the nature of the documents, or from the fact that seignorial consent was so general a requirement that its granting need not be recorded. Men sometimes worried that the lord of their land might prevent a transaction.[23] Yet other evidence suggests that to

[19] *Dare* appears in three of his twelve relevant documents. PRO, E 164/22, fos. 10ᵛ–11 concerned a death-bed gift by John, the earl's valet: here the circumstance of the gift may explain the unusual granting verb, as may the position of the donor; see e.g. *Regesta*, ii, No. 1327 for a use of *dare* in a confirmation by Henry I of a grant by John the Larderer. British Library, MS Cotton Vitellius, A i, fos. 42ᵛ–43 confirms a gift by Thorbert son of Aethelwulf, obviously an Englishman; on the position of Englishmen during this period, see P. R. Hyams, *Kings, Lords, and Peasants in Medieval England* (Oxford, 1980), 251–3. British Library, MS Add. 47677, fos. 242ᵛ–243 concerns land which firstly his wife and then Nigel de St Maria and the rustics of Walton, 'with their assent granted and gave' to the church of Wellesbourne. A wife's gifts were often also attributed to her husband; e.g. *Regesta*, iii, Nos. 845–7, 850–1, grants by Stephen and his queen. The mention of the rustics is more striking. Their lands may have been peculiarly closely associated with their lord.

[20] e.g. *Select Documents of the English Lands of the Abbey of Bec*, ed. M. Chibnall (Camden Soc., 3rd Ser. 73; 1951), No. XXVI, *The Charters of the Anglo-Norman Earls of Chester*, ed. G. Barraclough (Rec. Soc. Lancs. and Cheshire, 126; 1988), No. 87; see also e.g. *EYC*, xii, No. 15.

[21] *Confirmare*; 1100–30: e.g. *Regesta*, ii, Nos. 602, 890, 1041, 1156 etc.; Stenton, *First Century*, No. 20; *Earldom of Gloucester*, No. 82; 1130–60: e.g. *Regesta*, iii, Nos. 85, 101, 104, 132, 138–9, 182–3, 193, 229, 237–8, etc.; Stenton, *First Century*, Nos. 9, 46; *Stoke*, No. 34; *Earldom of Gloucester*, Nos. 13, 51, 68.

[22] Liebermann, *Gesetze*, i. 522.

[23] For an example from as late as *c.*1200, see *The Cartulary of Worcester Cathedral Priory*, ed. R. R. Darlington (PRS, NS 38; 1968), No. 38.

some lords alienation of land without their permission was all too conceivable. Henry de Lacy not only failed to do service to Hugh Bigod for the vill of Barnoldswick, but also gave the land to the abbot of Fountains for the foundation of an abbey.[24] At the beginning of Henry I's reign, a settlement between Abingdon and William the king's chamberlain granted William certain land on the condition that he become the abbey's man, and that 'he should not sell, or gage, or give that land in fee or fee farm to anyone'.[25]

The lord's participation in alienation is better taken as a norm, the strength of which varied with circumstances, rather than as a mandatory requirement.[26] We must look at the functioning of this norm from all the concerned parties' points of view. In addition to lords seeking to exercise their lordship by ensuring that they controlled their vassal's grants—or at least that their vassals showed respect for their position when making grants—both donors and donees sought seignorial confirmation for gifts. In 1135, Stephen, count of Brittany, addressed to Henry I a charter recording his gift of lands in Cambridge to Bury Abbey. He prayed that Henry 'grant this and make it hold in perpetual stability'.[27] Donees' desire for confirmations is clear, for example from gifts they gave the confirmer and from their obtaining charters by which a lord confirmed all his men's gifts to them.[28]

Lords' participation was connected with a whole range of obligations and interests, but with respect to land-holding, it had two main purposes. It was intended both to protect the lord's own interests, by preventing grants to his enemies or loss of services, and to increase the security of the gift. It constituted a promise that the lord would not interfere with the gift and that he would attempt to maintain the gift against threats from the donors, the donors' heirs, and outsiders. As such, it resembled the donor's warranty,

[24] 'The Foundation of Kirkstall Abbey', ed. E. K. Clark, in *Thoresby Society, Miscellanea*, 2 (1895), 173–4.

[25] *CMA*, ii. 128; note that this is a narrative rather than a charter, and hence could be influenced by the chronicler's own views.

[26] Some lords may have sought to assert their claim to control of alienation by broadcasting their assent to gifts which were going to be made whether they liked it or not; see also P. Dalton, 'Feudal Society in Yorkshire', Ph.D. thesis (Sheffield, 1989), esp. p. 228. E. Z. Tabuteau, *Transfers of Property in Eleventh-Century Norman Law* (Chapel Hill, NC, 1988), 171–2, 179–87, concludes that in 11th-cent. Normandy a lord's consent was not legally necessary, but advisable in practice.

[27] *EYC*, iv, No. 11.

[28] e.g. *Stoke*, Nos. 23, 37; on gifts to the confirmer, see below, p. 221.

and occasional charters use the term warrant for the lord's confirmation.[29] In many cases donor, donee, and lord would all have
been happy with a transaction. In others, for example gifts to the
lord's enemy, to the Church, or grants detrimental to estate structures, negotiations would be needed and conflict could arise.

Against whom was seignorial consent sought? From the donor's
and the donee's points of view, the lord himself might be the main
threat to any gift which displeased him, and hence his consent was
desirable. From his own point of view, insistence on regulating his
vassals' gifts was prudent lordship. Some power of regulation was
certainly claimed. Explicit grants that a donee might do as he wished
with the land indicate a sacrifice of future seignorial control by the
donor.[30] Unfortunately, only records of completed gifts generally
survive, so information is very scarce on lords refusing to permit
grants, or seizing back gifts to which they had not consented.[31]
We therefore may be rather ignorant of the strongest objections
which lords might present to their vassals' proposed alienations. For
example, the Norman *Très Ancien Coutumier* mentions mortal enmity
with the donee as good grounds for a lord to refuse to consent to his
vassal's gift. The provision in Henry I's Coronation Charter that the
king would not forbid his men to give their relatives to anyone in
marriage, 'except if they wish to join her to my enemy', encourages
one to see this as a widely applicable norm.[32] It may well have
allowed a lord to forbid any alienation contravening it, although his
ability to enforce his decision could be limited by the power of the
alienor and alienee.

Charters present the fulfilment of services as the lord's main

---

[29] e.g. *Sir Christopher Hatton's Book of Seals*, ed. L. C. Loyd and D. M. Stenton
(Northants Rec. Soc. and Oxford, 1950), No. 84. Cf. the idea of positive and negative
aspects of warranty discussed above, pp. 52–8.

[30] e.g. Madox, *Formulare Anglicanum*, No. II, on which see below, p. 223; British
Library, MS Cotton Julius C vii, fo. 218. Cf. also e.g. *Regesta*, ii, No. 1522.

[31] The 12th-cent. examples in Pollock and Maitland, i. 341 n. 3 all concern
alienations by churches without the king's permission. For the 13th cent., see D. W.
Sutherland, *The Assize of Novel Disseisin* (Oxford, 1973), 86–96; at p. 88 he states that
he found only one example between 1215 and *c.*1250 of the king's court upholding the
right of a lord to seize back his tenant's gift made to a church at greatly reduced
service. D. Walker, 'Miles of Gloucester, Earl of Hereford', *Trans. Bristol and Glos.
Arch. Soc.* 77 (1959), 81–3, argues that 'Charters of the Earldom of Hereford,
1095–1201', ed. D. Walker in *Camden Miscellany*, xxii (Camden Soc., 4th Ser. i;
1964), No. 72 is linked to a lord refusing to consent to his vassal's grant, but the
evidence for this is far from conclusive.

[32] *TAC*, xci, Tardif, 101. Coronation Charter, c. 3, Liebermann, *Gesetze*, i. 521.

concern with regard to his tenant's alienations.[33] They concentrate on gifts to the Church, and to a lesser extent family gifts. Particularly the former but also the latter were very often made for reduced or no service. Such gifts left the donor and his heirs fewer resources with which to fulfil his total services. Often the lord may have judged that his tenant's remaining resources sufficed, and hence have consented to the gift. Sometimes indeed the obvious sufficiency of the remaining land may have rendered any seeking of consent unnecessary. On other occasions, however, the man's capacity to fulfil his services would be endangered. If the donor or his heirs defaulted, the lord or his heirs might distrain them by their lands and in the last resort disinherit them. This involved all lands the vassal held of the lord and hence threatened those granted away. Such was a considerable incentive for the vassal making the gift to obtain quittance of the relevant service, and the beneficiary probably shared the donor's concern. It is very notable that a charter of Robert earl of Leicester speaks of the earl quitclaiming the service pertaining to the land given because [*quia*] the donor had made the gift with Robert's assent.[34] The tenant who acted respectfully to his lord thus received a reward.

However, if the donor and donee did not consult the lord, or indeed if they ignored his opinion, the lord might face considerable problems. Maitland's statement that 'nothing that the tenant can do without his lord's concurrence will remove from the land the burden of that service which is due to his lord from him and from it' no doubt contains considerable truth, particularly if one takes it as representing the lord's point of view. The lord should simply exact the services. Yet in practice this might be difficult. A strong opinion existed against churches forfeiting lands or being distrained,[35] and distraining a powerful lay tenant brought very real problems of a different kind. The prudent lord might prefer to prevent the potentially time- and resource-consuming business of enforcing ser-

---

[33] See also J. C. Holt, 'Notions of Patrimony', *TRHS*, 5th Ser. 33 (1983), 202–3, noting his citation of Huntington Library, San Marino, BA 42/1526; Tabuteau, *Transfers of Property*, 184; c. 39 of the 1217 issue of Magna Carta.

[34] Bodleian Library, MS Dugdale 12, p. 259. On distraint, see above, Ch. 2.

[35] Charters record lords' promises not to distrain lands given in alms by their vassals; see e.g. *Regesta*, ii, No. 1738. If a man made a gift to a church at a fixed rent, the lord might promise not to distrain the church except for that rent; see e.g. *Earldom of Gloucester*, Nos. 126, 134. See below, p. 219, for seignorial confirmations being intended to protect donees against forfeiture by the donor or his heirs.

vices in future, and to insist that the gift be reasonable if it were
to receive his consent. Occasional descriptions of gift ceremonies
involving the lord's consent show real negotiation. In 1147 × 83
William earl of Gloucester granted and by his charter confirmed
Walter de Claville's gifts of alms to Canonsleigh Abbey. He did so at
the petition of Walter and his son and heir, made in his court in the
presence of his barons. Walter and his son then undertook to acquit
the alms against the earl and his heirs of all secular service. It appears
that the confirmation was made in return for the donor's promise to
retain responsibility for the services.[36]

Many charters recording lords' confirmations of tenants' gifts to
the Church in fact state that they released the donor from the
services due from the gift.[37] The freeing from services did not
necessarily coincide with the original gift, and clearly could concern
not only the donor's immediate lord but all superior lords. Thus a
charter of William de Braose from 1150 × 69 records that Humphrey
de 'Changhetona' had granted specified lands to William Bernehus in
fee farm for 12*d.* a year and service to the king. Approaching his
death, William Bernehus gave these lands in alms to the monks of
Sele, and Humphrey granted this, saving his own right. Afterwards,
Humphrey granted the same land to the monks quit of the rent and
royal service. William de Braose, in whose presence this grant was
made, granted it and confirmed it by his charter.[38]

Another mid-twelfth-century charter is of especial interest in this
context. Earl Roger of Warwick granted and quitclaimed from himself and his heirs in perpetual alms the gift of all Cawston, which
Ingelram Clement, Ralph his brother, Thurkill of Cawston, and their
heirs had given to the abbey of Pipewell, with the consent of Henry
of Arden and his heirs. Roger himself and his wife and heirs gave,
granted, and quitclaimed to the abbey all the service from Cawston
which Henry of Arden and his heirs owed to him and his heirs.[39]
Here the overlord is not seen as a co-donor of the land; rather he is
seen as donor of the services, his sub-tenant as donor of the land. At
least in this instance, therefore, the superior's association appears
essential not so much for the man to make any gift, but rather for the

[36] *Earldom of Gloucester*, No. 44. See also *Danelaw Documents*, No. 5; *Glanvill*, ix. 1,
Hall, 104, on men acting to the disinheritance of their lord.

[37] See e.g. *Regesta*, ii, Nos. 1740, 1741.

[38] *Oxford Charters*, No. 10.

[39] British Library, MS Cotton Calig. A xiii, fos. 85ᵛ–86.

man to make a gift at reduced service without himself having to
continue to do full service.

Such a concern with services does not, however, exhaust the
reasons for the lord's participation in alienation. The lord's confirmation could provide protection against the misdeeds or mishaps of
the donor himself. Between *c.*1155 and 1177 Robert fitzHugh of
Tattershall confirmed a gift by William fitzHervey to the Templars.[40]
If William or his heirs were unwilling to hold to the gift, at William's
request Robert and his heirs were to 'justice' them to do so. In
addition, the lord's confirmation might secure the gift against the
donor's forfeiture or escheat. The Norman *Très Ancien Coutumier* of
*c.*1220 states that 'if the donor dies without heir or forfeits his land,
the whole fee will return to the lord, unless he shows his assent.'[41]
Charters suggest that this is applicable to twelfth-century England. In
1123 × 53 Earl Roger of Warwick 'granted' Hugh fitzRichard's gift
of Bearley to John of Kington, to be held of Hugh and his heirs: 'if it
falls into my hand, it is to be held in a similar way from me and my
heirs.'[42]

The lord's help was also requested to force the donor's heirs to
maintain the gift. A royal writ of 1130 illustrates the danger of the
lord and the donor's heir co-operating against a gift: Walter Espec
and Eustace fitzJohn were to ensure that whatever Robert Fossard or
Bertram of Bulmer had seized since the death of Ansketil of Bulmer
was to be entirely restored to Nostell Priory. Robert was Ansketil's
lord, Bertram his son.[43]

Lords also provided protection against other parties. In 1164 × 81
Richard de Rollos confirmed the abbey of Hambye's gift to Easby, of
the alms which he had given Hambye. No one, 'either heir or anyone
else at all', was to molest the canons.[44] The lord might provide
further protection by not simply confirming the gift but also adding

[40] *EYC*, v, No. 389.
[41] *TAC*, lxxxix, Tardif, 100.
[42] *Reading Abbey Cartularies*, ed. B. R. Kemp (2 vols.; Camden Soc., 1986–7), No.
578. See also *Book of Seals*, Nos. 84, 105; on which see also J. H. Round, *Feudal
England* (London, 1895), 470–1, and *Geoffrey de Mandeville* (London, 1892), 304–12.
[43] *Regesta*, ii, No. 1662. The dispute may have continued in Henry's reign, or
revived under Stephen, for *EYC*, ii, No. 1017 records Bertram's grant and confirmation in 1148 × 53 to Nostell of the alms his father had given. Note also Orderic
Vitalis, *Ecclesiastical History*, ed. and tr. M. Chibnall (6 vols.; Oxford 1969–80), vi. 174
for Henry I's confirmation to St Evroul being aimed against greedy heirs seeking to
seize back their relatives' alms.
[44] *EYC*, v, No. 194.

privileges. Thus Henry I ordered that the abbey of Romsey hold various gifts from Stephen fitzArard, especially the tithe of Whitsbury, and not be impleaded concerning it except by the king's command.[45] A lord who had confirmed his vassal's gift might reinforce it by standing as witness to the grant.[46]

Outside interference might well result from a claim against the lord for the land. The lord's confirmation constituted a promise that the land had been his, or his predecessors', to give in the first place. Thus in 1157 × 8 Warin fitzGerold and his brother, Henry, gave land in Sawbridgeworth, Hertfordshire, to Robert Blund of London. Geoffrey de Mandeville III, earl of Essex, confirmed the gift. Geoffrey may have been routinely acting as a good lord, his confirmation the more necessary because the lands were Warin and Henry's acquisitions. However, it is also notable that whilst Sawbridgeworth had been held by Geoffrey de Mandeville I in 1086, it was later lost to the family and only returned to Geoffrey in *c*.1141.[47] Geoffrey's confirmation thus emphasized that the land had been his to give, despite earlier tenurial quarrels.

The effect of a lord's confirmation was not entirely limited to his own time. It might encourage his successors to intervene in a dispute, even if they could not be forced by law to do so. In 1156 × 66 Geoffrey de Mandeville wrote to his brother Ernulf.[48] The abbot and monks of Colchester had complained to Geoffrey that Ernulf had unjustly and without judgment disseised them of land in Nuthampstead, Hertfordshire, which Ralph de Nuers had given them and placed on the altar in alms, and which they had held in Geoffrey's father's time and since. Ernulf was to reseise them or do them full justice in his court 'since my father loved and maintained the church of Colchester and confirmed their tenures. And I have confirmed and wish to maintain them in similar fashion for the love of God.' Conversely, the lord's consent might be aimed at preventing his own heirs from harming the gift. In the 1150s Roger of Aske founded the convent of Marrick. Warner fitzWimard, steward of the earl of Richmond, confirmed the gift by his charter, 'lest it pass into oblivion by the

---

[45] *Regesta*, ii, No. 811.

[46] See *Earldom of Hereford*, No. 74, an interesting written testimony to a gift.

[47] *Facsimiles of Royal and Other Charters in the British Museum*, i. *William I–Richard I*, ed. G. F. Warner and H. J. Ellis (London, 1903), No. 43; C. W. Hollister, 'The Misfortunes of the Mandevilles', *History*, 58 (1973), esp. 20, 27.

[48] *Cartularium Monasterii S. Johannis Baptiste de Colecestria*, ed. S. A. Moore (2 vols.; Roxburghe Club, London, 1897), i. 176.

length of time, or any of my heirs presume to deny this'.[49] Again, the major concern may have been not so much that the heirs would simply seize back the gift but that they would seek services and eventually confiscate the land concerned.[50]

The incentives for the donor and donee to obtain the lord's consent or confirmation are thus clear enough, but why did the lord agree to give such consent or confirmation? In part, no doubt, it was just assumed that men would grant away lands. Furthermore, man and lord's interests were not necessarily conflicting, but rather coincided. The lord could benefit from the prestige brought by an increased number of sub-tenants, by his vassal's enlarged following. In addition, hardly surprisingly, confirmations did not come free. Thus the 1130 Pipe Roll records that Richard Guiz owed the king two destriers for the grant of the land which Hugh de Laval had given him. Occasionally charters record gifts to the lord confirming, and these may have been not merely payments but also a way of symbolically making the confirmation binding.[51]

Confirmations also reinforced the bond between lord and vassal. They were manifestations of good lordship. The mutuality of the relationship of lord and man could be emphasized, as well as its hierarchy. Hugh earl of Shropshire travelled to his father Roger's tomb at Roger's foundation of Shrewsbury Abbey, and, at the request of the abbot and convent, made a grant for the completion of the church. Standing next to him was one of his barons, Hamo Peverel, who made a similar gift at Hugh's request. Hugh then strengthened both gifts by his seal. Hugh had thus both requested and confirmed Hamo's gift.[52]

Furthermore, the lord might also benefit from the closer link established with the grantee. We are well aware of the king's desire to exercise links with his sub-tenants, as manifested, for example, in the Oath of Salisbury. Other lords too may have cultivated such ties with

[49] *EYC*, v, Nos. 173, 174 respectively; see also No. 175.

[50] Late in the 1150s, Peter of Studley confirmed Nicholas of Bearley's gift to Bordesley Abbey, in perpetual right, to be held 'absque ulla heredum meorum uexatione'; *Book of Seals*, No. 153. The word *uexatio*, reminiscent of the writ *ne uexes*, may suggest that the immediate concern was with demands for service.

[51] *PR 31 HI*, 34; BL Add. Chart. 21493; *Book of Seals*, No. 84.

[52] *Monasticon Anglicanum*, ed. W. Dugdale (6 vols. in 8; London, 1817–30), iii. 520. See also *Stoke*, No. 533 for a man's charter granting his lord's gift and recording the same lord's confirmation of the man's gift. William of Poitiers, *Histoire de Guillaume le Conquérant*, ed. and tr. R. Foreville (Paris, 1952), 122, praised William I for his willingness to grant his authority to anyone wishing to confer a gift on the Church.

their sub-tenants.[53] If the grantee was a church, the lord would expect his share of spiritual benefits in return for his confirmation.[54] Confirmation to a church might be important in maintaining the relationship of the lord's family and that church, upon which rested some of their hopes of salvation. In addition, such confirmations, such protections, showed the lord acting in a way that justified his status, a point occasionally made explicit in charter introductions.[55] In such a context, it is not surprising that some seignorial confirmations included spiritual threats, in addition to the physical support they offered.[56]

Donors who included their lords in *pro anima* clauses must have hoped for such confirmations. In 1152 × 73 William son of Angot made a gift to Stoke by Clare, for the soul of Earl Gilbert de Clare and the salvation of Earl Roger his lords, and for his own salvation and that of his ancestors. His charter, addressed to Roger and all friends and neighbours, closed

I wish, desire, pray, and on behalf of God and St John the Baptist I implore with all my strength, in so far as you maintain this alms to the said monks in faith and love for the salvation of you and yours, that together in unanimous supplication they may more attentively and devotedly prevail upon the mercy of Christ for the salvation of my lords and myself.[57]

Religious benefit, good lordship, and the securing of gifts were thus united.

Such were the general considerations which underlay the seeking and granting of seignorial consent and confirmation to alienation. As they have led us to expect, their impact varied with the circumstances of any particular instance. First, as we have seen, the lord's concern with alienation varied with the donee. A charter of Earl Roger of

[53] *Book of Seals*, No. 84, 105 provide an unusual instance of the relationship of sub-tenant and confirming lord being sealed by the sub-tenant becoming the confirmer's man and giving him a good horse; on these charters, see the literature cited above, n. 42. For a lord making an arrangement with his new sub-tenant concerning the payment of relief, see *Earldom of Gloucester*, No. 151.

[54] e.g. *CMA*, ii. 102. The lord was the first witness of Henry I's charter confirming the same gift, *CMA*, ii. 103 (= *Regesta*, ii, No. 893). One wonders how important was his influence at court in obtaining this confirmation. See also e.g. *EYC*, v, No. 194, where Richard de Rollos hoped for a double profit by confirming a gift from the monks of Hambye to the canons of Easby.

[55] e.g. *EYC*, iv, No. 27.

[56] e.g. *Earldom of Gloucester*, No. 51.

[57] *Stoke*, No. 381.

Warwick clearly illustrates that alienation to the Church particularly
worried lords, at least by the mid-twelfth-century. Hugh fitzRichard,
with his son's assent, gave William Cumin the whole manor of
Snitterfield in fee and inheritance, in such a way that William could
give the manor to whomsoever he wished by hereditary right, 'whether to a cleric, a layman, or even, if he wished, to religion'. Hugh
and his heirs were to acquit William or those who held the manor
of all services pertaining to the earl and his heirs. Just as donors'
heirs felt that they retained greater control over a gift to a layman
than to a church, so too did lords, and for similar reasons: the loss
of services, of jurisdiction, and of possible reversion and other occasional profitable rights of lordship.[58]

Lords also played an unusually large part in family gifts. Many were
by substitutions, but charters recording family subinfeudations also
seem to mention seignorial participation with unusual frequency.[59]
Lords had good reason to desire some family gifts. Some they may
have suggested, for example that a weak man give up his land to a
stronger but younger brother. Other family gifts might be welcome
for different reasons, for example to simplify estate structures.[60]
However, on some occasions family gifts may have been less welcome
to the lord since they were often made at reduced service. In such
circumstances, record of the lord's consent was therefore desirable in
order to prevent later trouble.

Secondly, the amount given must have affected a lord's willingness
to consent. I have already cited Gilbert de Clare's provision that his
men's gifts to Stoke by Clare should not be to the disinheritance of
their successors.[61] Some others limit the amount or proportion of
their land which a man might alienate. In 1094 Roger of Poitou
granted that anyone desiring to make a grant to the monastery of
Lancaster might give up to half his land, or if he had no heir from a

[58] Madox, *Formulare Anglicanum*, No. II. Note also *Danelaw Documents*, No. 76, a
charter from late in Henry II's reign, which contains a provision against alienation to
the Church, and No. 77, which records the grant of that land to the Church.
[59] e.g. *Danelaw Documents*, Nos. 502–4; *Northants*, No. XXXb. See also above, pp.
210–11 on substitutions.
[60] e.g. Robert earl of Leicester 'granted and by his charter confirmed' Geoffrey
Ridel's gift, made with the earl and his son's consent, to Geoffrey's brother Ralph
Basset of all the land which Geoffrey had held of the earl; BL MS Harley 294, fos.
249ᵛ–250. Ralph and his heirs were to hold of Geoffrey and his heirs by the same
service as Geoffrey held of the earl. The purpose appears to have been to divide up the
Basset holdings according to honours, and this may well have benefited the earl.
[61] *Stoke*, No. 137 (ii), see above, p. 193.

woman, could give all his land and become a monk.[62] In contrast with such grants of large proportions of land, which might threaten the lord's services, it is conceivable that lords would not have troubled themselves about their tenants' very small gifts.

Thirdly, the relative power of lord and tenant must have been important. As we have seen, sometimes great men were tenants of lesser ones, sometimes lords had enfeoffed most of their lands to one tenant, sometimes clear evidence survives of the lord's problems in controlling a strong tenant. Did such powerful vassals really need their lords' consent for alienation? I have found no charters recording consents or confirmations in relationships of this sort, and this is surely not simply a result of the surviving evidence. A weak lord would have had great difficulty in preventing a gift by a strong vassal. Nor would the consent of an inferior lord increase the security of a great man's gift. In contrast, lesser men may often have made their gifts in their lords' courts; perhaps they had no courts of their own, or perhaps they desired the publicity of a greater assembly, together with the consent of their lord. At the same time, the lord could more easily regulate alienations by such lesser men.

Fourthly, the vassal's tenure might affect the lord's control. The lord's participation may have been especially needed for alienation of acquisitions, possibly because a man's hold on his acquisitions was weaker in relation to the lord and donor than was his hold on his inheritance.[63] It is furthermore possible that lords might particularly resist grants of lands seen as the head of a man's estates.[64] Ministerial lands were also peculiarly closely linked to the relationship of man, and lord. Charters confirming officials' gifts are notably common, and the verb *dare* was used with unusual frequency in their confirmations.[65] In the thirteenth century 'a tenement held by serjeanty is treated as inalienable and impartible', although it is also notable

---

[62] *CDF*, No. 665. See also Tabuteau, *Transfers of Property*, 181–2 for 11th cent. Norman charters.

[63] e.g. *BM Facsimiles*, No. 43. See also above, p. 210, below, p. 277.

[64] e.g. Huntington Library, San Marino, BA 42/1526, cited Holt, 'Notions of Patrimony', 202–3. See Stenton, *First Century*, 61–4 on the *caput honoris*, and for a Norman instance from 1059, Tabuteau, *Transfers of Property*, 183. See also for restrictions on the chief messuage *Glanvill*, vii. 3, Hall, 75–6 on socage and on division amongst female heirs, vi. 17, xii. 20, pp. 67, 145 on dower; S. F. C. Milsom, 'Inheritance by Women in the Twelfth and Early Thirteenth Centuries', in M. S. Arnold *et al.*, *On the Laws and Customs of England* (Chapel Hill, NC, 1981), 70. Cf. Pollock and Maitland, i. 280 on restrictions on the *caput baroniae*.

[65] e.g. *Earldom of Gloucester*, No. 77. See above, p. 213 on *dare*.

that such a restraint on alienation was often disregarded in practice even in the more rule-bound legal circumstances of that century.[66]

Fifthly, the lord's consent was particularly desirable when the gift was in special need of protection. The lands might have had a difficult history.[67] Or the donor might be a woman.[68] Similarly, seignorial confirmation was desirable for death-bed gifts, and for gifts by men entering monasteries, on the brink, as it were, of worldly death. Roger earl of Warwick confirmed Robert de Montfort's gift to Thorney Abbey, made on the day Robert gave himself to that church. Robert later made another gift 'in his illness' and specifically asked that Roger confirm it. In this case, even the earl's confirmation did not stop Robert's brother from disturbing the gift in Stephen's reign.[69] As with all the means of securing gifts, seignorial participation did not guarantee success.

CONCLUSIONS

The lord's was thus a particularly important interest affecting alienation. Often the interests of donor and lord would be shared so that consent might either be automatic or unnecessary. However, on occasions, it clearly was considered worth obtaining and recording the lord's consent, and on others the lord's wishes were not decisive. A picture of lords specifically and decisively involved in every gift exaggerates both the necessities and sometimes the capacity of seignorial control.

These conclusions are also compatible with the increasingly common grants, usually to a specific grantee, whereby lords confirmed in advance all future gifts. For ecclesiastical beneficiaries, these begin in Normandy and England before 1100, and then between *c*.1120 and

[66] Pollock and Maitland, i. 290, 334–5; E. G. Kimball, *Serjeanty Tenure in Medieval England* (New Haven, Conn., 1936), ch. IX; Simpson, *Land Law*, 10.

[67] See above, p. 220, for the grant of Sawbridgeworth. See also e.g. *Stoke*, No. 540.

[68] See *Regesta*, ii, Nos. 1006, 1550; also *EYC*, v, No. 228, and above, p. 196, for an instance involving Tiffany daughter of Roald the constable.

[69] Bodleian Library, MS Dodsworth 85, fo. 26. For the dispute, see *Regesta*, iii, Nos. 885–8. See also e.g. *Regesta*, ii, No. 1307. Note further that the one example which Tabuteau found to suggest that lords could block alienation by refusing to consent concerned a death-bed grant, *Transfers of Property*, 171–2. For a donor requesting his lord Henry II's confirmation of a death-bed gift, see J. C. Holt, 'Patronage and Politics', *TRHS*, 5th Ser. 34 (1984), 24.

1135 occurs a sharp increase amongst royal charters.[70] At least by
Henry II's reign, advance confirmations were also granted to laymen.
In 1154 × 62 Henry granted to Robert Basset all the lands which his
lords reasonably gave him or which he could reasonably acquire.[71] At
the same time appear the first grants to a man and his heirs and
assigns, suggesting choice as to the disposal of the lands.[72] Modern
scholars generally take assignment to refer to substitution, in which
case the lord's participation was needed, but it is uncertain that early
mentions of 'assigns' necessarily had such a particular meaning.
Glanvill wrote that 'a son can be "forisfamiliated" by his father in his
father's lifetime if the father assigns a certain part of his land to the
son and gives him seisin of it in his lifetime'.[73] This clearly is not
substitution. Early grants mentioning assigns could, therefore, simply
be advance confirmations of a man's gifts.

The increased frequency of advance confirmations in the latter
part of Henry I's reign coincides with the appearance of statements
that the gift should be made *iuste*, or *rationabiliter*, or *legaliter*, justly,
reasonably, or lawfully.[74] I do not wish to imply that without such
words advance confirmations could later force a lord to accept and
protect an 'unjust' gift. As so often, draftsmen found themselves
giving express wording to common sense. Still, the choice of vocabulary in advance confirmations is notable. In royal charters, *iuste*
appears in the first twenty years of Henry I's reign, and may be part
of a general change in royal charter drafting.[75] Between 1120 and
1135 *legaliter* and *rationabiliter* begin to appear.[76] Then *rationabiliter*
becomes common in Henry II's confirmations,[77] and also appears

[70] Pre-1100: see e.g. *Regesta*, i, No. 421, *EYC*, viii, No. 7 (1088 × 1118), Holt,
'Notions of Patrimony', 202–3 and refs. On Normandy, Holt, 'Notions of Patrimony',
202, Tabuteau, *Transfers of Property*, 180–1; her examples are largely from the last
twenty years of the 11th cent., but a few are earlier. 1120–35: e.g. *Regesta*, ii, Nos.
1285, 1327, 1428, 1536, 1742.

[71] Bodleian Library, MS Dugdale 12, p. 133.

[72] See e.g. *EYC*, i, No. 422, a charter of Henry II.

[73] *Glanvill*, vii. 3, Hall, 78. He goes on to discuss the different case of the son who
does homage to the chief lord for the paternal inheritance during his father's lifetime.

[74] e.g. *Regesta*, ii, No. 1810 *iuste*; No. 1742 *legaliter*; No. 1827 *rationabiliter*.

[75] *Regesta*, ii, No. 682 dates from 1105; R. C. van Caenegem, *The Birth of the English
Common Law* (2nd edn., Cambridge, 1988), 38–40 discusses the emergence of the
word *iuste* in writs.

[76] Orderic, iv. 184 seems to use the two words as near synonyms.

[77] e.g. *The Cartulary of Shrewsbury Abbey*, ed. U. Rees (2 vols.; Aberystwyth, 1975),
No. 47; Bodleian Library, MS Dugdale 12, p. 133; grants other than advance confirmations also used it, e.g. *Danelaw Documents*, No. 1; *CChR*, iv. 183–4.

in private charters, at least for the 1140s.[78] It is unclear how far *rationabiliter* was a technical term. Orderic uses it to signify that a man was *compos mentis*.[79] The word certainly had a canonical usage,[80] and appears early in the twelfth century in ecclesiastics' charters.[81] Often the word can have meant little more than *iuste*, but it did possess the advantages of its respectable pedigree and its resonances of fashionable *ratio*. The criteria by which the justice or reasonableness of the gifts would be determined are again surely those considered above with regard to confirmations of specific gifts.

Such advance confirmation may be seen as a sign of the limits and increasing weakness of seignorial control of alienation. Certainly, as Holt has pointed out, even in the early thirteenth century, 'the general licence to alienate was still not so strong that detailed confirmation would not strengthen it'.[82] However, the lord does seem to be saying that, although he retains a retrospective control, permission for individual gifts is no longer necessary. Such advance confirmations therefore indicate a less regular part for the honorial court and surely do suggest a relaxation of seignorial control over alienation.

Donors and donees were not restricted to securing their gifts in any one of the ways I have discussed in the last three chapters. Other people participated in alienation. In eleventh-century Normandy, it seems that tenants could sometimes refuse to agree to grants whereby their lord 'attorned' them and their land and services to a new lord.[83] In England, we have some examples of families who held extensive lands being transferred to great magnates in the late eleventh century.[84] Perhaps these tenants agreed to the rearrangements, or perhaps the conditions following the Conquest allowed at least the

---

[78] e.g. *EYC*, ix, No. 165. See also *Mowbray*, No. 155.

[79] Orderic, vi. 154 on Philip I of France; see also *Glanvill*, vii. 1, Hall, 70.

[80] See e.g. the *Prologus* to Ivo's *Decretum*, with its emphasis on *ratio*; G. Lésage, 'La "Ratio Canonica" d'après Alexandre III', in *Proceedings of the 4th International Congress of Medieval Canon Law*, ed. S. Kuttner (Vatican City, 1976), 95–106. P. Stein, *Regulae Iuris: From Juristic Rules to Legal Maxims* (Edinburgh, 1966), comments on *ratio* in Roman Law.

[81] e.g. *Worcester*, No. 264.

[82] Holt, 'Notions of Patrimony', 204.

[83] Tabuteau, *Transfers of Property*, 171, 187–8.

[84] See *CMA*, ii. 20–1; *Book of Seals*, 110 for the Domesday tenancy in chief of William son of Corbucion being divided in Rufus's reign between the new earldoms of Warwick and Buckingham.

king greater scope for changing tenurial arrangements than the duke
had enjoyed in Normandy. However, early twelfth-century evidence
clearly shows that great men felt they should not be treated thus, and
by the second half of the century, lords were promising that they
would not forcibly attorn even fairly minor men.[85] Again we may be
seeing lords' control of their men's lands being reduced.

More generally, it was also sometimes thought useful specifically to
record that a gift was made by the counsel of the donor's barons or
men.[86] Potential claimants might be persuaded to consent to a grant,
often no doubt in return for a suitable reward.[87] Most notably, wives
often joined in grants.[88] Overlords confirmed gifts with the same
purposes and motives as had immediate lords. Geoffrey de Clinton
reserved for himself the rent owed by a lord who had consented to
his tenant's gift.[89] Grantees sought other high-level confirmations.
Churches turned to bishops and the Pope, and occasional records
survive of laymen gaining ecclesiastical confirmation of their gifts of
alms.[90] Roger archbishop of York gave the confirming churchman's
perspective: for its future security, whatever has justly been given to a
church by gift of the faithful 'should be confirmed by episcopal
authority'.[91] Best of all, the king would confirm the gift, bringing

---

[85] Orderic, vi. 58; see also *PR 31 HI*, 62. *EYC*, i, Nos. 628–9. On attornment in the
13th cent., see Pollock and Maitland, i. 346–9, ii. 93–4.

[86] e.g. *Chester*, Nos. 2, 104, *Reading*, No. 236, *Stoke*, Nos. 21—a gift also counselled
by God—333, *Book of Seals*, No. 3; see also *EYC*, v, Nos. 186, 222, Stenton, *First
Century*, No. 46, which include the donor's friends amongst those counselling the gift,
and in the former cases assenting to it; *The Registrum Antiquissimum of the Cathedral
Church of Lincoln*, ed. C. W. Foster and K. Major (10 vols.; Lincoln Rec. Soc.,
1931–73), No. 316 for a gift made 'diuina inspirante clementia . . . bonorum uirorum
consilio'. See also D. Postles, 'Securing the Gift', *Archives*, 19 (1990), 188.

[87] e.g. *English Lawsuits from William I to Richard I*, ed. R. C. van Caenegem (Selden
Soc., 1990–1), No. 240; *Registrum Antiquissimum*, No. 149.

[88] Sometimes a wife had a personal claim to the gift, be it her inheritance, the
maritagium which she had brought into the marriage, or her dower; e.g. *Earldom of
Gloucester*, No. 119, *EYC*, iv, No. 73, Stenton, *First Century*, No. 46 respectively. The
effect of consenting to a donation from her dower was presumably to prevent her
reclaiming it as such after her husband's death; on dower, see now J. Biancalana,
'Widows at Common Law', *Irish Jurist*, NS 23 (1988), 255–329. A preliminary survey
(see Hudson, 'Legal Aspects of Seignorial Control of Land', D.Phil. thesis (Oxford,
1988), 178–80) suggests that generally charters of great men rarely mention their
wives' consent, especially after 1150. Amongst lesser men's charters, the proportion
recording wives' participation remains fairly stable, or increases slightly, in the second
half of the 12th cent.

[89] *Oxford Charters*, No. 71, see also e.g. *EYC*, viii, No. 16.

[90] e.g. *CMA*, ii. 190–200; *Reading*, Nos. 139–53; *EYC*, xii, No. 76.

[91] *EYC*, v, No. 175; note also e.g. *Northants*, No. LVI.

both personal power, the aura of royal authority, and the possibility of royal justice. Thus a church might benefit greatly from a royal order that a gift be treated 'as my demesne alms'.[92]

Such a piling up of methods of securing a gift can be seen as particularly characteristic of a world in which royal justice, although influential, still did not provide regular, automatically available remedies for infringement of the grant. They sought both to reconcile in advance potential grievances and to gather a variety of men who were pledged to supporting the gift in the case of any future dispute.[93] Yet at the same time, the limitations of such methods, including seignorial consent, are significant, especially in comparison with the Continent.[94] They can again be linked to the various features of Anglo-Norman society, including the degree of royal power, which also rendered the tenant quite secure during his lifetime and his heir in a strong position to succeed after his death.

[92] See e.g. *Regesta*, i, No. 237a; ii, No. 1459.

[93] See e.g. Geoffrey de Mandeville's foundation charter for Hurley Priory, P. M. Barnes and C. F. Slade (edd.), *A Medieval Miscellany for Doris Mary Stenton* (PRS, NS 36; 1960), 107; above, pp. 196–7 for the gift of Tiffany daughter of Roald; Van Caenegem, *Lawsuits*, No. 343. Note also the variety of authorities which became involved in disputes involving the tithes of Belvoir Priory: *Regesta*, ii, Nos. 1277 (spurious), 1458, 1495, iii, Nos. 82–3; HMC, *Rutland*, iv. 158–60.

[94] Mentions of seignorial participation seem to have been less common in England compared with other closely connected lands; see e.g. Tabuteau, *Transfers of Property*, 179–187, J. Boussard, *Le Gouvernement d'Henri II* (Paris 1956), 234 and n. 1. As with the *retrait lignager*, the *retrait féodale*, which gave the lord first right of purchase, did not become general in England; for an exceptional instance, see *Danelaw Documents*, No. 544. On Norman precursors of the *retrait féodale*, see Tabuteau, *Transfers of Property*, 184. See below, p. 276, for comments on the further decline in participation in alienation.

8

Bishops, Abbots, and the Alienation of Church Lands

> The authority of the holy canons orders that no bishop or abbot
> alienate church possessions [*res*] or transfer them into the power
> of princes or other persons, and if it happens it is to be held
> void.
>
> Eugenius III to Bishop Nigel and the prior and chapter of Ely,
> 1150 × 3[1]

THUS far I have concentrated primarily on lay lords. Yet no examination of lordship and land-holding can afford to neglect the control of
church lands, which in 1086 constituted a quarter of the lands in
England. Their alienation was subject to the additional rules of
Canon Law and to different obligations. These lands had been given,
for example, 'to God, Saint Mary, the abbot, and his monks'.[2] Gifts
were sometimes made in the hand of the abbot, but placed on the
altar of the saint. Rannulf bishop of Durham referred to St Cuthbert
as his lord.[3] To all these associated beneficiaries, and to the donor,
who might well have stressed the perpetuity of his gift in order to
protect his spiritual benefits, the prelate had obligations, and these
had an effect on alienation and thus on lordship.

I now consider the background of Canon Law and of political
circumstances, and analyse three connected ways of enforcing these
obligations: alienation of church lands might be totally prohibited; the
church's lands might be divided between prelate and chapter, with
each fully controlling their own share; or alienation might only be
permitted with consent from the chapter. I then discuss the connected

---

[1] *Liber Eliensis*, ed. E. O. Blake (Camden Soc., 3rd Ser. 92; 1962), 344,
Papsturkunden, ii, No. 63. In this chapter I shall use the word prelate to cover abbots as
well as bishops, rather than in its more limited sense of just bishops.

[2] *CMA*, ii. 141. See e.g. *Chronicon Abbatiae Rameseiensis*, ed. W. D. Macray
(London, 1886), 253–4 for reference to the lands of St Benedict.

[3] *Durham Episcopal Charters, 1071–1152*, ed. H. S. Offler (Surtees Soc. 179; 1968),
Nos. 14, 16, 17, 24.

issue of royal control of alienation of church lands. Finally I argue that church land-holding, and notably the emphasis on the Church's lasting control of land and the close control exercised by the king, played an essential role in wider developments affecting land-holding and law.

CANON LAW AND INALIENABILITY

The canonical collections of the late eleventh and early twelfth centuries work on the basic premiss that 'it is not permitted for bishops to alienate church possessions [*res*] in any way'. The *Collectio Lanfranci*, Ivo's *Decretum*, and Gratian, all include such statements, and they treat the subject fairly consistently.[4] The restriction contrasts with their general emphasis on the bishop or abbot's power over the affairs of his church.[5]

However, the prohibition in the canons was qualified, first by the exceptions of necessity and utility. Lanfranc and Gratian's collections included the seventh canon of the Council of Agde, which began by prohibiting alienation, but went on

if need compels, so that for the need or the use of the church anything is dispersed as a usufruct or in direct sale, the cause of the necessity to sell is first to be proved in the presence of two or three bishops of the same province or neighbouring bishops, so that after priestly discussion the sale which has been made may be strengthened by their subscription.[6]

Such problems fall under the general question of the effect of necessity on rules which greatly exercised canonists in this period.[7] A second qualification is that the canons were most concerned with

---

[4] Trinity College, Cambridge, MS B 16 44, pp. 285–6, Hinschius, 333; *Decretum*, pars iii, cc. 172, 242; Gratian, *Decretum*, C. x, q. ii, cc. i, viii. Ivo's *Pannormia* has a slightly different emphasis, see below, p. 232.

[5] e.g. Gratian, *Decretum*, C. x, q. ii. See also *The Monastic Constitutions of Lanfranc*, ed. D. Knowles (Edinburgh, 1951), 74.

[6] Trinity College, Cambridge, MS B 16 44, pp. 285–6, Hinschius, 332–3; Gratian, *Decretum*, C. x, q. ii, c. i. The Council of Agde took place in 506. It is unclear whether the manuscript reads 'in directa uenditione' or 'indirecta uenditione'; with advice from Mark Philpott, I have chosen the former reading here.

[7] For necessity, see the Prologues to Ivo's *Pannormia* and *Decretum*. See also Gratian, *Decretum*, C. xii, q. ii, c. xv on the freeing of captives. On necessity generally, see also Hugh the Chantor, *The History of the Church of York, 1066–1127*, ed. and tr. C. Johnson (Edinburgh, 1961), 49–50. Sawyer, No. 1424, shows an Anglo-Saxon prelate, in 1022, apparently using necessity to justify a temporary alienation.

long-term alienations.[8] A third qualification might permit alienation with the consent of the clergy. This is most clearly stated in the short section on alienability in Ivo's *Pannormia*, the most popular canonical collection in England for at least the first fifty years of the twelfth century: 'a gift, sale, or exchange of church possessions by a bishop will be void if made without the consent and subscription of the clergy'.[9] This statement also appeared in Ivo's *Decretum* and in Gratian, but in neither collection do mentions of alienation by consent predominate as in the *Pannormia*.[10]

Canon Law collections concentrated on bishops and episcopal obligations, but they were also applied to abbots. In England as elsewhere, abbots on their benediction swore to prevent future alienations and to resume past ones. Thus the officiating bishop asked the abbot whether he wished to gather, as much as he could, the possessions of the church which had previously been unjustly dispersed; the abbot replied 'uolo', 'I wish.'[11] The good ecclesiastic might then investigate the situation of his church's estates and take appropriate action.[12]

Pressures for inalienability may well have grown during the twelfth century. The new monastic orders adopted different methods of land use.[13] Other churches sought outside protection against the possible

---

[8] See Ivo, *Decretum*, pars iii, c. 183: 'alienationis ... uerbum continet uenditionem, donationem, permutationes, emphiteuseos perpetuum contractum.' These would probably be seen as including grants of knights' fees and fee farm, but not less permanent grants. See M. Cheney, 'Inalienability in Mid-Twelfth Century England: Enforcement and Consequences', *Proceedings of the Sixth International Congress of Medieval Canon Law*, ed. S. Kuttner and K. Pennington (Vatican City, 1985), 470, 472 on fee farm.

[9] Ivo, *Pannormia*, lib. ii, c. lxxxvi. On the popularity of Ivo's *Pannormia*, see Z. N. Brooke, *The English Church and the Papacy* (Cambridge, 1931), 41. On early post-Conquest Canon Law collections in England, see also P. Cramer, 'Ernulf of Rochester and Early Anglo-Norman Canon Law', *JEcclH* 40 (1989), 483–510.

[10] Ivo, *Decretum*, pars iii, c. 231; Gratian, *Decretum*, C. xii, q. ii, c. lii. The wider implications of Ivo's particular selection of texts for the *Pannormia* requires further study, preferably in conjunction with analysis of the practical application of Canon Law.

[11] *The Pontifical of Magdalen College*, ed. H. A. Wilson (Henry Bradshaw Soc. 39; 1910), 81; for similar oaths by bishops and deacons, see *Statutes of Lincoln Cathedral*, ed. H. Bradshaw and C. Wordsworth (3 vols.; Cambridge, 1897), ii. 34–5.

[12] e.g. *Liber Eliensis*, 287; another such investigation presumably lay behind the trial at Penenden Heath.

[13] See e.g. M. D. Knowles, *The Monastic Order in England* (2nd edn., Cambridge, 1963), 632–4, B. D. Hill, *English Cistercian Monasteries and their Patrons in the Twelfth Century* (Urbana, 1968), ch. 2. When dealing with monasteries, my concern in this chapter is therefore primarily with Benedictine houses.

activities of their heads, and complete prohibition of alienation is implied, for example, by some royal documents ordering the resumption of church lands.[14] Similarly, between 1101 and 1114, Paschal II damned with eternal malediction all who infringed or diminished, sold or distributed the lands of Westminster Abbey.[15]

However, although these prohibitions restricted ecclesiastical lords' power to alienate, they never threatened to abolish it. Circumstances were often unfavourable to the strict application of canonical doctrine. Although records of the post-Conquest councils do not deal directly with alienation by bishops and abbots, they do mention a connected matter also prominent in the canons, lay seizure of church possessions. Such invasions were, of course, a particular problem in periods of political disturbance.[16] Some were hard to distinguish from unjust alienations; lands seized might be retrieved only by enfeoffing the oppressor,[17] and such enfeoffments would have constituted alienation through fear, which the canons condemned.[18] Other laymen brought subtler pressure in order to obtain lands, whilst keepers of churches during vacancies were sometimes profligate with the lands in their charge.[19]

Churches anyway had their military obligations to fulfil. Reliance entirely on household knights rarely lasted long, and lands were therefore alienated.[20] Even after the initial period of enfeoffment, churches continued to grant lands to laymen whose support they desired.[21] Moreover, many ecclesiastical lords, like their lay counterparts, rewarded their families and followers with land. Nepotism was a common charge after any prelate's death. The chronicler Hugh Candidus accused Thorold, abbot of Peterborough from 1069 to

---

[14] e.g. *Regesta*, i, No. 330; ii, No. 650.

[15] *Papsturkunden*, i, No. 9. See Cheney, 'Inalienability', esp. 477 on Waltham Abbey in the late 12th cent.

[16] e.g. *Councils and Synods*, i, ii. 581, the Legatine Council at Windsor in May 1070, c. 11. For a mention in the *Collectio Lanfranci*, see e.g. Trinity College, Cambridge, MS B 16 44, p. 45, Hinschius, 178–9.

[17] e.g. F. Du Boulay, *The Lordship of Canterbury* (London, 1966), 54; J. A. Raftis, *The Estates of Ramsey Abbey: A Study in Economic Growth and Organization* (Toronto, 1957), ch. 2, esp. p. 31. See also e.g. *Regesta*, ii, Nos. 546, 626.

[18] Gratian, *Decretum*, C. xii, q. ii, c. xviii. See also *Regesta*, i, No. 98 on alienation because of fear.

[19] e.g. *CMA*, ii. 42–3; H. M. Chew, *The English Ecclesiastical Tenants-in-Chief and Knight Service, especially in the Thirteenth and Fourteenth Centuries* (Oxford, 1932), 118.

[20] e.g. *CMA*, ii. 3–4; *Liber Eliensis*, 217; Chew, *Ecclesiastical Tenants-in-Chief*, 114–16.

[21] e.g. *CMA*, ii. 43.

1098, of squandering the abbey's lands amongst his relations and the knights whom he had brought with him, to such an extent that only one-third of the abbey's land remained in demesne. In his *Carta* of 1166, the archbishop of York complained that nepotism had led his predecessors to enfeoff more knights than the king required.[22]

Thus the prelate's personal view of his powers and obligations could differ from that of his chapter, and the resultant tension sometimes produced disputes over alienation. The *Abingdon Chronicle* provides a gallery of contrasting abbots: Reginald, apparently careless of the convent's will, and intent on providing for his own family; Faritius, in harmony with the convent as he used his influence towards the resumption of alienated lands; Ingulf, incapable of withstanding the pressures brought on by Stephen's reign, and in the face of his problems neglecting the opinion of the monks. In many churches, internal tension and external pressures similarly combined against the maintenance of the demesne.

THE RESTRICTION OF ALIENATION

If alienation, to no one's surprise, continued to take place, what methods were employed to restrict it? One strategy, the attempted restriction of grants to the tenant's life or an even shorter period, has already been discussed.[23] A second method was the division of lands between prelate and chapter, one purpose of which was to ensure the preservation of possessions required for the sustenance of the church. It removed them from the prelate's direct control, reduced his powers of lordship, and entrusted their administration to the prior or dean and chapter.

The division was gradual, and varied between churches.[24] Some

---

[22] Hugh Candidus, *Chronicle*, ed. W. T. Mellows (Oxford, 1949), 84–5; see also e.g. pp. 88–9; *Red Book*, i. 413. See also e.g. *CMA*, ii. 35–40; *Chronicon Abbatiae de Evesham*, ed. W. D. Macray (London, 1863), 98; Adam of Domerham, *Historia*, ed. T. Hearne (2 vols.; Oxford, 1727), ii. 306, 308–9.

[23] See above, Ch. 3; also *Reading Abbey Cartularies*, ed. B. R. Kemp (2 vols.; Camden Soc., 1986–7), Nos. 1, 27; B. F. Harvey, 'Abbot Gervase de Blois and the Fee Farms of Westminster Abbey', *BIHR* 40 (1967), 127–42, which is of general interest for this chapter. Desire to prevent losses arising from an inability to raise rents may have increased concern over long-term alienation.

[24] Historians discussing division of revenues have not always distinguished between two situations: (i) certain lands being administered with the rest of the abbey's possessions, the revenues then providing for the monks, and (ii) a full division whereby the convent itself had independent control of the lands. Note the careful account of M.

Anglo-Saxon charters record gifts made for the monks' food, or 'as their very own'.[25] In Domesday, some monastic lands are specified as, for example, 'from the monks' food', and the secular canons of Chichester Cathedral are recorded as holding sixteen hides in common.[26] However, such statements do not prove a strict division of possessions. In 1086 an abbey or monastic cathedral's lands were generally all administered together, and this may even be true of secular cathedrals.[27] In a monastery, the cellarer would control the supply of food both for monks and abbot. Other revenues might be set aside for the monks or clerks, again from sources administered with the rest of the church's lands. Domesday several times referred to Lanfranc as holding lands ascribed to the monks' supply: 'Sandwich lies in its own Hundred. The archbishop holds this borough. It is for the clothing of the monks.'[28] In many abbeys, such arrangements probably continued into the early twelfth century.

However, major administrative changes were taking place. These probably began at cathedrals before 1100. At the secular cathedral of Chichester, prebendal organization may have started under Stigand, bishop between 1070 and 1087.[29] In 1106 an enquiry in the county court concerning the cathedral church of York stated that

the land of the canons is called St Peter's own table. . . . The archbishop has this right only in the possessions of the canons, that when a canon dies he

---

Howell, 'Abbatial Vacancies and the Divided *Mensa* in Medieval England', *JEcclH* 33 (1982), esp. 173–81. She considers, *inter alia*, the various reasons for the division of revenues, notably the desire to limit royal control of the Church's lands during vacancies. For this and the following paragraph, see also J. Barrow, 'Cathedrals, Provosts and Prebends: A Comparison of Twelfth-Century German and English Practice', *JEcclH* 37 (1986), esp. 552–63.

[25] e.g. Sawyer, Nos. 843, 1259.

[26] e.g. *Domesday*, i, fos. 58a, 78a, 143b. See also *The Letters of Lanfranc Archbishop of Canterbury*, ed. and tr. H. Clover and M. Gibson (Oxford, 1979), No. 56. For Chichester, see *Domesday*, i, fo. 17a. On Worcester, see J. D. Hamshere, 'Domesday Book: Estate Structure in the West Midlands', in J. C. Holt (ed.), *Domesday Studies* (Woodbridge, 1987), 168–71.

[27] See e.g. *Regesta*, i, No. 104, William I ordering that Abbot Aethelwig of Evesham have his land in Warwickshire to hold for the use of the monks.

[28] *Domesday*, i, fo. 3a. Domesday Book on occasion uses the phrase 'ad uictum' or 'ad uestitum monachorum' to emphasize a claim to disputed lands rather than to indicate a separation of lands between prelate and chapter, e.g. this entry concerning Sandwich includes the phrase 'the men of this borough testify . . .', suggesting a dispute. See also V. H. Galbraith, 'An Episcopal Land-Grant of 1085', *EHR* 44 (1929), 363–7.

[29] *The Acts of the Bishops of Chichester, 1075–1207*, ed. H. Mayr-Harting (Cant.–York Soc. 130; 1964), 41–2.

grants the prebend to another, but not however without the counsel and assent of the chapter.[30]

A Canterbury charter and Eadmer record that Anselm placed the possessions of monks of ChristChurch at their own disposal.[31] In both cathedrals and other monasteries, the division of lands and their administration generally grew clearer in Henry I's reign and beyond.[32] Offices such as the sacristy, the chamber, and the almonry were further endowed.[33] A separate administration was being created for the house. Meanwhile, abbots started to live more distantly from their monks.

By the mid-twelfth century, priors or deans and chapters of cathedrals had their own seals, and were granting lands. In 1143 × 5 Prior David and the convent of Worcester granted various lands to William Rupe, and in 1146 × 89 Prior Ralph, 'by the unanimous favour of the whole chapter of Worcester', granted half a virgate to Richard of Grimsley to possess 'by hereditary right'.[34] Here we have control of the church's lands divided between bishop and prior, and the latter now subject to the requirement of acting with the consent of the monks. It is less certain whether non-cathedral monastic chapters had their own seals in this period. The *Abingdon Chronicle* records Abbot Ingulf's misuse of the church's seal in Stephen's reign. It is unclear whether the abbey still had only one seal, which Ingulf was using against the will of the monks, or two seals—one for the abbot and one for the prior and chapter—and that Ingulf

[30] *Visitations and Memorials of Southwell Minster*, ed. A. F. Leach (Camden Soc., NS 48; 1891), 192–3.

[31] *Les Régistres de Grégoire IX*, ed. L. Auvray (4 vols.; Paris, 1896–1955), ii, No. 3233; Eadmer, *Historia Nouorum in Anglia*, ed. M. Rule (London, 1884), 219.

[32] *Feudal Documents from the Abbey of Bury St Edmunds*, ed. D. C. Douglas (London, 1932), No. 35; E. King, *Peterborough Abbey 1086–1310* (Cambridge, 1973), 88; Raftis, Ramsey, 37–8; Knowles, *Monastic Order*, 405. On cathedrals, monastic and secular, under Henry I, M. Brett, *The English Church under Henry I* (Oxford, 1975), 191–8; also on secular cathedrals, see *Chichester*, 42–8; *English Episcopal Acta, I. Lincoln, 1067–1185*, ed. D. M. Smith (London, 1980), p. xlix; *English Episcopal Acta, V. York, 1070–1154*, ed. J. E. Burton (Oxford, 1988), p. xli, Hugh the Chantor, 11; *Early Charters of the Cathedral Church of St Paul, London*, ed. M. Gibbs (Camden Soc., 3rd Ser. 58; 1939), No. 219.

[33] See e.g. Hugh Candidus, 122–3, 130, concerning Stephen's reign.

[34] *The Cartulary of Worcester Cathedral Priory*, ed. R. R. Darlington (PRS, NS 38; 1968), Nos. 439, 440 respectively. By the 1150s, the prior and monks of Ely were recalling the time of Bishop Hervey, who died in 1131, when they did not have a copy of their own seal; E. Miller, *The Abbey and Bishopric of Ely* (Cambridge, 1951), 287–8.

was making personal use of the latter. Neither narratives nor seal impressions from other monasteries allow firmer conclusions.[35]

Other associated distinctions sometimes supplemented the main division of lands. One resembled the lay distinction between inheritance and acquisitions. The *Evesham Chronicle* records of Abbot Aethelwig that

from those lands which he acquired in his own time, he gave to certain good men for the great necessity and good of the church, and they faithfully served God and him for them as long as he lived. Of the other lands which his ancestors acquired he gave none at all, but held them honourably in his hand until his death for the needs of the brothers.[36]

Another distinction singled out certain lands as alienable. Thus at Abingdon, in the reign of the Conqueror, the intention seems to have been to make grants from what the chronicler, a century later, calls the lands of vavassours. Such may well be the lands which thegns had held from the church before 1066.[37]

However, the separation of lands was not wholly satisfactory as a method of preventing alienation. Disputes arose, and outside mediation or judgment was sometimes needed. Thus Henry I on occasion helped to enforce such emerging divisions of lands.[38]

[35] *CMA*, ii. 208–9. In the second half of the 12th cent. appear seals bearing the abbot's personal name, rather than simply his title. This may be a sign of his growing separation from the house, and may have been accompanied by the appearance of seals of the convent: e.g. W. de G. Birch, *Catalogue of Seals in the Department of Manuscripts in the British Museum* (6 vols.; London, 1887–1900), Nos. 2802, 3149, 3946, 4010, 4254; see also No. 4280. For secular chapters, see e.g. Nos. 1785, 1786 from Lincoln; also *St Paul's*, No. 176. Separate seals was not a complete solution; note *Papsturkunden*, ii, No. 47, which shows a bishop issuing charters sealed by his own and the church's seals, without the permission of the convent.

[36] *Evesham Chronicle*, 95; I here take ancestors to mean previous abbots. Note also B. Dodwell, 'The Honour of the Bishop of Thetford/Norwich', *Norfolk Archaeology*, 33/2 (1963), 186–7, for the Domesday distinction whereby the recent acquisitions of the bishop of Thetford were referred to as his *feudum*; however, Domesday does not show that such estates had been alienated.

[37] See *CMA*, ii. 3, 35; note *Regesta*, i, Nos. 276, 383, distinguishing thegnlands from demesne. I do not, of course, wish to imply that thegnlands were held in the same way as later knights' fees; on 'thegnlands' and for Domesday references, see P. Vinogradoff, *English Society in the Eleventh Century* (Oxford, 1908), 81, 85, 87–8, 370–2, R. W. Finn, *An Introduction to Domesday Book* (London, 1963), esp. 138–40, Miller, *Ely*, 51–3. For 'vavassour' as a translation of 'thegn', see *Leges Willelmi*, 20 2, Liebermann, *Gesetze*, i. 507, cf. II *Cnut*, 71 2.

[38] See e.g. *Regesta*, ii, No. 1079, *Worcester*, Nos. 260–2 (charters of Henry I and Queen Matilda not included in *Regesta*); also *Annales Monastici*, ed. H. R. Luard (5 vols.; London, 1864–9), ii. 46–7 for royal mediation between the bishop of

Moreover, separation might, in the eyes of the chapter, leave an un-satisfactorily large proportion of lands potentially under the prelate's sole control. In addition, disputes soon arose over alienations from the chapter's portion by the will of the head of the chapter alone.

As we have seen, Ivo of Chartres in particular pointed to a further method of controlling alienation, the requirement for the consent of the clergy. Specific papal orders reinforced the point: in 1159 × 63 Alexander III forbade that the bishop or prior of Worcester alienate lands without the counsel and assent of the whole chapter, or the weightier [*sanior*] part of it.[39] More generally, to take counsel, to have respect for the long-term interests of the church was a sign of a good prelate,[40] although again of course there were occasions when consent was less than willing.[41]

Before 1066, convents in both England and Normandy consented to grants, and throughout the following century the requirement for such participation carried considerable weight.[42] By the twelfth century, the charters of some churches regularly mention participation. Those of St Mary's, York, from the 1120s onwards, generally include a statement such as 'with the common counsel and assent of our chapter'.[43] Other phrases might record participation. A few charters of St Mary's present the chapter as joint donors with the

Winchester and his monks. For other disputes, see e.g. William of Malmesbury, *De Gestis Pontificum Anglorum*, ed. N. Hamilton (London, 1870), 172, 195. For intervention by a papal legate, see *Councils and Synods*, i, ii. 812–3. Note the problems at Durham, where Rannulf Flambard took lands belonging to his church, only restoring them at the end of his life: *Durham*, Nos. 24, 25.

[39] *Worcester*, No. 77, *Papsturkunden*, ii, No. 109. For a later example, *The Letters of Pope Innocent III concerning England and Wales*, ed. C. R. and M. G. Cheney (Oxford, 1967), No. 113.

[40] See *The Chronicle of Battle Abbey*, ed. and tr. E. Searle (Oxford, 1980), 172 where the abbot reminds the convent that he would do nothing without their counsel and licence, for he was a mortal and would die, but the church would live on thereafter.

[44] See e.g. *Battle Chronicle*, 314; also *Gesta Abbatum Monasterii Sancti Albani*, ed. H. T. Riley (3 vols.; London 1867–9), i. 182, where the abbot made the convent confirm two agreements 'importunitate sua'.

[42] England: e.g. Sawyer, Nos. 1420, 1423, 1425, 1426. Normandy: see esp. the case turning on consent recorded in Fauroux, No. 148, *CDF*, Nos. 711–12, *Regesta*, i, No. 92. After 1066, mentions of the chapter's consent appear as soon as charters survive: e.g. *EYC*, i, Nos. 41–2; *Feudal Documents*, No. 104.

[43] *EYC*, i, Nos. 310–11; ix, No. 134; from the mid-12th cent., e.g. i, Nos. 264, 414, 540. Other houses of regular canons: e.g. *Cartulary of Oseney Abbey*, ed. H. E. Salter (6 vols.; Oxford Hist. Soc. 89, 90, 91, 97, 98, 101; 1929–36), iv, Nos. 106, 414b; v, No. 538a; vi, No. 1087. Monasteries: e.g. *CMA*, ii. 136–7; *Ramsey Chronicle*, 236, 237, 258.

abbot.[44] From the time of Henry I onwards appear charters in the name of the chapter confirming episcopal acts.[45] At Bury, between 1121 and 1156, the prior regularly appeared as the first witness of abbatial documents, continuing to do so thereafter, but less frequently.[46] Such witnessing may have constituted the record of the chapter's consent. Similarly, many charters of the bishops of Chichester either record the chapter's consent, or are witnessed by the dean, or both.[47] Consent was not only obtained for permanent grants. At Bury in 1160, Abbot Hugh and the whole convent 'by their unanimous counsel' granted Ralph Brian their clerk two manors for twelve years, whereafter they were to return to the church except the harvests and the buildings. The first witness was the prior.[48]

An Abingdon case from early in the century illuminates the effect of this requirement for consent. With the convent's permission, Abbot Reginald gave his son, William, the church of Marcham. He also made him some other gifts without consulting the convent. In 1101 × 3 all these gifts were adjudged to be from the church's demesne; William therefore gave back and quitclaimed them to Abbot Faritius. However, he was allowed to keep the church of Marcham for life. Various considerations may have shaped this settlement. Possibly Marcham church was not considered part of the abbey's demesne, or had from the first only been given for life. However, it was the convent's consent for the gift of the church which the chronicler emphasized.[49]

I have treated the division of lands and the obtaining of consent separately, and they might be seen as alternatives. The earlier division

[44] *EYC*, i, No. 460; iii, No. 1303; ix, No. 135; see also e.g. *Documents Illustrative of the Social and Economic History of the Danelaw*, ed. F. M. Stenton (London, 1920), Nos. 249, 306, *CMA*, ii. 212, 233.
[45] Brett, *English Church*, 197–8.
[46] *Feudal Documents*, Nos. 111, 113–14, 116–21, 123–4, 128–31, 133–4, 140–2, 144–6, 152–3, 155–8, 167.
[47] e.g. *Chichester*, Nos. 9, 16, 24–7, 32, 63 (chapter joint party with bishop), 65 (*coram capitulo*), 87. See also No. 6, a document described as 'suspicious', for the chapter confirming the grant by giving a book of the letters of St Jerome in testimony. Among other sets of charters, for example those of the bishops of Lincoln, there are few grants for which the assent of the chapter would seem particularly necessary, but the bishops from Alexander onwards often included in their charters clauses saving the dignity of the church of Lincoln in all things; e.g. *Lincoln Acta*, Nos. 68, 72, 111, 135; for Lincoln examples of the consent of the chapter, see e.g. Nos. 37, 44, 234.
[48] *Feudal Documents*, No. 145.
[49] *CMA*, ii. 40, 130–1.

of lands of cathedral churches may help to explain why the chapter's participation is mentioned less frequently in grants by bishops than those by abbots.[50] However, the two methods could also act together. Hilary of Chichester considered it prudent to obtain the consent of the chapter for the alienation even of lands which he proclaimed as his own acquisition; as with laymen alienating lands, ecclesiastics were keen to pile up justifications and reinforcements for their actions. Moreover, in both abbeys and cathedral churches, before the division of lands was complete, a vaguer attribution of certain lands to the monks must still have discouraged their alienation, and if they were to be granted, have given the convent's counsel greater weight. For example, it is significant that at Abingdon the early twelfth-century cases in which the question of consent was most important were also those involving lands of the monks' supply.[51]

THE RESUMPTION OF ALIENATED LANDS

If such methods failed to prevent unjust alienations and disputes arose, how were the lands to be regained? Problems were obviously greatest if the prelate was still intent on maintaining the alienation. In such circumstances, the chapter no doubt relied on prayer, and also looked for external support, which could be provided by records and also by great men, lay or ecclesiastical.[52] Some general ecclesiastical confirmations prohibited the seizure or other unjust diminution of church lands, and diminution could conceivably be taken to refer to prelates as well as outside aggressors.[53] The convent might also turn to the Pope against its bishop. Thus in 1156, Hadrian IV suspended Nigel bishop of Ely from office because he had failed to restore to the

---

[50] Cathedral convents participating in prelates' grants; Canterbury: e.g. *Ancient Charters Royal and Private Prior to A.D. 1200*, ed. J. H. Round (PRS 10, 1888), No. 9, prior as first witness; *Durham*, No. 1 convent as joint grantor; No. 11 convent consent; Nos. 22, 33, 38, 41 prior as first witness.

[51] See esp. *CMA*, ii. 35–40, 208–10; this conclusion seems justified even bearing in mind that the chronicler was writing when the division of lands may have been clearer. *Feudal Documents*, No. 151 may be another relevant case.

[52] See e.g. A. Saltman, *Theobald, Archbishop of Canterbury* (London, 1956), No. 103.

[53] e.g. *The Charters of Norwich Cathedral Priory*, ed. B. Dodwell (2 vols.; PRS, NS 40, 46; 1974, 1985), i, No. 260, Round, *Ancient Charters*, No. 8, by Archbishops Anselm and Ralph of Canterbury respectively.

church possessions alienated by him.[54] Alternatively, the clergy might forge a papal letter.[55]

The convent or chapter's best hope, however, seems to have been that either the offending prelate or a successor would come round to their cause. A dispute which began as one between convent and prelate might become one between prelate and chapter on the one side, and the donee on the other. In the late eleventh century, Abbot Reginald of Abingdon gave a demesne manor at Dumbleton to his nephew. Soon, however, a record of Archbishop Aelfric's original gift of Dumbleton to Abingdon was found in the abbey's archive, and was read to the abbot. According to the chronicler, writing in the 1160s, it forbade that Dumbleton be removed from the monks' use. The abbot unsuccessfully urged his nephew to return the land. Both parties sought royal support, but Rufus apparently accepted their offerings whilst taking no positive action. With the highest source of worldly justice providing no solution, it required God's intervention to break the deadlock. The nephew fell ill and lost the use of his tongue; he restored the land, recovered, and henceforth lived properly.[56] Here we see the impact of documents upon a dispute, and also the effect of religious pressure. At least on occasion divine intervention was decisive.

Once prelates were intent on resuming grants, they could rely simply on their own strength, but such an approach could be dangerous. The *Evesham Chronicle* records that Walter, abbot from 1077, 'did not wish to take homage from many good men whom his predecessor had had, deciding to take away the lands of all of them if he could'.[57] The chronicler saw this not as a heroic defence of the church's rights, but as youthful imprudence, resting on bad advice from relatives, and soon resulting in serious loss of lands. Crucially, the abbot had failed to take notice of his own power relative to that of his potential opponents.

In order to provide sufficient power, outside help was frequently

---

[54] *Liber Eliensis*, 373–9; *Letters of John of Salisbury*, ed. W. J. Millor, H. E. Butler, C. N. L. Brooke (2 vols.; Edinburgh and Oxford, 1955–79), Nos. 39–43.

[55] See e.g. Harvey, 'Abbot Gervase', 129.

[56] *CMA*, ii. 35–6. In France, Suger recorded how his knowledge of the abbey's charters, acquired by burrowing in the archive during his youth, helped him to resume the abbey's rights; *Œuvres Complètes de Suger*, ed. A. Lecoy de la Marche (Paris, 1867), 160–1. For another instance of illness leading to the restoration of lands, see *CMA*, ii. 12–15. For restoration at the death of a tenant, see *Feudal Documents*, No. 151.

[57] *Evesham Chronicle*, 96.

needed. Donors often promised to 'maintain' their alms.[58] However, whilst lords sometimes protected their own or their recent ancestors' foundations from outside attack, no surviving evidence suggests that they were extensively involved in enforcing the prelate's obligations to his church with regard to alienation.[59] The king, on the other hand, was the particular protector of the Church. Preambles of royal diplomas occasionally mentioned this duty.[60] The *Leges Edwardi* state that 'the king who is vicar of the highest King is constituted for this purpose, that he rule the realm and the people of the Lord and above all the Church, and defend them from wrong-doers, and destroy and pluck out the wicked'.[61] Such protection could extend against not only outside attack, but also sinful or unwise prelates. Duke William had helped to enforce the requirement for the convent's consent to alienation in Normandy before 1066.[62] In England in 1077, he ordered his sheriffs to return to his bishoprics and abbeys all the demesne and demesne lands which 'my bishops and abbots have given to them whether by softness, or fear, or greed, or have consented that they have, or which the sheriffs have taken by their own violence'.[63]

Evidence exists of Rufus helping churches to regain lost lands,[64] but instances from Henry I's reign are much more plentiful. Newly appointed prelates often received grants like that to Archbishop William of Canterbury in 1123: he might 'seise into his demesne' all

[58] Note e.g. *Monasticon Diocesis Exoniensis*, ed. G. Oliver (Exeter, 1846), 23, No. 1, for the earl of Cornwall taking a church 'under the protection of God and of the lord Henry king of England and of myself'. See also S. M. Wood, *English Monasteries and their Patrons in the Thirteenth Century* (Oxford, 1955), ch. viii. Cf. below, p. 250, on churches seeking to restrict other aspects of the tenurial bond with the donor; they desired the benefits of having a lord without the restrictions—see also P. R. Hyams, 'Warranty and Good Lordship in Twelfth Century England', *L&HR* 5 (1987), 442.

[59] Control over other types of church, for example colleges of secular canons, might be much closer; see e.g. D. B. Crouch, *The Beaumont Twins* (Cambridge, 1986), 205–7.

[60] e.g. *Regesta*, i, No. 237a.

[61] *Leges Edwardi*, 17, Liebermann, *Gesetze*, i. 642. Note also e.g. the opinions of the *Norman Anonymous* on the position of the king in relation to the Church.

[62] See above, n. 42.

[63] *Regesta*, i, No. 50; on the date, see *English Historical Documents, ii. 1042–1189*, ed. D. C. Douglas and G. W. Greenaway (2nd edn., London, 1981), 463. Other royal orders deal with similar problems, and the major recorded trials of the reign concern the restoration of church lands; see *Regesta*, i, Nos. 155, 177; E. Miller, 'The Ely Land Pleas in the Reign of William I', *EHR* 62 (1947), 438–56; D. Bates, 'The Land Pleas of William I's Reign: Penenden Heath Revisited', *BIHR* 51 (1978), 1–19.

[64] *Regesta*, i, Nos. 329–31; see also Nos. 388, 418.

lands pertaining to the archbishopric, whoever held them, as they were in demesne at Anselm's death, unless he chose not to do so.[65] Other writs specifically concentrated on grants made without the chapter's consent; for example, in 1121 Henry ordered 'that Herbert abbot of Westminster make to be seised into his hand all those lands which have been placed or given outside the church without the assent and consent of the chapter'.[66] The king also issued confirmations concerning specific estates which had been successfully resumed.[67]

Stephen intervened in some disputes,[68] but was significantly absent from others. Thus it was the Pope, not the king, who provided most help for Bishop Nigel of Ely in his attempts at resumption.[69] Stephen's death left many disputes unresolved, and the new king soon asserted his influence in the same ways as had his grandfather. For example, in 1155 × 8 he announced that he was reseising into the hand of St Edmund, his church, and of Henry himself, all demesne lands given or in any way taken from the abbey 'without the assent of the chapter' since the death of Henry I.[70]

Such a survey of royal involvement might suggest that the king altruistically and decisively favoured the Church in all disputes. This was not so. First, monasteries had to pay for royal help. The 1130 Pipe Roll provides a notable echo of the abbot's benediction when it records that the abbot of Westminster rendered account of one thousand marks of silver 'that he gather the goods of his church which had been unjustly dispersed and guard them once gathered'.[71]

[65] *Regesta*, ii, No. 1417; also e.g. Nos. 650, 885, 1101. See also *Red Book*, i. 210; and below, pp. 244–5, on a dispute over Yaxley. Other instances of Henry I helping churches to regain demesnes: e.g. *Regesta*, ii, Nos. 721, 929.

[66] *Regesta*, ii, No. 1252; see also e.g. No. 1131.

[67] See e.g. Hugh Candidus, 88–9, a case in which he had already been involved at an earlier stage; note, however, p. 99, where following the death of the abbot, the king granted the estate to Richard Basset. The struggle for control of the estate continued more successfully under Abbot Martin, p. 123.

[68] See *Regesta*, iii, Nos. 771, 773, for intervention in a dispute between the abbot and monks of Bury St Edmunds.

[69] See below, p. 246. See also *CMA*, ii. 208–10, disputes between abbot and monks with no sign of royal involvement.

[70] *Feudal Documents*, No. 81. See also e.g. *Reading*, Nos. 18, 27; *Ramsey Chronicle*, 298; *Royal Writs in England from the Conquest to Glanvill*, ed. R. C. van Caenegem (Selden Soc. 77; 1958–9), No. 99; on the royal licence granted to Becket to resume land, *MTB*, iii. 43. Note the 13th-cent. writ of entry 'sine consensu capituli', e.g. *Early Registers of Writs*, ed. E. de Haas and G. D. G. Hall (Selden, Soc. 87; 1970), R. 850; *Bracton*, fo. 323, Thorne, iv. 35.

[71] *PR 31 HI*, 150; also pp. 37–8.

244

Part Three

Hugh Candidus records Peterborough paying 60 marks for a royal confirmation of a successfully resumed estate.[72] As always, money was very useful in bringing a satisfactory outcome to a dispute. Secondly, although most sources concentrate on examples where the king supported the restoration of alienated lands, he sometimes refused to help either side decisively,[73] or supported specific lay grantees. The few surviving examples of the latter tend to concern unsuccessful claims, for otherwise they would not have been preserved in church archives, but are indicative of the variety of support which could be obtained from the king.[74] Awareness of the power of the king to help or hinder resumption is revealed by a charter of Archbishop Theobald concerning Jocelin bishop of Salisbury:

the king gave the bishop the power of recalling what had been dispersed and of making his bishopric whole again, as it was in the time of Bishop Osmund and on the day on which King Henry was alive and dead. And the lord king will not hinder but help and maintain the bishop in recalling these things.[75]

Several of these points are well illustrated by Abbot Robert of Thorney's lengthy efforts to regain land at Yaxley and Sibson, which his predecessor Gunter had given to his nephew. The case seems to have started, perhaps soon after Robert became abbot in 1113, with an enquiry into his predecessor's gifts, where he learnt that the grant had been made 'contrary to the will and prohibition of the general chapter'. He refused the nephew's homage and demanded the return of the land. When his requests were unproductive, the abbot disseised the nephew, 'broke his houses and stubbed up his holt'. Here we have clear evidence that ecclesiastics were not all pacific men. However, the abbot did not rely solely on his own resources:

that the matter might be more quickly settled, he crossed the sea and from our lord the king he sought through his own efforts and those of his friends a writ ordering that he should be reseised of that land by the king's justices and should hold it in peace if [the nephew] was unable to show that it had

---

[72] Hugh Candidus, 89.
[73] See above, p. 241.
[74] See e.g. Adam of Domerham, ii. 306. Note also Miller, *Ely*, 66–9, on William I helping the abbot to extract services from those who had invaded Ely lands, but not to bring those lands back into demesne. Herbert the king's chamberlain succeeded in continuing to hold an estate from Abingdon despite general royal orders for restoration of the church's demesne, perhaps suggesting royal favour to the official; *CMA*, ii. 43, 86, 134–5.
[75] Saltman, *Theobald*, No. 241.

been given to him by grant of the chapter and that it was not appropriated to the support of the monks.

Such pressure, and the intercession of friends, may have had some effect on the nephew but he too had obtained a writ, which produced a hearing in the shire court of Huntingdon. There he had to restore the land at Sibson 'by the rod of Odo Revel which is kept in the treasury of the church', and quitclaimed all suits he might have against the abbot for the latter's forceful action. However, he also with considerable formality received two marks of silver, and retained the land at Yaxley for which he became the abbot's man. The settlement was publicized by a series of ceremonies, and also recorded in several documents including a royal confirmation.[76]

In addition to worldly powers, church authorities also sometimes helped enforce the prelate's obligations. The evidence until the mid-twelfth century is very limited. However, it is notable that before the 1150s, no surviving charters of the archbishops of Canterbury specifically order the resumption of unjust alienations. Then in 1155 × 61 a letter of Archbishop Theobald ordered the abbot of Tavistock to recall all the lands which his predecessor had taken for himself without consulting the convent, or had given to laymen.[77] Theobald was also, for example, involved in a dispute between the bishop and chapter of Worcester which affected the division of property between them.[78]

Most significant is the increased assertion of papal power from the late 1130s, examined by Mary Cheney.[79] Certainly earlier popes had been intent on preventing alienation, and even in the latter part of the century not all prelates sought papal support. However, it is notable that from the pontificate of Eugenius III some papal confirmations to bishops included a new formula:

since the pastors of the Church are, according to the apostle, constituted for building not destroying, we grant you free power [*liberam facultatem*] of canonically recalling to the right and demesne of this place the possessions of the same church which have unjustly been taken away, laying down that neither you nor your successors be allowed to alienate these things or

---

[76] D. M. Stenton, *English Justice between the Norman Conquest and the Great Charter 1066–1215* (Philadelphia, 1964), 24–5, app. IV; *Regesta*, ii, No. 1457.

[77] Saltman, *Theobald*, No. 260.

[78] Saltman, *Theobald*, No. 282; see also No. 299 and Supplementary Documents H.

[79] Cheney, 'Inalienability'.

possessions from the church or transfer them from the control of the church by giving them in fee.[80]

The standardized wording in bulls to different bishops confirms that the papacy provided at least part of the impetus. Such papal orders brought some results. Bishop Nigel of Ely resumed Impington and probably also Pampisford, which Bishop Hervey had given to Archdeacon William, his nephew. However, despite continuing papal support, circumstances forced Bishop Nigel to give up his efforts, and in 1166 Pampisford appears amongst the lands of the new enfeoffment, alienated since 1135.[81] Papal orders, therefore, provided extra strength but did not ensure success.

Thus Canon Law prohibited the alienation of church lands, with certain qualifications. In practice, this doctrinal pressure, together with requirements for the chapter's participation and the gradual division of church lands, merely restricted alienation by prelates. The differing priorities of prelate and chapter, the internal politics of the honour and pressures from beyond it ensured that alienation did occur. Grants placed laymen in possession who might well regard themselves as having thus acquired a justified title, and others might well sympathize with them. Resumption therefore could require considerable effort. It was difficult whilst tensions within the house remained, frequently until the coming of a new prelate. Even if they were resolved, outside help was often needed. The prelate who failed to calculate the balance of power correctly in disputes might lose the estates, as did Abbot Walter of Evesham, or even any hope of future outside support, as did Becket. Often compromise proved the best answer. After a struggle, Henry of Blois succeeded in regaining a church and three manors which his predecessor as abbot of Glastonbury had granted to a certain knight called Odo who was married to the abbot's niece: 'but since it rang in my ears that a bruised reed should not be broken, I promised him, on the intervention of some people, lands worth forty shillings a year and the service of a knight of Ashbury'.[82]

[80] e.g. *Papsturkunden*, ii, No. 54.
[81] Miller, *Ely*, 168–72.
[82] Adam of Domerham, ii. 306; see also the cases cited above, pp. 244–5.

KINGS AND CHURCH LANDS

The Anglo-Norman kings not only helped to enforce prelates' obligations to their churches, but also claimed that church lands should not be alienated without royal permission. In the 1180s *Glanvill* wrote that 'neither a bishop nor an abbot can give any part of their demesnes permanently [*ad remanenciam*] without the assent and confirmation of the lord king, since their baronies are from the alms of the lord king and his ancestors.'[83] This concerns land held in respect of the office of prelate, as opposed to family land, which would not have been referred to as royal alms. *Glanvill*'s terms probably reflect the late twelfth-century situation, with a far clearer distinction between the prelate's barony and the other lands of the church, and he does not discuss the alienability of the latter. However, earlier evidence shows that the provision against prelates alienating church lands without royal permission pre-dates the clearer distinction. In *c*.1092 William Rufus issued a writ concerning the abbot of Ramsey, forbidding that he grant any land of his demesne to any man, 'without my license and counsel', since he wished the abbot to hold honourably.[84] Further charters record prelates obtaining royal assent for alienation. In 1155 × 8 Abbess Dameta of Holy Trinity, Caen, made a grant to Simon of Felstead 'by the counsel and consent of Henry, king of England'. Henry himself granted to Simon and his heirs the tenements 'in fees and farms and all things', as Abbess Dameta's charter witnessed.[85]

Grants made without royal permission could be revoked. The Abingdon chronicler recorded that in the first years of Henry I's reign, a certain Rainbald gave back lands to the abbey since he held

[83] *Glanvill*, vii. 1, Hall, 74.
[84] *Regesta*, i, No. 329. On Henry I, see the speech placed into the abbot of St Albans mouth, *Gesta Abbatum Monasterii Sancti Albani*, i. 173–4, stating that in the time of Henry I, new monasteries and convent churches needed only a royal charter. No one could found a house without royal permission, and the Church was to be answerable concerning temporal matters to the king alone. Cf. Eadmer's comment, *Historia Nouorum*, 9, that under Rufus 'cuncta . . . diuina simul et humana ejus nutum expectabunt'. See also E. M. Hallam, 'Henry II as a Founder of Monasteries', *JEcclH* 28 (1977), 113–32.
[85] *Recueil des Actes de Henri II*, ed. L. Delisle and E. Berger (4 vols.; Paris, 1909–27), No. XLV. Also from Henry II's reign: *Feudal Documents*, Nos. 80, 92, the former but not the latter concerning grants made 'hereditarily'. See Adam of Domerham, ii. 306–7, for Henry of Blois claiming that a gift made without the convent's consent was improper despite the king granting it.

them 'without the consent of the king and the monks'.[86] In 1116, Henry I ordered that no abbot of Tavistock give anything to anyone, except with his confirmation and the assent of the whole chapter. Then in $c.1129 \times 30$ he ordered that the abbot and monks 'have back and reseise in the demesne of their church all those lands which have been placed outside that demesne without my consent and confirmation, since the death of my father William'.[87] The king clearly could choose to view the requirement for his consent as mandatory.

Why did the king insist that prelates obtain his permission for alienation? In part it may simply have been the right of any lord to control lands he had given. A founder may have exercised considerable influence over his house. Hope of further gifts and protection must have ensured that churches did not often flout the wishes of donors and their families by alienating their gifts. Very occasionally a charter specifies that the alms given were not to be alienated.[88]

Yet, for reasons to be cited below, lordship over church lands may have been less extensive than over those given to laymen, and royal control of ecclesiastical alienation had other elements. It extended to all the churches' demesnes, not just lands given by the king. The king was protector of the Church, a role which had a long tradition.[89] In addition, kings had particularly close relations to certain churches, notably for example Battle Abbey. They also granted confirmations to numerous others. A charter of Henry I to Great Malvern Priory, probably drafted by the beneficiary, specified that all lands which had been given to it were to be held 'as my demesne alms'.[90] The spread

---

[86] *CMA*, ii. 130.

[87] *Regesta*, ii, Nos. 1131, 1663. The king might also order the regathering of all lands alienated since a specific time, perhaps implicitly showing royal control of ecclesiastical alienation of land: e.g. *Regesta*, ii, Nos. 607, 1417.

[88] e.g. *Facsimiles of Early Charters in Oxford Muniment Rooms*, ed. H. E. Salter (Oxford, 1929), No. 52.

[89] See e.g. Carolingian Capitularies on the preservation of church lands: *MGH, Capitularies I* (Hanover, 1883), Nos. 18, 24, 28, 59. In England, note also writs forbidding alienation, e.g. *Anglo-Saxon Writs*, ed. F. E. Harmer (Manchester, 1952), No. 55 (= Sawyer, No. 1105). Such provisions may imply that the ruler had a dispensing power to allow alienation. Some pre-1066 English and Norman charters mention royal or ducal consent for alienation by prelates: see Fauroux, No. 14; see also No. 220, although this may concern a prelate granting his personal lands; *Anglo-Saxon Charters*, ed. A. J. Robertson, (2nd edn., Cambridge, 1956), Nos. XCIV, CXII (= Sawyer, Nos. 1394, 1406) both leases for three lives.

[90] *Regesta*, ii, No. 1489.

of such confirmations could easily further the idea that church lands generally were royal alms, and therefore under royal protection and control.[91]

Furthermore, the king was seeking to protect not only the Church but also the spiritual and material benefits of himself, his family, and his realm. The lands concerned were alms and intended to be perpetual. Alienation endangered the desired spiritual benefits. Rufus's writ to Ramsey shows concern for the support of the monks, who did the praying for souls and the safety of the realm.[92] In addition, even though the lands could be referred to as alms, some might also be burdened with military service.[93] If the alienation was for military service the king might be more willing to allow it. Thus the same writ by which Henry I forbade that the abbots of Tavistock alienate their demesne without his permission, also ordered that no one should hold anything of the church's demesne, except those whom Abbot Geoffrey had given lands for military service.[94] The king could exercise discretion in enforcing the norm. In contrast, he might particularly oppose alienations at nominal service which could lead to loss of revenue from vacancies.[95]

Thus royal control of ecclesiastical alienation stems partly from interests similar to those of any powerful lord controlling vassals' gifts, partly from a special obligation to the Church. This obligation, the wider emphasis on restricting alienation of church lands, added to the balance of power between ecclesiastical donor and king, together gave the norm sufficient weight to be observed and enforced as binding.

---

[91] See also *Regesta*, i, No. 104.

[92] *Regesta*, i, No. 329, cited above, p. 247. See also Wood, *English Monasteries*, 155.

[93] See E. Kimball, 'Tenure in Frank Almoign and Secular Services', *EHR* 43 (1928), 341–53; also A. W. Douglas, 'Tenure *in elemosina*', *AJLegH* 24 (1980), 95–132. Even writing in the 1180s, *Glanvill* did not see the terms *baronia* and *elemosina* as mutually exclusive; see above, p. 247.

[94] *Regesta*, ii, No. 1131, cited above, p. 248.

[95] By the time of *Glanvill*, only the lands of the prelate fell into the king's hand during a vacancy, and not those of the convent; see e.g. Knowles, *Monastic Order*, 614–15. Hence any grant by a prelate to the chapter would later deprive the king of revenue from a vacancy. However, it is far from certain that kings would regard such grants as constituting alienations from the Church, and hence falling under the type of control I have been discussing.

CONCLUSIONS: ALIENABILITY, THE CHURCH, AND THE DEVELOPMENT OF LAND LAW

The prelate's powers of alienation provide parallels and contrasts with the lay land-holder. The layman had obligations to his kin and followers, the prelate to his *familia*, the clergy of his church. However, the canons worked from strict rules of inalienability, tempered by exceptions of necessity, whereas lay custom rested on reasonableness. In practice, this exaggerates the contrast. The variety of statements in the canons permitted flexibility. In particular, whilst the canons might require at least the chapter's consent for alienation, the giving of that consent would be determined by norms of reasonableness. Furthermore, other means of enforcing the prelate's obligations, notably the division of lands between prelate and chapter, had little to do with canonical rules. The effect of all such obligations rested on the balance of power in each case.

The prelate was subject to various superior authorities, including the saint of the church, and through the saint God. Those giving lands to churches retained some interest in them, yet such a relationship of donor and church might be less formalized than that between lay lord and lay tenant. For example, very few charters mention the tenurial bond with the donor and his heirs. More stress the freedom with which alms were to be held; 'as freely and quit as can be said or thought or understood by man' ran a grant of William earl of Gloucester to Tewkesbury Abbey.[96] Moreover, private control of ecclesiastical alienation was further limited by the fact that the families responsible for giving most of the land before 1066 had been destroyed.

On the other hand, we have also seen that the king asserted his lordship of church lands. In *c.*1078 × 82 William de Warenne and his wife gave the church of St Pancras, Lewes, to Cluny, by the counsel and consent of William I. Their charter ended with a clause in the king's name: 'I grant this gift thus that I have the same lordship in it as I have in the other alms which my great men make by my will [*meo nutu*].'[97] Generally, it appears to have been the king, more than the original donor or his descendants, who sought to control the alienation of church lands.

---

[96] *Earldom of Gloucester Charters*, ed. R. B. Patterson (Oxford, 1973), No. 177. However, note the elements of the donor's continuing interest discussed by E. Mason, 'Timeo Barones et Donas Ferentes', *Studies in Church History*, 15 (1978), 61–75.

[97] *Regesta*, i, No. 192.

These conclusions are clearly of great importance when considering the nature of land-holding and its development. The 'vertical' connection with lords was often weak, the connection to the king important. Also, grants to churches were lasting, again partly because of royal power. We have furthermore seen that churchmen were thinking in abstract terms about land-holding. Thus in the century after the Conquest, at least church land-holding was far from being based on a personal relationship of lordship, rather closer to the type of property relationship which some have seen as emerging only in the following century.

Yet the churches' attitudes and actions with regard to their land may be of still broader importance. As well as contributing to the refinement of ideas concerning land-holding, their relations to the king may have contributed to wider royal involvement within honours in matters concerning land. Even under Henry I, it may well be that laymen saw the methods being employed by churches, and sought to benefit from them. In some instances, they may have had little choice, for the only answer to a church with a royal writ might be the obtaining of a royal writ of one's own. Others too looked to the king. They may have been royal servants, or weak lords incapable of controlling their tenants, or powerful vassals, perhaps themselves tenants in chief. Or they may simply have wished to use every available weapon. Once men became accustomed to the effectiveness of royal support, increasing numbers must have sought it. The king too became accustomed to acting in land cases, and would intervene the more readily not just in ecclesiastical but also lay honours. Procedures for royal action also developed. Writs were already establishing a key position in judicial affairs, a position which was to remain a distinguishing feature of English law. Their drafting was growing more sophisticated, often more explicit in their provisions.[98] Royal involvement thus obtained a momentum of its own even before the Angevin reforms.

---

[98] Van Caenegem refers to this process as judicialization, whereby writs ceased to order executive action, instead requiring court hearings. However, the change was less dramatic than he makes out. Supposedly executive orders sometimes led to court hearings. Hence my emphasis on change in diplomatic rather than in general intent. See also J. Boorman, 'The Sheriffs and the Shrieval Office in the Reign of Henry II', Ph.D. thesis (Reading, 1989), 202. For a possible instance of executive action against disseisin by Henry II late in his reign, see *The Cartulary of Cirencester Abbey*, ed. C. D. Ross and M. Devine (3 vols.; Oxford, 1964–77), No. 36.

9

Henry II's Legal Reforms and the Development of Land Law, 1066–1189

THE history of law has too often been written as the progress of the administration of justice or the genealogy of legal doctrine. I have sought to examine the concerns of the land-holder, as lord and tenant, and analyse the ways in which considerations of power and developments in thought affected methods of controlling land. This final chapter, however, differs from its predecessors in that it turns primary attention to the royal administration of justice. Also, it does not pretend to be a definitive investigation of the greatly increasing amount of primary material for the period of the Angevin reforms. What it seeks to provide is an interpretative essay on the reforms of Henry II and their effect on land-holding and law. Inevitably there will be some overlap with what has already been said of the period 1154–66, but the change of perspective reveals further aspects of legal development. I attempt to reconcile the evidence that the Anglo-Norman world was not one of autonomous lordships but of considerable royal involvement, and that the social effects of customs in Anglo-Norman England did not differ greatly from those of Common Law rules, with the continuing impression that Henry II's and subsequent reforms really did make a difference.

Henry II succeeded to a realm in which the disturbances of Stephen's reign had reduced royal influence. Force had played a greater part in disputes. Churches had turned away particularly to papal help, although often this was not decisive.[1] Nevertheless, political circumstances had not swiftly reversed ideas concerning land-holding. Thus, for example, Stephen's chancery had enforced certain classifications of land-holding when recording the grants of others. Similarly notions

---

[1] Conceivably Henry II drew some notion of the desirability of increased central control of justice from the papal example. However, particularly bearing in mind my arguments concerning Henry I's reign, such a model seems unnecessary. Papal and English royal developments are better seen as parallel processes, sharing some underlying elements.

of the correctness of succession had not declined; indeed they had been extended to areas such as the holding of certain offices for which previous kings had not promised heritability.

Interpretations of the acts of Henry II and his advisers and servants concerning justice and laws, and of their effects, have differed greatly. For many writers, genius was at work, producing a better, more rational royal law, at the expense of feudal irrational justice.[2] For others, Henry and his advisers were simply seeking to make the old seignorial world work according to its own terms, but the unintentional product of their actions was the emergence of Common Law, and notably Common Law property.[3]

After briefly sketching a chronology of the reforms, I shall deal with the judicial aspects of his reforms, and then with their effect on land-holding. I argue that certainly Henry had no overall policy for English law, that experimentation took place, but that his intentions for the administration of justice went well beyond making a feudal framework function properly according to its own terms. Moreover, the judicial aspects of the reforms gathered their own impetus, and consumer demand further ensured that the effects of his actions snowballed. However, I close by re-emphasizing the importance of developments before 1135, and the limits to the changes resulting from the reforms.

THE CHRONOLOGY OF REFORM

To begin with a chronology for Henry's reforms; I seek to gather not merely legislation but all types of action concerning law and justice. Immediately there are analytic problems. How far were the measures introduced by legislation, how far by the king's administrative decisions, how far by the hardening of custom, and how far by, say, individual decisions in the chancery on the drafting of writs? The narrative sources were often not interested in such details, and the documentary material is not necessarily more helpful. In addition, there are problems of terminology, for example do words such as *decretum* point to legislation? This difficulty may also suggest atti-

---

[2] e.g. *Royal Writs in England from the Conquest to Glanvill*, ed. R. C. van Caenegem (Selden Soc. 77; 1958–9), 355.

[3] See esp. S. F. C. Milsom, *The Legal Framework of English Feudalism* (Cambridge, 1976), 186.

tudes dissimilar to the modern separation of legislation from other judicial and legal acts. Nevertheless, a preliminary chronology can be constructed.[4]

Significant, often neglected, steps took place in the general reconstruction of royal authority in the 1150s and early 1160s. The first important move came in 1153–4, when Henry, together with Stephen, promised to restore the disinherited to their lands.[5] This may well have encouraged unprecedented royal participation in land cases, and have increased demand for writs concerning justice in land cases, writs *de recto*, perhaps even to a degree which encouraged regularization of procedure.[6] At the same time, many sought to

[4] On the legislative, the judicial, and the administrative in Henry's reforms, see above, p. 28, on *statutum*; M. G. Cheney, 'A Decree of Henry II on Defect of Justice', in D. E. Greenway *et al.* (edd.), *Tradition and Change* (Cambridge, 1985), 183; H. G. Richardson and G. O. Sayles, *Law and Legislation from Aethelbert to Magna Carta* (Edinburgh, 1966), ch. V; J. C. Holt, 'The Assizes of Henry II: The Texts', in D. A. Bullough and R. L. Storey (edd.), *The Study of Medieval Records* (Oxford, 1971), 85–106; D. J. Corner, 'The Texts of Henry II's Assizes', in A. Harding (ed.), *Law-Making and Law-Makers in British History* (London, 1980), 7–20. Walter Map, *De Nugis Curialium*, ed. and tr. M. R. James (Oxford, 1983), 476, describes Henry II as 'in legibus constituendis et omni regimine corrigendo discretus, inusitati occultique iudicii subtilis inuentor'. Some of Henry's moves in the Becket dispute might be referred to as legislation of at least a temporary nature; e.g. *MTB*, v. 152; vii. 147–9. Other difficulties, for example of dating, mean that some elements cannot be fitted into this chronology; see e.g. the new writs mentioned in P. R. Hyams, 'Warranty and Good Lordship', *L&HR* 5 (1987), 478, and Hall, p. xxxv, on otherwise unknown legislation in *Glanvill*. Note also the controversy over the development of the custom that no one need answer about their free tenement without a royal writ', below, n. 6. For further discussion of Normandy, including remarks on chronology, see R. C. van Caenegem, *The Birth of the English Common Law* (2nd edn., Cambridge, 1988), 57–9; J. Yver, 'Le Bref Anglo-Normand', *TVR* 29 (1961), 313–30, 'Le "Très Ancien Coutumier" de Normandie, miroir de la législation ducale?', *TVR* 39 (1971), 333–74.

[5] See above, p. 135; see also more generally G. J. White, 'The Restoration of Order in England, 1153–1165', Ph.D. thesis (Cambridge, 1974), ch. 5. Henry's restoration of the royal demesne must also have generated land litigation; the *Gesta Abbatum Monasterii Sancti Albani*, ed. H. T. Riley (3 vols.; London, 1867–9), i. 123 suggests that Henry promulgated an edict on the subject. The relationship of this resumption to the views of the inalienability of church lands discussed in Ch. 8 requires further study.

[6] D. M. Stenton, *English Justice between the Norman Conquest and the Great Charter 1066–1215* (Philadelphia, 1964), 29, suggests that at this time Henry laid down a 'general rule that his writ must be sought before the lord's court could entertain actions of right and that if the lord's court failed to do justice the Sheriff should do it'. This would be the basis of the custom stated by *Glanvill*, xii. 25, Hall, 148, in the form 'secundum consuetudinem regni nemo tenetur respondere in curia domini sui de aliquo libero tenemento suo sine precepto domini regis uel eius iusticie capitalis'. A lost ordinance or orders to officers are of course possible, but I favour a more gradual

rectify the uncertainty of their position by obtaining royal confirmations. It seems that the beneficiaries included a substantial number
of sub-tenants, who thereafter could call on royal justice. Such
confirmations therefore extended royal involvement within honours in
matters concerning land-holding.[7]

It is also partly in this connection that Henry's concern with
disseisins in the early years of his reign must be seen. From between
1155 and 1162 come two references to an edict and an assize
concerning dispossession. Both involve disputes over advowsons, and
this may reflect a limit to the applicability of the royal action.[8]
Nevertheless, one can see circumstances connected with the solution
of land disputes after Stephen's reign which would require action on
disseisin. For example, if an honour was restored to a claimant, what
was to happen to the existing sub-tenants? The new lord might well
wish to disseise them and give the lands to his own followers. It may
be that the king provided actions concerning disseisin with the aim of
protecting the existing men's tenure in order to prevent conflicts
between tenants in chief spreading down the tenurial scale.[9]

Other legislation survives from the same period, including decrees
on distraint for services and on default of justice which I have
discussed in earlier chapters.[10] A *statutum* of before 1162 was taken
to mean that Englishmen could only recover their lands if they could
prove that their ancestors had been seised on the day of Henry I's

emergence of the custom, which would be compatible with the view of judicial change
outlined in the following pages; see also Van Caenegem, *Writs*, 212–31, Milsom, *Legal
Framework*, 57–64, and J. Biancalana, 'For Want of Justice: Legal Reforms of Henry
II', *Columbia Law Review*, 88 (1988), 448 n. 56, who links it to the 'routinization of
novel disseisin'. Note that the custom was not known in Normandy, Yver, 'Bref', 319.

[7] See Hyams, 'Warranty', 476–7, T. A. M. Bishop, *Scriptores Regis* (Oxford, 1961),
30–1.

[8] *Letters of John of Salisbury*, ed. W. J. Miller *et al.* (2 vols.; Edinburgh and Oxford,
1955–79), i, Nos. 102, 115. On these and the origins of novel disseisin, see D. W.
Sutherland, *The Assize of Novel Disseisin* (Oxford, 1973), 7–8; Stenton, *English Justice*,
34; Biancalana, 'Legal Reforms of Henry II', 473–7; M. G. Cheney, 'The Litigation
between John Marshal and Archbishop Thomas Becket in 1164: A Pointer to the
Origin of Novel Disseisin?', in *Law and Social Change in British History* (London,
1984), 23–4; Van Caenegem, *Writs*, 284 n. 2, 331; C. H. Haskins, *Norman Institutions*
(New York, 1918), 332–3. That such an action began in connection to churches may
encourage one to see at least an indirect influence of Canon Law upon novel disseisin;
see below, p. 267.

[9] I owe this point to Professor J. C. Holt, who intends to develop a much fuller
argument in print.

[10] See above, pp. 28, 139.

death and afterwards.[11] Also already of concern in the late 1150s were unsupported accusations made against laymen in church courts, upon which Henry had legislated by the beginning of 1158.[12]

So far all of these have been, at least as far as we can tell, piecemeal acts concerning individual issues. However, there are signs of a wider-ranging ordinance in Normandy in 1159. The Bec annalist seems to provide a summary of this legislation by its headings: subjects include unsupported accusations of the laity by deans, other judgments without testimony of neighbours, the keeping of peace, punishment of criminals, and peaceful holding of possessions by laity and Church.[13] Thus even before the years 1164–6, often seen as the start of 'the Angevin Legal Reforms', many changes were deliberately being made in the administration of justice. Further administrative changes, such as the disappearance of the local justiciars, may also be hidden within this period.[14]

In England, the extant wider-ranging ordinances begin with the Constitutions of Clarendon in 1164. These referred to themselves as 'a record or recognition of part of the customs and dignities of his ancestors, that is of his grandfather King Henry and of others, which ought to be observed and held in his realm'. They concern customs and dignities in relation to the Church, but particularly notable for the later development of land law was the first laying down of regular assize procedure:

If a claim emerges between clerk and lay or lay and clerk, about any tenement which the clerk wishes to draw to alms, the lay person to lay fee, it

[11] Van Caenegem, *Writs*, No. 169; see Hyams, 'Warranty', 499–500, *Kings, Lords, and Peasants in Medieval England* (Oxford, 1980), 252; Stenton, *English Justice*, 31–2; van Caenegem, *Writs*, 216–18. Note that the text of the writ does not specify that the *statutum* only concerned claims by Englishmen; rather, it mentions claims 'contra statutum meum' by Englishmen, perhaps a specific application of a more general decree.

[12] Haskins, *Norman Institutions*, 331–2; see R. C. van Caenegem, 'Public Prosecution of Crime in Twelfth-Century England', in C. N. L. Brooke *et al.* (edd.), *Church and Government in the Middle Ages* (Cambridge, 1976), 68–70.

[13] Haskins, *Norman Institutions*, 329–31.

[14] Stenton, *English Justice*, 68–9. See also T. Keefe, *Feudal Assessments* (Berkeley, Calif., 1983), 10–12 on an enquiry in 1163 concerning services; J. Boorman, 'The Sheriffs and the Shrieval Office in the Reign of Henry II', Ph.D. thesis (Reading, 1989), 20–1 on notable changes amongst sheriffs in the early 1160s; pp. 180–91 on the increasing importance in writs of clauses specifying that if the order was not carried out, the sheriff was to do it. Note also references to the king's assize in *Register of Abbey of St Benet of Holme*, ed. J. R. West (2 vols.; Norfolk Rec. Soc. 2, 3; 1932), Nos. 36, 39, the meaning of which is unclear.

will be terminated by recognition of twelve lawful men, by consideration of the chief justiciar of the king.[15]

Similar, although not identical, procedures were to multiply for a range of land cases; again an action concerning the Church led the way.

The Constitutions of Clarendon were a key issue in the dispute between Becket and Henry II, and the dispute may also provide the background—to be discussed later—for the extension of assize procedure through the assize of novel disseisin. This extension can also be associated with the Assize of Clarendon of 1166. The primary purpose of the Assize of Clarendon, at least as far as revealed by its text, was the pursuit of a crack-down on crime, which extended throughout the realm.[16] It must be taken to fit in with the gradual process of experimentation and development. As Corner has written

There are indications . . . that Henry II, late in 1165 or early in 1166, ordered the local officials of all counties to implement an assize, the contents of which were very similar to those of the surviving text of the Assize of Clarendon; and that in 1166, by issuing the Assize of Clarendon as we know it, Henry took control of the procedures detailed in that assize away from these officials and gave it to justices in eyre initially intended to tour the entire country.[17]

Administrative activity in 1166 also included the enquiry into knight service which produced the *Cartae baronum*. Henry was absent from England for four years from March 1166, and no legislation exists from this period, but this did not mean the end of judicial innovation, which Henry's servants were well capable of producing. For example, an extensive forest eyre was undertaken in 1167; Hyams has suggested that 'the first block of pipe-roll payments for warranty default etc. in 1169 could mark an increase in royal interest'; and the eyre of 1168–70 has been described as 'certainly the most thorough and exhaustive eyre that had yet been carried out'.[18] It has also been

[15] Constitutions of Clarendon, c. 9, *SSC*, 165–6.
[16] On the question of whether the Assize of Clarendon was meant to be a temporary measure (perhaps in contrast to the Assize of Northampton) or a permanent one, see Stenton, *English Justice*, 72, who concludes that it was to be a lasting one, as does Sutherland, *Novel Disseisin*, 8–9, concerning the 1166 measure on disseisin; cf. Van Caenegem, *Writs*, 285.
[17] Corner, 'Henry II's Assizes', 19–20.
[18] Hyams, 'Warranty', 478; H. G. Richardson and G. O. Sayles, *The Governance of Medieval England* (Edinburgh, 1963), 203; Stenton, *English Justice*, 38, 73.

suggested that the late 1160s was the point at which many writs concerned with justice started to be sealed closed in form, and to be 'returned' to a specified court where the writ's specifications of the issue and the trial form would be read out.[19]

Henry's return in 1170 produced moves perhaps as important as the more famous ones of 1166.[20] It was the year of the Inquest of Sheriffs, an enquiry which may have been underestimated by historians on account of the survival of only a few of the returns, and its usual title: it was in fact an enquiry into the activities not only of royal but also of baronial administration. It also included a clause which was later described as an 'Assize of Essoiners', concerning the giving of gage and surety by essoiners in not only the king's court but also those of the shire and of barons.[21] The Inquest resulted in the replacement of a large proportion of the sheriffs, and this probably marked a stage in reducing any independent power enjoyed by the sheriff, making them more servants of royal justice.[22]

The 1170s saw continuing experimentation with new forms of judicial organization, although there was no eyre in the early years of

---

[19] Hyams, *King, Lords, and Peasants*, 229 n. 33, van Caenegem, *English Common Law*, 47, 53, W. L. Warren, *Henry II* (London, 1973), 340. Stenton, *English Justice*, 33, suggests that the returnable writ may go back to the early years of Henry II, and p. 32 describes it as 'the real leap forward'. P. Chaplais, *English Royal Documents: King John–Henry VI, 1199–1461* (Oxford, 1971), 7–12, argues that Henry's chancery often issued writs close from the 1160s.

[20] Note that van Caenegem, *Writs*, 232–3 shows a peak in 1170 of payments 'pro recto': this is notable whether or not they concern payments for a particular 'writ of right'. There is no such peak in 1170 in his other graphs based on Pipe Roll payments, *Writs*, 252–3, 295–6. See Stenton, *English Justice*, 47 n. 79 for the problems of using Pipe Roll evidence.

[21] *PKJ*, i. 153–4; also Stenton, *English Justice*, 48. The same year may have seen the regular appearance of the deforciant clause in the *breue de recto*, mentioning not just lord and claimant but also the tenant. Of course no precise conclusions can be drawn from such a diplomatic change, but this increased emphasis on the 'horizontal' aspect of disputes is notable; see Hyams, 'Warranty', 477–8, van Caenegem, *Writs*, 212, and Biancalana, 'Legal Reforms of Henry II', 449 and n. 59, who, with more caution than Hyams, cites the evidence from 1170 and earlier instances. Note also article 'XIV' of the Inquest of Sheriffs as printed in *PKJ*, i. 153: 'If anyone complains about any plea which is ended in the lord king's court before himself or his justiciar thus that the case is renewed, and the complainant is convicted or confesses, he is to be taken and held in prison until the king orders him to be freed.'

[22] See Warren, *Henry II*, 291; memory of the Inquest and its results no doubt acted as a constraint on actions by sheriffs after 1170. Some historians have placed greater emphasis on the changes of 1170, but note that Boorman, 'Sheriffs', tends to play down the changes in the position of sheriffs resulting from the 1170 Inquest and the legal reforms. See Ralph de Diceto, *Opera Historica*, ed. W. Stubbs (2 vols.; London, 1876), i. 434 for a later investigation of sheriffs' activities.

the decade. 1175, or possibly 1174/5, brought a more complete eyre than ever before, and thereafter such country-wide eyres occur on average every other year for the remainder of the reign.[23] The form of the Assize of Northampton of 1176 is instructions to royal justices on eyre, and includes enquiry concerning, for example, crown rights and the swearing of fealty to the king. In particular, it renewed and revised the crack-down on crime specified by the Assize of Clarendon. It also made clear provision concerning land law, on the subjects of inheritance—the assize *mort d'ancestor*—and on disseisin. The mid-1170s may also have seen a major step forward in the creation of royal judicial records, perhaps even the beginning of the plea rolls, a development generally accredited to Richard's reign.[24]

In his account of 1177, Roger of Howden mentions that Henry laid down [*statuit*] that no one was to take a man's possessions [*res*] for the debt of his lord, unless the man was a debtor or surety concerning that debt; only the man's rents were to go to the creditor.[25] It was not permitted to distrain men's other possessions for their lord's debt. Howden states that the king ordered this decree and custom to be held in all his vills and everywhere in his power, that is in Normandy, Aquitaine, Anjou, Maine, Touraine, and Brittany. It is thus unclear whether it applied to England, but the *Dialogue of the Exchequer* mentions a royal 'constitution' whereby the chattels of a lord's knights could no longer be sold for the lord's personal debts, except if they were for scutage. This suggests the existence, perhaps the earlier existence, of related legislation in England.[26]

---

[23] P. A. Brand, 'Multis Vigiliis Excogitatam et Inventam', *Haskins Society Journal*, 2 (1990), 203–4; see also Stenton, *English Justice*, 76–7 on eyres in the 1180s. Note also H. G. Richardson, 'Richard fitz Neal and the *Dialogus de Scaccario*', *EHR* 43 (1928), 170–1, on the lack of fixed circuits for eyres: 'everything was provisional and subject to alteration and revision, even while the eyre was in progress'. W. L. Warren, 'Royal Justice in England in the Twelfth Century', *History*, 52 (1967), 174, suggests that an eyre 'of limited commission for jail delivery and assizes' occurred as early as 1186, in contrast to the argument that they became common under John, as perhaps implied by *The Earliest Lincolnshire Assize Rolls, 1202–1209*, ed. D. M. Stenton (Lincoln Rec. Soc. 22; 1926), pp. xxxvii–xxxviii. The Pipe Roll evidence cited by Warren seems to me inconclusive as to the nature of this 1186 eyre.

[24] Richardson and Sayles, *Governance*, 185; Brand, 'Multis Vigiliis', 215–16; R. V. Turner, *The English Judiciary in the Age of Glanvill and Bracton* (Cambridge, 1985), 13 n. 45.

[25] Roger of Howden, *Chronica*, ed. W. Stubbs (4 vols.; London, 1868–71), ii. 146.

[26] Richard Fitz Nigel, *Dialogus de Scaccario*, ed. and tr. C. Johnson (Oxford, 1983), 112; Richard's statement that, 'though not yet hoary headed' when writing at the end of the 1170s, he could remember this suggests that the *constitutio* was made earlier than 1177.

From 1178 comes the famous appointment by Henry II of two clerks and three men of his household to hear and do justice concerning complaints from all over England. This used to be taken as the origin of the Common Bench—the most important of all courts for civil pleas in the later Middle Ages—but recent scholarship rejects this view, seeing the bench as only emerging from the exchequer in the 1190s.[27] Again the impression is not of once and for all change, but variation and development, determined by pressure from above and below.[28]

From the end of the 1170s comes another new provision on procedure, the Grand Assize, probably established at the Council of Windsor in 1179 and described by *Glanvill* as 'a royal benefit granted to the people by the goodness of the king on the advice of his magnates'.[29] The dispute, instead of being settled by battle, could alternatively be determined before the king's justices by twelve lawful knights of the neighbourhood who declared on oath as to 'which of the parties has the greater right in the land in question'.[30] Legislation continued into the 1180s, although measures affecting England concerned areas less intimately connected with land-holding, for example the Assize of Arms in 1181, and the Assizes of the Forest in 1184–5.[31] Moreover, judicial change affecting land law continued. For example, it seems to have been in the last years of Henry's reign that control of the administration of replevin passed from the justices in eyre—by now possibly overburdened—to the sheriff.[32]

[27] *Gesta Regis Henrici Secundi Benedicti Abbatis*, ed. W. Stubbs (2 vols.; London, 1867), i. 207; see also the comment of J. H. Round, *Feudal England* (London, 1895), 576. Brand, 'Multis Vigiliis', 206; B. R. Kemp, 'Exchequer and Bench in the Later Twelfth Century—Separate or Identical Tribunals', *EHR* 88 (1973), 559–73; cf. Turner, *Judiciary*, 70–4.

[28] Note e.g. the account in Diceto, i. 434–5.

[29] *Glanvill*, ii. 7, Hall, 28.

[30] *Glanvill*, ii. 10, Hall, 30. Note though that the procedure was quite cumbersome; Yver, 'Bref', 321.

[31] Corner, 'Henry II's Assizes', 9–13, places the legislation concerning the forest into the context of administrative development. The *Rotuli de Dominabus* fits neatly into this concern with establishing royal rights.

[32] See above, p. 40. In addition, Lady Stenton noted that 'from 1181 onwards the pipe rolls show a rapid increase in the number of payments made for licence of being brought into agreement—*pro licencia concordandi*', and suggested that royal justices were encouraging such concords; *English Justice*, 49–51, quotation at p. 51. Cf. P. R. Hyams, 'The Charter as a Source for the Early Common Law', *Journal of Legal History*, 12 (1991), 185, who places a rush for royal hearings and licences to concord in the mid-1170s. See Hyams, *King, Lords, and Peasants*, 230, on the development of writs of naifty late in Henry's reign.

Thus although the regular pattern of the overall administration of justice seems to have been settling in these years, change continued, and further developments occurred after Henry's death.[33]

THE NATURE OF REFORM

Such a chronology is necessarily approximate and incomplete, but forms a basis for the following analysis. I examine first the general attitude of Henry and his advisers towards the administration of justice and law; secondly, the way in which specific political situations and administrative problems led to wider changes; thirdly, the general nature of administration under Henry II; and fourthly, consumer demand and response.

It is extremely unlikely, if not impossible, that Henry had any precise views on what he would like substantive law to be, let alone that the eventual results would have been expected. Nor should Henry be seen as having a consciously anti-feudal or anti-baronial policy. Henry, like his grandfather, could be happy to let a reliable magnate continue to deal with his own affairs. *Glanvill* describes a situation

when a baron has a plea in his court concerning which there arises a reasonable difficulty which his own court is incompetent to settle. In such a case the lord may adjourn his court into the court of the lord king, in order to have the advice and assent of that court as to the proper legal course in the difficulty. The lord king owes it as of right to his barons to allow them in such circumstances to adjourn their courts thus into his court, so as to enable them to take advice in his court from learned men. When their difficulties have been resolved in the court of the lord king, the lord may return with his plea, and try and determine it in his own court.

Royal and baronial interests did not necessarily clash.[34]

Yet in view of claims that increased royal control of land-holding was not the product of royal intention, it is necessary to reassert that Henry II was seeking to exercise his authority in this and other areas of justice, and that his predecessors had probably done likewise.

---

[33] Note e.g. the further development of writs of entry: Stenton, *English Justice*, 50–1; R. C. Palmer, 'The Origins of Property in England', *L&HR* 3 (1985), 24–50.

[34] *Glanvill*, viii. 11, Hall, 102–3. Whether Henry brought from Anjou any different attitudes to the magnates, or indeed to kingship, is a point which might repay further study.

They held certain ideas incongruous with a purely passive role, ideas expressed for example in their Coronation oaths. Enforcement of royal rights, performance of royal duties, led the king to seek to settle disputes. The profit arising therefrom was welcome, but it should not be exaggerated as a motive for judicial involvement.[35] Indeed, the moral motivation behind Henry's judicial activities may have been stronger and more general than legal historians have allowed. It is probably no coincidence that Henry in the early years of his reign was concerned not only with crime and violence but also with the prevention of heresy and the regulation of prostitution.[36] Such were the activities of a just king, the grandson of one regarded as the 'Lion of Justice'.

We must, moreover, take Henry at his word, and suggest that at least at first he was seeking to restore the situation as in his grandfather's reign. In this sense, he was seeking to make the system work according to its own terms, but it was a system in which the king had been very much involved. Furthermore, Henry was enforcing his own perception of his grandfather's time, it was his royal view of the correct functioning of the system that counted. Such retrospection may have led to generalizations about royal action not necessarily justified by past practice, but of considerable future effect.

Central to these royal rights and duties would have been those of maintaining the peace and doing justice, especially hearing cases of default of justice. Maintenance of the peace clearly could be linked to questions of land-holding. Henry must have feared that those who had now lost lands to the once 'disinherited' would take matters into their own hands. In this sense he had to protect rightful title and seisin.[37] Concern with disseisins, which as we have seen was some-times associated with violence, must also surely be connected with

---

[35] See van Caenegem, *English Common Law*, 103–4. For criticisms of Henry's innovations on the grounds that they were motivated by gain, see *Radulfi Nigri Chronica*, ed. R. Anstruther (Caxton Soc., London, 1851), 168. The accusation forms part of a famous diatribe against Henry.

[36] See R. I. Moore, *The Formation of a Persecuting Society* (Oxford, 1987), 96, 111, 130–1, 135–6. See also William of Canterbury's 'Life of St Thomas', in *MTB*, i. 12, for Henry prosecuting a canon 'forsan zelo justitiae ductus, et ne flagitia praesumerentur in regno suo'.

[37] It is only to this degree that I consider it certain that Henry had any 'policy on seisin', and it was an attitude not dissimilar to that of previous or later kings: see also N. D. Hurnard, 'Did Edward I reverse Henry II's Policy upon Seisin?', *EHR* 69 (1954), 539.

the drive against crime from the mid-1160s.[38] Moreover, the maintenance of peace and the doing of justice were closely associated. Decrees on default of justice and unjust distraint, together with the moves against disseisins, can be associated with attempts to prevent such recourse to violence as occurred under Stephen.

In addition, default of justice provided a possible means of reconciling royal action with seignorial jurisdiction. Biancalana has powerfully argued that the notion of 'want of justice' lay at the heart of Henry's reforms, and permitted a workable arrangement with lords. Henry, he suggests, ensured that each of his reforms respected the role of seignorial courts, whilst establishing the legitimacy of his own court's role, according to the shared principle that 'the king did not have jurisdiction unless a lord had failed to hear a plaintiff's claim'.[39] Even so there was a tension: whilst lords used this principle to protect their courts, Henry used it as a justification for new royal jurisdiction.[40]

This last statement of Biancalana's itself shows that Henry's approach was not passive, and one may wonder whether Henry and his advisers and officials really felt themselves so bound.[41] The so-called 'principle' was not always happily accepted in practice. Barons complained about Henry's decree concerning default of justice: 'the king had made a constitution, which he thought would be very advantageous to himself'. The barons seem to have suspected Henry's motives, and may have felt that plaintiffs were exploiting the new procedure to obtain royal justice, whether or not they had a convincing

[38] See above, p. 42. In the light of Biancalana, 'Legal Reforms of Henry II', 481, I suspend comment on the possible criminal stage of novel disseisin, but Biancalana, 475, agrees that 'the royal ordinances against disseisins without hearing and judgment were general peace keeping measures'. On violence and royal action concerning disseisin, see Sutherland, *Novel Disseisin*, 27–9.

[39] Biancalana, 'Legal Reforms of Henry II', 436; note also 437, 441, 461; see 457 for an example of what might be considered unjust judgment.

[40] Note that the *Leges Henrici*, 10 1, Downer, 108, presents the king's hearing cases 'for want of right' as a royal right; also 59 19, p. 188. On these, see M. T. Clanchy, 'Magna Carta and the Common Pleas', in H. M. Mayr-Harting and R. I. Moore (edd.), *Studies in Medieval History presented to R. H. C. Davis* (London, 1985), 221–2. Biancalana, 'Legal Reforms of Henry II', 467, writes in the context of novel disseisin that the king's justices 'developed criteria of a just judgment of a lord's court', criteria which were new, and that 'in adopting them, royal justices defined the role of lords in the feudal framework as conceived by royal administration'.

[41] Biancalana, 'Legal Reforms of Henry II', 466, 509–11, himself argues that from 1176 one finds a writ *praecipe* which 'usurped seignorial jurisdiction' in female inheritance cases, with no regard for notions of default of justice.

complaint of default of justice. Quite possibly Henry and his advisers had always known that such was the likely outcome. At least after this disagreement between king and barons, the notion of 'want of justice' can hardly have been a shared principle: both sides were too aware of its flexibility. Henry and his advisers may well have frequently resorted to the principle for self-justification, but it was only one guiding factor in judicial activities.

As time passed, Henry's claims may have become more assertive. The momentum of reform could be self-perpetuating. The Becket dispute had led to a royal circle expressing strong views of kingship. The Inquest of Sheriffs represents a striking assertion of the king's authority. As with some of Edward I's acts in his assertion of royal power, enquiry into local and magnate administration can be seen as not only restoring royal rights but also obtaining support from a wider constituency. Within such a wider constituency could be found some of those who were benefiting from, and increasingly administering, Henry's new judicial measures.[42]

The question of general motivation thus blurs into my second theme, that of the impact of political circumstances and particular administrative problems. Actions which were originally formed in specific political circumstances and intended for fairly specific purposes, such as the provision of justice to sort out disputes arising from Stephen's reign, came to have much larger effects. A similar conclusion is reached in Mary Cheney's stimulating analysis of the origins of novel disseisin. She is far from suggesting a monocausal solution: 'once the initial impetus was provided, many motives will surely have influenced the discussions that shaped the assize of Novel Disseisin'. Rather, she argues that the initial impetus stems from Archbishop Thomas Becket's early actions of reclaiming Canterbury's lands which had been granted out to the laity, most notably certain lands held by John Marshal.

John Marshal's case could have provided the immediate incentive for the assertion of a new royal concern with disseisin effected without judgment, and directly or indirectly for the formulation of a new civil procedure in the lines of the recognition known to Glanvill.[43]

---

[42] Similarly, in 1176 Henry was careful to obtain the fealty of all freemen and above, and ordered his justices to enforce the swearing of homage and fealty.

[43] Cheney, 'Novel Disseisin', 25–6; see also above, p. 139 n. 115. Another example of a reaction to a rather different ecclesiastical measure is suggested by van Caenegem,

Moreover, as reforms developed, new measures were sometimes needed to cope with the problems arising. For example, the first writs of entry can be seen as emerging to supplement assizes such as novel disseisin, to deal with any anomalies they produced.[44]

The way in which reforms produced in specific political circumstances came to have a lasting effect must be linked to my third theme, the general nature of administration under Henry. It was an administration of experiment, but also of increasing regularity. Such regularization worked, for example, through the general eyre, and the returnable writ. It manifested itself, for instance, in the custom reported by *Glanvill* that no one need answer about their free tenement without a royal writ.[45] Linked to this standardization may have been the increasing accumulation of information in royal hands. The Assize of Clarendon laid down that all the sheriffs were to cause a record to be made of all fugitives from their county 'and let them do this before the county courts and carry the names of those written therein before the justices, when next they come to them, so that these men may be sought throughout all England, and their chattels be seized for the needs of the king'.[46] The 1166 enquiry concerning knight service and the 1170 Inquest of Sheriffs also collected information which might have inspired, or at least influenced, future royal judicial and legal activity.

Most important, though, in the process of standardization may have been a change in the role and personnel of royal justices. They became less presidents of the courts in which they sat, more judges in the sense of themselves deciding the cases.[47] Certainly presidents of

---

Writs, 332–3, who sees the assize of darrein presentment as stemming from a decree of the Third Lateran Council giving the presentation of a benefice to the bishop if it was not filled within three months. A speedy, if temporary, way of dealing with disputes about advowsons was therefore in the interest of patrons.

[44] See Hurnard, 'Policy upon Seisin?', 537–9. See also Biancalana, 'Legal Reforms of Henry II', 487, for the argument that 'mort d'ancestor ... removed an awkward situation created by the pleading rule for the writ of right', that the ancestor had to be seised in the reign of Henry I. On the unintended effects of the assize *utrum*, see A. Nicol (ed.), 'Changes in the Assize *Utrum* between the Constitutions of Clarendon and Bracton', in R. F. Hunnisett and J. B. Post (edd.), *Medieval Legal Records Edited in Memory of C. A. F. Meekings* (London, 1978), 17–24.

[45] See above, p. 255 n. 6.

[46] Assize of Clarendon, c. 18, *SSC*, 172.

[47] See Brand, 'Multis Vigiliis', 203; these changes, he argues at 211, also meant that 'judgment making was, for the first time, in these courts in the hands of men directly appointed (and directly removable) by the king'. His argument is based

courts had held considerable sway over their activities, and justices continued to rely heavily on answers provided by assizes and juries.[48] However, growing control by a core of regular and increasingly full-time justices must have affected the law enforced in the courts.[49] Their own opinions on law and justice may have led to some standardization. Some would have a varying degree of learning in Roman or Canon Law. Knowledge of these could help to clarify thought, to conceptualize existing patterns of royal action. Take the development of separate processes, some to deal with right, others with seisin alone. Writs of the Anglo-Norman kings had sometimes ordered reseisin whilst allowing for the possible bringing of claims in future.[50] Then, by early in Henry II's reign, we see at least ecclesiastics differentiating between the possessory and the proprietary, categories from Canon and Roman Law.[51] Such ideas must have facilitated the development of actions such as novel disseisin, but the assizes, as far as we can tell, were not formulated in the language of learned law. Signs of a policy based on a new theory, rather than on the development of old processes and ideas, are scarce.[52] Thus the royal advisers' approach to certain judicial and legal problems was influenced by the learned laws, but they did not seek solutions in the

primarily on the language of final concords and on the Assize of Northampton, c. 7, *SSC*, 180. Note that the legal significance of the diplomatic of Final Concords is very hard to interpret; e.g. earlier writs to the shire court name only the sheriff, but the suitors played a part in the judgment. Pipe Rolls from the mid-1170s show a slight change in form of entry, but not one which backs Brand's point: until *c.22 HII* the heading generally refers to the pleas 'of' the justices; thereafter, the first entry for each set of justices is usually headed 'per' the justices, but subsequent entries sometimes use the genitive; see e.g. *PR 22 HII*, 20, 21, 73, *PR 23 HII*, 130–1.

[48] See e.g. *CMA*, ii. 229 for justices of Henry I seemingly acting like judges rather than presidents of a court in a case concerning a hundred and a market. On the limited control later exercised by royal officials concerning criminal offences, see T. A. Green, *Verdict According to Conscience* (Chicago, 1985).

[49] Brand, 'Multis Vigiliis', 214. See Stenton, *English Justice*, 74 on new and inexperienced justices.

[50] See van Caenegem, *Writs*, Nos. 52–61.

[51] See *Letters of John of Salisbury*, No. 102; van Caenegem, *English Common Law*, 123 n. 59 on papal letters to England; Cheney, 'Novel Disseisin', 13. See also *Early Charters of the Cathedral Church of St Paul, London*, ed. M. Gibbs (Camden Soc., 1939), No. 163, above p. 104, for Theobald allowing the question of right to remain after a case had been settled; note the comments of van Caenegem, *English Common Law*, 124 n. 65.

[52] Cf. the arguments that Henry II had a policy upon seisin, esp. F. Joüon des Longrais, 'La Portée politique des réformes d'Henry II en matière de saisine', *RHDFE*, 4th Ser. 15 (1936), 540–71.

adoption of learned procedures.[53] Other measures may even have
been 'devised as a protection' against the 'alien system' of Canon
Law.[54] Standardization, routinization, could emerge without learned
models.

Meanwhile, the learned laws did also help to give form to the
administrators' opinions on the role of royal government, an ex-
pansive view best expressed in the Prologues to *Glanvill*—which
contains a eulogy to this very circle of the king's advisers—and to the
Dialogue of the Exchequer. The leading men in the circle, such as
Robert earl of Leicester, Richard de Lucy, Richard of Ilchester,
Richard fitzNigel, Ranulf de Glanvill, and Hubert Walter were, at
least in some aspects of their lives, servants of the *king*, their loyalty
highly personal and their functions manifold, not specialized.[55] The
increasing reliance on king's men particularly in the late 1170s is
clear in Howden's chronicles. In 1177 Henry replaced the keepers of
the castles of England, and handed them over for keeping to knights
who were from his own private household, in 1178 an enquiry led to
the removal of the excessive number of justices, and their replacement by five men, 'all from his private household'.[56]

The measure of 1177 was taken with the counsel of the great
men. However, there may have been growing up a group of administrators who, owing everything to the king, pursued his claims more
rigorously than he did, and whose attitude to the magnates was more

[53] See e.g. Sutherland, *Novel Disseisin*, 21–4, 32–3; Biancalana, 'Legal Reforms of
Henry II', 473, 476 on Canon Law and disseisin, also 501; van Caenegem, *Writs*,
360–90. Such ideas could also influence the interpretation of land-holding and justice
by men, particularly ecclesiastics, beyond the royal circle: see above, n. 51. On the
general intellectual context, see also Biancalana, 'Legal Reforms of Henry II', 433–4.

[54] Cheney, 'Novel Disseisin', 24; see also pp. 15, 21, where she argues that the laity
could defend itself against the claims of Canon Law 'only by refining its notions of
tenure and lordship' and by 'devising new procedures'.

[55] See e.g. Turner, *Judiciary*, 39–51; note the similarity of career patterns between
the men discussed in his ch. 2 and those of Henry I in J. A. Green, *The Government of
England under Henry I* (Cambridge, 1986), ch. 7. Palmer, 'Origins of Property', closely
connects the emergence of bureaucracy, the state, and property, all occurring *c.*1200;
however, bearing in mind Weber's discussion of bureaucracy, Henry II's regime was
only bureaucratic to a limited extent, bureaucratization a very gradual process; M.
Weber, *Economy and Society*, ed. G. Roth and C. Wittich (2 vols.; Berkeley, Calif.,
1978), ii, ch. XI, esp. 956–63. Certainly some families had traditions of royal service,
and men served one king after another but this does not prevent their loyalty from
having been personal; Henry II's men would have felt it their duty to Henry, apart
from anyone else, to serve his heir faithfully.

[56] Benedict, i. 160, 207. See also Turner, *Judiciary*, 271 on royal servants' defence
of the king's rights.

antagonistic than his.[57] According to Hyams, Henry's advisers 'included men familiar with the established ecclesiastical tradition that princes ought to support the *pauper* against the oppression of the *potentes*'. The clearest evidence of this may come in Richard fitzNigel's statement in the *Dialogue of the Exchequer* that lords were their men's 'domestic enemies'.[58] Other views, for example concerning trial by battle, may also have been peculiarly those of king's men, and perhaps out of harmony with those of the lay nobility.[59]

There must have been men within the royal administration, men perhaps of lower status than the earl of Leicester or Richard fitzNigel, who had to work out solutions to increasing numbers of particular problems. Their thoughts on these subjects might come to produce some kinds of policy, for example an attempt to provide remedies which allowed for fewer essoins and thus speeded justice.[60] Whilst we have seen that many earlier court cases were far from irrational in their methods, Henry's administrators may well have prided themselves in bringing reason to bear upon the problems they faced.[61] Such possibilities relate to the increasing regularity of royal administration. Red tape, and administration for the sake of the administrators, were emerging. For the first time, perhaps, certain administrators felt that England should in some sense be ruled in a more standardized way, that local administrative variation, even liberties, could in some cir-

---

[57] Note also the possibility that men rising from lowly positions had particularly rigorous attitudes; in a discussion of the harshness of clerical justices and their lowly origins, Walter Map, *De Nugis*, 14, cites Claudian: 'nothing is harsher than the lowly when he rises to high degree'.

[58] *Dialogus*, 101; Hyams, *Kings, Lords, and Peasants*, 261; see also Diceto, i. 434 on the king seeking to protect the weak. Note *TAC*, vii. 1, Tardif, 7, which presents the *recognitio de saisina patris* as a means of protecting the weak against the strong; see also Yver, 'Bref', 330. Cf. complaints on the expense of justice, see Turner, *Judiciary*, 5; also *English Lawsuits from William I to Richard I*, ed. R. C. van Caenegem (2 vols.; Selden Soc., 1990–1), No. 422, for poverty preventing the pursuit of a case early in Henry II's reign. Such complaints obviously reveal the ideal of readily accessible and affordable justice.

[59] See Sutherland, *Novel Disseisin*, 35–6. See Stenton, *English Justice*, 82 ff. on the education of Henry II's justices, and on the lay origins of many; also R. V. Turner, 'Who was the Author of *Glanvill*? Reflections on the Education of Henry II's Common Lawyers', *L&HR* 8 (1990), 97–127.

[60] The concern with essoins is obvious from their prominence in *Glanvill*; see also Stenton, *English Justice*, 47.

[61] For background, see e.g. M. T. Clanchy, '*Moderni* in Education and Government in England', *Speculum*, 1 (1975), 671–88. I am far from suggesting that a rational system replaced an irrational, aided by the great appeal of the 'modern' methods.

cumstances be overruled. This feeling manifested itself in the Assize of Clarendon, with its statements such as

let there be no one in a city or borough or a castle or outside, not even in the honour of Wallingford, who shall forbid the sheriffs to enter into their land or their soke to arrest those who have been accused or are notoriously suspect of being robbers or murderers or thieves or receivers of them, or outlaws, or persons charged concerning the forest; but the king commands that they shall aid the sheriffs to capture them.[62]

Such standardization is a key element in legal development. England came to have a Common Law not because of legislation on issues of substantive law, but because an increasingly regularized royal justice took over a considerable part of the administration of law.

Finally, let us look at consumer demand and response. People liked the availability of royal remedies, even if they disliked royally imposed justice.[63] The cost of writs involving land cases early in Henry II's reign was very similar to that suggested by the 1130 Pipe Roll, but a fall occurred from the middle of the reign.[64] Some of the actions, most notably the Grand Assize, were designed to be popular. Novel disseisin may also have been popular in order to expedite justice, whilst being acceptable because it did not produce irreversible decisions. In addition, longer-term causes such as social change and the vastly growing number of religious houses must have been increasing the demand for royal justice.[65] But why did men accept other royal actions? One must not of course assume that they always did. As has already been noted, complaints concerning the decree on default of justice give a hint that some magnates felt that the power of the king had increased, was increasing, and ought to be diminished. Yet most of the reforms proved popular to men, if not in their role as lords, at least in their role as tenants of other lords. This dual role may be one

---

[62] Assize of Clarendon, c. 11, see also c. 9; *SSC*, 171.

[63] See Howden, iv. 62 on eyres as a burden and on the fantastic way litigants flock to chancery for writs. Also Stenton, *English Justice*, 75 on complaint about the Assize of Northampton.

[64] Green, *Government*, 103, who assumes that payments 'pro recto' recorded in 1130 were for writs. The best comparison is with the figures of payment 'pro recto' given by van Caenegem, *Writs*, 231–2. Note that column 4 of van Caenegem's table suggests that payments may have remained steady for similar amounts of land. On the other hand, writs for new processes were cheaper; see e.g. van Caenegem, *Writs*, 393–5. See Stenton, *English Justice*, 30 on the appearance of writs 'of course', first mentioned in 1200.

[65] See above, p. 152, on the increasing frequency of confirmations to sub-tenants.

vital key. Cheney suggests the following specific political circumstances which made novel disseisin more acceptable. The laity faced
the threat of loss of lands to the increasingly strong claims of church
landlords, as manifested most clearly in the case of John Marshal and
Thomas Becket: the lay barons'

attitude becomes understandable if there were many who as tenants wel-
comed the security offered by the new procedures; for all but the greatest,
the gain would have appeared to outweigh any possible loss of jurisdiction,
about which indeed some already lamented, but as yet in secret.[66]

Such was a particularly controversial issue. In other potentially un-
popular instances, royal justice could at least have the attraction of
being definitive, certainly for the laity without the option of appeal to
Rome. For these reasons, once a fairly regular source of royal justice
was available, its superior jurisdiction may inevitably have been likely
to predominate over lesser ones. One such instance may again be the
decree on default of justice. The provision that cases should pass
to each higher lord's court in turn until it reached the royal court
may have made this initially acceptable, but the end result was to
strengthen not all overlords but the king.[67] And here we have another
answer to the question 'Why did Henry get away with it?'—because
men did not realize what was happening. Once change had taken on
a great momentum, they had to learn to use the new situation for
their own purposes.[68]

REFORM AND LAND-HOLDING

What were the results of all these changes with regard to land-
holding? As has been argued, the administration of justice, the development of law, and the control of land are intimately connected. In
terms of lordship, with Henry II's reforms the degree of discretion

[66] Cheney, 'Novel Disseisin', 24.
[67] Cheney, 'Decree', 193. Note how at the end of the 13th cent. control of
alienation into mortmain fell into the king's hands, although the Statute of Mortmain
provided for action by the alienor's lord. See also Milsom, *Legal Framework*, 185,
'controlling jurisdictions have a habit of taking over the functions they control'.
[68] Further research might reveal signs of confusion in response to the legal changes;
see below, p. 272, for an apparent instance of surprise at the widening access to royal
writs. There may of course have been some political give and take in the adoption of
certain measures.

which a lord might exercise was more tightly defined, unless he was
the king, who had no superior lord. In terms of the administration of
justice, baronial courts retained extensive jurisdiction, but gradually
lost that over crucial land cases.[69] Areas where the routine form
of royal justice did not apply came to be more clearly defined as
franchises or palatinates.[70] On the other hand, royal administration of
justice was greatly extended, becoming routine, rather than *ad hoc*
even if frequent as it probably was under Henry I. Increasing numbers of individuals came into contact with royal government.[71] In the
mid- or late 1160s Bishop Gilbert Foliot was shocked to find one of
his canons summoned by a writ concerning a case brought, in his
eyes, by one who was 'almost a peasant' and involving a mere half-
virgate, rent 12*d*. He even wondered whether the document was
genuine.[72]

In terms of law, norms governing land-holding had been applied in
earlier cases, but the reforms affected these norms, reduced any
flexibility. The routine Common Law actions increasingly excluded
the broader social circumstances of disputes.[73] Informal agreements
started to be ruled out of court by royal justices. *Glanvill* wrote that
'the court of the lord king is not accustomed to protect private
agreements, nor does it even concern itself with such contracts as can

---

[69] Note esp. the replacement of the action of right in the lord's court by the assizes.
If one believes Magna Carta, c. 34, the lords in 1215 still saw their courts as worth
protecting. On continuing baronial jurisdiction, see e.g. *The Court Baron*, ed. and tr. F.
W. Maitland and W. P. Baildon (Selden Society, 4; 1891). More generally, the
declining importance of the honour with regard to land-holding, and perhaps other
matters, may be reflected in a shift in charter diplomatic from addresses to the men of
the honour to broader addresses; see Hyams, 'Charter', 180, who gives no specific
chronology, and Hudson, 'Diplomatic and Legal Aspects of the Charters', in A. T.
Thacker (ed.), *The Earldom of Chester and its Charters* (Jnl. of Chester Arch. Soc. 71;
1991), 156–9, which also reveals that such a change also affected future palatinates.
Again the relationship of legal change and diplomatic is far from simple.

[70] See e.g. N. D. Hurnard, 'The Anglo-Norman Franchises', *EHR* 64 (1949),
289–327, 433–60; G. Barraclough, 'The Earldom and County Palatine of Chester',
Hist. Soc. of Lancs. and Cheshire Trans. 103 (1951–2), 23–57; H. M. Cam, 'The
Evolution of the Medieval English Franchise', *Speculum*, 32 (1957), 427–42; J. W.
Alexander, 'The Alleged Palatinates of Norman England', *Speculum*, 56 (1981), 17–27.

[71] In a context other than land law, note A. L. Poole, *Obligations of Society in the
Twelfth and Thirteenth Centuries* (Oxford, 1946), ch. 5, esp. p. 81: 'an examination of an
eyre roll leaves one with the impression that it was almost impossible, however much
he might strive to do his duty, for a man to escape amercement at some stage'.

[72] *Letters and Charters of Gilbert Foliot*, ed. A. Morey and C. N. L. Brooke (London,
1967), No. 196, and see Hyams, *King, Lords, and Peasants*, 249–50.

[73] Note, however, the reservations expressed below, p. 281.

be considered to be like private agreements'.[74] Jocelin of Brakelond may provide further information. He complains of his abbey, Bury St Edmunds, losing a case because the local knights acting as royal jurors stated that they knew nothing 'about our charters nor about private agreements', but relied instead on the tenants' long tenure. Perhaps Bury was the victim of a general stance taken by justices towards the exclusion of certain materials from influence in court.[75]

How did such changes come about? Royal justices were coming to operate to an increasing degree by a set of discrete legal rules, distinguished from other considerations. Sessions of the shire court before the justices of the general eyre were regarded as sessions of the king's court. Such justices might favour 'a more general custom of the king's court, which was of nationwide applicability' rather than local custom,[76] although the mentality of nation-wide rules might be slow to develop and royal justices could take notice of local custom.[77] Still, the very fact that these justices were outsiders may have made them less receptive to local opinion, customs, and informal arrangements. Increased business might lead to reflection and thence to more standardization.[78]

Other factors were also working towards a more rule-based mentality. The administrative self-righteousness which I have suggested existed may have encouraged administrators to apply their norms more rigidly. Some of the justices were familiar with the universally applicable, and to a degree systematic, rules of Roman or Canon

---

[74] *Glanvill*, x. 18, Hall, 132; x. 8, p. 124, makes a similar statement about such agreements 'whether made out of court or in courts other than that of the lord king'. It sounds as if the royal court may have been growing overburdened and the royal advisers were having to think of ways in which to stem the flow of business. However, in order now to get royal protection, one had to make agreements in the royal court, again promoting the superior jurisdiction. See also Brand, 'Multis Vigiliis', 216 on the limitation of royal courts to specific categories of litigation.

[75] *The Chronicle of Jocelin of Brakelond*, ed. and tr. H. E. Butler (London, 1949), 124; Hyams, 'Charter', 180–1. However, note that *Bracton*, fo. 34, Thorne, ii. 109 in the 1220s or 1230s could still state that 'though it is not routine, the necessity of considering *privatae conventiones* is sometimes imposed upon the king's court'.

[76] Brand, 'Multis Vigiliis', 206; also 219–22. For detailed study of some methods by which such control came to be increased, see L. E. M. Walker, 'Some Aspects of Local Jurisdiction in the 12th and 13th Centuries, with Special Reference to Private and County Courts', MA thesis (London, 1958).

[77] For a more gradualist conclusion on the changes in the nature of trials, see P. R. Hyams, 'Henry II and Ganelon', *Syracuse Scholar*, 4 (1983), 35.

[78] Hyams, 'Warranty', 478 suggests that 'the 1170s look to be the first decade when royal land actions reached a critical mass that compelled judicial reflection on the nature, proof and enforcement of private warranty, and property right in general'.

Law.[79] The very existence of administrative manuals, such as *Glanvill*, could have had a profound effect. *Glanvill* had probably to define in his own mind some customs of the king's court—future students could learn them more mechanically, as if rules, from his text.[80] The development itself of a literate mentality led to a greater rigidity of norms. Increasingly frequent drafting of documents could lead to standardization, and to notions of set actions to fit set circumstances. What lawyers call 'strict construction' is already apparent in the first surviving court rolls in the mid-1190s: being the close reading of texts, strict construction is only really possible in a literate situation.[81] Meanwhile the start of regular royal record-keeping facilitated the belief that rules should have a temporally unlimited effect, and might encourage their retrospective application. We find men seeking to correct, according to the rigid pattern of their own rules, the socially perfectly acceptable arrangements of the past—generally made in exceptional circumstances, for example the succession of a younger son because of the feebleness of the elder.[82]

Such a shift of mentality also affected the nature of argument in court. Rules involve inclusion and exclusion. Justices accepted some evidence and arguments as permissible, ruled others out of court.[83] This differs from the more all-embracing nature of earlier lawsuits. Certainly many earlier cases had involved the concentration on a key issue, but the new processes probably encouraged such focusing on one vital question, which could be put to an assize jury.[84] Also, technicalities came to be more important. Writs were subjected to increasingly close scrutiny, so that defendants might have them ruled ineffective on technicalities.[85] This tendency became self-perpetuating, for such technicalities required increasingly specialist advice, and

---

[79] See above, n. 59, on the education of Henry's justices; but see Turner, *Judiciary*, 31: 'their biographies reveal them to be mainly men of practical experience in other branches of royal government, not "learned" men in the academic sense', cf. on later decades pp. 150–2, 226–39.

[80] A. Murray, *Reason and Society in the Middle Ages* (Oxford, 1978), 121–4 discusses the importance of manuals. For an anthropologist's view of the influence of writing on the emergence of rules, see J. R. Goody, *The Logic of Writing and the Organization of Society* (Cambridge, 1986), ch. 4. See also van Caenegem, *Writs*, 355.

[81] See also Hyams, 'Warranty', 479.

[82] See above, p. 126.

[83] Hyams, 'Charter', 180. The returnable writ also probably contributed to the limitation of the ground covered by court hearings: see van Caenegem, *Writs*, 357 n. 6.

[84] See e.g. Stenton, *English Justice*, 50 on the Grand Assize, 140–1 for a case of 1113 × 27 concentrating on a specific issue.

[85] Brand, 'Multis Vigiliis', 216–17.

these specialists—unlike earlier wise men—would gain their power not just from their wisdom and eloquence but also from their strictly legal skills:

Old style *consilium* from one's friends no longer sufficed. For effective implementation learned 'translation' was required, out of the language of everyday experience and mundane choice into the voice of an artificial reason to which the courts would listen.[86]

Perhaps the best evidence of all for the arrival of such a rule-based mentality comes from clause 43 of the 1217 version of Magna Carta, which forbade that anyone 'give his land to any religious house thus that he resume the land to hold from the same house'. The situation seems to be that a tenant was conspiring with the monastery to avoid his lord's rights such as wardship and relief. Here we have the type of skilled legal device which in the later Middle Ages—in forms such as the enfeoffment to use—employed the strict application of legal rules to facilitate socially desired action, in ways which were not intended by the general thrust of other rules of law. Such playing with rules would not have been possible in the earlier, more custom-based period, where for law not to fit social reality in this way would have seemed impossible.[87]

CONCLUSION

Thus Henry's reforms affected lordship, the administration of justice, and the nature of norms affecting land-holding. However, it is not with the degree of change caused by Henry II's reforms that I wish to end. As I have argued with regard to the Anglo-Norman period, men already enjoyed considerable security of tenure. The descent patterns of lands did not alter greatly after 1154, although importantly some marginal cases were affected by the Angevin reforms. The require-

---

[86] Hyams, 'Charter', 184; cf. Turner, *Judiciary*, 35 on the continuing importance of the eloquent knightly pleader in the 13th cent. Stenton, *English Justice*, 86–7, 149–50 on increasingly professional attorneys and essoiners. I would emphasize that developments, especially at first, were gradual; also, that the earlier role of men such as the *causidici* mentioned in *CMA*, ii. 2 must not be underestimated and requires further study. The essential discussion is now P. A. Brand, *The Origins of the English Legal Profession* (Oxford, 1992), esp. ch. 1.

[87] Hyams, 'Charter', 183. One is reminded of Bede's complaint in his letter to Egbert about laymen buying land under the pretext of founding monasteries, but the action forbidden in 1217 seems legally subtler than that in Bede's time.

ments for consent to alienation seem weak in comparison to at least some areas of France. Thereafter, the decline in participation in alienation usefully illustrates key themes in my argument. First, it again loosens the association of legal change with Angevin reforms. Secondly, it re-emphasizes the importance in legal development, before, during, and after the Angevin administrative changes, of society's thought on land-holding, rather than the impetus given by some 'judicial logic' or even administrative change.

Legal explanations of the decline in participation have commonly rested on the homage and warranty bars: when these were regularly enforced by royal power, they prevented lords and heirs from discontinuing gifts. This development is generally dated to the last quarter of the twelfth century.[88] Yet the evidence does not support this close association with the Angevin reforms. Consent clauses had always been less usual in Anglo-Norman England than on the Continent. Moreover, even in the charters of lesser men, clauses recording the consent of heirs may well have been declining from *c.*1150 × 60. Such a picture fits with the security which donees and their heirs enjoyed well before Henry II's reign.

Furthermore, as I have argued, participation expressed the social and religious interests and relationships of all who might be concerned with the gift. That gifts often involved not just an individual but rather a group act reinforced notions of mutual obligation and ideals of harmony. Similarly religious, social, and economic causes existed for the decline of participation. Perhaps there were changes in piety, or in the occasions of giving, or an increasingly active land market.[89] Increasing distinction between tenures may have led men to associate restrictions on alienation with, for example, life-holdings, and have encouraged the feeling that they might dispose as they wished of lands granted them in fee and inheritance.[90] Underlying

---

[88] See e.g. S. E. Thorne, 'English Feudalism and Estates in Land', *CLJ* (1959), 206–9, Milsom, *Legal Framework*, 121–42; Hyams, 'Charter', 182–3 links the decline with royal justices' disregard for private agreements, on which see above, p. 272; note also S. D. White, *Custom, Kinship, and Gifts to Saints* (Chapel Hill, NC, 1988), 205 on state administration rendering the *laudatio* redundant.

[89] For the situation in western France, see White, *Gifts to Saints*, ch. 6 and esp. pp. 191–2.

[90] By the early 13th cent., lack of freedom to alienate was associated with villein tenure. This sharp distinction was the product of legal change during the period *c.*1170–1220; Hyams, *Kings, Lords, and Peasants*, ch. 5, 13. See Hyams, *Kings, Lords, and Peasants*, 5–10; Pollock and Maitland, ii. 93 on the attornment of land held in villeinage. Hence they may have been seen as less free to dispose of lands, the lord

the decline in seignorial control of alienation were further pressures, which also affected security of tenure and heritability. Long occupation strengthened the link felt between tenant and land, as opposed to tenant and lord, weakened the personal element in land-holding.[91] Some vassals, and probably an increasingly influential number, were notably powerful in relation to their lords. To credit the vassal with such power and views complements other explanations as to why the tenant became, in *Bracton's* words, the *uerus dominus*, the true lord, of the land.

More generally, when dealing with changing social relations and mentalities rather than statutory change, one might expect development to be gradual. It is therefore also notable that Henry II's reforms do not immediately lead to the disappearance of consent clauses, and they continued occasionally to appear well into the thirteenth century.[92] Other indications of mentalities similarly take the focus away from the Angevin period. If shifts in vocabulary— admittedly primarily Latin vocabulary—are taken as one of the best indications of mentality, a key shift came between *c.*1050 and 1130, rather than under the Angevins.[93] Pre-Angevin views of land-holding were sophisticated and developing. The Norman conquerors, bringing with them their own changing and influential notions, had to consider the varying modes of land-holding which arose in their newly acquired land, a process of definition in which the Domesday survey must have played a significant part. Further developments in thought, both abstract and gut-feeling, may have been working to restrict any seignorial discretion over land-holding. Henry II's reforms could not have functioned, could not have been conceived of in the form they took, had there not been norms by which they might work. Those working out the limits of *mort d'ancestor*, for example, knew the customary patterns of secure succession, and no one would have

freer to dispose of them. The correlative may be that other tenants increasingly felt lands to be their own and that they should be free to alienate them. Previous distinctions were less precise, but by the time Richard fitzNigel was writing in the late 1170s, the land of villeins was already seen as peculiarly belonging to the lord: See above, p. 214, for the verb *dare* being used to describe a lord's confirmation of a gift by his *rustici*.

[91] See above, pp. 60–1, 150–1.
[92] See above, pp. 186–7. See also P. A. Brand, Review of S. F. C. Milsom, *Studies in the History of the Common Law*, *L&HR* 6 (1988), 202–3, on the continuing importance of seignorial influence in the 13th cent.
[93] See above, Ch. 3.

disagreed with their view.[94] Even if the effect of the reforms was to provide further regularity, definition, and formalization, developments before Henry II's reign must be taken as a necessary, although not sufficient, explanation for the nature of land-holding in Common Law.

Similarly with regard to jurisdiction, one may argue that Angevin acts were prefigured in the Anglo-Norman period. Reaction to Henry II's decree concerning default of justice shows that at least great men early in Henry's reign felt their courts should have an important role, which the king was now restricting.[95] However, this need not compel us to posit some earlier world of autonomous honours. Little evidence exists of adjudication in honour courts except those of great lords. In any case, the complaining magnates' recent past, Stephen's reign and the early years of Henry II, may have been the golden age of the English honour court. It is on documents of this unusual period that Stenton based his view of the honour as a 'feudal state in miniature'.[96] Such a description of the honour does not fit well the Anglo-Norman period as a whole, its politics, its administration of justice, or its land-holding.[97] Even in cases between man and lord, the honour court was not always autonomous. For example, a man who felt he had been denied right by his lord could turn to the king and obtain either a hearing in the royal court or a writ.[98] Some such writs were addressed to the sheriff, suggesting at least some role for him in these hearings.[99] Courts could be of mixed form, made up partly of men of the honour, but afforced by the sheriff, royal justices, or

---

[94] See also Biancalana, 'Legal Reforms of Henry II', 486, 508.

[95] *MTB*, iv. 40–1; Cheney, 'Decree of Henry II', also 'Novel Disseisin', 15–16. *Letters and Charters of Gilbert Foliot*, No. 196, shows a lord feeling that his court was being unfairly bypassed in a minor land dispute.

[96] Stenton, *First Century*, 47–55.

[97] Note the direct relationship of king and sub-tenants, on which see e.g. the comment of Biancalana, 'Legal Reforms of Henry II', 440; also royal control of profitable rights other than land, e.g. tolls.

[98] On transfer of cases under Henry I, see above, p. 136. For the early years of Henry II's reign, see p. 139. For another land case before royal justices early in Henry I's reign, see *Chronicon Abbatiae Rameseiensis*, ed. W. D. Macray (London, 1886), 252.

[99] e.g. *Regesta*, ii, Nos. 654, 1551; see also Nos. 581, 975, *Facsimiles of Early Charters from Northamptonshire Collections*, ed. F. M. Stenton (Northants Rec. Soc. 4; 1930), 12–15; from the first twelve years of Henry II's reign, *St Benet of Holme*, No. 34 (and No. 164 which relate to it). See also e.g. *CMA*, ii. 129, where a sheriff, with no tenurial connection to the abbey, witnesses a settlement apparently in the seigniorial court. The other witnesses named may be present for their importance as officials rather than simply as tenants.

other great men.[100] Nor were land disputes confined within honours. Clashes over land between neighbours, tenants of different lords, were common, particularly because of the complexity of tenurial arrangements in England.[101] Henry I provided that border disputes or invasions of other men's lands should be dealt with in shire courts if between sub-tenants of different lords.[102] The existence of such a court, under royal control, formed an influential part of the legacy of Anglo-Saxon government. With the presence of royal justices it was also to provide the key forum through which the Angevin reforms would work.

Such provisions and actions are signs of royal involvement in justice, and of changes in the nature and degree of seignorial control of land. Construction of a chronology is very difficult. Information before 1100 in this regard is very scarce, apart from Domesday Book, but I lean to a view that constraints from outside the honour upon lords' control of their lands were fewer than in the twelfth century. The balance of power between vassal and lord—together with their potential supporters—would therefore have been particularly important.[103] Under Henry I, however, there are indications that Henry was involved even in some fairly minor disputes. Men were increasingly having to take the king into account in their dealings concerning land. If these various arguments concerning customs and thought, courts, royal involvement, and the consequent limitation of

[100] See e.g. above, pp. 5, 136; *Regesta*, ii, No. 1751; F. M. Stenton, 'The Danes in England', *PBA* 13 (1927), 221–2; Biancalana, 'Legal Reforms of Henry II', 459 n. 115. Note *Regesta*, ii, No. 529, Henry I granting the abbot of Battle that any plea against the abbey's tenants take place in the abbot's court; the proviso is added that if the case could not be determined there, it was to be transferred to the royal court to be settled in the presence of the justiciar and the abbot. *Leges Edwardi*, 9 2, Liebermann, *Gesetze*, i. 633, provides that if a baron hears a plea about the men of other barons in his court, a royal justice was to be present. This need not refer to cases involving land.

[101] See e.g. *CMA*, i. 491–2, ii. 118. Note also *Dialogus*, 63: Domesday Book had been compiled 'that each, content with his own right, should not usurp another without punishment'.

[102] *Regesta*, ii, No. 892, Liebermann, *Gesetze*, i. 524. A minimal interpretation of this provision on cases concerning pleas 'de diuisione terrarum, uel de preoccupatione' would limit it to minor boundary disputes. However, 'preoccupatio' may well be synonymous with 'usurpatio' or 'inuasio' and hence cover a wider range of disputes. Even if only boundary disputes are meant, they need not have been minor affairs. On *preoccupatio*, see also Hudson, 'Milsom's Legal Structure: Interpreting Twelfth-Century Law', *TVR* 59 (1991), 54–5.

[103] The one major post-Conquest seizure of land from Abingdon mentioned in its chronicle from which no case arose is that of Fyfield and Kingston by Henry de Ferrers in the Conqueror's reign, *CMA*, i. 484–5, 490–1.

seignorial discretion, are correct, Henry I's reign was probably one of major change. Certainly flexibility remained, royal regulation of justice was not complete, and the position of lord and tenant varied according to their power. The Church may still have been leading developments in relation to land-holding and royal justice. Yet by 1135 for laymen as well as ecclesiastics, the threat, if not the routine, automatic administration, of royal justice had already been shaping the norms of seignorial action and of land-holding.[104]

If one can argue that the nature of land-holding under Henry I renders the impact of the Angevin reforms less dramatic, so too can the situation after Henry II's reign. Certain groups were excluded at least partially from the reforms. Most notable are villeins, who came to be definable as those without recourse to the usual royal remedies.[105] Also excluded, although to a lesser extent, were the king's tenants in chief. The political consequences of this anomaly is reflected in Magna Carta's attempts to restrict the king's now peculiar power.[106] Yet even later, they did not have, for example, the full freedom to alienate their land which other men enjoyed.[107]

Change from Henry II's reign was also limited in other ways. Self-help could still play a significant part in the control of land, and it is conceivable that in the second half of the thirteenth century some land cases were still brought to lord's courts by plaint.[108] Nor must it be assumed that the procedures laid down in *Glanvill* and its associated manual, the *Dialogus*, were always followed. Take the example of distraint. As we have seen, the distrainee's goods were not supposed to be sold. However, Jocelin of Brakelond records a dispute in 1196 in which the abbot of Bury, with the tacit backing of the king's justiciar Hubert Walter, was seeking to enforce the services his knights owed him. All eventually admitted their obligations, apart

---

[104] Note the similar, although independent, view of Biancalana, 'Legal Reforms of Henry II', 497.

[105] Hyams, *King, Lords, and Peasants*, has argued strongly that the clear jurisdictional division of villeins from free men stemmed from the reforms of Henry II's reign.

[106] J. C. Holt, *Magna Carta* (2nd edn., Cambridge, 1992), ch. 5; cf. J. E. A. Jolliffe, *Angevin Kingship* (London, 1955).

[107] See e.g. J. M. W. Bean, *The Decline of English Feudalism* (Manchester, 1968), 66–79. On the royal lord manipulating inheritance, see e.g. K. B. McFarlane, 'Had Edward I a "Policy" Towards the Earls?', *History*, 1 (1965), 145–59.

[108] Hurnard, 'Policy upon Seisin', 535; Sutherland, *Novel Disseisin*, 4, 97–125; *Select Cases of Procedure without Writ under Henry III*, ed. H. G. Richardson and G. O. Sayles, (Selden Soc. 60; 1941), pp. lxxi–lxxii, who note, however, that the defendant could invoke the rule requiring a royal writ before he answered concerning freehold. See also above, n. 75, on *Bracton* concerning *privatae conventiones*.

from Aubrey de Ver, who, having been abroad on the king's service, continued to resist. The abbot, therefore, took and sold his beasts. This had the desired effect of bringing him to court, and having taken counsel, he acknowledged the right of St Edmund and the abbot.[109] Presumably the length of Aubrey's resistance was seen to justify the extreme move. Flexibility thus remained in the norms of reasonable distraint. Much procedure was still a matter of custom not rule.

Even where rules do exist, some rest on criteria of reasonableness, ensuring that they can function in certain circumstances rather like earlier customary norms. Others leave what some legal philosophers have called a *penumbra*, a grey area particularly exposed by hard cases. Now these *penumbrae* may be much more confined than those left by earlier customs, but they do suggest that early Common Law rules and the customs of, for instance, Henry I's reign may be less qualitatively different than is sometimes suggested.[110] Linked to this are limits to any shift in the form of dispute settlement, from compromise to decision for one party, which is sometimes associated with increased royal judicial activity. Pre-Common Law England knew decisions as well as compromises; later medieval England knew compromise as well as outright decision. For negotiation, compromise, and even decisions outside court, general attitudes to land-holding were important before but also after the emergence of more precise and discrete legal rules.

Indeed, especially in such activities outside court, one might find that thought and actions had changed little between, say, the reign of William I and the death of Henry II. Lords had similar desires for the use of their lands in relation to their vassals. A man in 1100, certainly in 1135, had the language with which he could readily have explained custom to a man two or three generations later, and the latter would no doubt have found the situation described not merely comprehensible but familiar. The developments of land law from *c.*1166 are of course striking, but they were most notably an acceleration of administrative change, not an unprecedented leap forward.

[109] Jocelin of Brakelond, 66–7.
[110] See above, p. 9; note also the continuing existence of hard cases such as the *casus regis*. For one set of thoughts on modern rules relevant in this context, see H. L. A. Hart, *The Concept of Law* (Oxford, 1961), ch. VII. Note how the petty assizes dealt primarily with central cases: see e.g. Biancalana, 'Legal Reforms of Henry II', 507 on *mort d'ancestor* leaving 'collateral claims beyond the close range of family relationships covered by the assize to seignorial courts'.

Select Bibliography

A: MANUSCRIPT SOURCES

Bodleian Library, MS Dodsworth 85.
Bodleian Library, MS Dugdale 12.
Bodleian Library, MS Dugdale 13.
Bodleian Library, MS Dugdale 17.
Bodleian Library, MS Film Deposit 912.
Bodleian Library, MS Laud misc. 625.
Bodleian Library, MS Lyell 15.
British Library, Additional Charter 21493.
British Library, Additional Charter 21494.
British Library, Additional Charter 47380.
British Library, Additional Charter 47381.
British Library, Additional Charter 47382.
British Library, Additional Charter 47384.
British Library, Additional Charter 48086.
British Library, Additional Charter 48488.
British Library, Additional MS 57677.
British Library, Additional MS 47677.
British Library, MS Cotton Calig. A xiii.
British Library, MS Cotton Julius C vii.
British Library, MS Cotton Vitellius A i.
British Library, MS Harley 294.
British Library, MS Harley 782.
British Library, MS Harley 1885.
British Library, MS Harley 3650.
British Library, MS Harley 4714.
British Library, MS Harley 4757.
British Library, MS Harley charter 84 H 18.
British Library, MS Harley charter 84 H 19.
British Library, MS Lansdowne 415.
British Library, MS Royal 11 B ix.
Chatsworth Library, Abingdon Cartulary.
Magdalen College, Oxford, MS 273.
Trinity College, Cambridge, MS B 16 44.
Trinity College, Oxford, MS 85.

Theses

BOORMAN, J., 'The Sheriffs and the Shrieval Office in the Reign of Henry II', Ph.D. thesis (Reading, 1989).

DALTON, P., 'Feudal Society in Yorkshire', Ph.D. thesis (Sheffield, 1989).

GARNETT, G. S., 'Royal Succession in England, 1066–1154', Ph.D. thesis (Cambridge, 1987).

HUDSON, J. G. H., 'Legal Aspects of Seignorial Control of Land in the Century after the Norman Conquest', D.Phil. thesis (Oxford, 1988).

PHILPOTT, M., 'Archbishop Lanfranc and Canon Law', D.Phil. thesis (Oxford, 1993).

WALKER, L. E. M., 'Some Aspects of Local Jurisdiction in the 12th and 13th Centuries, with Special Reference to Private and County Courts', MA thesis (London, 1958).

WHITE, G. J., 'The Restoration of Order in England, 1153–1165', Ph.D. thesis (Cambridge, 1974).

B: PRINTED SOURCES

(i) Primary Sources

Acts of the Bishops of Chichester, 1075–1207, ed. H. Mayr-Harting (Cant.–York Soc. 130; 1964).

Adami de Domerham Historia de Rebus Gestis Glastoniensibus, ed. T. Hearne (2 vols.; Oxford, 1727).

Ancient Charters Royal and Private Prior to A.D. 1200, ed. J. H. Round (PRS 10; 1888).

Anglo-Saxon Charters, ed. and tr. A. J. Robertson (2nd edn., Cambridge, 1956).

Anglo-Saxon Chronicle, ed. D. Whitelock, with D. C. Douglas and S. I. Tucker (London, 1961).

Anglo-Saxon Wills, ed. and tr. D. Whitelock (Cambridge, 1930).

Anglo-Saxon Writs, ed. F. E. Harmer (Manchester, 1952).

Annales Monastici, ed. H. R. Luard (5 vols.; London, 1864–9).

ANSELM, *S. Anselmi Cantuariensis Archiepiscopi Opera Omnia*, ed. F. S. Schmitt (6 vols.; Edinburgh, 1938–61).

Beauchamp Cartulary: Charters 1100–1268, ed. E. Mason (PRS, NS 43; 1980).

Book of the Beasts, tr. T. H. White (London, 1954).

Borough Customs, ed. M. Bateson (2 vols.; Selden Soc. 18, 21; 1904, 1906).

'BRACTON, HENRY DE', *De Legibus et Consuetudinibus Regni Anglie*, ed. and tr. S. E. Thorne (4 vols.; Cambridge, Mass., 1968–77).

Bracton's Note Book, ed. F. W. Maitland (3 vols.; London, 1887).

Calendar of Charter Rolls Preserved in the Public Record Office (6 vols.; 1903–27).

Calendar of Documents Preserved in France illustrative of the History of Great Britain and Ireland, ed. J. H. Round (London, 1899).

Calendar of Patent Rolls Preserved in the Public Record Office (in progress, 1891–present).

CANDIDUS, HUGH, *The Chronicle of Hugh Candidus, a Monk of Peterborough*, ed. W. T. Mellows (Oxford, 1949).

Carmen de Hastingae Proelio of Guy Bishop of Amiens, ed. C. Morton and H. Muntz (Oxford, 1972).

Cartae Antiquae, Rolls 1–10, ed. L. Landor (PRS, NS 17; 1939).

Cartae Antiquae, Rolls 11–20, ed. J. C. Davis (PRS, NS 33; 1960).

Cartulaire noir de la cathédrale d'Angers, ed. C. Urseau (Paris and Angers, 1908).

Cartularium Abbathiae de Rievalle, ed. J. C. Atkinson (Surtees Soc. 83; 1889).

Cartularium Abbathiae de Whiteby, ed. J. C. Atkinson (2 vols.; Surtees Soc. 69, 72; 1879, 1881).

Cartularium Monasterii de Rameseia, ed. W. H. Hart and P. A. Lyons (3 vols.; London, 1884–93).

Cartularium Monasterii S. Johannis Baptiste de Colecestria, ed. S. A. Moore (2 vols.; Roxburghe Club, London, 1897).

Cartularium Prioratus de Colne, ed. J. L. Fisher (Essex Arch. Soc., Occ. Publications, 1; 1946).

'Cartularium Prioratus S. Johannis Evang. de Brecon', ed. R. W. Banks, *Archaeologia Cambriense*, 4th Ser. 13 (1882), 275–308; 14 (1883), 18–49, 137–68, 221–36, 274–311.

The Cartulary of Cirencester Abbey, ed. C. D. Ross and M. Devine (3 vols.; Oxford, 1964–77).

The Cartulary of Missenden Abbey, ed. J. G. Jenkins (3 vols.; Bucks. Arch. Soc., Rec. Branch, 2, 10; 1939, 1955; vol. 3 jointly with HMC, 1962).

Cartulary of the Monastery of St Frideswide at Oxford, ed. S. R. Wigram (2 vols.; Oxford Hist. Soc. 28, 31; 1895–6).

Cartulary of Oseney Abbey, ed. H. E. Salter (6 vols.; Oxford Hist. Soc. 89, 90, 91, 97, 98, 101; 1929–36).

The Cartulary of the Priory of St Denys near Southampton, ed. E. O. Blake (2 vols.; Southampton Rec. Soc. 24, 25; 1981).

The Cartulary of Shrewsbury Abbey, ed. U. Rees (2 vols.; Aberystwyth, 1975).

Cartulary of Tutbury Priory, ed. A. Saltman (Staffs. Rec. Soc., 4th Ser. 4; HMSO, 1962).

The Cartulary of Worcester Cathedral Priory, ed. R. R. Darlington (PRS, NS 38; 1968).

The Charters of the Anglo-Norman Earls of Chester, c.1071–1237, ed. G. Barraclough (Rec. Soc. of Lancs. and Cheshire, 126; 1988).

Charters and Documents illustrating the History of the Cathedral, City, and Diocese of Salisbury, in the Twelfth and Thirteenth Centuries, selected W. H. Rich Jones, ed. W. D. Macray (London, 1891).

'Charters of the Earldom of Hereford, 1095–1201', ed. D. Walker, in *Camden Miscellany*, xxii (Camden Soc., 4th Ser. 1; 1964).

Charters of the Honour of Mowbray, 1107–1191, ed. D. E. Greenway (London, 1972).

The Charters of Norwich Cathedral Priory, ed. B. Dodwell (2 vols.; PRS, NS 40, 46; 1974, 1985).

Charters and Records of Hereford Cathedral, ed. W. W. Capes (Cantilupe Soc., Hereford, 1908).

'Charters relating to the Priory of Sempringham', ed. E. M. Poynton, *Genealogist*, NS 15 (1899), 158–61, 221–7; 16 (1900), 76–83, 153–8, 223–8; 17 (1901), 29–35, 164–8, 232–9.

CHRÉTIEN DE TROYES, *Cligés*, ed. W. Foerster (Halle, 1884).

The Chronicle of Battle Abbey, ed. and tr. E. Searle (Oxford, 1980).

The Chronicle of Jocelin of Brakelond, ed. and tr. H. E. Butler (London, 1949).

Chronicles of the Reigns of Stephen, Henry II, and Richard I, ed. R. Howlett (4 vols.; London, 1884–9).

Chronicon Abbatiae de Evesham ad annum 1418, ed. W. D. Macray (London, 1863).

Chronicon Abbatiae Rameseiensis, ed. W. D. Macray (London, 1886).

Chronicon Monasterii de Abingdon, ed. J. Stevenson (2 vols.; London, 1858).

Corpus Iuris Canonici, ed. Ae. Friedberg (2 vols.; Leipzig, 1879–81).

The Coucher Book of Furness Abbey, ed. J. C. Atkinson and J. Brownhill (2 vols. in 6 parts, Chetham Soc. NS 9, 11, 14, 74, 76, 78; 1886–1919).

Councils and Synods with other Documents relating to the English Church, i, ed. D. Whitelock, M. Brett, and C. N. L. Brooke (2 vols.; Oxford, 1981).

The Court Baron, ed. and tr. F. W. Maitland and W. P. Baildon (Selden Soc. 4; 1891).

Coutumiers de Normandie, i. Le Très Ancien Coutumier de Normandie; ii. La Summa de Legibus Normannie in Curia Laicali, ed. E.-J. Tardif (Société de l'Histoire de Normandie, Rouen et Paris, 1881, 1896).

Curia Regis Rolls (in progress, 1922–present).

Decretales Pseudo-Isidorianae, ed. P. Hinschius (Leipzig, 1863).

Documents Illustrative of the Social and Economic History of the Danelaw, ed. F. M. Stenton (London, 1920).

Domesday Book seu Liber Censualis Wilhelmi Primi Regis Angliae, ed. A. Farley and H. Ellis (4 vols.; vols. i–ii, London, 1783; vols. iii–iv, London, 1816).

The Domesday Monachorum of Christ Church Canterbury, ed. D. C. Douglas (London, 1944).

Durham Episcopal Charters, 1071–1152, ed. H. S. Offler (Surtees Soc. 179; 1968).

EADMER, *Historia Nouorum in Anglia*, ed. M. Rule (London, 1884).

286   *Select Bibliography*

EADMER, *The Life of St. Anselm, Archbishop of Canterbury*, ed. and tr. R. W. Southern (2nd edn., Oxford, 1972).

Earldom of Gloucester Charters: The Charters and Scribes of the Earls and Countesses of Gloucester to A.D. 1217, ed. R. B. Patterson (Oxford, 1973).

The Earliest Lincolnshire Assize Rolls, 1202–1209, ed. D. M. Stenton (Lincoln Rec. Soc. 22; 1926).

Early Buckinghamshire Charters, ed. G. H. Fowler and J. G. Jenkins (Records Branch of Bucks. Arch. Soc. 3; 1939).

Early Charters of the Cathedral Church of St Paul, London, ed. M. Gibbs (Camden Soc., 3rd Ser. 58; 1939).

Early Registers of Writs, ed. E. de Haas and G. D. G. Hall (Selden Soc. 87; 1970).

Early Yorkshire Charters, vols. i–iii, ed. W. Farrer (Edinburgh, 1914–16); index to vols. i–iii, ed. C. T. and E. M. Clay; vols. iv–xii, ed. C. T. Clay (Yorks. Arch. Soc. Rec. Ser. Extra Ser., 1935–65).

Ecclesiastical Documents, ed. J. Hunter (Camden Soc., 1st Ser. 8; 1840).

An Eleventh-Century Inquisition of St Augustine's, Canterbury, ed. A. Ballard (London, 1920).

English Episcopal Acta:

  (i) *Lincoln, 1067–1185*, ed. D. M. Smith (London, 1980).
  (ii) *Canterbury, 1162–90*, ed. C. R. Cheney and B. E. A. Jones (London, 1986).
  (v) *York, 1070–1154*, ed. J. E. Burton (Oxford, 1988).

English Lawsuits from William I to Richard I, ed. R. C. van Caenegem (2 vols.; Selden Soc. 106, 107; 1990–1).

'Epistulae Fiscannenses: Lettres d'amitié, de gouvernement, et d'affaires', ed. J. Laporte, *Revue Mabillon*, 43 (1953), 5–31.

Eynsham Cartulary, ed. H. E. Salter (2 vols.; Oxford Hist. Soc. 49, 51; 1908–9).

Facsimiles of Early Charters from Northamptonshire Collections, ed. F. M. Stenton (Northants Rec. Soc. 4; 1930).

Facsimiles of Early Charters in Oxford Muniment Rooms, ed. H. E. Salter (Oxford, 1929).

Facsimiles of English Royal Writs to A.D. 1100 presented to Vivian Hunter Galbraith, ed. T. A. M. Bishop and P. Chaplais (Oxford, 1957).

Facsimiles of Royal and Other Charters in the British Museum, i. *William I– Richard I*, ed. G. F. Warner and H. J. Ellis (London, 1903).

FANTOSME, JORDAN, *Chronicle*, ed. and tr. R. C. Johnston (Oxford, 1981).

Feodarium Prioratus Dunelmensis, ed. W. Greenwell (Surtees Soc. 58; 1872).

Feudal Documents from the Abbey of Bury St Edmunds, ed. D. C. Douglas (London, 1932).

The First Register of Norwich Cathedral Priory, ed. and tr. H. W. Saunders

(Norfolk Rec. Soc. 11; 1939).

FLORENCE OF WORCESTER, *Chronicon ex Chronicis*, ed. B. Thorpe (2 vols.; London, 1848–9).

FOLIOT, GILBERT, *The Letter and Charters of Gilbert Foliot*, ed. A. Morey and C. N. L. Brooke (London, 1967).

Formulare Anglicanum, ed. T. Madox (London, 1702).

'The Foundation of Kirkstall Abbey', ed. E. K. Clark, in *Thoresby Soc., Miscellany*, 2 (1895), 169–208.

GAIMAR, *L'Estoire des Engleis*, ed. A. Bell (3 vols.; Anglo-Norman Texts Soc. 14–16; 1960).

GEOFFREY OF MONMOUTH, *The Historia Regum Britannie of Geoffrey of Monmouth, i. Bern Burgerbibliothek, MS. 568*, ed. N. Wright (Cambridge, 1985).

GERALD OF WALES, *Giraldi Cambrensis Opera*, ed. J. S. Brewer, J. F. Dimock, and G. F. Warner (8 vols.; London, 1861–91).

GERVASE OF CANTERBURY, *Historical Works*, ed. W. Stubbs (2 vols.; London, 1879–80).

Die Gesetze der Angelsachsen, ed. F. Liebermann (3 vols.; Halle, 1903–16).

Gesta Abbatum Monasterii Sancti Albani, ed. H. T. Riley (3 vols.; London, 1867–9).

Gesta Regis Henrici Secundi Benedicti Abbatis, ed. W. Stubbs (2 vols.; London, 1867).

Gesta Stephani, ed. K. R. Potter, intro. R. H. C. Davis (Oxford, 1976).

'GLANVILL, RANULF DE', *Tractatus de Legibus et Consuetudinibus Regni Anglie qui Glanvilla vocatur*, ed. G. D. G. Hall (Edinburgh, 1965).

The Great Chartulary of Glastonbury, ed. A. Watkin (3 vols.; Somerset Rec. Soc. 59, 63, 64; 1947–56).

GUILLAUME DE JUMIÈGES, *Gesta Normannorum Ducum*, ed. J. Marx (Paris and Rouen, 1914).

GUILLAUME DE POITIERS, *Histoire de Guillaume le Conquérant*, ed. and tr. R. Foreville (Paris, 1952).

The Guthlac Roll, ed. G. F. Warner (Roxburghe Club, Oxford, 1928).

Hemmingi Chartularium Ecclesie Wigorniensis, ed. T. Hearne (2 vols.; Oxford, 1723).

HENRY OF HUNTINGDON, *Historia Anglorum*, ed. T. Arnold (London, 1879).

Historia et Chartularium Monasterii Sancti Petri Gloucestriae, ed. W. H. Hart (3 vols.; London, 1863–7).

HMC, *The Manuscripts of his Grace The Duke of Rutland* (4 vols.; London, 1888–1905).

—— *Ninth Report, Appendix* (London, 1883).

—— *Report on the Manuscripts of Lord Middleton* (London, 1911).

HUGH THE CHANTOR, *The History of the Church of York, 1066–1127*, ed. and tr. C. Johnson (Edinburgh, 1961).

Inquisitio Comitatus Cantabrigiensis subiicitur Inquisitio Eliensis, ed. N. E. S. A. Hamilton (London, 1876).

IVO OF CHARTRES, *Opera Omnia* (*PL* 161, 162).

JOHN OF SALISBURY, *The Letters of John of Salisbury*, ed. W. J. Millor, H. E. Butler, C. N. L. Brooke (2 vols.; Edinburgh and Oxford, 1955–79).

—— *Historia Pontificalis*, ed. and tr. M. Chibnall (Oxford, 1986).

JOHN OF WORCESTER, *Chronicle*, ed. J. R. H. Weaver (Anecdota Oxoniensia, Med. and Mod. Ser. 13; 1908).

Kalendar of Abbot Samson of Bury St Edmunds and Related Documents, ed. R. H. C. Davis (Camden Soc., 3rd Ser. 84; 1954).

Lancashire Pipe Rolls and Early Lancashire Charters, ed. W. Farrer (Liverpool, 1902).

Leges Henrici Primi, ed. and tr. L. J. Downer (Oxford, 1972).

The Letters of Lanfranc Archbishop of Canterbury, ed. and tr. H. Clover and M. Gibson (Oxford, 1979).

Letters of Pope Innocent III concerning England and Wales, ed. C. R. and M. G. Cheney (Oxford, 1967).

Liber Eliensis, ed. E. O. Blake (Camden Soc., 3rd Ser. 92; 1962).

Liber Rubeus de Scaccario, ed. H. Hall (3 vols.; London, 1896).

Life of Christina of Markyate, a Twelfth-Century Recluse, ed. and tr. C. H. Talbot (Oxford, 1959).

The Lincolnshire Domesday and the Lindsey Survey, ed. C. W. Foster and T. Longley (Lincoln Rec. Soc. 19; 1924).

Luffield Priory Charters, ed. G. R. Elvey (2 vols.; Northants Rec. Soc. 22, 26; 1968, 1975).

MAP, WALTER, *De Nugis Curialium*, ed. and tr. M. R. James, rev. C. N. L. Brooke and R. A. B. Mynors (Oxford, 1983).

Materials for the History of Thomas Becket, ed. J. C. Robertson (7 vols.; London, 1875–85).

The Monastic Constitutions of Lanfranc, ed. and tr. D. Knowles (Edinburgh, 1951).

Monasticon Anglicanum, ed. Sir William Dugdale, rev. J. Caley, H. Ellis, B. Bandinel (6 vols. in 8; London, 1817–30).

Monasticon Diocesis Exoniensis, ed. G. Oliver (Exeter, 1846).

'Mordak Charters in possession of Lord Willoughby de Broke with certain additional documents from other sources', *Miscellanea Genealogica et Heraldica*, 5th Ser. 6 (1926), 97–103.

NIGEL, RICHARD FITZ, *Dialogus de Scaccario*, ed. and tr. C. Johnson, rev. F. E. L. Carter and D. E. Greenway (Oxford, 1983).

Notitia Conciliorum Hispanie, atque Noui Orbis, ed. J. Saenz de Aguirre (Salamanca, 1686).

Novae Narrationes, ed. S. F. C. Milsom (Selden Soc. 80; 1963).

OFFLER, H. S., 'A Northumberland Charter of King Henry I', *Archaeologia*

Aeliana, 4th Ser. 45 (1967), 181–8.

ORDERIC VITALIS, *The Ecclesiastical History of Orderic Vitalis*, ed. and tr. M. Chibnall (6 vols.; Oxford, 1969–80).

—— also ed. A. le Prévost (5 vols.; Société de l'histoire de France, Paris, 1838–55).

Papsturkunden in England, ed. W. Holzmann (3 vols.; Berlin and Göttingen, 1930–52).

PETER OF BLOIS, *Opera Omnia* (*PL* 207).

Pipe Rolls, published by Pipe Roll Society.

Placita Anglo-Normannica: Law Cases from William I to Richard I, ed. M. M. Bigelow (Boston, Mass., 1879).

Placitorum in Domo Capitulari Westmonasterii Asservatorum Abbreviatio: Richard I–Edward II (Record Commission, 1811).

Pleas before the King or his Justices, 1198–1202, ed. D. M. Stenton (4 vols.; Selden Soc. 67, 68, 83, 84; 1952–67).

The Pontifical of Magdalen College, ed. H. E. Wilson (Henry Bradshaw Soc. 39; 1910).

Radulfi Nigri Chronica, ed. R. Anstruther (Caxton Soc., London, 1851).

RALPH OF DICETO, *Opera Historica*, ed. W. Stubbs (2 vols.; London, 1876).

Raoul de Cambrai, ed. and tr. S. Kay (Oxford, 1992).

Reading Abbey Cartularies, ed. B. R. Kemp (2 vols.; Camden Soc., 4th Ser. 31, 33; 1986, 1987).

Recueil des Actes des Ducs de Normandie, ed. M. Fauroux (Mémoires de la Société des Antiquaires de Normandie, 26; Caen, 1961).

Recueil des Actes de Henri II, ed. L. Delisle and E. Berger (4 vols.; Paris, 1909–27).

Regesta Regum Anglo-Normannorum, 1066–1154:

(i) *1066–1100*, ed. H. W. C. Davis, with the assistance of R. J. Whitwell (Oxford, 1913).

(ii) *1100–1135*, ed. C. J. Johnson and H. A. Cronne (Oxford, 1956).

(iii) *1135–1154*, ed. H. A. Cronne and R. H. C. Davis (Oxford, 1968).

(iv) *Facsimiles of Original Charters and Writs of King Stephen, the Empress Matilda, and Dukes Geoffrey and Henry*, ed. H. A. Cronne and R. H. C. Davis (Oxford, 1969).

Register of Abbey of St Benet of Holme, 1020–1210, ed. J. R. West (2 vols.; Norfolk Rec. Soc. 2, 3; 1932).

The Register of St Osmund, ed. W. H. Rich Jones (2 vols.; London, 1883–4).

Les Régistres de Grégoire IX, ed. L. Auvray (4 vols.; Paris, 1896–1955).

The Registrum Antiquissimum of the Cathedral Church of Lincoln, ed. C. W. Foster and K. Major (10 vols.; Lincoln Record Soc., 1931–73).

Registrum Roffense, ed. J. Thorpe the elder (London, 1769).

ROGER OF HOWDEN, *Chronica*, ed. W. Stubbs (4 vols.; London, 1868–71).

Rotuli Curiae Regis: Rolls and Records of the Court held before the King's Justiciars or Justices, ed. F. Palgrave (2 vols.; Record Commission, 1835).

Royal Commission on Historical Manuscripts, Reports and other Publications (London, 1870–present).

Royal Writs in England from the Conquest to Glanvill, ed. R. C. van Caenegem (Selden Soc. 77; 1958–9).

Rufford Charters, ed. C. J. Holdsworth (4 vols.; Thoroton Soc. Rec. Ser. 29, 30, 32, 34; 1972–81).

'The Rydeware Chartulary', ed. I. H. Jeayes, *William Salt Arch. Soc.* 16 (1895), 257–302.

The Sandford Cartulary, ed. A. M. Leys (2 vols.; Oxfordshire Rec. Soc. 19, 22; 1938, 1941).

Select Cases of Procedure without Writ under Henry III, ed. H. G. Richardson and G. O. Sayles (Selden Soc. 60; 1941).

Select Charters and Other Illustrations of English Constitutional History from the Earliest Times to the Reign of Edward I, ed. W. Stubbs (9th edn., Oxford, 1913).

Select Documents of the English Lands of the Abbey of Bec, ed. M. Chibnall (Camden Soc., 3rd Ser. 73; 1951).

SIMEON OF DURHAM, *Opera Omnia*, ed. T. Arnold (2 vols.; London, 1882–5).

Sir Christopher Hatton's Book of Seals, ed. L. C. Loyd and D. M. Stenton (Northants Rec. Soc. and Oxford, 1950).

The Song of Roland: An Analytical Edition, ed. G. J. Brault (2 vols.; Pennsylvania, 1978).

'The Staffordshire Chartulary', ed. R. W. Eyton and G. Wrottesley, *William Salt Arch. Soc.* 2 (1881), 178–276; 3 (1882), 178–231.

Statutes of Lincoln Cathedral, ed. H. Bradshaw and C. Wordsworth (3 vols.; Cambridge, 1897).

Stoke by Clare Cartulary, BL Cotton Appx. xxi, ed. C. Harper-Bill and R. Mortimer (3 vols.; Suffolk Charters, 4–6; 1982–4).

SUGER, *Œuvres Complètes*, ed. A. Lecoy de la Marche (Paris, 1867).

Textus Roffensis, ed. T. Hearne (Oxford, 1720).

—— Facsimile edn., P. H. Sawyer (2 vols.; Early English Manuscripts in Facsimile, 7, 11; 1957, 1962).

THOMAS OF ELMHAM, *Historia Monasterii S. Augustini Cantuariensis*, ed. C. Hardwick (London, 1858).

Transcripts of Charters Relating to the Gilbertine Houses of Sixle, Ormsby,

Catley, Bullington and Alvingham, ed. F. M. Stenton (Lincoln Rec. Soc. 18; 1922).

Two Cartularies of Abingdon Abbey, ed. C. F. Slade and G. Lambrick (2 vols.; Oxford Hist. Soc., NS 32, 33; 1990–2).

Two Chartularies of the Priory of St Peter at Bath, ed. W. Hunt (Somerset Rec. Soc. 7; 1893).

Visitations and Memorials of Southwell Minster, ed. A. F. Leach (Camden Soc., NS 48; 1891).

WACE, *Le Roman de Brut*, ed. I. O. Arnold (2 vols.; Société des Anciens Textes Français, Paris, 1938–40).

—— *Roman de Rou*, ed. A. J. Holden (3 vols.; Société des Anciens Textes Français, Paris, 1970–3).

Westminster Abbey Charters, 1066–c.1214, ed. E. Mason (London Rec. Soc. 25; 1988).

The Will of Aethelgifu, ed. and tr. D. Whitelock (Roxburghe Club, 1968).

WILLIAM OF MALMESBURY, *De Gestis Pontificum Anglorum Libri Quinque*, ed. N. E. S. A Hamilton (London, 1870).

—— *De Gestis Regum Anglorum Libri Quinque*, ed. W. Stubbs (2 vols.; London, 1887–9).

—— *Historia Novella*, ed. K. R. Potter (Edinburgh, 1955).

(ii)   Secondary Sources

ADAMS, G. B., *Councils and Courts in Anglo-Norman England* (New Haven, Conn., 1926; repr. New York, 1965).

ALEXANDER, J. W., 'The Alleged Palatinates of Norman England', *Speculum*, 56 (1981), 17–27.

AULT, W. O., *Private Jurisdiction in England* (Newhaven, Conn., 1923).

BAILEY, S. J., 'Warranties of Land in the Thirteenth Century', *CLJ* 8 (1942–4), 245–99; 9 (1945–7); 82–106.

—— 'Warranties of Land in the Reign of Richard I', *CLJ* 9 (1945–7), 192–209.

BARLOW, F., *Edward the Confessor* (London, 1970).

—— *The English Church, 1066–1154* (London, 1979).

—— *William Rufus* (London, 1983).

BARNES, P. M. and SLADE, C. F. (edd.), *A Medieval Miscellany for Doris Mary Stenton* (PRS, NS 36; 1960).

BARRACLOUGH, G., 'The Earldom and County Palatine of Chester', *Hist. Soc. of Lancs. and Cheshire Trans.* 103 (1951–2), 23–57.

BARROW, J., 'Cathedrals, Provosts and Prebends: A Comparison of Twelfth-Century German and English Practice', *JEcclH* 37 (1986), 536–84.

BATES, D., 'The Land Pleas of William I's Reign: Penenden Heath Revisited', *BIHR* 51 (1978), 1–19.

BATES, D., 'The Origins of the Justiciarship', *A-NS* 4 (1982), 1–12.
—— *Normandy Before 1066* (London, 1982).
BERMAN, H. J., *Law and Revolution: The Formation of the Western Legal Tradition* (Cambridge, Mass., 1983).
BIANCALANA, J., 'For Want of Justice: Legal Reforms of Henry II', *Columbia Law Review*, 88 (1988), 433–536.
—— 'Widows at Common Law: The Development of Common Law Dower', *Irish Jurist*, NS 23 (1988), 255–329.
BIGELOW, M. M., *The History of Procedure in England, 1066–1204* (Boston and London, 1880).
BIRCH, W. DE G., *Catalogue of Seals in the Department of Manuscripts in the British Museum* (6 vols.; London, 1887–1900).
BISHOP, T. A. M., *Scriptores Regis: Facsimiles to Identify and Illustrate the Hands of Royal Scribes in Original Charters of Henry I, Stephen, and Henry II* (Oxford, 1961).
BLOCH, M., *Feudal Society*, tr. L. A. Manyon (2 vols.; London, 1961).
BOURDIEU, P., *Outline of a Theory of Practice*, tr. R. Nice (Cambridge, 1977).
BOUSSARD, J., *Le Gouvernement d'Henri II Plantagenêt* (Paris, 1956).
BRAND, P. A., 'Control of Mortmain Alienation in England, 1200–1300', in J. H. Baker (ed.), *Legal Records and the Historian* (London, 1978), 29–40.
—— 'New Light on the Anstey Case', *Essex Archaeology and History*, 16 (1983), 68–83.
—— ' "Multis Vigiliis Excogitatam et Inventam": Henry II and the Creation of the English Common Law', *Haskins Society Journal*, 2 (1990), 197–222.
—— 'Lordship and Distraint in Thirteenth Century England', in P. R. Coss and S. D. Lloyd (edd.), *Thirteenth Century England III* (Woodbridge, 1991), 1–24.
—— *The Origins of the English Legal Profession* (Oxford, 1992).
—— and HYAMS, P. R., 'Seignurial Control of Women's Marriage', *P&P* 99 (1983), 123–48.
BRETT, M., *The English Church under Henry I* (Oxford, 1975).
BROOKE, C. N. L., 'Gregorian Reform in Action: Clerical Marriage in England, 1050–1200', *CHJ* 12 (1956), 1–21.
—— *The Mediaeval Idea of Marriage* (Oxford, 1989).
BROOKE, Z. N., *The English Church and the Papacy, from the Conquest to the Reign of King John* (Cambridge, 1931).
—— and BROOKE, C. N. L., 'Hereford Cathedral Dignitaries in the Twelfth Century; Supplement', *CHJ* 8 (1944–6), 179–85.
—— 'Henry II, Duke of Normandy and Acquitaine', *EHR* 61 (1946), 81–9.
BROWN, R. A., 'The Status of the Anglo-Norman Knight', in J. Gillingham and J. C. Holt (edd.), *War and Government in the Middle Ages* (Cambridge, 1984), 18–32.
BROWN, S. D. B., 'Military Service and Monetary Reward in the Eleventh and Twelfth Centuries', *History*, 74 (1989), 20–38.

CAM, H. M., 'The Evolution of the Medieval English Franchise', *Speculum*, 32 (1957), 427–42.

CAMPBELL, J., 'Observations on English Government from the Tenth to the Twelfth Century', *TRHS* 5th Ser. 25 (1975), 39–54.

—— 'The Significance of the Anglo-Norman State in the Administrative History of Western Europe', *Beihefte der Francia*, 9 (Munich, 1980), 117–34.

—— 'Some Agents and Agencies of the Late Anglo-Saxon State', in J. C. Holt (ed.), *Domesday Studies* (Woodbridge, 1987), 201–18.

—— 'The Sale of Land and the Economics of Power in England: Problems and Possibilities', *Haskins Society Journal*, 1 (1989), 23–37.

CARABIE, R., *La Propriété foncière dans le très ancien droit normand*, i. *La Propriété domaniale* (Caen, 1943).

CHAPLAIS, P., 'The Original Charters of Herbert and Gervase Abbots of Westminster (1121–1157)', in P. M. Barnes and C. F. Slade (edd.), *A Medieval Miscellany for Doris Mary Stenton* (PRS, NS 36; 1960), 89–110.

—— *English Royal Documents: King John–Henry VI, 1199–1461* (Oxford, 1971).

—— 'Henry II's Reissue of the Canons of the Council of Lillebonne of Whitsun 1080 (?25 February 1162)', *JSA* 4 (1973), 627–32.

CHARLES-EDWARDS, T. M., 'The Distinction between Land and Moveable Wealth in Anglo-Saxon England', in P. H. Sawyer (ed.), *Medieval Settlement* (London, 1976), 180–7.

CHENEY, C. R., *English Bishops' Chanceries, 1100–1250* (Manchester, 1950).

—— *From Becket to Langton* (Manchester, 1956).

CHENEY, M. G., 'The Compromise of Avranches of 1172 and the Spread of Canon Law in England', *EHR* 56 (1941), 177–80.

—— 'The Litigation between John Marshal and Archbishop Thomas Becket in 1164: A Pointer to the Origin of Novel Disseisin?', in J. A. Guy and H. G. Beale (edd.), *Law and Social Change in British History* (London, 1984), 9–26.

—— 'Inalienability in Mid-Twelfth Century England: Enforcement and Consequences', *Proceedings of the Sixth International Congress of Medieval Canon Law*, ed. S. Kuttner and K. Pennington (Vatican City, 1985), 467–78.

—— 'A Decree of Henry II on Defect of Justice', in D. E. Greenway, C. Holdsworth, J. Sayers, (edd.), *Tradition and Change: Essays in Honour of Marjorie Chibnall* (Cambridge, 1985), 183–93.

CHEW, H. M., *The English Ecclesiastical Tenants-in-Chief and Knight Service, especially in the Thirteenth and Fourteenth Centuries* (Oxford, 1932).

CHEYETTE, F. L., 'Suum Cuique Tribuere', *French Historical Studies*, 6 (1970), 287–99.

CHIBNALL, M., 'Ecclesiastical Estates and the Growth of Feudal Estates at the time of the Norman Conquest', *Annales de Normandie*, 8 (1958), 103–18.

CHIBNALL, M., 'Charter and Chronicle', in C. N. L. Brooke *et al.* (edd.), *Church and Government in the Middle Ages* (Cambridge, 1976), 1–17.

—— 'Military Service in Normandy before 1066', *A-NS* 5 (1983), 65–77.

—— *The World of Orderic Vitalis* (Oxford, 1984).

—— *Anglo-Norman England* (Oxford, 1986).

—— *The Empress Matilda* (Oxford, 1991).

CLANCHY, M. T., 'Magna Carta, Clause 34', *EHR* 79 (1964), 542–8.

—— 'The Franchise of Return of Writs', *TRHS* 5th Ser. 17 (1967), 59–79.

—— 'Remembering the Past and the Good Old Law', *History*, 55 (1970), 165–76.

—— 'A Medieval Realist: Interpreting the Rules at Barnwell Priory, Cambridge', in E. A. G. Attwooll (ed.), *Perspectives in Jurisprudence* (Glasgow, 1977), 176–94.

—— *From Memory to Written Record* (London, 1979).

—— *England and its Rulers, 1066–1272* (London, 1983).

—— 'Law and Love in the Middle Ages', in J. Bossy (ed.), *Disputes and Settlements: Law and Human Relations in the West* (Cambridge, 1983), 47–67.

—— 'Magna Carta and The Common Pleas', in H. M. Mayr-Harting and R. I. Moore (edd.), *Studies in Medieval History presented to R. H. C. Davis* (London, 1985), 219–32.

CLAY, C. T. and GREENWAY, D. E. (edd.), *Early Yorkshire Families* (Yorks. Arch. Soc. Rec. Ser. 135; 1973).

COLVIN, H. M., 'Holme Lacy: An Episcopal Manor and its Tenants in the Twelfth and Thirteenth Centuries', in V. Ruffer and A. J. Taylor (edd.), *Medieval Studies Presented to Rose Graham* (Oxford, 1950), 15–40.

Complete Peerage of England, Scotland, Ireland, Great Britain, and United Kingdom, ed. G. E. C[okayne], rev. V. Gibbs, H. A. Doubleday, *et al.* (12 vols. in 13; London, 1910–59).

CONWAY, A. E., 'The Owners of Allington Castle, Maidstone (1086–1279)', *Archaeologia Cantiana*, 29 (1911), 1–39.

CORNER, D. J., 'The Texts of Henry II's Assizes', in A. Harding (ed.), *Law-Making and Law-Makers in British History* (London, 1980), 7–20.

COWDREY, H. E. J., 'The Peace and the Truce of God in the Eleventh Century', *P&P* 46 (1970), 42–67.

CRAMER, P., 'Ernulf of Rochester and Early Anglo-Norman Canon Law', *JEcclH* 40 (1989), 483–510.

CRONNE, H. A., 'The Office of Local Justiciar in England under the Norman Kings', *University of Birmingham Historical Journal*, 6 (1958), 18–38.

—— *The Reign of Stephen, 1135–54: Anarchy in England* (London, 1970).

CROUCH, D. B., 'Geoffrey de Clinton and Roger, Earl of Warwick: New

Men and Magnates in the Reign of Henry I', *BIHR* 55 (1982), 113–24.

—— 'Robert Earl of Gloucester and the Daughter of Zelophehad', *JMedH* 11 (1985), 227–43.

—— *The Beaumont Twins* (Cambridge, 1986).

—— 'The Foundation of Leicester Abbey, and Other Problems', *Midland History*, 12 (1987), 1–13.

DARBY, H. C., *Domesday England* (Cambridge, 1977).

DAVIS, R. H. C., 'What Happened in Stephen's Reign, 1135–1154', *History*, 49 (1964), 1–12.

—— *King Stephen* (3rd edn., London, 1990).

DEARAGON, R., 'The Growth of Secure Inheritance in Anglo-Norman England', *JMedH* 8 (1982), 381–91.

DODWELL, B., 'The Honour of the Bishop of Thetford/Norwich in the Late Eleventh and Early Twelfth Centuries', *Norfolk Archaeology*, 33/2 (1963), 185–99.

—— 'Holdings and Inheritance in Medieval East Anglia', *EcHR*, 2nd Ser. 20 (1967), 53–66.

DONAHUE, C. 'The Policy of Alexander III's Consent Theory on Marriage', *Proceedings of the Fourth International Congress of Medieval Canon Law*, ed. S. Kuttner (Vatican City, 1976), 251–81.

DOUGLAS, A. W., 'Frankalmoin and Jurisdictional Immunity: Maitland Revisited', *Speculum*, 53 (1978), 26–48.

—— 'Tenure *in elemosina*: Origins and Establishment in Twelfth-Century England', *AJLegH* 24 (1980), 95–132.

DOUGLAS, D. C., 'A Charter of Enfeoffment under William the Conqueror', *EHR* 42 (1927), 245–7.

—— *The Social Structure of Medieval East Anglia* (Oxford, 1927).

—— 'Some Early Surveys from the Abbey of Abingdon', *EHR* 44 (1929), 618–25.

—— *William the Conqueror: The Norman Impact upon England* (London, 1964).

DU BOULAY, F. R. H., *The Lordship of Canterbury* (London, 1966).

DUBY, G., *La Société aux xi͞ et xii͞ siècles dans la région Mâconnaise* (2nd edn., Paris, 1971).

—— 'The Evolution of Judicial Institutions', in *The Chivalrous Society*, tr. C. Postan (London, 1977), 15–58.

DUPARC, P., 'Le Tensement', *RHDFE* 40 (1962), 43–63.

DWORKIN, R. M., *Law's Empire* (London, 1986).

—— (ed.), *The Philosophy of Law* (Oxford, 1977).

ENEVER, F. A., *History of the Law of Distress for Rent and Damage Feasant* (London, 1931).

EYTON, R. W., *Court, Household and Itinerary of King Henry II* (Dorchester, 1878).

FAITH, R. J., 'Peasant Families and Inheritance Customs in Medieval England', *Agricultural History Review*, 14 (1966), 77–95.

FARRER, W., 'An Outline Itinerary of King Henry the First', *EHR* 34 (1919), 303–82, 505–79 (repr. separately, 1920).

—— *Honors and Knights' Fees* (3 vols.; London, 1923).

FLEMING, D., 'Landholding by *milites* in Domesday Book: A Revision', *A-NS* 13 (1991), 83–98.

FLEMING, R., *Kings and Lords in Conquest England* (Cambridge, 1991).

FOULDS, T., 'The Lindsey Survey and an Unknown Precept of King Henry I', *BIHR* 59 (1986), 212–15.

FOURNIER, P., and LE BRAS, G., *Histoires des collections canoniques en Occident depuis les Fausses Décrétales jusqu'au Décrets de Gratien* (2 vols.; Paris, 1931–2).

GALBRAITH, V. H., 'An Episcopal Land-Grant of 1085', *EHR* 44 (1929), 353–72.

—— 'Monastic Foundation Charters of the Eleventh and Twelfth Centuries', *CHJ* 4 (1932–4), 210–19.

GARNETT, G. S., 'Coronation and Propaganda: Some Implications of the Norman Claim to the Throne of England in 1066', *TRHS*, 5th Ser. 36 (1986), 91–116.

GILLINGHAM, J., 'Love, Marriage and Politics in the Twelfth Century', *Forum for Modern Language Studies*, 25 (1989), 292–303.

GOEBEL, J., *Felony and Misdemeanor: A Study in the History of English Legal Procedure* (New York, 1937).

GOLD, P. SCHINE, *The Lady and the Virgin: Image, Attitude and Experience in Twelfth-Century France* (Chicago, 1985).

GOLDING, B., 'Simon of Kyme, the Making of a Rebel', *Nottingham Medieval Studies*, 27 (1983), 23–36.

GOODY, J., *The Development of the Family and Marriage in Europe* (Cambridge, 1983).

—— *The Logic of Writing and the Organization of Society* (Cambridge, 1986).

GRANSDEN, A., *Historical Writing in England c.550 to c.1307* (London, 1974).

GREEN, J. A., ' "Praeclarum et Magnificum Antiquitatis Monumentum": The Earliest Surviving Pipe Roll', *BIHR* 55 (1982), 1–17.

—— 'The Sheriffs of William the Conqueror', *AN-S* 5 (1983), 129–45.

—— *The Government of England under Henry I* (Cambridge, 1986).

—— 'Unity and Disunity in the Anglo-Norman State', *Historical Research*, 62 (1989), 115–34.

—— *English Sheriffs to 1154* (HMSO, 1990).

GUEST, A. M. (ed.), *Oxford Essays in Jurisprudence* (Oxford, 1961).

GUREVIC, A., 'Représentations et attitudes à l'égard de la propriété pendant le Haut Moyen Âge', *Annales ESC* 27 (1972), 523–47.

HARDING, A., 'Medieval Brieves of Protection and the Development of the Common Law', *Juridical Review*, NS 11 (1966), 115–49.

—— *The Law Courts of Medieval England* (London, 1973).

HARPER-BILL, C., 'The Piety of the Anglo-Norman Knightly Class', *A-NS* 2 (1980), 63–77.

HART, H. L. A., *The Concept of Law* (Oxford, 1961).

HARVEY, B. F., 'Abbot Gervase de Blois and the Fee Farms of Westminster Abbey (1138–1158), *BIHR* 40 (1967), 127–42.

—— *Westminster Abbey and its Estates in the Middle Ages* (Oxford, 1977).

HARVEY, S., 'The Knight and the Knight's Fee in England', *P&P* 49 (1970), 3–43.

HASKINS, C. H., *Norman Institutions* (New York, 1918).

HILL, B. D., *English Cistercian Monasteries and their Patrons in the Twelfth Century* (Urbana, 1968).

HOLLISTER, C. W., *The Military Organization of Norman England* (Oxford, 1965).

—— 'The Misfortunes of the Mandevilles', *History*, 58 (1973), 18–28.

—— 'The Anglo-Norman Succession Debate of 1126: Prelude to Stephen's Anarchy', *JMedH* 1 (1975), 19–39.

HOLT, J. C., 'The Assizes of Henry II: The Texts', in D. A. Bullough and R. L. Storey (edd.), *The Study of Medieval Records* (Oxford, 1971), 85–106.

—— 'Politics and Property in Early Medieval England', *P&P* 57 (1972), 3–52.

—— 'Politics and Property in Early Medieval England: A Rejoinder', *P&P* 65 (1974), 127–35.

—— *What's in a Name? Family Nomenclature and the Norman Conquest* (Stenton Lecture, 1981; University of Reading, 1982).

—— 'Feudal Society and the Family in Early Medieval England:'

(i) The Revolution of 1066', *TRHS*, 5th Ser. 32 (1982), 193–212.
(ii) Notions of Patrimony', *TRHS*, 5th Ser. 33 (1983), 193–220.
(iii) Patronage and Politics', *TRHS*, 5th Ser. 34 (1984), 1–26.
(iv) The Heiress and the Alien', *TRHS*, 5th Ser. 35 (1985), 1–28.

—— 'The Introduction of Knight Service in England', *A-NS* 6 (1984), 89–106.

—— 'More Battle Forgeries', *Reading Medieval Studies*, 11 (1985), 75–86.

—— 'The *Casus Regis*; The Law and Politics of Succession in the Plantagenet Dominions 1185–1247', in E. B. King and S. J. Ridyard (edd.), *Law in Mediaeval Life and Thought* (Sewanee, 1990), 21–42.

—— *Magna Carta* (2nd edn., Cambridge, 1992).

—— (ed.), *Domesday Studies* (Woodbridge, 1987).

HOWELL, M., 'Abbatial Vacancies and the Divided *Mensa* in Medieval England', *JEcclH* 33 (1982), 173–92.

HUDSON, J. G. H., 'Life-Grants of Land and the Development of Inheritance in Anglo-Norman England, *A-NS* 12 (1990), 67–80.

—— 'Milsom's Legal Structure: Interpreting Twelfth-Century Law, *TVR* 59 (1991), 47–66.

—— 'Diplomatic and Legal Aspects of the Charters', in A. T. Thacker (ed.),

The Earldom of Chester and its Charters (Journal of the Chester Arch. Soc. 71; 1991), 153–78.

HURNARD, N., 'Magna Carta, Clause 34', in R. W. Hunt, W. A. Pantin, R. W. Southern (edd.), *Studies in Medieval History Presented to F. M. Powicke* (Oxford, 1948), 157–79.

—— 'The Anglo Norman Franchises', *EHR* 64 (1949), 289–327, 433–60.

—— 'Did Edward I Reverse Henry II's Policy upon Seisin?', *EHR* 69 (1954), 529–53.

HYAMS, P. R., *Kings, Lords, and Peasants in Medieval England* (Oxford, 1980).

—— 'Trial by Ordeal: The Key to Proof in the Early Common Law', in M. S. Arnold *et al.* (edd.), *On the Laws and Customs of England: Essays in Honor of Samuel E. Thorne*, (Chapel Hill, NC, 1981), pp. 90–126.

—— 'The Common Law and the French Connection', *A-NS* 4 (1982), 77–92, 196–202.

—— 'Henry II and Ganelon', *Syracuse Scholar*, 4 (1983), 22–35.

—— 'Warranty and Good Lordship in Twelfth Century England', *L&HR* 5 (1987), 437–503.

—— '"No Register of Title": The Domesday Inquest and Land Adjudication', *A-NS* 9 (1987), 127–41.

—— 'The Charter as a Source for the Early Common Law', *Journal of Legal History*, 12 (1991), 173–89.

JOLLIFFE, J. E. A., *Angevin Kingship* (London, 1955).

JONES, M., *The Creation of Brittany* (London, 1988).

JOÜON DES LONGRAIS, F., *La Conception Anglaise de la saisine du xiie au xive siècle* (Paris, 1925).

—— 'La Portée politique des réformes d'Henry II en matière de saisine', *RHDFE*, 4th Ser. 15 (1936), 540–71.

KEEFE, T., *Feudal Assessments and the Political Community under Henry II and his Sons* (Berkeley, Calif., 1983).

KEETON, G. W., *The Norman Conquest and the Common Law* (London and New York, 1966).

KEMP, B. R., 'Hereditary Benefices in the Medieval English Church: A Hereford Example', *BIHR* 43 (1970), 1–15.

—— 'Exchequer and Bench in the Later Twelfth Century—Separate or Identical Tribunals', *EHR* 88 (1973), 559–73.

KIMBALL, E., 'Tenure in Frank Almoign and Secular Services', *EHR* 43 (1928), 341–53.

—— 'The Judicial Aspects of Frank Almoign Tenure', *EHR* 47 (1932), 1–11.

—— *Serjeanty Tenure in Medieval England* (New Haven, Conn., 1936).

KING, E., *Peterborough Abbey 1086–1310: A Study in the Land Market* (Cambridge, 1973).

—— 'The Tenurial Crisis of the Early Twelfth Century', *P&P* 65 (1974), 110–17.

—— 'Mountsorel and its Region in King Stephen's Reign', *Huntington Library Quarterly*, 44 (1980), 1–10.

—— 'The Anarchy of King Stephen's Reign', *TRHS*, 5th Ser. 34 (1984), 133–53.

—— 'Dispute Settlement in Anglo-Norman England', *A-NS* 14 (1992), 115–30.

KNOWLES, M. D., *The Monastic Order in England* (2nd edn., Cambridge, 1963).

—— and HANCOCK, R. N., *Medieval Religious Houses: England and Wales* (rev. edn., London, 1971).

LALLY, J. E., 'Secular Patronage at the Court of Henry II', *BIHR* 49 (1976), 159–84.

LAMBRICK, G., 'Abingdon Abbey Administration', *JEcclH* 17 (1966), 159–83.

LATIMER, P., 'Grants of "Totus Comitatus" in Twelfth-Century England: Their Origins and Meaning', *BIHR* 59 (1986), 137–45.

LE GOFF, J., *Time, Work and Culture in the Middle Ages*, tr. A. Goldhammer (Chicago, 1980).

LEMARIGNIER, J.-F., *Recherches sur l'hommage en marche et les frontières féodales* (Lille, 1945).

LENNARD, R. V., *Rural England, 1086–1135: A Study of Social and Agrarian Conditions* (Oxford, 1959).

LE PATOUREL, J., 'The Reports of the Trial on Penenden Heath', in R. W. Hunt, W. A. Pantin, R. W. Southern (edd.), *Studies in Medieval History Presented to Frederick Maurice Powicke* (Oxford, 1948), 15–26.

—— *The Norman Empire* (Oxford, 1976).

LÉSAGE, G., 'La "Ratio Canonica" d'après Alexandre III', *Proceedings of the Fourth International Congress of Medieval Canon Law*, ed. S. Kuttner (Vatican City, 1976), 95–106.

LEWIS, C., 'The Norman Settlement of Herefordshire under William I', *A-NS* 7 (1985), 195–213.

LITTLE, L. K., 'La Morphologie des malédictions monastiques', *Annales ESC* 34 (1979), 43–60.

LOENGARD, J., 'The Assize of Nuisance: Origins of an Action at Common Law', *CLJ* 37 (1978), 144–66.

MAITLAND, F. W., *Domesday Book and Beyond* (Cambridge, 1897).

—— *The Collected Papers of Frederic William Maitland*, ed. H. A. L. Fisher (3 vols.; Cambridge, 1911).

—— *The Forms of Action at Common Law* (Cambridge, 1936).

MARTINDALE, J., 'Succession and Politics in the Romance-Speaking World, c.1000–1140', in M. Jones and M. Vale (edd.), *England and her Neighbours, 1066–1485: Essays in Honour of Pierre Chaplais* (London, 1989), 19–41.

MASON, E., 'William Rufus; Myth and Reality', *JMedH* 3 (1977), 1–20.

MASON, E., 'Timeo Barones et Donas Ferentes', *Studies in Church History*, 15 (1978), 61–75.

MAUSS, M., *The Gift*, tr. I. Cunnison (London, 1954).

MILLER, E., 'The Ely Land Pleas in the Reign of William I', *EHR* 62 (1947), 438–56.

—— *The Abbey and Bishopric of Ely* (Cambridge, 1951).

MILSOM, S. F. C., 'Reason and the Development of the Common Law', *LQR* 81 (1965), 496–517.

—— 'Law and Fact in Legal Development', *University of Toronto Law Journal*, 17 (1967), 1–19.

—— *The Legal Framework of English Feudalism* (Cambridge, 1976).

—— 'Inheritance by Women in the Twelfth and Early Thirteenth Centuries', in M. S. Arnold *et al.* (edd.), *On the Laws and Customs of England: Essays in Honour of S. E. Thorne* (Chapel Hill, NC, 1981), 60–89.

—— *Historical Foundations of the Common Law* (2nd edn., London, 1981).

—— *Studies in the History of the Common Law* (London, 1985).

MOREY, A., and BROOKE, C. N. L., *Gilbert Foliot and his Letters* (Cambridge, 1965).

MORRIS, W. A., *The Medieval English Sheriff to 1300* (Manchester, 1927).

MORTIMER, R., 'The Beginnings of the Honour of Clare', *A-NS* 3 (1981), 119–41.

—— 'Land and Service: The Tenants of the Honour of Clare', *A-NS* 8 (1986), 177–97.

MURRAY, A., *Reason and Society in the Middle Ages* (Oxford, 1978).

NEWMAN, C. A., *The Anglo-Norman Nobility in the Reign of Henry I: The Second Generation* (Philadelphia, 1988).

NICHOLS, J., *The History and Antiquities of the County of Leicester* (4 vols. in 8; London, 1795–1815).

NICOL, A. (ed.), 'Changes in the Assize *Utrum* between the Constitutions of Clarendon and Bracton', in R. F. Hunnisett and J. B. Post (edd.), *Medieval Legal Records Edited in Memory of C. A. F. Meekings* (London, 1978), 17–24.

OFFLER, H. S., 'The Tractate *De Iniusta Vexacione Willelmi Episcopi Primi*', *EHR* 66 (1951), 32–41.

OLIVIER-MARTIN, F., *Histoire du droit Français des origines à la Révolution* (Paris, 1951).

ORMEROD, G., *The History of the County Palatine and City of Chester* (3 vols.; London, 1819).

PAINTER, S., *Studies in the History of the English Feudal Barony* (Baltimore, 1943).

—— 'The Family and the Feudal System in Twelfth-Century England', *Speculum*, 35 (1960), 1–16.

PALMER, R. C., 'The Feudal Framework of English Law', *Michigan Law Review*, 79 (1981), 1130–64.

—— *The County Courts of Medieval England, 1150–1350* (Princeton, NJ, 1982).

—— 'The Origins of Property in England', *L&HR* 3 (1985), 1–50.

—— 'The Economic and Cultural Impact of The Origins of Property: 1180–1220', *L&HR* 3 (1985), 375–96.

PLANIOL, M., *La Très Ancienne Coutume de Bretagne* (Rennes, 1886).

PLUCKNETT, T. F. T., *A Concise History of the Common Law* (5th edn., London, 1956).

—— *Early English Legal Literature* (Cambridge, 1958).

—— *The Legislation of Edward I* (Oxford, 1962).

POLLOCK, SIR FREDERICK, and MAITLAND, F. W., *The History of English Law before the Time of Edward I* (2 vols.; 2nd edn. reissued with a new introduction and select bibliography by S. F. C. Milsom, Cambridge, 1968).

POSTLES, D., 'Choosing Witnesses in Twelfth-Century England', *Irish Jurist*, NS 23 (1988), 330–46.

—— 'Securing the Gift in Oxfordshire Charters in the Twelfth and Early Thirteenth Centuries', *Archives*, 19 (1990), 183–91.

—— 'Gifts in Frankalmoin, Warranty of Land, and Feudal Society', *CLJ* 50 (1991), 330–46.

POWELL, W. R. 'Essex Domesday Topography since 1903: Place Name Identification and Problems', *Essex Archaeology and History*, 16 (1984–5), 40–7.

PRESTWICH, J. O., 'The Treason of Geoffrey de Mandeville', *EHR* 103 (1988), 283–312.

RABAN, S., *Mortmain Legislation and the English Church* (Cambridge, 1982).

RAFTIS, J. A., *The Estates of Ramsey Abbey: A Study in Economic Growth and Organization* (Toronto, 1957).

RAZ, J., *Practical Reason and Norms* (London, 1975).

REDSTONE, L. J., 'The Liberty of St. Edmund', *Proceedings of the Suffolk Institute of Archaeology*, 15 (1913–15), 200–11.

REEDY, W. T., 'The Origin of the General Eyre in the Reign of Henry I', *Speculum*, 41 (1966), 688–724.

REYNOLDS, S. M. G., *Kingdoms and Communities in Western Europe, 900–1300* (Oxford, 1984).

—— 'Bookland, Folkland, and Fiefs', *A-NS* 14 (1992), 211–27.

RICHARDSON, H. G., and SAYLES, G. O., *The Governance of Medieval England from the Conquest to Magna Carta* (Edinburgh, 1963).

—— *Law and Legislation from Aethelbert to Magna Carta* (Edinburgh, 1966).

ROBERTS, S., *Order and Dispute* (Harmondsworth, 1979).

ROBINSON, J. A., *Gilbert Crispin, Abbot of Westminster* (Cambridge, 1911).

ROSENWEIN, B. H., *To be the Neighbor of Saint Peter: The Social Meaning of Cluny's Property, 909–1049* (Ithaca, NY, 1989).

ROUND, J. H., *Geoffrey de Mandeville* (London, 1892).

ROUND, J. H., *Feudal England* (London, 1895).

—— 'Bernard, The King's Scribe', *EHR* 14 (1899), 417–30.

—— *Studies in Peerage and Family History* (Westminster, 1901).

—— 'The Burton Abbey Surveys', *EHR* 20 (1905), 275–89.

—— *The King's Serjeants and Officers of State* (London, 1911).

SALTMAN, A., *Theobald, Archbishop of Canterbury* (London, 1956).

SANDERS, I. J., *English Baronies: A Study of their Origin and Descent* (Oxford, 1960).

SEARLE, E., *Lordship and Community: Battle Abbey and its Banlieu 1066–1538* (Toronto, 1974).

—— 'The Abbey of the Conquerors: Defensive Enfeoffment and Economic Development in Anglo-Norman England', *AN-S* 2 (1980), 154–64, 197–8.

—— 'Women and the Legitimization of Succession at the Norman Conquest', *A-NS* 3 (1981), 159–70, 226–9.

SHEEHAN, M. M., *The Will in Medieval England* (Toronto, 1963).

SIMPSON, A. W. B., *The History of Land Law* (Oxford, 1986).

SOUTHERN, R. W., *Saint Anselm and his Biographer* (Cambridge, 1966).

—— *Medieval Humanism and Other Studies* (Oxford, 1970).

—— *Saint Anselm: A Portrait in a Landscape* (Cambridge, 1990).

STENTON, D. M., *English Justice between the Norman Conquest and the Great Charter 1066–1215* (Philadelphia, 1964).

STENTON, F. M., 'The Danes in England', *Proceedings of the British Academy*, 13 (1927), 203–46.

—— *Latin Charters of the Anglo-Saxon Period* (Oxford, 1955).

—— *The First Century of English Feudalism, 1066–1166* (2nd edn., Oxford, 1961).

STRINGER, K. J., 'A Cistercian Archive: The Earliest Charters of Sawtry Abbey', *JSA* 6 (1980), 325–34.

STUBBS, W., *The Constitutional History of England* (3 vols.; Oxford, 1874–8).

SUTHERLAND, D. W., *The Assize of Novel Disseisin* (Oxford, 1973).

TABUTEAU, E. Z., *Transfers of Property in Eleventh-Century Norman Law* (Chapel Hill, NC, 1988).

THORNE, S. E., 'Livery of Seisin', *LQR* 52 (1936), 345–64.

—— 'English Feudalism and Estates in Land', *CLJ* (1959), 193–209.

TURNER, R. V., *The English Judiciary in the Age of Glanvill and Bracton, c.1176–1239* (Cambridge, 1985).

—— 'Who was the Author of *Glanvill*? Reflections on the Education of Henry II's Common Lawyers', *L&HR* 8 (1990), 97–127.

VAN CAENEGEM, R. C., 'Public Prosecution of Crime in Twelfth-Century England', in C. N. L. Brooke *et al.* (edd.), *Church and Government in the Middle Ages* (Cambridge, 1976), 41–76.

—— *The Birth of the English Common Law* (2nd edn., Cambridge, 1988).

VAUGHAN, R., *Matthew Paris* (Cambridge, 1958).

VINOGRADOFF, P., *English Society in the Eleventh Century* (Oxford, 1908).

VODOLA, E., *Excommunication in the Middle Ages* (Berkeley, Calif., 1986).

VOSS, L., *Heinrich von Blois, Bischof von Winchester, 1129–1171* (Historische Studien, 210; Berlin, 1932).

WALKER, D., 'Miles of Gloucester, Earl of Hereford', *Trans. Bristol and Glos. Arch. Soc.* 77 (1959), 66–84.

—— 'Ralph son of Pichard', *BIHR* 33 (1960), 195–202.

WARREN, W. L., *Henry II* (London, 1973).

—— 'The Myth of Anglo-Norman Administrative Efficiency', *TRHS*, 5th Ser. 34 (1984), 113–32.

WAUGH, S., 'Tenure to Contract', *EHR* 101 (1986), 811–39.

—— 'Women's Inheritance and the Growth of Bureaucratic Monarchy in Twelfth- and Thirteenth-Century England', *Nottingham Mediaeval Studies*, 34 (1990), 71–92.

WHITE, S. D., 'Politics and Property in Early Medieval England: Succession to Fiefs in Early Medieval England', *P&P* 65 (1974), 118–27.

—— '"Pactum … Legem Vincit et Amor Iudicium": The Settlement of Disputes by Compromise in Eleventh-Century Western France', *AJLegH* 22 (1978), 281–308.

—— 'Inheritances and Legal Arguments in Western France, 1050–1150', *Traditio*, 43 (1987), 55–103.

—— *Custom, Kinship, and Gifts to Saints: The* Laudatio Parentum *in Western France, 1050–1150* (Chapel Hill, NC, 1988).

WIGHTMAN, W. E., *The Lacy Family in England and Normandy, 1066–1194* (Oxford, 1961).

WILLIAMS, A., 'The Knights of Shaftesbury Abbey', *A-NS* 8 (1986), 214–42.

WOOD, S. M., *English Monasteries and their Patrons in the Thirteenth Century* (Oxford, 1955).

YVER, J., 'Le Bref Anglo-Normand', *TVR* 29 (1961), 313–30.

—— 'Une boutade de Guillaume le Conquérant: Note sur la genèse de la tenure en aumône', in *Études d'histoire du droit canonique, dédiées à Gabriel le Bras* (2 vols.; Paris, 1965), 781–91.

—— 'Autour de l'absence de l'avouerie en Normandie', *BSAN* 57 (1965), 194–213.

—— 'Le "Très Ancien Coutumier" de Normandie, miroir de la législation ducale?', *TVR* 39 (1971), 333–74.

Index

Hugh, son of 125
Bolingbroke (Lincs.) 127
Book of Numbers 112
Bordesley abbey 221 n. 50
Borne, Robert 165–6
  Ralph, son of 166
Bosco, Ernald de 20
Bosco, William de 49 n. 159
Boulogne, honour of 127
Brackley, hospital of 170
'Bracton', *De Legibus* 16, 43, 69, 85, 103,
  212, 277
Brakelond, Jocelin of 273, 280
Bramhope, Baldwin fitzRalph of 200
  Ralph and Peter, sons of 200
Brand, P. A. 28, 29
Braose, William de 133 n. 96, 218
Breteuil, William de 121
  Eustace, son of 121
Bretons 110
Brian fitzCount 111
Brian, Ralph, clerk of Bury St
  Edmunds 239
Brittany, legislation concerning 111 n.
  11, 260
Brobury, Robert of 132, 133
'Broch' (Bucks.) 125
  Robert of 125
Broi, Robert de 171
Brompton in Pickering Lyth (Yorks.,
  NR) 97
Buckingham, earldom of 227 n. 84
  see also Giffard
Bullington priory 187, 189
Bully, Roger de 143 n. 129
Bulmer, Anseketil of 219
  Bertram, son of 199, 219
Burgh, in Banstead (Surrey) 141
  John of 141
Burneville, William de 159
Bury St Edmunds, abbey of 36, 53 n.
  175, 94, 95, 215, 239, 243, 273
  Hugh, abbot of (1157–80) 239
  Samson, abbot of (1182–1211) 280

Caen, St Stephen's abbey 105 n. 180
Calne, church of (Wilts.) 88
Calne, Nigel of (royal chaplain) 88
Cambridge, lands in 215
Camville, Hugh de 165
Candidus, Hugh 233–4, 244
Canon Law 2, 32, 84, 86, 92 n. 119, 122,
  170, 181, 193, 206, 227, 230–3,

245–6, 250, 267–8, 273
Canonsleigh abbey 218
Canterbury, archbishopric of 141, 245,
  265
  Aelfric, archbishop of (995–1005) 241
  William, archbishop of (1123–36) 242
  Theobald, archbishop of (1138–
    61) 104, 120, 122, 158, 187, 192,
    193, 244, 245
  see also Anselm; Becket
Canterbury, monks of Christ Church 236
caput honoris 224
Carbunel, Ralph 191
  Ernald, brother of 191
Cartae baronum (1166) 33, 35, 36, 37, 45,
  49–50, 199, 234, 258, 266
castles 117
  Bedford 117–18, 144
  of bishop of Durham 26
  castle guard 31, 38
  Gainsborough 83 n. 80
  inheritance of 71, 82, 115 n. 33,
    117–18, 144
  keepers of 117, 268
  Lincoln 84 n. 82
  Windsor 38
casus regis 114, 118, 123 n. 65
Cawston (War.) 218
  Thurkill of 218
ceremony:
  asserting lord's control of
    inheritance 69
  burial 189; translation of mother 189
  gift 4, 84, 103, 157–66, 188, 190–1,
    195, 214, 218; objects used in 162;
    placing on altar 161–2, 188, 190,
    196, 220; swearing on altar 173
  nomination of heir 125
  in settlement 138, 160, 210, 245
  concerning spiritual penalties 168
  see also countergift; homage; monastery,
    entering; oaths; seisin
Chaddleworth (Berks.) 196
Chahaines, Ralph de 49 n. 159
champions 47
chancery 74, 77, 90, 253–4
'Changhetona', Humphrey de 218
charters:
  beneficiary-drafting 89, 90, 170, 184,
    187, 190, 205, 248
  as external authority 70, 72, 84, 104,
    130
  granting verbs 149; *concedere* 72–7,